Includes a 90-minute DVD of three ghost in...

PICTURE YOURSELF Ghost Hunting

Step-by-Step Instruction for Exploring Haunts and Finding Spirits, Spooks, and Specters

Christopher Balzano, Foreword by Jeff Belanger

COURSE TECHNOLOGY
CENGAGE Learning™

Picture Yourself Ghost Hunting: Step-by-Step Instruction for Exploring Haunts and Finding Spirits, Spooks, and Specters
Christopher Balzano

Publisher and General Manager, Course Technology PTR:
Stacy L. Hiquet

Associate Director of Marketing:
Sarah Panella

Manager of Editorial Services:
Heather Talbot

Marketing Manager:
Jordan Casey

Acquisitions Editor:
Megan Belanger

Project Editor:
Jenny Davidson

Technical Reviewer:
Jeff Belanger

PTR Editorial Services Coordinator:
Erin Johnson

Copy Editor:
Sandy Doell

Interior Layout Tech:
Shawn Morningstar

Cover Designer:
Mike Tanamachi

DVD-ROM Producer:
Brandon Penticuff

Indexer:
Sharon Hilgenberg

Printed in the United States of America
1 2 3 4 5 6 7 11 10 09

Library of Congress Control Number: 2008929252
ISBN-13: 978-1-59863-498-3
ISBN-10: 1-59863-498-4

Course Technology
25 Thomson Place
Boston, MA 02210
USA

Cengage Learning is a leading provider of customized learning solutions with office locations around the globe, including Singapore, the United Kingdom, Australia, Mexico, Brazil, and Japan. Locate your local office at: **international.cengage.com/region**

Cengage Learning products are represented in Canada by Nelson Education, Ltd.

For your lifelong learning solutions, visit **courseptr.com**
Visit our corporate website at **cengage.com**

To my friend Jeff Belanger, who proves it is not enough to be a trailblazer. Sometimes you have to show people down the path.

Foreword by Jeff Belanger

PICTURE YOURSELF LURKING through a dark, dank, and dusty basement full of spider webs, who knows what other kinds of creepy-crawly creatures, and ghosts. That's right, ghosts—a bonafide haunting—at least if you're to believe the owners of the property. Picture yourself part of a new breed of explorer: a paranormal investigator, out in the haunted boneyards, battlefields, and homes of the world looking for proof of life after death.

Today, more people than ever are on the quest for spooks. There are thousands of organizations and clubs around the world that specialize in ghost hunting, and there are many individuals who are called in when something goes bump in the night.

We've arrived at an incredible time in history—because of the popularity of the supernatural in mainstream culture, we're allowed to openly discuss our encounters and explore the notion of what happens after we die. Then there are those of us who actively go looking for these specters of lore and legend. Armed with equipment like cameras, digital thermometers, EMF meters, dowsing rods, audio recorders, and even psychics, we try to wrap our hands around a subject that's been perplexing humans for many millennia.

Paranormal investigation is a field of research that is still wide open to discovery and innovation. People from all walks of life have something they can bring to the subject, whether it's an understanding of home construction and what can cause those creaks and pops on the staircase, to electrical engineers who can help pinpoint disturbances in the electromagnetic field, to folks with a sympathetic ear who can really connect with victims of a haunting who may be frightened because they don't understand what is happening around them.

The field is open to everyone, but that doesn't mean anyone can be a good ghost investigator. Understanding where the field has been, where it is now, and where it's going is paramount to getting yourself involved. Knowing the techniques and equipment being used and what the results have been is critical before you to jump in. But more than just jumping in and trying to reproduce an investigation you may have seen on television, you have an opportunity to make this your own—to bring your own personality and expertise to a field that's hungry to grow. Mainstream science has ignored the millions of reports of paranormal phenomena, so it's left to the rest of us to document, explore, and try to better understand this enigmatic subject.

Picture Yourself Ghost Hunting is not only the best starting point for any budding paranormal investigator, it's also a valuable resource for people who may have already gotten their start from watching a television show, but who are eager to learn something new and better understand the equipment and techniques employed by intrepid explorers of the unexplained.

I've had the pleasure of knowing and working with Chris Balzano for several years now, and I've always appreciated his objectivity, sincerity, and straightforward approach to this important work. This book and accompanying DVD he's put together is highly recommended for those who have long sat on the sidelines of paranormal research and who are now ready to get more involved.

You've already taken the next step. The book is in your hands and you've read this far. Keep going. Read, learn, and get involved. When you start getting results, share them. Tell others about what you've discovered and where you found it. If you have questions, ask! You will be amazed at how easy it is to correspond with many paranormal experts.

I look forward to bumping into you at a haunt real soon.

Supernaturally yours,

Jeff Belanger

Founder of Ghostvillage.com and
author of *The World's Most Haunted Places.*

Acknowledgments

WHILE WRITING THIS BOOK I wanted to present as many sides of the story as possible. I am grateful for the following people and groups who offered their insight and opinion on the paranormal: Shawn Blaschka from the Wausau Paranormal Research Society, Brian J. Cano from the SCARED! crew, Dale Kaczmarek from the Ghost Research Society, Kathleen Popola of Blue Moon Paranormal Investigations, Jeffrey Stewart of the Paranormal Investigators of New England, Gregg Cable and Circle City Paranormal Exploration, Nicole Ardonlino from Northeastern Paranormal Investigations, Tim Harte and the MESA Project, Jason Jrakeman, Mystic of VanPort Paranormal Research Agency, Gary Manley and the Massachusetts Paranormal Team, Adam Cadabona from the Southern California Paranormal Detectives, Tina Carlson and the Las Vegas Society of Supernatural Investigations, Bruce J. Duarte of South Coast Paranormal Investigations, Luann Joly of Whaling City Ghosts, who also contributed pictures to the book, and Maureen Carrol of South Jersey Ghost Research. Many of the pictures from the book were provided by some great people out there in the field, including: Thomas D'Agostino and Arlene Nicolson, Brianne Pouliot, Jamie Chesterson and the Texas Paranormal Society, Anita Tallbull and the Native American Ghost Society, John M. Nevulis, Elizabeth Russell, Justin Mycofsky, Brooke Huchel, Brendon Paulson of Eidolic Paranormal Research Association, Carrie Shimkus from Massachusetts Area Ghost Investigation Coalition, and Josh Mantello of the Berkshire Paranormal Group.

A special thanks goes out to Tim Weisberg from the Spooky Southcoast radio show for support, pictures, and ideas, as well as his co-host Matt Moniz, who in addition to submitting pictures and constantly challenging my ideas about the paranormal, also allowed me to film his investigation. Also helping on the DVD were Thomas D'Agostino and Arlene Nicolson, Ron Kolek and the New England Ghost Project, Aaron Cadieux of Big Operations Productions, who endured much helping out, and John Horrigan. The biggest thanks go to Andrew Lake of Greenville Paranormal Research. The DVD would not have been done without his dedication, vision, and persistence. I am forever better for having met him.

As always, my wife, Jill, and my son, Devin, are my constant muses, always encouraging and always willing to let me go out and get the story. A special thanks goes to all those other investigators who have taught me what I know, and for the families who have allowed their stories to become part of my story.

About the Author

CHRISTOPHER BALZANO is a teacher and writer from the Boston area. He is the founder and director of Massachusetts Paranormal Crossroads, an online collection of legends and ghost stories from Massachusetts and the surrounding states.

He has been investigating the paranormal for more than ten years and has been writing about those experiences for the past five. He has been a contributor to Jeff Belanger's *Encyclopedia of Haunted Places* and *Weird Massachusetts* and was one of the writers behind *Weird Hauntings.* His writing has been featured in *Haunted Times* and *Mystery Magazine* and has been covered by the *Boston Globe,* the *Boston Herald,* the *Standard Times,* and *Worcester Magazine.*

Christopher is the author of several books about regional hauntings, including *Dark Woods: Cults, Crime, and Paranormal in the Freetown State Forest* and *Ghosts of the Bridgewater Triangle,* as well as the collection of true ghosts stories *Ghostly Adventures.* He has appeared on radio stations in Boston and throughout the Internet, as well as being called upon by several local television shows to comment on ghosts and urban legends.

Table of Contents

You're Not Alone in the Dark

I'M STANDING ONLY A FEW feet away from the spot where dead people have been retrieved from a near bottomless pond. I have a camera, a tape recorder, and a flashlight, and I'm waiting for an investigative group that has been lost in the woods for over an hour. At the top of the ledge there are some teenagers drinking beer, partying only feet away from where more than a dozen people have committed suicide, ghost lights have been seen hovering in the air, and a mysterious woman in black has replayed the moment of her faithful leap into the water.

Andrew Lake, investigator for Greenville Paranormal Research and a documentary filmmaker, is standing next to me shaking his head. "I never thought I'd be here a year ago," he says. I know what he means. He only knows a fraction of the ghost reports from where we are standing and only half the stories of the people who have been brought to the forest and killed right where we wait. I try to contact the group again with the walkie-talkies, but again their voices come over more static than language.

Finally, a member of the team I'm out with comes up the path. He's out of breath, half from the walk up the steep path and half from excitement. He tells us the psychic member of his team was attacked by a type of demon.

It's another night out in the field.

Ghost hunting is not like other hobbies people can get into. You learn the rules, and how often the rules bend and snap, and then go out and try to answer a question people have been challenged by since the beginning of mankind. You quickly learn the only thing typical about paranormal investigating is nothing is typical. From different obstacles when you're in the location to the stories behind the haunting to that moment something happens that gets your adrenaline moving, there are no two investigations exactly alike.

The best way to prepare for that is to learn what is out there and how to find it. Think of this book as just that. It is a teacher, a field guide, a reference book, and hopefully a whisper in your ear as you hit the field looking for the unknown. It's a daunting task, searching for that which few have captured, and along the way you'll come across variables not talked about in this book. I have tried to share as much of the information that is out there, and tried to show you how some of the best people in the field handle themselves, but ultimately it comes down to you.

A good ghost hunter is like an all-star baseball player or a world-class bassoon player. Listen to the coach and follow the conductor, but within those lines allow who you are to come through. With the help of this book, you add something to the paranormal field. You take the baton from such greats as Sir Arthur Conan Doyle, Harry Price, and Hans Holzer, and continue the tradition.

As a teacher I am forced to check students' textbooks at the end of every year and mark the wear and tear that has accumulated. If I see highlighter or pen marks, I have to force them to buy the book. I want the opposite with this one. Dog-ear a section you want to flip back to, cross out a section you think is a sign of my insanity, fill the margins with notes and ideas. This is your book, but it is a conversation between us. And if you ever find yourself in a dark woods or an abandoned insane asylum, you'll feel I'm there with you, tape recorder in one hand and a pen in the other.

A face caught during an investigation in an asylum.
Photo courtesy of Sheryl Vartanian and www.visceralaxis.net.

1

Learn
Before You Look

I WAS SPENDING SOME TIME WITH MY PARENTS because I hadn't seen them in a few weeks. We were just finishing our coffee, my son playing with his toy cars at our feet, when my phone rang. My wife gave me that look, shrugged her shoulders, and nodded. I looked at the number and recognized the part of the state it came from. On the other end was a woman who had been suffering from a haunting for years, which was now being experienced by her daughter. Things were getting serious, and the more I talked with her, the more it sounded like a possible demonic infestation.

After 45 minutes of listening to her story, most of which came as one long sentence with no breaks, she asked me to meet with her the next day—anytime that would work for me. I thought about my coming week. As a full-time high school teacher, my time was at a premium and we were entering midterms. I had three interviews scheduled to promote my latest book, and a deadline for the one I was finishing. There was not much time to breathe, but the little girl was seeing the man and he was telling her he was going to strangle her.

It was another day as a paranormal investigator. Ghosts don't have a schedule, and the calls seem to come at the worst possible time. I could move this other appointment, I thought, and correct my midterms in class. I could make it work. After all, this was why I got into the work in the first place.

Why Are You Doing This?

IT SOUNDS LIKE AN ODD question, but it might not be an easy one to answer at first. Some are looking for spiritual enlightenment, while others are looking for the newfound fame that comes along with being a ghost hunter. Some want that piece of evidence that will prove there is life after death, even if they don't quite know what that will mean for them. Most have had some kind of personal experience and are looking to find the answer to what happened to them. More often than not, the investigators are pulled in by reasons they do not know, an experience as unexplainable as ghosts themselves.

Then there is that rush. There is something to be said for bringing yourself to the edge of the unknown and waiting with anticipation for something to happen. When you crouch next to a tombstone, full moon with a slight chill in the air, and turn on all five of your senses, anything can happen. Call it that sixth sense, or the opening of your third eye, but there is something that ignites your body and your mind.

Many who investigate the paranormal are adrenaline junkies, and there is no bigger high than being hot on the trail of a ghost. In the same

Figure 1.1
A haunted tunnel, the definition of the adrenaline rush.

way the hormone can make a 100-pound mother lift a car off her child, adrenaline pumping through the body of a ghost hunter creates almost superhuman perception. You hear every snap of a twig, every creak of the floorboard. Every smell enters your brain for analysis, and straining to see in the dark makes shadows almost dance. You are highly sensitive, and when you have felt like that, the rest of the day seems a bit boring.

The good news is you don't need to know the answer quite yet, but it will be one you will need to address eventually, so it is important to start thinking about it now. Sometimes the important thing is the journey and not why you're on it or where you end up. That's just what you've started with this book. You have a rough idea of what a ghost is and have maybe seen a show or two. It's a fit for you, and all you need now is the information, some signposts on the journey. Some of the information is based in science and some in mere theory. It can be intimidating to dive into, but knowing what is out there will help you find what people have been telling you is not out there.

The journey starts with a question. Why are you doing this? The question really asks you two things, and both will test your commitment level and your approach to investigating. The first is the easier of the two. How much time and money are you willing to invest in looking for ghosts? How serious are you about becoming an investigator? Of course, over time, your answers might change, but going in you should know a few things. Ghost hunting can be a very time-consuming and expensive hobby, and it may not offer the immediate rewards of stamp collecting or model cars. While many retailers are designing tools to help the investigator, most equipment you'll use was created for an entirely different reason and can get pricey. There is technical information you'll need to know to get the job done, as well as information about religion, history, psychology, and parapsychology.

The Investigation Equation

It takes a significant amount of time to gather information and then analyze it. Television shows make it seem instantaneous but use this simple equation. For a true paranormal researcher:

evidence = investigation × 3.5 × equipment

or

E =3.5IQ.

For those who are not experts in math, think of it this way. Take how long you are out in the field and multiply it by the evidence gathering equipment you use (cameras, sound recorders), and then allow for time to look at the evidence carefully. For example, an hour investigation with two cameras will take you seven hours to complete. Add to this interviewing witnesses and conducting research on the location at the library and hall of records, and you are looking at a pretty steep investment of time.

Now, you can spend an hour at a place and listen to the recording you made for EVPs and be done with it. No matter what anyone tells you, that is fine. The true measure of your time and money is always what you feel comfortable with. The nature of the work might lead you to spend more time than you want, and if you see all of your paychecks going to Geiger counters and your family has issued a missing person report on you, it might be time to scale back.

Is it worth it? I think it is, but that leads us to the next part of the question. What is your motivation for investigating the paranormal? Most investigators reply the same way when asked. They were always into ghost stories and creepy tales, and then something happened to them. That is not what I'm asking. I want to know where you think it will lead.

What Are You Trying to Prove?

Why are you doing this? What do you think it will prove, or more importantly, what do you hope to prove? Most investigators have some angle about making the world understand or accept the paranormal that sends them out there. They believe it will take different things to make the non-believer finally bend to the truth they understand, but most feel they will have to experience something themselves to ever believe. This means the evidence you gather will never be taken seriously outside the paranormal community.

Some investigators do the work to help others. By understanding the things that go bump in the night, they can shed some light on the unknown. When you begin to gain a name in your community and people start seeking you out, there is an element of satisfaction knowing you helped someone sleep a little bit easier at night. Maybe that is enough for you; although the odds you will spend much time with clients is very slim and usually takes a few years.

The popularity for ghost hunters comes and goes, and the most recent craze has made rock stars out of investigators. There is a belief that looking for ghosts and starting a group is the first step to fame and fortune. At some point, the bubble will burst, and those along for the ride trying to get famous will drop out. Of course, there is also a romantic element to ghost hunting, and from afar, it appears very glamorous. There are many glamorous parts, but what interests us is somewhat off center from what the rest of the public thinks is interesting. Except to each other, we're not cool. Recently, a Hollywood producer was working on a new reality show about the paranormal. He asked me if I knew of any well-known, good-looking investigators. I told him that was pretty hard to find, and he asked why there was a lack of beauty in the paranormal world. "Are you kidding?" I asked him. "Most of us got into this stuff in high school because we had no dates on Saturday night."

That's hyperbole, but there is an element of truth to it. A ghost hunter spends hours in a cemetery and then days in a room in front of a screen looking closely for a small movement of the curtain or a shadow or listening for a stray sound. Then again, it is kind of cool to wear black and walk through an old insane asylum.

Don't Know Much about History

Okay, maybe this is my favorite reason: I *am* a teacher. I look for anything I can to get students involved and get them curious. I always try to find a hook for a new lesson, something that makes them forget they are there to learn something. I have often used a good ghost story to teach them something about English or literature, but one of the easiest connections to make is between the paranormal and history.

Most people who have investigated for some time will tell you they were doing something else when they stumbled upon the paranormal. They were scientists who had a personal experience, or musicians who started experiencing strange sounds and then took it to the next level. Many were people just interested in history. The dead make history come alive and may tell us more about who we were in the past than answering the questions of life after death. True research will always touch upon some aspect of the past, and some people enjoy it just for that reason.

Religion and the Paranormal

It's there and you can't avoid it. There are religious undertones to the paranormal. You may be the biggest believer in absolutely nothing and secure in your place in the universe, but the questions you are facing are so big there is no way to avoid the "R" word.

As you ask yourself the questions you need to move forward, you will eventually come to wonder about the meaning of all of this. Do we have a soul? Is there something after this life?

Figure 1.2
The entrance of a church.

Figure 1.3
An old church candle stand thought to be a magnet for ghostly activity.

These are questions of psychology and philosophy, but also of religion. There is no way to ask if there is something more without also asking if there is someone who controls it all. That means some kind of higher power, which leads you to some kind of god. So much of modern day ghost hunting is about taking the religion out of the ghost question, and no one wants to trample on the thoughts of anyone else. Again, to not consider the questions religion poses for humans is to leave an aspect of an investigation outside. It might be a key to unlocking the door.

There is another reason to confront religion. If a ghost can be the personality of a person, who they were when they were living and conscious of what was going on, they might be influenced by what their idea of god was when they were breathing. Witnesses might filter their experience through their religion, or even be more open, or more closed off, to something because of their belief system. It might influence how you want to conduct yourself. All of these are legitimate reasons to be aware of this side of the paranormal. Do not, however, enter the world of ghost hunting thinking you are going to get answers to these questions. Don't get me wrong: Some find a spiritual answer in the search and the evidence. If you start because you want to understand God's plan or know the secrets of the soul, you may have entered the wrong business. Demonologists might say becoming involved in the work lets you know your creator on a different level, but most investigating will only bring about new questions and not solve the old.

You're Never Wrong

All of these are good answers, and if you think about it carefully, you probably have some combination of these reasons in different degrees. That is okay. Never let anyone tell you your reasons are not good enough or up to the standards of other groups. You determine your level of commitment, how much money you spend, and how much time you devote, and as long as you never pretend you are doing more than you are, you'll be fine. One does not need to be noble or have noble reasons for being out in the field.

What Is a Ghost and Why Ask the Question?

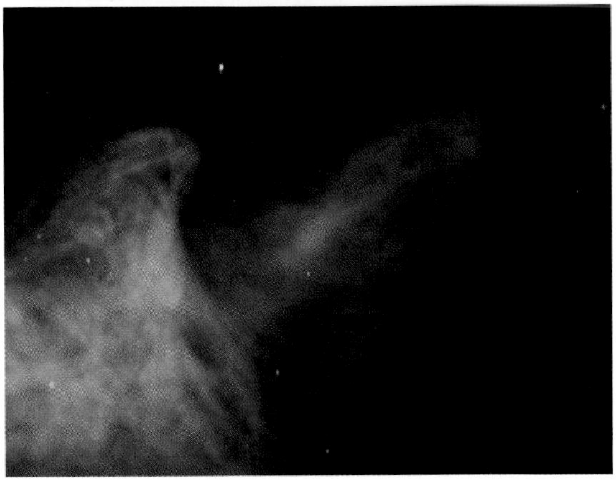

Figure 1.4
Ghostly interference during an investigation.
Picture courtesy of the Native American Ghost Society.

"The disincarnate personality of a once living human being whose energy and personality is able to exist beyond the human body."

—Shawn Blaschka, WPRS

"...a ghost or haunting is something left over from life, an echo."

—Brian J. Cano, The SCARED! Crew

"A ghost is a disembodied spirit of a once living person that hasn't quite made the transition from this world to the next often due to an untimely, sudden or violent death."

—Dale Kaczmarek, Ghost Research Society

"I believe ghosts are either emotional imprints in time and space, replaying themselves over and over until they finally fade out, or at times they are souls that choose to stay on Earth for one reason or another. Maybe because they don't realize they're dead or they have unfinished business that needs to be taken care of."

—Kathleen Popola, Blue Moon Paranormal Investigations

"To me a ghost is the life force of someone whom has died. They then try to interact with the living for whatever reason. Some people say they have unfinished business or just come back from wherever they were to contact someone special."

—Nicole Ardolino, Northeast Paranormal Investigations

"I believe that every living thing is made up of energy, and while our outer shell may die, the energy lives on. Most times it crosses over to the next realm of existence and sometimes it stays retaining the same emotions and experiences it had when it was in a body."

—Tina Carlson, Las Vegas Society of Supernatural Investigations

"...someone or thing that is no longer of our present time frame, and will always remain within the fabric of time until it has decided to move on to where it needs to go."

—Bruce J. Duarte, S.C.P.I.

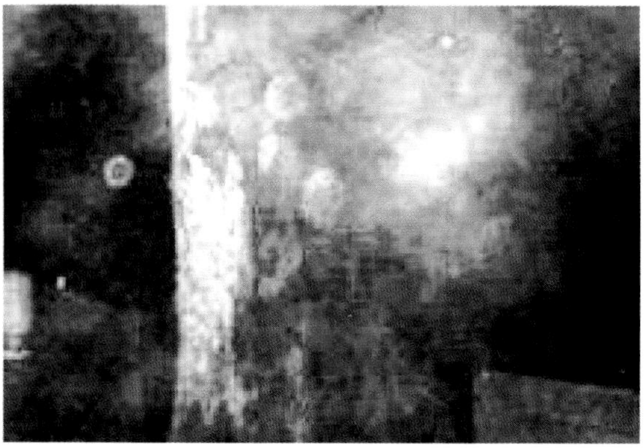

Figure 1.5
An unexplained mist during a hunt at a Native American Reservation.
Picture courtesy of the Native American Ghost Society.

Here's the part where many authors pull out their favorite dictionary, give you the definition and the appropriate way to pronounce the term, and then spend some time telling you why the wisdom of Webster's is incomplete. I'm just going to skip to the third part to save some time. There is no clear-cut definition that can be settled on, and part of ghost hunting, or at least the role of a good ghost hunter, is to keep challenging the accepted view of what a ghost is. A good investigator will challenge his own views and make sure his way of seeing it is not getting in the way of answering the question.

Ghost hunters today cannot settle on what a ghost actually is, and since the beginning of man, people have struggled with the question of death and life after death. The two are connected in our minds, or the prevailing idea is that a ghost is somehow an alternate reflection of a human who was once alive and who now is dead. Let's leave that behind as we look at the question. It is best to look at the question in the broadest terms. Later we'll look at the types of ghosts that have been reported, so my definition will only look at those hauntings I believe involve a ghost and only a ghost.

For me, a ghost is the disembodied essence of someone. Short, to the point, and encompassing as many of the kinds of spirits as are out there. As soon as you provide a solid description for anything viewed by so many in abstract terms, people will be lining up to tell you why your answer is incomplete. This is the one I'm comfortable with and that I work from. There are traces of science and the esoteric, leaving me open to the possibility of both and allowing me to understand that the real answer might be where the two meet up.

Disembodied?

Ghosts are not real. Ghost hunters may argue with that on its surface, but by its definition, ghosts belong to another world we do not understand, and even if you can talk to one and take a picture of it, it does not make it any more real. Leaving out some of the more fringe ideas, and everything in this field is fringe to someone, ghosts have no real body with a heartbeat and brain activity you can monitor. There have been instances where some kind of biological function can be heard or seen, but there is no breath coming out of a specter.

This does not mean whatever a ghost is does not exist; it just means ghosts do not have some of the characteristics needed to apply for social security. The personality and the grief and happiness might be real, but the body is not. Anything they are able to move or influence comes from manipulation of energy, not because a hand can grip it.

Protons and Electrons

Let's look at some science, or at least popular science. This means taking some understood truths and making some assumptions based on them. Essence is a muddy word, and I like it because it does not try to pinpoint what exactly we are sensing when a haunting happens. Many feel a ghost is energy, and much of ghost hunting is centered on tracking and trying to record that power. The science, while not proven, makes some sense, so it is worth looking at its ideas.

Figure 1.6
An orb caught at a haunted boarding school.
Picture courtesy of the Native American Ghost Society.

In a twist on its laws, people put forth that energy can't be created or destroyed. If your personality, or everything you are, is really only a collection of the impulses and energy running through your brain and your neurons, that personality has the potential to remain as pure energy after you die. Detecting a ghost means finding a way to register this, and getting rid of a ghost means interrupting it somehow.

This is sound, but it allows for a bit of bending of what the rule actually says. Energy can't be destroyed, but it can be converted. Think of power from a windmill. It's harnessed, changed, and then you can turn on your blender. The juice making your daily shake is nothing like the wind it started from. It has been converted into something different. The human personality, with all of its subtlety and complexity, can be shifted by the slightest short circuit or a simple head injury. With all of the tumblers having to be perfect for you to be you, the energy reason might not be the perfect solution to the problem.

The fact of the matter is electric equipment can read unusual amounts of energy where people have experienced ghosts, and some of the evidence gathered confirms or reflects the narrative of people's experiences, so the connection between energy and the paranormal can't be set aside. Instead, think of that essence as having the ability to manipulate, or at least to be detected as, energy. It is easier to define a ghost by how we can become aware of it. When we discuss the equipment ghost hunters use, we'll get more specific about those individual connections.

Riding the Wave

There is an entire spectrum to look at, not just traditional electricity. Some feel the reason for the increased level of ghostly activity is the increased level of microwaves in our society today. Others put their eggs into the magnetic and electromagnet end of the spectrum. Still others use the same equipment frequently utilized in looking for radiation. When looking for ghosts, investigators have tried using infrared and ultraviolet, the extremes of the visible light spectrum. Paranormal investigating also taps into other forms of waves that are not as clearly defined.

Much of it has to do with manifestation and not the origin of the specter. Much of audio work, like EVP recording, has to do with acoustic energy. This is similar to radio waves and can be detected by the human ear without equipment or with something used to capture it, like a recorder. This seems easily manipulated by ghosts, resulting in many reports of hearing a ghost instead of seeing one, and it explains why one can capture sounds on tape.

Figure 1.7
Thomas D'Agostino sweeping for acoustic energy during an investigation.
Picture courtesy of Arlene Nicholson.

These same waves might even draw in people to investigate. During one investigation, we found a bass guitar in the basement of the home. One of us picked it up and another said he played bass in a band when he was younger. A third investigator reminisced about his days playing the instrument before I came forward to tell about my good old days as a bass player. Four investigators all playing the same instrument that, by its nature, utilizes low frequencies. That might be more than coincidence.

Sometimes that acoustic energy might provide the juice for other kinds of manifestations. I recorded the case of a musician who heard about a woman who died in the apartment he was living in. Upon hearing her story, he wrote a song about her, and would often play the basic cords of it and marvel at how the words came to him. He started to notice that the environment shifted when he played the song, and he could feel someone there with him. He eventually saw her ghost and noted she returns when he plays that song. Another man had poltergeist activity whenever he played a certain song on a particular violin. Both might be cases where the acoustic energy fed the presence already there, allowing it to come forth.

But Ghosts Are Dead, Right?

There have been many cases where a ghost turned out to be something completely contradictory to the traditional idea of one. Most involve someone who was alive and has now passed, but while that may be the standing rule, I use the term "most" because of those stories that lie on the outside. I heard of a case where a little boy was abused and left alone in the dark basement. He invented an imaginary friend to keep him company in those long hours. Jackie Barrett, a renowned psychic, went into the house and discovered the imaginary friend was still there, but rather than the product of his imagination, he had actually drawn in a demon. That was unusual, but she also found the little boy remained in the room he was abused in as a ghost. The nature of the abuse was so traumatic, his essence imprinted itself in the environment, and the demon was still feeding off of it years later. The man still lived upstairs, but the ghost of his childhood owned the basement.

Figure 1.8
The ghost of a person or a collection of the energy in the room?
Picture courtesy of Brooke Huchel.

These non-dead ghosts mainly fall into the realm of a residual haunting, or non-intelligent energy received by a human source. There are some examples that are not so easily taken in. People have reported being visited by loved ones who were thousands of miles away but who somehow left their own bodies. By my definition, these are ghosts.

The Reasons or the Excuses

If a ghost can be anyone for any reason, if you can live a full life and die in your sleep with all of your affairs in order, it makes the world of the paranormal less romantic. It also makes becoming a spirit something everyone has to fear. To make ourselves feel better, we create a mystique about ghosts that may be fantasy. A very common theme in investigators' ideas of spirits is that they have died a horrible death or have some kind of unfinished business. Something draws us in about a brutal murder or suicide and makes us live in the haunting and the backstory. These things, many feel, are needed for a paranormal event. This is not the case. While we may like the idea that we can right our wrongs in the next life, there are too many cases that have no origin or purpose. It is more of our human mind's need to fit everything inside of a neat box.

It might also have to do with our own human condition. Someone once posed to me the question, "Why are there so many ghosts from the Victorian Era?" While many battlefields of the Civil War are haunted, the trend is much more involved than that. I said something on the spot, but a few days later I discovered *This Republic of Suffering: Death and the American Civil War* by Drew Gilpin Faust. It is an account of the horrors of the war and far from a ghost book. In it, she discusses the idea of Ars Moriendi or the good death. The idea was not new, having been explored centuries earlier in Europe, but in the decades before the war, the notion of your death influencing your afterlife became very popular in America. A violent death far away from the people you loved meant you were less likely to get into heaven. Relatives wanted to know how their sons and nephews passed because it clued them into how they would spend eternity, and the dying would try to recreate their homes as they lay bleeding in the field, going so far as to place pictures of their family around them before they expired.

The concept became the foundation for a new religion called Spiritualism that had its rise around the same time. It is still around today. Most people look to die in a predictable, peaceful way where they see it coming and have time to transition in their mind before their body does it for them.

This does not mean a bad death is the key to a disturbed afterlife full of haunting, but it might be a strong enough idea to hold some people to this plane. There is something to be said for some spirits needing to deal with something and move on, and the good death may be something that sets them free. Take away that honor, and they might be less inclined to let go. It accounts for many of the romantic stories of unfinished business and even explains someone who died suddenly not being ready to transition.

Defining the Ghost Hunter

I SAT WITH THREE REPORTERS asking me questions in a cemetery. Actually, it was one reporter and her friend who came along in case I was actually a serial killer. A third heard why they were going out and insisted on coming as well. The reporter's friend laughed and asked a question I had heard too many times before. "Are you a Ghostbuster?" I made sure I was not wearing a proton pack and assured her I wasn't. The reporter broke in, "No. They like to be called ghost hunters." Time was passing too quickly in the graveyard, but I wanted to have the record set straight.

"Actually, I consider myself a paranormal investigator."

"What's the difference?"

I thought about it, and shrugged before giving in. The next day I was referred to as a ghost hunter. It was fine with me. My name was in the paper.

Besides from the obvious connotation from the television show *Ghost Hunters*, there really is no difference between any of the names people are using these days to identify themselves.

Figure 1.9
Investigator Brian Paulson.
Picture courtesy of Brian Paulson and the Eidolic Paranormal Research Association.

Usually they don't call themselves anything and let other people decide the label. My favorite is a man from Kentucky who refers to himself as a spectral detective or a Spi-Eye. I've seen what he does and can assure you he is a ghost hunter. I use the terms interchangeably, and it might be more important to define what you do and let the names sort themselves out.

Defining the Job

A ghost hunter is someone who actively looks for the paranormal. There are different ways of going about it, but the end pursuit remains constant. There's a weight to the term today, especially given the success of the television show, but what a ghost hunter does extends way beyond this. The words conjure up images of people who see life through night vision and walk around with thousands of dollars' worth of equipment. There is some truth to that. Many people who consider themselves ghost hunters are more on the scientific side of things. They believe the best way to answer the questions posed in this book is to find hard evidence and present it to the general public. They abide by some sort of loose scientific process and try to recreate something solid.

Figure 1.10
Investigator Andrew Woods from Greenville Paranormal Research.
Picture courtesy of Arlene Nicholson.

Figure 1.11
Thomas D'Agostino preparing for an investigation.

This is not the only definition. Hans Holzer, for example, is considered by many to be the father of modern ghost hunting, and his methods more often than not strayed from the scientific. Many of the original investigators used nothing more than a tape recorder, their wits, and some kind of belief in their own psychic ability. Many, like Harry Price, the definitive paranormal researcher in the 1930s and 1940s, had nothing more than a pen, a notebook, and a library card. Today we revere these investigators, but many look down on current investigators who don't have a scientific approach. There is pressure to conduct an investigation as a scientist. Do what you do.

Figure 1.12
The Native American Ghost Society catches something unexplained on film.

Some of the best advances in the field are made by people with quick minds and good eyes, not necessarily heavy equipment or psychic ability.

A ghost hunter looks, analyzes, and documents. There are some who believe it is in the job description to rid families of whatever might be in their houses, and this may be something you eventually would feel comfortable doing. There is a danger in this. We don't fully understand what a ghost is, and where the line is between an entity and other types of supernatural things, so it is almost impossible to say you can get rid of anything that might be haunting someone. Instead of claiming to clean a house, think of yourself as a counselor who might be able to lessen the supernatural load.

Living the Life

When people hear what I do, I get two reactions and they usually happen right after one another. The first is a turned up nose and the classic ambiguous question, "You're into that?" The second comes more slowly, but the person will tell me a story they heard or an experience from when they were younger. Right at that moment, I turn from a bar patron enjoying a beer and the game into a ghost hunter. The change happens that quickly and you have to be ready.

Living the life means taking your level of commitment right to the cusp of what is comfortable. A cop can never fully turn off being a cop, and a paranormal investigator never sleeps. A handheld tape recorder designated for interviews and ideas only will serve you well. Stories and leads can come at any time, and he who hesitates is lost.

You get the story down, but you would be surprised how much people remember when someone is taking them so seriously. It makes what has been on the edge of reality real for them.

There are the late night calls. Many people live with a haunting for years without saying anything until something big happens or they see something in a movie or in a book that touches a nerve. If you don't pick up the phone, you may never hear from them again. I could fill a book with cases I tried to follow up on where the people refused to talk about it again.

Many believe investigating is about aligning all of your equipment on a table, planning out what to do, assembling a team, and hitting the field. Most experiences happen when the witness least expects it. The same will happen to you. Being caught setting up may cause you to lose the most extraordinary evidence you might ever get.

For example, while working on the DVD for this book, I was setting up my video camera. As I made note of the fact my camera battery had been drained, the camera shooting the DVD picked up an EVP on its audio track. This would have been lost if we did not have tape running.

Figure 1.13
An investment of thousands of dollars' worth of equipment.
Picture courtesy of Jamie Chesterson and the Texas Paranormal Society.

Is This a Job?

We will discuss in detail in Chapter 7 whether to charge for the work you do, but even if you do, there is very little chance you will get rich or even make a living doing this. There are about as many investigators who make a comfortable living doing this as there are convincing orb photos (but we'll talk about that later), and despite some recent attempts, there is no union securing medical benefits and overtime. Most people who make the paranormal a major part of their lives do something else. The majority are writers who tell of their cases or of general paranormal knowledge. Others might have a radio show or speak at conferences for a few hundred dollars an event. In the very rare case they work on a television show as the talent or behind the scenes.

The image has become the reality for some. People buy lottery tickets because they see the pictures of people holding big checks. The odds of winning are so stacked against people, but they still play their numbers. It may look like everyone has a book deal or a television show, but I can count ten groups within five miles of where I live, and there is only so much money to go around.

There's a Downside

There is a standing rule in my house. We only put the baby monitor on when we are about to fall asleep and anything we hear over it that is not my son's voice is a stray radio transmission, even if it calls us by name and asks us for help. We once heard my son talking to someone with the same name as my wife's deceased father. We promptly convinced ourselves he had a new kid at the daycare we didn't know yet. We shared a strained smile and never spoke of it again.

Prepare to have your life invaded. It is better to be safe than sorry, but there is a good chance someone might come to visit you. There is a classic story by Han Holzer of a ghost who bothered a man until a psychic was called in. The ghost crossed to the other side with the help of a dead friend, and as they walked towards the light, the friend asked him why he had bothered the poor guy. He replied, "He was the only one who could see me."

Paranormal investigators see because they seek out. There is a theory that you stand out like a bright light in darkness when you start to look for spirits. That is a great comfort for them, but might be freaky to you. Looking for a spirit in a haunted house is one thing, but waking up to find one in your room is another. It is something you will have to deal with if you want to start doing this. There are ways to keep ghosts out of your house, so you might want to practice what you preach and start building walls and a moat around your bedroom.

There is also a theory that something is out there looking to get in. It is cunning and sinister and not very apt at making friends. Not all in the supernatural world was once a living and breathing person, and these other beings can be dangerous. They are drawn to you for the same reason a human entity is, so be on guard. Some religions strictly forbid ghost hunting because it leaves one open to these forces. There are investigators I know who have backed down from actively looking for cases because they felt something else coming in. Again, protect yourself and know they are out there, but most people will never suffer from an attack or unwanted attention.

The New Ideas on Ghosts

AS SCIENCE AND TECHNOLOGY kill the gods of old and turn religion on its head, the same advances force people to rethink what a ghost might be. You want to approach investigating with as open a mind as possible, so you will need a crash course in some of these new ideas. No one out there is demanding you get a doctorate in quantum physics to look for ghosts, but knowing a few scientific ideas can't hurt, and it lets you see the ever changing scope of what a ghost hunter does. These ideas should challenge your mind and test your religion, and hopefully move your understanding forward. There is good work being done to advance ghost research that has nothing to do with the investigators we see on television. These ideas are on the fringe of paranormal research and some aren't even accepted by all scientists.

Rather than read about advanced science, it will be considerably easier to break it down to what we need. *Superstring theory* tells us the world is a collection of strings moving at incredible speeds and encompassing alternate realities, levels of consciousness, and dimensions. Ghosts may be people somehow caught in between these levels or able to jump between them. A ghost in one reality is a human walking and talking in another.

Advanced chaos theory put forth the idea that millions of decisions over the course of a minute radically change what happens to an individual and all of mankind. You turn left and a car hits you, or you sneeze and a man dies thousands of miles away. This interconnectedness means a ghost may be someone who has jumped the track of one timeline and landed in another. Stuck between the two, their physical appearance and behavior would seem dreamlike or ghostly. In fact, you may be the ghost in their world for a brief moment. These experiences, called time slips, will be discussed later.

There are some ideas on the outer edges of the fringe, so close to the edge they have one leg dangling. People have put forth theories that all ghosts are aliens looking to test the human race. Another hypothesis says they come from below the surface of the Earth for the same reason. These kinds of ideas will always be around, and they come and go quickly, but do not dismiss them. I was contacted by a man who believed all of the supernatural activity in his area was caused by the government using the mentally disabled people in a hospital in bizarre experiments trying to perfect mind control and remote viewing. I wanted to laugh it off, but the next day someone I worked with called me crazy for believing any of this. It's all relative.

Not all the ideas come from science. Religions have tossed their hats into the ring, and one of the dominant ideas put forward is that all ghosts are just demons in sheep's clothing. Another idea says the essence of a person can escape from a person either living or dead and manipulate energy, much like spiritual telekinesis.

Some of these religious beliefs are so strong entire sects form around them. The best way to deal with them, and any of the new ideas about the paranormal, is to listen and put the information away for a rainy day. You never know when it will be useful.

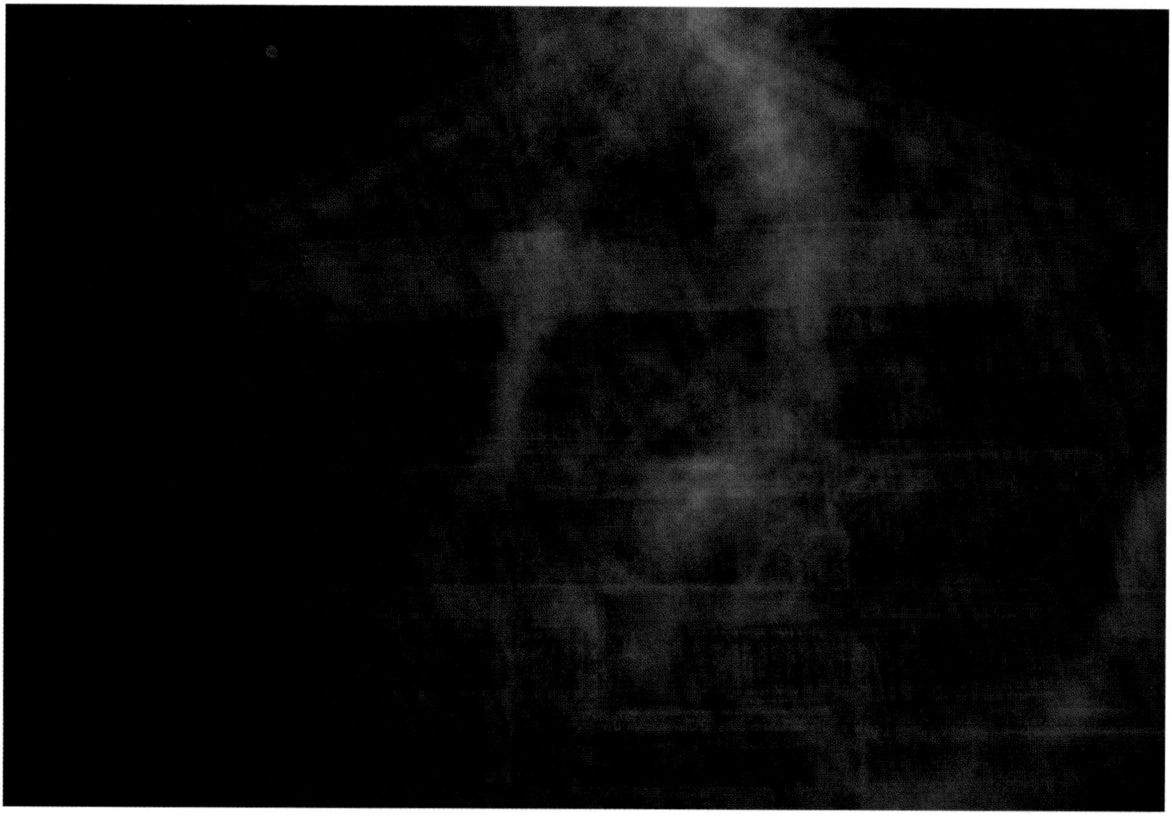

Figure 1.14
A darker energy seen at an old building.
Picture courtesy of Brian Paulson and the Eidolic Paranormal Research Association.

Looking for the Dead: Where to Look When They Don't Come to You

As you become a more experienced paranormal investigator, people will begin to find you. It may be someone who sees your website and needs someone to explain the weird creaks they are hearing at night, or a business like a hotel or restaurant looking to make the leap to being certified haunted to draw in business. As I discussed earlier, it will be up to you whether you call these cases and the people involved clients, but they are people who become the heartbeat of what you do. Between these situations and the ghosts that find their way to you, your docket might be full.

In reality, the majority of the ghosts you investigate will have to actually be looked for. Cases, even for the more well known investigators and groups, come in bunches during certain times of the year, and when it rains it pours. Most of the time, you will be anxiously sitting around, waiting for a case and working to perfect your craft. During these times, it's best to go out and find your own ghosts. Whether you get evidence you can use or determine a ghost may not be present in the location, these are the places where you pay your dues.

Cemeteries

Three ghost hunters are playing poker on a Saturday night, and, as the last rake comes in, a yawn hits the room. Where is the excitement? Where is that rush of adrenaline and the satisfied feeling of knowing you're doing your part to solve one of life's great mysteries? They need to get out into the field. You need permission to get into that old hospital, and they've investigated Johnny's house seven times. Where can they call back on?

There is something inherently paranormal about a cemetery, and when the pickings are lean, investigators go back to the well. In many ways, a graveyard can be the ideal place to get in contact with spirits, or at least try to get in touch, and ghost hunters hit the headstones with vigor.

Figure 1.15
A haunted cemetery in Boston, Massachusetts.

We'll discuss more about how to look into a graveyard in Chapter 6, but there are some things that are important to cover before then. What you do reflects on all paranormal investigators. There is a famously haunted cemetery in New Hampshire that is now closed to the public after dusk because people were taking pieces of a headstone said to glow blue at night. A vandal is a vandal, no matter what his motive.

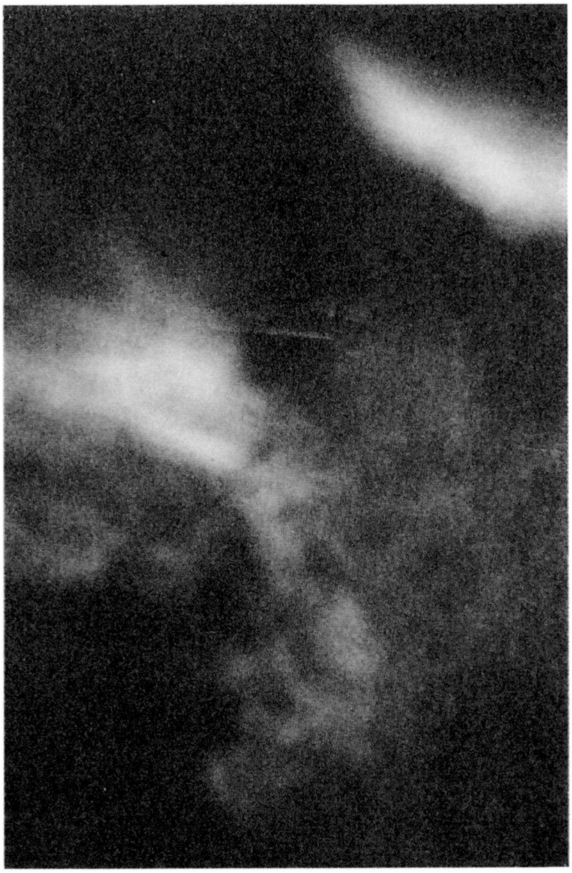

Figure 1.16
A picture taken at the famous Vale End Cemetery in New Hampshire.

Looking into a graveyard can be productive and give you all you need to curb your hunger, but remember these simple rules:

- **Know the rules of your state and town. Most cemeteries are closed after dark, and it is trespassing to be in there.**
- **No gate does not mean a cemetery is open.**
- **Respect the living. Don't investigate a well visited cemetery in the day when people are visiting loved ones.**
- **Respect the dead. Ghosts or no ghosts, people who once had proud lives are buried there. Treat them with honor and reverence even if they are nothing but dust to you.**
- **What you take in, take out.**

Empty Places

Investigations are oftentimes crimes of opportunity. Ghost hunters go where the story is, and when they can't get in legally, they sneak in. This should never be done, but there are ways to get permission to get into an abandoned place that has a reputation of being haunted. Take advantage of these buildings when you can, especially if there is a history of tragedy you can track down that may provide confirmation of your evidence. There are some major obstacles we'll discuss later, but empty places are one of the most exciting locations you can get into.

Some of the best empty places are as follows:

- **Old mills and factories, especially if something traumatic happened there**
- **Hospitals, asylums, and sanitariums**
- **Old schools**
- **Farms**
- **Warehouses**
- **Jails**

Figure 1.17
The famous haunted Fort Adams in Rhode Island.

Figure 1.18
The haunted Fort Smith.
Picture courtesy of the Native American Ghost Society.

The Prepackaged Paranormal

Ghosts are big business these days. I was drawn to an old Army fort in Newbury, Rhode Island, a town known for its paranormal history. I heard the place might be haunted from a few scattered stories and went there to check it out. I took one look and knew it had to be haunted. There was no way it couldn't be. It fit the part perfectly, but looks can be deceiving. I found it was one of the most mundane places in the town, with no solid reports or history to point at something left behind. The fort had begun capitalizing on its appearance, its visual eeriness, and billed it as haunted for yearly events where they would share its history and then hint at something still going on today. It made for a fun time, but as a research subject it fell short.

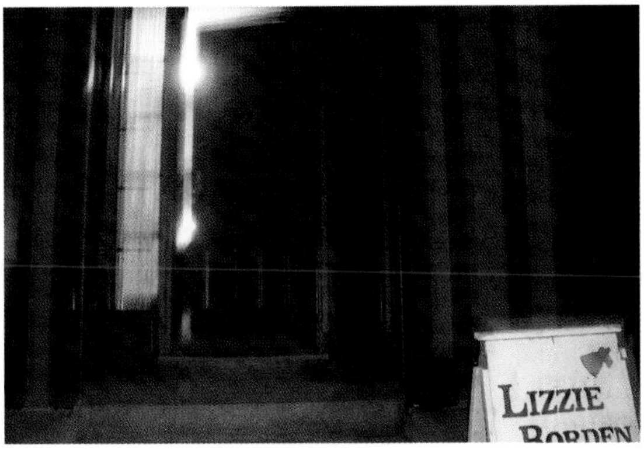

Figure 1.19
The Lizzie Borden Bed and Breakfast. You can stay the night and hunt for any of the ghosts reported there.

These kinds of events are popping up everywhere, and they make for a good night out. Most large cities have tours focused on the ghosts living there. They are a mix of history, urban legend, and whispers, and some even invite people to come with equipment to try to gather evidence. This is, of course, a marketing ploy. Not only does it draw the investigators in, but it makes it feel more haunted for the others on the tour, and if any evidence is gathered, it builds their credibility. By all means, attend these tours and events. Keep in mind you should be critical any time you put your money down for a chance to see a ghost. It might be better just to sit back and let someone else hand the stories to you for a change.

If you are planning a trip to a town, do a bit of online research and fit in a ghost tour. There are websites out there for any place you may want to go, but one of the best might be Haunted America Tours at www.hauntedamericatours.com. They offer the best from each state and provide other valuable paranormal information.

One of the new commodities on the ghost market is the ghost investigation of a known haunted site. These are usually sponsored by a group or some kind of paranormal media entity and are becoming more and more popular. For a fee, you can meet real life investigators, sometimes a big name, and look for phantoms at the Lizzie Borden Bed and Breakfast or Eastern State Penitentiary. These are a mixed bag at best. They usually hit the purse pretty hard and it's not exactly easy to gather good evidence with 20 other people snapping pictures. On the other hand, some really convincing evidence has been produced from these places and special events.

Every Place Is Haunted

Just because a place does not have a reputation does not mean there are not ghosts there. As you get more involved, ghosts find you. They might hang around, waiting for their turn at the microphone, regardless of the location. Some people just draw in ghosts, but more often, people who do the work find odd things happen around them. This might be a quiet spirit trying to get your attention. They might not be tied down by time or place, so always feel free to contact the dead after watching the basketball game or when you first wake up in the morning. All you have to lose is a bit of time and some videotape.

You'll need to know what you're doing though. You've taken the first leap, now it's time to get your hands dirty and find out what a ghost is and how to look for them. Think of every page after this as another step, with some stumbles thrown in for good measure. Press forward, but remember to carry a flashlight and have an extra set of batteries.

2

It Takes All Kinds

KNOW WHAT YOU'RE GETTING INTO. Ghosts have many faces, not all of them pretty. If it is becoming increasingly harder for investigators to agree about what a ghost actually is, it should be an even stickier situation trying to classify the different types of characters who inhabit the paranormal world. With so many different traits and with so many variants, it can become more confusing to figure out what might be haunting a location than it is to find the courage to search for it. As investigators become better known in certain communities, they are asked to diagnose problems, often over the phone or through e-mail. I am frequently asked, "Well, what's haunting me?" Some might want an immediate answer, even if it is only for their own peace of mind. The answer is almost never clear-cut, but I have created a system to deal with the difficult task of judging what might be haunting the location.

Like many things in life, entities from the realm of the afterlife should be classified by what they do. The traditional method might suggest listing spirits by their intentions or what they look like or the type of evidence gathered from them. I choose to let their actions speak for themselves.

Who's Doing the Watching?

THE FIRST MAJOR GROUPING of spirits deals with the intelligence of the phantom. A ghost might have been a valedictorian in life, but as a ghost, it might be nothing more than a mere shadow. Instead, think of intelligence as how well it can relate to others. Is it aware of the world around it? Is it a part of the world around it? Ghosts can really be broken down into two major groups: Conscious hauntings and psychic recordings.

Conscious Hauntings

Can a spirit cry or laugh or get angry when you ignore it? An affirmative answer indicates a haunting, which may be more frightening, and at times more heartbreaking, than hauntings you read about in books. The truth is most ghosts are nothing more than misguided energy, but a good percentage have some kind of intelligence to them. They're living, breathing people; they're just not living and breathing. They might be perfect reflections of what they were in life, or only a dominant part of their personality has survived, but they can react and interact with their surroundings and with you. They might be confused or not see things clearly, but they have a relationship with the world, or maybe even the dimension, they are in. We'll get into these kinds of ghosts a bit later in this chapter.

Psychic Recordings

Most investigators and researchers will tell you the majority of paranormal activity making people lose sleep is of a nonintelligent nature. The ghost is only energy somehow trapped in an environment. The right situation and circumstance triggers the activity, and at times it's witnessed by people. We call this a psychic recording, otherwise known as a residual haunting because it denotes the trapped energy somehow still left in the floors and ceilings. Although ideas on supernatural topics may run the gamut of theory and belief, this one is pretty much universal to people in the field and one of the first distinctions investigators try to make.

In the 1970s, a theory was proposed that forms the basis for many investigators' beliefs about trapped energy. The stone tape theory put forth moments that could be caught in an environment if the right natural conditions were present. Since then, many believe water, especially running water, absorbs human emotion somehow, which is often used as the foundation for so many spirits to be present near water supplies. The same holds true for rocks such as granite and metal, which is then used to explain why an object moved from one place to another. While based in some science, the explanation is also convenient. There are very few places that don't have these types of objects in them.

Think of walking into a friend's house right after he has had an argument with his wife or girlfriend. Both are smiling and offering you a drink, but there is something lingering in the air. You may not be able to put your finger on it, and you may not be able to measure it with any kind of equipment, but something is just not right. There is similar electricity in the air after a physical altercation. The fistfight was broken up, but the energy of the violence has somehow left its imprint in the room.

Psychic recordings work much the same way. A strong personality or an emotional event creates so much energy it literally stays in the air. It may be from the emotional weight or the speed and the pop of the episode. It becomes a trapped moment playing in a loop, sometimes experienced and other times working with too little juice to be observed. The right combination of energy, either electrical or emotional, or both, triggers a replay of the event. A person does not even need to be present for it to happen.

A man falls down the stairs on his way to his son's baseball game. As he slips on the top stair, his wife turns the corner and sees him start to go down. She screams for him and reaches out, but it is too late. He hits every other step on the way to the bottom, until he crashes. His wife runs down after him and collapses at the base of the stairs on top of her beloved. She screams out his name and holds his lifeless body close.

Figure 2.1
A road where the residual energy of a mysterious woman appears.

This kind of event is the perfect set of conditions for a potential psychic recording. So tragic and sudden the event, and with so many different sounds and sights, it may mark itself on the environment. Twenty years later a family moves in. Every Saturday afternoon during the spring they hear an unseen voice scream, and then odd noises coming from the front steps, and then finally a disembodied voice yell a man's name.

There is another possible root for a psychic recording. Repetition may lead to a memory becoming trapped. Like a path through the woods made clean by continued movement over it, the activity becomes so mindless to the person who does it that they leave a bit of themselves there.

In Massachusetts, there is a place in the town of Lynn known as Dungeon Rock. A man walked the same path every day as he marched up a hill and down a tunnel to dig for gold. He did the same thing for decades until he died, eventually recruiting his son who did it until he too expired. People have seen this man and his son marching up the hill and disappearing underground, and all attempts to communicate with them are met with a deaf ear. They are nothing more than a recording linked and working together even in death.

Don't feel bad for them though. To the investigator, the psychic recording is both clear-cut and frustrating. On one hand, you know what they are and what to say about them, but on the other they are almost impossible to stop and hard to gather evidence from. The energy left in the place may be so strong it could last for decades. There is no rationalizing or talking with the spirit the way you can in an intelligent haunting. Furthermore, the possibility of any harm coming from a psychic recording is almost nonexistent and it usually does not intensify. You also can save yourself the emotional roller-coaster because you do not need to weep. The people in the recording are no longer suffering, at least not in that location.

Psychic recordings are not limited to a single person or an enclosed experience. They sometimes play themselves out on a much grander scale. There are old battlefields in Europe where airplane battles are still going on years after all the planes have landed. At Gettysburg, the site of the most infamous battle of the Civil War, many people have reported hearing or seeing parts of the fighting happening, many times thinking it was some kind of reenactment. One of the most mysterious hauntings in America takes place in Hawaii where an entire battalion of ghost soldiers marches towards its final battle. Many believe it to be nothing more than a recording because people cannot interact with the soldiers. Of course, it is said if you see them at all, you will die shortly afterwards, so the existence of these warriors is still up in the air.

Ghosts More Precisely

LET'S TAKE THIS A BIT DEEPER and fine-tune the characterization of ghosts. Understanding that there are crossovers on every level and that many of the spirits we are going to talk about can fall into the intelligent or psychic recording column, let's define the actions of a ghost.

Ones You See

Do you trust your eyes? People say you can imagine a floating figure if you are under stress or overtired. Scrooge blamed his visitation on bad food. All that makes sense to you, especially in the light of day, but you just saw something, and they can't take that away.

While they're the ghosts you are least likely to come into contact with, spirits you can actually see are the most dramatic paranormal occurrence you can have. It is easier to pass off a smell or a random noise, but seeing is often believing. There are always reasons why a ghost is not a ghost, but observing something might be the most solid evidence of life after death. They're the only type of ghost that should be called an apparition, especially when you consider the word literally means something seen.

Full-Bodied Apparitions

Full-bodied apparitions are the holy grail of paranormal investigating. The ghost is just what it sounds like, an apparition whose whole body is on our plane. It wears clothes of the time-period it lived in and can perform many of the tasks it was used to in life, although it more often than not can't manipulate its environment. While most of these spirits are nothing more than psychic recordings, there are reports of full-bodied apparitions that are intelligent and speak. They are the most vivid paranormal experience for a witness to come across, and usually enough to change ideas about ghosts. For the ghost hunter they are the rarest evidence captured and many an investigative hour has been spent scanning pictures for them.

What the body can do varies. At times, there is a glow around it and the witness can tell almost immediately he is looking at something not of this earth. Other times, the living can hold an entire conversation with a person only to realize later the person they were talking to was dead. Time and again, full-bodied apparitions who make contact don't know they are dead and have a hard time dealing with our reality.

Part of a Whole and Little Things Out of the Corner of Your Eye

More often than not, seeing a ghost involves watching some part of it rather than the whole. The most common seems to be the head of the dead person, but feet, arms, and torsos have also been reported. There are often stories told of clothes being the only visible part of the ghost. While it may be unsettling to see a head floating in the air without a body, you have to ask yourself, why. Why would this spirit come as only a head instead of a full person?

Figure 2.2
The image of a face that appeared during a séance.

The first reason may be due to the nature of the person's death. He may have lost the body part and that is what led to his demise. The headless body or the bodiless head of Anne Boleyn would make sense. There might also be a reason or some significance to the partial formation. Perhaps the feet tell us we need to move out of the house, or eyes tell us we need to watch for something. The ghost might also be responding to its environment. I remember reading about a ghost with no feet, and when research was done, they found out the floor had been a few inches lower before it had been remodeled. The ghost didn't know things had changed. The most common reason, however, may just be a lack of power. Perhaps the spirit just doesn't have the juice to show itself completely.

This might also account for the appearance of those little critters that dash just out of the range of your peripheral vision. Many of the stories I hear about everyday people who experience ghosts involve seeing something out of the corner of their eye at some point. They dismiss what they see because they can explain it away, but there is usually something else paranormal to go with it. These spirits can be seen going in and out of shadows or seen for only a split second in a mirror or a window. There is almost always something else happening, like unexplained noises or weird feelings, and the sighting confirms for the witness that he is being haunted. Some of these might be shadow people, but we'll get to them later in this chapter.

In Rod We Trust

In some of the theories put forth, the energy that makes us who we are can become a concentrated form. This is echoed by many alternative religions who speak of our energy as a ball of powerful light. Native American and European traditions talk of the soul as a light that can be harvested by evil, sometimes known as Will o' the Wisp or Tei-Pai-Wankas. Science invites us to look at all of our body as energy impulses. That energy may be seen by a witness or an investigator as an orb of energy, or a ball of bright light. Investigators strive to capture these in pictures and base their investigations around them, but at times they are seen with the human eye. While most are white or yellow, some people have experienced different shades of blue, red, and green. The reason for a particular color is unknown and has no effect on how the shape moves, but of course observers feel enlightened by the white lights and scared of the red ones.

Figure 2.3
Haunted rod or camera strap?
Picture courtesy of Josh Mantello and the Berkshire Paranormal Group.

Unlike swamp gas and St. Elmo's Fire, which can be explained, or even orbs caught on camera that are often dismissed as dust or moisture, these spheres have a personality and move in unconventional and unpredictable ways. They are often accompanied by an electrical smell, as opposed to the rot of a swamp. Lore attached to them include the trainman who walks the track late at night with his lantern to check for people looking to hop a ride.

Not all are round though. People also have seen the lights streak across their line of sight. Again, the majority of the evidence is found in pictures, and many can be explained away. Still, there is a small percentage of the population who see them with the naked eye. The most rampant variant of these streaks is the rod of light popular at the beginning of this century. There were hundreds of reports of one- to two-foot rods of light that would float in the air and then sprint across the room and vanish into the wall. Many felt they were related to UFOs or something else supernatural. They are not talked about as much today, but they are important enough to at least think about.

Doppelgangers

Over the years the word doppelganger has come to be known as someone who looks similar to another person, but in the paranormal world the meaning has remained the same for centuries. A doppelganger is a vision of yourself, often as a harbinger of your own demise. Seeing one does not mean you will automatically die, but rather that your end will come in that location. Imagine sitting on your front steps and then watching yourself cross the street. This may mean you will someday be hit by a car crossing that very street.

The evidence for the existence of these ghosts is sketchy. Instead, the stories are passed down through second-hand reports or through journal entries. Someone conveys the story and then one day it comes to pass. Think of it as a variant of the crisis apparition, but the one in trouble is you and it might not happen for decades.

There Is More Than Meets the Eye

In many ways, a haunting can be dealt with better if you see someone walk through your living room. Your eyes may be playing tricks on you, but for the most part there is some proof inside your own head screaming that you are not completely crazy. Most of the paranormal is more elusive than that. For one reason or another, ghosts invade our other sense, many times being too subtle for us to notice or being dismissed as imagination or something natural. The haunting may intensify because of this, like a problem becoming bigger when disregarded or a child raising the stakes so you'll pay attention. Even people who have died hate to be ignored.

Did You Smell That?

Smell is our most powerful sense, even if we don't know how it fully works or understand the way it plays with our head. Catch a whiff of vanilla from a candle, and you remember being a small child waiting for Grandma to finish the cookies. Smell a highlighter and it reminds you of the hours you spent in detention. The general idea is that smells vibrate at certain frequencies, which is why some can have a calming effect on you and others can make you excited. If this is true, smells can be produced or manipulated by the same forces that manipulate other forms of energy. Ghosts might not have their own scent, but they can sometimes haunt through our nose.

A smell might be particular to the person doing the haunting. Perhaps this person always smoked a cigarette in the bathroom before going to bed. Now you can smell someone lighting up every night around nine before you climb into bed. Aunt Joanne's perfume was like sweet violet, even if she wore so much you could taste it in the back of your throat. When her ghost comes around, her perfume is in the air. If the odor is relevant to the person, if it somehow defines who they were when they were alive, it might be recognized by the living. They know who the ghost is, and if they didn't believe in spirits before, smelling may be believing.

Figure 2.4
A haunted Native American reservation where odd smells have been detected along with unexplained drums and ghostly visions.

There are some standards investigators put forth. The smell of different flowers is the sign of a positive spirit. The smell of garbage or excrement hints at the demonic, or something dark or evil. Be careful of making generalizations. Too often, people smell garbage and assume the worst when in actuality the house is built downwind from the town dump or there is a dead animal in the walls. Scents might seem to be solid evidence, especially if they go hand in hand with some other paranormal element, but you would be surprised how far scents travel and how they move throughout a house.

With One Ear to the Ground

It is far more likely you will hear a ghost rather than see one. Whether it is through a listening device like a radio or television or with your own ears, it might take less energy to produce results from the dead through sound waves. There are relatively few hauntings that do not involve sound of some kind, although we are quick to laugh off the majority of evidence we might get based on noise until something else happens and we can link it to other evidence. If the contact is dramatic, we might raise an eyebrow, but so much auditory communication from the spirit world is ignored.

Many sounds come as part of a psychic recording. There might be a consistent footstep or a scream heard, but these can also be signs of an intelligent haunting. People sometimes report moans, cries, or talking, usually loud enough to be heard but not so much that they can hear what is being said. This usually adds frustration for the witness, and seems to give the spirit needed energy for the haunting to intensify later.

People who live in a haunted house may experience their names being called. Unless it's a great coincidence, this is a sign of an intelligent haunting. Unlike other types of ghosts, this may be a sign that contact is being requested. Like many things having to do with the paranormal, this might be dangerous. Sometimes dark things have sweet voices and say all the right things. Approached with the same caution as other types of spirit communication, this type of talking should be encouraged and not shied away from. Simply respond the same way you would if someone called your name in real life.

Knocks are one of the great harbingers and a staple of folklore and superstition. Spirits are said to tap or knock on the door of someone who is about to die, usually in sets of three, almost like death is asking to come in. Others claim it to be relatives or friends coming to help the newly departed cross over with ease. Not all knocks are messages of death, however. There have been reports of people hearing a pounding on the door only to find no one there when they open it. Think of Poe and his chamber door. This can be very disturbing for the witness because it conveys a sense of invasion, like something is just outside the door, waiting for its chance to get in.

Other sounds range from confusing to terrifying. For some reason, coughing is always popular, and singing and laughing happen frequently when children are involved. Moaning is a very traditional ghostly sound, but some people have heard clapping, crying, and even passing gas.

The Ghost Effect

Paranormal activity often happens off camera when no one is observing and no one is around with a digital camera with an infrared filter. Instead of something solid to hold onto, the haunted only sees the effect of the presence of the ghost. Instead of hearing footsteps across the floor or a floating spirit making dinner, the witness finds his car keys on his nightstand when he knows he put them on the counter before he left the room. There is something more unnerving about only living through the end result. You may start to question your sanity because you shouldn't be seeing what you are seeing, but when the haunting is subtle, it can really grind away at your mind.

Ghosts have a tendency to play around with electronics, and the connection between the paranormal and energy is well defined for those who investigate. It seems like a marriage made in heaven and probably the easiest way for a spirit to make itself known. This is an excellent example of the ghost effect. You do not see a ghost change the channel on the television or turn off a monitor. Instead, it happens when you get up to get a cup of coffee or answer the phone.

This kind of haunting can go on for years and come to no resolution. The typical pattern suggests the ghost may be learning how to manipulate the world it lives in, and as it becomes acclimated to its new existence, it can do more and make itself known more. There is usually an escalation and eventually a twist to the haunting, which brings about another aspect of the paranormal. It starts with a flicker of the lights and then one night she is standing over you when you wake up. It is not until things start to get more intense that you look back and realize something had been happening for quite some time.

The nature of the haunting also has an element of the sinister to it. A psychic recording can't help being what it is, and there is always sympathy for the ghost of a small child. An effect haunting plays with you, toying with your emotion, and begging for you to spend an increasing amount of time thinking about what you might be living with. It points to one of the many nonhuman spirits we'll be discussing later.

I Just Know It's There

You are not alone. There is no sound and nothing you can see, but it is like the room is breathing. There is a heaviness you can't explain except with abstract words like "sorrow" or "melancholy." Investigators too wrapped up in science might laugh at you or ask you to move on to the next detail, but the moment should not be overlooked. You have just experienced a common paranormal event. There might just be something looking at you when you feel those eyes on you.

Study of the paranormal has shifted from a psychic to an instrumental science-based field, and with the change of approach, an important aspect of ghostly experiences has been tossed aside. Many hauntings begin with simply feeling something or the feeling of being watched. Witnesses have a hard time putting it into more specific words, but they talk of not feeling alone in the room or that there were eyes they could not see staring at them. You can't measure that experience or record it to look at more closely, but it is there and acts as a precursor to something more.

As an investigator you should always note these feelings and ask witnesses about them if they don't mention them. They are not just dramatic setup. It may be a clue as to what is going on in a haunting or give you a location you might want to check on. For example, a homeowner tells you he always felt he was being watched while working on model planes in the basement. It continued for a while, and then one day he saw the ghost of a little boy in the bathroom. You would want to check the bathroom, but it is worth your while to spend more time in the basement.

The feeling of a place can have a dramatic effect on someone's mood, and some theorize it might even play on their personality. Haunted places have been known to change a person. At the very least, that energy can often be felt, almost as if you are reliving a moment of a violent or emotional event.

Poltergeists

People who know very little about the supernatural know what a poltergeist is, mainly due to the 1982 film about a family from California living on an old cemetery, and no single factor is more responsible for confusing investigators about what one is. Unlike the haunting experienced in that movie, poltergeist activity almost completely exists as an auditory event with intense elements of an effect haunting. The difference is you see the effect but you also see the dish fly across the room and shatter against the wall. The name "noisy spirit" itself is so broad many people in and out of the field mislabel any haunting where there is extreme activity a poltergeist.

In fact, there are rules, or at least standards, the noisy ones must follow to fall into this category. The ghost must be intelligent, and throughout the records of poltergeist activity, they seem to want to communicate when other spirits shy away. They are not seen. They are heard in the form of knocks against the wall or as footsteps but not as a voice. They can manipulate electronic devices, but unlike other types of ghosts, they can play with solid matter. This is the scariest and the most definitive factor of a poltergeist. While it is rare to see spirits move things, and you are almost never in danger of getting physically assaulted by a ghost, this is what poltergeists do best. They wreak havoc on a household, often focusing their attention on one or two members of a family and breaking anything not tied down. Then they untie it and break that too.

Figure 2.5
An area that reported poltergeist-like activity.

Here's the clincher. Most who investigate the paranormal don't think poltergeists are ghosts at all. When cases are placed next to each other, certain traits stand out. A significant number of the cases involve a family with a child, many times a female (although the numbers are evening out in recent reports), in a certain stage of development. Puberty creates poltergeists. There are whispers of abuse against that person, and the abuser can be the focus of the ghostly attacks. There is an energy we don't understand, often classified as telekinetic energy, that builds up during the abuse, or just in times of stress, and releases as physical energy. This can be enough to throw a grown man across the room.

Barnes & Noble Refund Policy Change

Beginning September 1st, 2008, Barnes & Noble will be changing our return policy to reflect the following:

All returns must be made within 14 days of purchase and accompanied with an original sales receipt. After 14 days or without an original sales receipt, returns or exchanges will not be permitted. Gift receipts will be accepted for up to 60 days from date of purchase for store credit.

BARNES&NOBLE
BOOKSELLERS

Not All That Haunts Is Human

Life would be too easy if paranormal investigators only had to deal with the souls of the human dead when they investigated. Theories abound about all the other creatures of the night a ghost hunter might encounter, and each and every one's existence is as possible and as insane as the existence of ghosts. Take these with a grain of salt, but don't be too quick to dismiss.

All Dogs Don't Go To Heaven

If you think you might have a ghost in your house, buy a dog and take a picture every time it looks curiously at a wall or starts to bark for no reason. Forget any equipment you can buy or a finely tuned psychic; a cat can find any ghost no matter where it is hiding. Investigators have learned to perk up their ears like a rabbit when they hear an animal is picking up on something in a suspected haunted place. It's no wonder there are so many reports of family pets and animals that come back from the dead to get their last pet in. Some also never leave.

Although people rarely call an investigator about a ghostly dog or cat, there is growing evidence that an animal might have the ability to come back. There are countless stories of people talking to pets that have passed or hearing a deceased bird still rattling a cage. If pet owners could take a step back, they might be able to concede that their fish probably doesn't have a soul. If not, that lends more credence to the idea that ghosts are reflections of energy rather than spirituality.

The Ghost in Your Rearview Mirror

There are common ghosts that may be more of an urban legend than ghostly occurrence. We will be looking at classic legends later in the book, but one makes an appearance often enough to at least deserve some consideration now. It has more of a conscious than a psychic recording, and it changes from story to story. For the past hundred years, cars have found their way out of the junk heaps and back on the road, rolling through some haunted history and reliving their glory days. Before the invention of the car there was the haunted stagecoach or train, but the car seems to stand alone among its travel peers. Unlike those haunted vehicles of old, cars often show a personality during a haunting. Lincoln's funeral train passively rides through the land on his anniversary, but the phantom car drives behind you and takes different turns and blares its horn at different times. It knows who you are. More importantly, it's dangerous.

That does not mean we can gloss over phantom trains and ships. Trains are still seen today, and a tragedy at sea is almost always going to generate rumors of a haunting. Ships might be even more prone to the paranormal than cars. Sailors stay on them for months and engage in dangerous activities under stressful conditions. Let's not overlook the water factor as well.

Real Monsters (Well Sort of) and Famous Fiends

Your mother put you back in bed, rubbed your head, and smiled that warm smile. She told you there were no such things as monsters, and you loved her and believed her. I'm sorry. She may have loved you, but your mother is a liar. There are creatures we have not yet documented and placed in zoos that you may come into contact with. They may be exaggerations of what we have been fed by the media, or they may just have not been acknowledged, but there are enough stories out there to start distrusting your mom.

Investigators are often asked to separate ghosts, UFOs, and odd monsters. Many times the three types don't get along. There might not be something under your bed, but something is out there. Haunted locations, such as cemeteries and forests, are home to many animals that might complicate the investigation, but there might also be some supernatural figures looking back at you.

In addition to the classic Bigfoot and werewolf stories, people have reported trolls, fairies, and vampires. Throw in stories of large birds, unearthly large snakes, and floating cat eyes, and it might be enough to make you spend your time inside, which is not any safer, by the way. Many groups employ someone they title a "cryptozoologist" to help handle these problems. Before you dismiss any of these stories, remember most of the people in this country feel the same way about ghost stories.

How do you deal with a monster? Document it, reassure the witness, and then move on.

Dark Figures

The world of the supernatural is a world of trends. Some do what they do because they are moved or driven to investigate, and others ride trends and make great strides while the focus is on a single aspect. If you follow the headlines,

Figure 2.6

An orb, which may be easily dismissed due to the rain, in an area known as a monster hotspot.
Picture courtesy of Jeff Belanger and Ghostvillage.

Figure 2.7
A cemetery where these dark figures have been seen.

what television shows are popular, and what movies bring in the most money, you can watch ideas come and go. Some trends take on a life of their own and fizzle out, like the haunted rods, but others stay and point us in a new direction that can't be ignored. Dark figures are a new trend and growing in lore.

Not quite a ghost and not quite a demon, dark figures are a secondary character in the paranormal world. They are watchers and observers and feed off the fear of people too scared to confront them. Sounds romantic or like something in a story, but they have been seen for years and are rarely talked about. In the past five years, with the rise of demonology and the continuation of paranormal investigating technology, they have become a common hanger-on at hauntings.

Not Ghosts, but Spooky Nonetheless

When does a haunting not involve a ghost? Better yet, when does a haunting not involve a haunting at all? Investigators do not have all of the answers, and when you deal with something not within the normal, most of your day is spent dealing with questions that have no answers. There are, however, some things that challenge categorization or do not fall within the lines. Stay in the field long enough and your miscellaneous folder will start to overflow.

Everyone's Time Comes

People do not need to be a believer in ghosts to become one. They say Harry Houdini told his wife of a special password he would communicate to her after he died. This was to be his way of cancelling out his life's work as a paranormal wet blanket. Séance after séance went by, and the password was never uttered. People who work with ghosts often make this pledge to the people they work with. I will come back to bring you proof. It has not happened yet beyond a shadow of a doubt.

Instead, the field is flooded with the exact opposite. Those who do not believe find some truth in the many stories of people who come back from the dead to say goodbye to the people they love. Commonly referred to as crisis apparitions, these ghosts are a one-time paranormal event that leaves the living person involved confused and yet ultimately uplifted. It often sets the witness on a path to try to understand what has happened, but it stands as some of the most solid proof that there is something more than we see. People who would never entertain the idea that ghosts exist believe crisis apparitions.

The story follows a pattern so closely some may feel it is urban legend. Someone is by himself when he suddenly sees a loved one in the room. At times, he turns around or looks up to see the loved one, but more often he wakes up to find the person standing over him. The person appears normal, although some also use the words, "not all there" or "something I couldn't explain" to describe them. The dead person passes on one last message of love or something the person needs to know and then walks out of the room or disappears. Somewhat disturbed about the experience, the witness tries to pass off what happens, but later finds out the person he loved had passed away at the precise moment he saw him.

There is no way to investigate that happening, but it can't be ignored. The witness is very rarely a strong believer and has no motive to share the story. In fact, he often opens himself up to ridicule when he does come forward. Unlike other paranormal occurrences, there is a source for the haunting because someone has died and the witness did not know. The fact that he receives that information afterwards both acts as another level of proof and a way to keep the person honest.

The other variant involves a last phone call, although this can happen for some time after the death. The basic story is the same, but instead of seeing the ghost, the person gets a phone call. The ringing phone can act as a harbinger of the person's death or a last communication for a person suffering from a recent loss.

The crisis apparition does not just benefit the living. Although it may be easier to get along with the business of living after an apparition, there is a theory that the dead must adjust to their new environment as well. Many ghost hunters, most notably Hans Holzer, believe the soul must remain for a certain amount of time to become accustomed to and prepare for the afterlife. They can't move on until things are settled. The process helps both sides.

Floating Women or a Case of the Nerves

We do not fully understand the human mind. We know there are things we will never know about the brain. There is too much unaccounted for and too many stories of how it adapts and overcomes. There are also times it's trapped. Perhaps there is actually a ghost holding it down. This is commonly known as the Old Hag syndrome, but people have been reporting the "floating ghost" for centuries. She sits on your chest and paralyzes you as you helplessly wait for her to go away. Ever since people have started writing down haunted tales, the old hag has been stealing people's air.

I know what you think. It can easily be explained away. Your brain wakes up before your body does, and you open your eyes but can't move your legs. Your mind is still coming off of a very vivid phase of images due to REM and dream stages, and you create a ghost holding you down in your bed. This is a very logical reason, and people have been diagnosed with sleep paralysis who never see the hag, but there are those selected number of reports that defy the simple story.

The different hags out there alone make you start to wonder if the legend might be something more than an old wives' tale. The hag has appeared as an old woman, but also as a beautiful young woman, a man, and just about every animal, real or imagined. Many experts say this is actually more of a demonic attack, especially when the hag appears for a long period of time or when there is some kind of physical damage. Of course, we all dream differently, so maybe we just choose the face of our tormentor.

Just Go Into the Light

People do not have to believe in an afterlife to be trapped by one. In hospitals around the world, people have reported leaving their bodies and being led through other places and dimensions before being told they still need to go back to the world of the living. The event, known as a near-death experience, or NDE, happens to people around the world, from different backgrounds and religious upbringings.

There are some common themes reported in the majority of NDEs. The dead person leaves his body and sees himself, oftentimes hearing people report him dead or watching doctors trying to bring him back. The dead person hovers before leaving the plane of things he recognizes and then enters a dark world, sometimes described as a tunnel. He may see an old friend or a dead relative, and there is some kind of mentor who knows the rules and shows the recently deceased the world that awaits him and begins to guide him into the light. It has become the subject of jokes and ridicule, but people may be asked to go into the light. Here, there is some disparity. Some people report going into the light and seeing Heaven, filled with beautiful angels and old friends and everything the person wants. Some say they see the other side, a place where Hell has taken over Earth and our future is bleak. Some are merely brought to the edge of the light and told how amazing it is. The person is then either told he has the choice to go back or is told he must go back. There is a feeling of being pushed forward and the dead person slams down to his body, snapping back to life.

What makes the experience so odd is that it crosses cultures almost intact. One does not have to believe in Heaven to be brought to the edge of it. There is a scientific reason for NDEs, and people who study them closely for both religious and scientific reasons admit there is something to the commonality of the occurrence. Perhaps there is life after death and a Heaven and a Hell, or maybe we just have a series of electrical pulses that create the same hallucination in all people.

Time Is Just Slipping Away

Think of a time slip as wasted time in the paranormal realm. We all lose track of time, and road hypnotism and other psychological issues might cause us to zone out once in a while. Time slips are more profound. In your normal day, you drive home from work, pull in your driveway, and do not remember anything that happened on the way there. Think of a time slip as an instantaneous recognition of lost time. For example, you look down at your clock and realize two hours have just gone by, or you get out of the shower and somehow you are three hours late for work. Time slips work the other way as well. During a haunting, a witness may actually find herself out of her own time and living in another.

There is a connection between these slips and the paranormal. Some ghostly occurrences happen in this wasted time where the witness sees a scene the way it was in the past. Here they may be the ghost. While they are unexplained, they also happen most often during investigations, almost as if a part of what you experienced has been erased. One of the other chief zones of time slips are places on the map that have a heightened level of paranormal activity. These are seen all across the country, and have been noted by local and national investigators, and within them time is more flexible than usual. People theorize there may be a thin veil between our world and other worlds or dimensions.

Demons and the Darkness

"Is there any danger to becoming a ghost hunter?" The question comes up often, and usually I want to answer with a laugh and a reassuring shake. Depending on your level of commitment and the attention you give to detail, nothing should ever harm you. Looking for ghosts and conducting investigations in a house should be as safe as looking for mice, and if you plan correctly and take the right steps, an outside investigation should be secure too. There is nothing to fear and there are no long lasting negative effects to looking into the paranormal.

When I'm asked that, I stop short before I tell stories of some of the researchers I know. I try not to think about the dark things I've heard about because sometimes I don't know where to start. There is another building block to the supernatural world, and playing around with these elements, especially without the knowledge and respect every investigator should have, is like tempting them to come out and play. There are harmful things in the dark. Demons are a part of our world.

Who Has the Answers?

Trying to define what a demon might be is much like navigating a minefield of religion and science while knowing there is no one single answer. Like ghosts, demons may be best defined by what they do rather than what they are, but there are religious undertones that must be squared with. The easiest definition is any spirit that was never human, but we have already seen that might be too broad. It is also too limiting to say any creature, unseen, who answers to the Devil, so again that might not work for us. There have been darker, more sinister figures in every religion and in every culture.

Even in the old days, before television shows and websites, people became experts in the world of spirits. Some were religious people, and their approach reflected their ideas that a ghost could be a demon in hiding or that a haunting could be the result of a demonic infestation. They were generally religious people and there was no separation between their religious life and their paranormal one. Times have changed. While there is still a spiritual side to a belief in demons, some of the religion has been left on the sidelines. Instead, many feel that demons are an older order of spirits still in this world with the ability to interact and influence our world. To the demonologist for whom this is still a religious calling, that is a dangerous way to go about it.

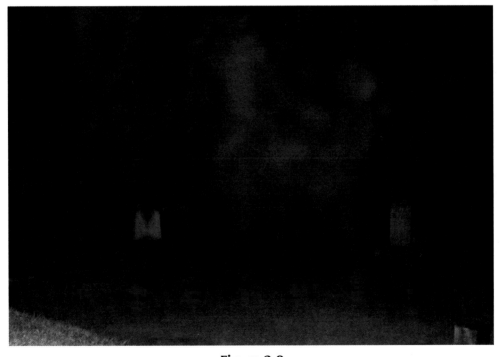

Figure 2.8
This cemetery is haunted by something darker and has been the site of physical assaults.
Photo courtesy of Brendan Marlborough.

Letting the Dark In

There are stages to a demonic infestation, and understanding them may at least give you a moment of pause when you encounter unknown spirits. The first is called obsession. The demon gains some kind of entrance into a person's life and takes advantage of the relationship. This often happens because of addiction or weakness, but the most common doorway is through experimentation with some kind of ghostly contact. People hold up the Ouija board as the easiest way to attract demons, but any kind of spirit communication or investigation makes you a target. Once contact has been made, the demon engages to keep the person interested.

A good example may be a spirit of a teenager who was killed by his abusive father. You feel for the ghost's story, so you continue to make contact with him. The spirit might even tell you there is something left on the property you can find or an old obituary you can look up that will give you more information. The demon is setting you up, and making you think more and more about it. You come to a point where you literally become obsessed with it. Trust is established and you go out of your way to make contact with the spirit.

Then things get scary. The demon has started to gain control over you and now decides to test and abuse this control. You are now asked to isolate yourself from other people and told over and over again that the world is against you. Only the demon truly cares for you. You give up everything and the demon moves in for the final takeover. Possession begins. During the more intense moments of possession, several demons might be joining in on your torment. While we know very little about demons, demonologists generally agree there is a hierarchy and low-level demons pave the way for more powerful spirits to feed off of your energy.

True or absolute possession means the demon has complete control of you all of the time, but this is a rarity. Instead, you give yourself over to the demon and it moves in and out of you when it wants to. Much like in the movies, the only way to bring a possessed person back is to conduct an exorcism.

Getting Back to Fine

Psychology and religion usually don't play nice. Religion, usually some variation of Christianity, believes an exorcism is hand-to-hand combat with evil spirits acting against God and trying to infect and manipulate God's plan. It is a direct attack on the Devil, and engaging in the activity is the work of an enlightened, experienced demonologist and there are lives on the line during the combat. Catholics believe an exorcism can only be done by an ordained priest with the blessing of the Church. During the ceremony, all involved are putting their lives in danger.

Psychology feels the suggestion of possession can be broken by the suggestion of someone who can drive the demon out. There is no dark force behind it all, but rather a mind game whose consequences can be serious and deadly. While they see the danger in allowing people to believe in such things, keeping up the illusion is a very powerful tool.

The answer might be somewhere in the middle. You will need to decide where you stand, and there are demonologists and references out there for you to explore along the way. Like many things about the paranormal, you will need to research and evaluate, but how you view demons will help determine what kind of investigator you are.

Figure 2.9
Another odd mist seen in the same cemetery.
Photo courtesy of Brendan Marlborough.

3

A Brief History of Looking for Ghosts

INVESTIGATORS WEAR THEIR TIME IN THE FIELD like a badge. The longer someone has been investigating ghosts, the more respect he tends to command from the rest of the community. Ghost hunting can be split into two periods of time, and people from the first era proudly proclaim they were into all of this long before it was popular. It's easy to be one of the old timers though. They date roughly from the beginning of humans on Earth to only a few years ago. In the paranormal world, there are pre-TAPS and those who have been spurred into action from watching the Atlantic Paranormal Society's work on the television show *Ghost Hunters*.

It might seem like ghost investigating is a new fad, and in many ways the modern approach is in its infancy. The actual practice of looking for ghosts, or trying to explain what a spirit might be and what it means for us as people, was first planted in our minds when the first people learned that sometimes people never wake up. It has been the foundation for religions and the basis of our approach to life. They may not have hit the field with investigative equipment in ancient Rome, but death and eternal life was a concern.

The brief history of ghost hunting is anything but brief, with each age defined by how it looked to answer the question. Answers have always been hard to come by, but the search continues. Down through the ages, those who search have taught something to the rest, but the closer we look through time to our own age, the less respect the paranormal investigator gets. Science has lifted the investigation to a new level but reduced the ghost hunter's impact on society.

Did You Know They Saw a Ghost?

THINK OF THIS CHAPTER AS A TOUR. Not only is it important to see what you are getting involved in as part of a larger picture, it also offers you something to research. The best ghost hunter is in touch with the past, including the paranormal past. The giants that have come before us have survived in bits and pieces, and often in a literary sense they have helped to shape what we think a ghost is and how it might act. Witnesses who may have never watched a paranormal television show grew up reading about spirits in Freshman English.

It's a typical promotional ploy. Whatever movie an actor is currently pimping is the best movie he's been a part of, or the project he has learned the most from. His fellow actors are the most professional or funny he has had the pleasure of working with. If the new movie is a horror movie, he will wait for the exact moment to tell the world he has seen a ghost himself, and that revelation, held close to his chest until the right time, had a profound effect on his life, and adds just the right amount of credibility to the performance.

I'm not saying to not trust actors and actresses. They may be telling the truth. In fact, throughout history people have reported seeing ghosts, even consulting ghosts to try to improve their lives. They are in good company. After all, ghosts are even in the Bible. King Saul went to the Witch of Endor to find out his future, and there is a reference to several apostles seeing Jesus walking with Moses and Elijah.

Figure 3.1
©istockphoto.com/susaro

It's a long tradition dating back thousands of years, but in the past it was quite normal for people to spot spirits. They were thought of differently back then, and it is not until the last hundred years or so that people have thought ghost spotters were loons. This did not make the hauntings stop; it merely drove them out of the public eye and made the witnesses less likely to believe what they saw.

Abraham Lincoln and members of his family frequently saw specters and consulted mediums, although he took their advice with a grain of salt. He might have done well to follow his own psychic side, for it is said he saw his own death in a dream a short time before he was assassinated. That didn't stop him from appearing to Winston Churchill in the Lincoln Bedroom years later.

Ronald Reagan was also familiar with the other side, even going so far as to change the course of Air Force One to follow ghost lights he saw in the sky. John Fitzgerald Kennedy was said to have seen a doppelganger shortly before his trip to Dallas. Queen Elizabeth II claims to have seen John Brown, the servant of Queen Victoria.

Musicians, often in touch with unseen forces while looking for inspiration, have sometimes gone over the edge and made contact. Reports say Jimmy Page, fresh from selling his soul to the Devil, saw the ghost of Aleister Crowley after he bought his house, and the Red Hot Chili Peppers say they frequently saw spirits in the haunted house they rented to record an album. Sting saw a whole ghost family in his bed, but another famous singer also has been known to enter other people's beds. Mama Cass sometimes is felt in Dan Ackroyd's bed.

Politicians have something to lose, musicians almost take pride in their phantoms, but actors and actresses use it as a publicity tool. Kate Hudson reported she has seen a ghost while on tour talking about her movie *Skeleton Key*. Hugh Grant says he encountered the dead Bette Davis in a Los Angeles home, and the ghost Nicolas Cage saw at Francis Ford Coppola's house drove him out. According to Unexplained.net, both Keanu Reeves and Matthew McConaughey had encounters that altered their lives.

More and more people report a belief in ghosts, and more everyday people are coming forward with their stories of unexplained encounters. Part of the shift is due to a changing attitude toward the paranormal. Statistically, you are more likely to see a ghost than get hit by a car, but still there are nonbelievers out there. Perhaps it is too easy to explain away the hauntings people have, too many reasons to think that what they saw is not what they think they saw. Perhaps the old saying is true: "Seeing, or at least experiencing, is believing."

The Literary Ghost —Metaphor or a Haunting?

SOME OF THE GREATEST WRITERS of all time worked in genres we would classify as horror or Gothic, and the first tales told beside the fires of our ancestors spoke of spirits in the night and things to be wary of from the other side. It made sense in the old days. Fear is a primal instinct and a means of burning the truth into someone and instructing them in the ways of the world. Old fairy tales and folklore spoke of Death as a person who could be fooled, and the dead as people to avoid lest they take part of your humanity back with them.

As understanding killed superstitions, the narrative power of scaring someone into believing stayed with us. It moved from the cities to the rural communities and lingered as old wives' tales and cautionary legends. There was still something about those ghost stories that stuck with people. Children often remember frightening tales from the Old Testament as opposed to the gentle teachings of other books because of the emotion evoked.

Figure 3.2
©istockphoto.com/Alina Solovyova-Vincent

From those humble beginnings, horror writers developed, and while it may be looked down upon by the modern literary elite, the horror story has been the field of choice for giants in days gone by. During the Romantic Age, a focus on nature and those things supernatural, became a powerful means of showing how far from God and the right order of the world we had strayed. Think of Naturalism, the offshoot of Transcendentalism, which gave us the great American authors Nathaniel Hawthorne and Edgar Allen Poe.

The genre survives today. Horror stories are often at the top of the bestseller lists, and as an extension, horror movies make studios big money but garnish few awards. Nothing strikes at the very heart of what it means to touch the immortal like a ghost. Through the years, people have called upon apparitions to represent that part of us that lives on in turmoil or at peace. The metaphor is easy, and in the hands of a great author, it can be a powerful tool of expression.

These ghosts are used as a convention, but they have taught us what a ghost is. For example, the line, "It was a dark and stormy night," from Edward Bulwer-Lytton in his 1830 novel, tells us when a ghost will appear. Knowing how writers use them, and how they have touched us, will help dispel some of your own prejudices and see the mistakes witnesses might make.

The Ghost Can Set Things Straight

Perhaps the most famous literary ghost is that of King Hamlet in Shakespeare's *Hamlet*. The king's spirit appears to his son to tell the tale of his murder and beseech Prince Hamlet to avenge his death. The play tackles death throughout, from the graveyard scene where the prince watches his friends slowly turning into dust or the prince's own debate on the value of suicide. It is his father's spirit, however, that resonates with the value of the paranormal in literature and presents the theme we still hold to today. He represents the dead setting things back in order, establishing some balance, and, like the paranormal theme we still hold to today, this allows the ghost to rest.

Figure 3.3
Photo courtesy of Karen Hatzigeorgiou and karenswhimsy.com/public-domain-images.

He commands his son, even at the risk of his own life, to avenge his death and reset the scales. The play reinforces two of the major themes in the paranormal. The first is that extreme tragedy, even one so passive as poisoning, forces the spirit to stay earthbound. The second is that spirits can't pass on to the afterlife until their death is set right, or their killer brought to justice. Both of these ideas resonate with modern ghost hunters who spend much of their time looking for the tragedy that is at the heart of a haunting. Many feel they, like Hamlet, can set things right for the ghost just by listening to or doing something for the spirit.

Love Springs Eternal: Ghosts as Passionate Energy

What is the greatest love story ever told? Answer the question and you may be giving someone a more precise insight into who you are as a person than you might like. It is easy to go with the easy answers where the couple embraces at the end and the violins start to play, or maybe the sacrifice for the greater love where one of the lovers dies to save the other. These types of stories make us weep and confirm that love can conquer all. Then there are the darker love stories. Suicide and murder replace symphonies and stolen kisses, and while these stories act as symbols and force us to challenge what we would do in situations, they also give a more exact look at the silliness that passion can sometimes be.

The Gothic Romance, *Wuthering Heights* by Emily Brontë, uses ghosts to express how deep love can be, including all the trappings and the idea that love can extend the soul and that passion is an elemental force, like the wind or lightning. Catherine and Heathcliff are not thrown into the storm; rather, they are the storm. If they were meant to be the way society would like them, they might find peace in the afterlife. Instead, they return as ghosts to extend that love and eventually walk through the moors as spirits to represent that love and the essence of a person, like those elemental forces we used to create legends about. The lovers find their way to each other, but even in death there is something detached or transcendent about their union. Their natural becomes supernatural, hinting that devotion can't be killed when the body stops breathing.

This is yet another motif that finds its way into paranormal investigating. A haunting might be real, but research time is spent trying to sift through the urban legends that are attached to it. Love, and the soul unable to find rest until that love is settled, is often the source of a haunted story. In Chapter 12 we will look at how legends and myths have influenced investigators. The idea of getting it right, especially in the face of love, sneaks into the back story of many hauntings. Don't allow it to unless it can be backed up. The lovers, who were kept apart, or a suicidal member of the couple who killed himself after a forced separation, leave residual energy in the air. If we can get those wacky kids together, the haunting will stop. If thoughts can exist after we die, why can obsession and fervor not? They are just another electrical pulse from the brain. Socially, it again invites us to see ghosts as emotional extensions of our mistakes and reinforces the idea that ghosts have to get it right before they can move on.

There Are Actually Four: Ghosts as Lessons and Helpers

It is a traditional literary device. If an old person appears in literature, they are there to teach you something. Joseph Campbell often talks of the mentor who takes the hero by the hand and shows him the way to his destiny. There are lessons to be learned, and only the one with experience can give the hero what he needs and cannot get from inside himself. These older characters fill that role, and at times ghosts make themselves known for the same reason.

Figure 3.4
©istockphoto.com/Diane Diederich

The story of *A Christmas Carol,* by Charles Dickens, is recycled so much, we often lose sight of the impact the four ghosts have in Ebenezer Scrooge's conversion from a lonely miser to an example of the miracle of Christmas. They are more than just messengers and tour guides. Marley acts as the cautionary tale, the man who has fallen down the hole and knows the way out, while the three Christmas ghosts all have knowledge of Scrooge's personality and how the events in his life play out and influence each other. As they take him from moment to moment, they offer information and insight inside of Scrooge but hidden to the rest of the world. The ghosts know what is in his heart, even as it hardens to the people he comes into contact with, and, more importantly, they know what buttons to push to warm it when most have given up on him. They have gained knowledge and power as ghosts, as if death is a secret way to authority.

This helps perpetuate the idea that a ghost has somehow grown as a person after it has stopped growing as a person. We often see the dead as having some perspective we can't even begin to understand as long as we are bound to this world. They are masters of the past, present, and future. One of the selling points of the Ouija Board is that using it will tell you what your job will be or if that boy in school likes you. This becomes our expectation of ghosts. We feel they will offer us something to advance our own lives, but this type of relationship with the paranormal will most likely lead to disappointment. It also becomes a way darker spirits might enter your life. By offering something you are missing or exchanging your time for a glimpse of your future, they keep you talking or even convince you to think things you wouldn't think of normally.

They're Talking for Us: Ghosts as the Voice of the Living

Nothing in the paranormal world is as scary as a ventriloquist and a freaky doll. It is not just the mouth and the solid expressions of the toy but the fact that the puppet master tends to lose himself completely in the illusion. The human is usually the straight man while the doll takes on the roll of his controller's subconscious, almost like a visual id, and the man is allowed to express the hidden part of who he is. Good writers and movie makers have used this to scare, but even the most innocent ventriloquist is unsettling.

The 1990s saw the rise of a new literary movement, although many of the writers who are considered its masters had been around for years. In Africa and South America more novelists were turning to a style known as magical realism to express the themes of oppression, cultural confusion, and political turmoil. They mixed highly sensitive issues with a deep connection to the spiritual world to stress the traditions of the old slipping away and to say things they could not come right out and express in literal terms. These stories often involved a very thin veil between the spirit world and the real world, and the direct influence of ghosts moved characters and became their motivation. For the characters in the story, the phantoms were a way to be inspired, or scared, into action, while the author used them to show the need for radical action against the government in Third World environments.

The Famished Road by Ben Okri, is a modern version of the Romantic literature written almost 200 years before. Both Magical Realists and Romantics showed a knack for using man's distance from or fear of nature as a way to express something wrong with society, and both were written during periods of political turmoil. The Magical Realists, however, used their writing to encourage their own people to rebel. Okri uses ghosts in *The Famished Road* as corruptors, symbolizing the corruptors who were keeping the people poor and weak. In a twist, he also uses them as a way to overcome those same oppressors by understanding that life is turmoil but the connection to tradition can prevail or at least offer peace while things straighten themselves out. He uses them to say what the people can't, and they become his characters' and his country's voice.

The Spiritualist Movement

America was a Puritan country that then developed its own sense of Christian ideal. By the early 19th century, these threads had started to come undone. The old religions, while still embraced by the majority, were being replaced by whispers in parlors and over spirit boards across the land. It was slow at first, but it took hold of the nation and went from being an American belief system to something appealing for others in different countries. While not as strong as it once was, it is still being practiced today. To think it all started with some ghosts and two young ladies from New York.

Near the Canadian border in the town of Hydesville, lived two sisters named Kate and Margaret Fox. One day in 1848, they began to communicate with spirits using a series of raps and knocks. News of their communications with the dead began to filter into the town and beyond, and before you could say psychic experience, the girls were being inundated with requests to prove their worth. They fed the public's need for the paranormal by conversing with several spirits while people looked on with amazement.

It might have ended there, but the two ladies soon saw an evolution of their own abilities. They could now talk directly to the dead, and people anxious to converse with their loved ones came from states away for the chance to meet the Foxes. If these two could somehow touch the other side, maybe anyone could. Prophets, now calling themselves mediums, sprouted all over the country and began to accumulate followings of large numbers of people, who remained loyal because they believed in the psychic ability of their leaders.

Figure 3.5
©istockphoto.com/Laurie Knight

Figure 3.6
The entrance to haunted Dungeon Rock, a Spiritualist meeting place.

They were a mixed bag of psychic giants and charlatans, but the followers were true believers. It was a dramatic shift from Christianity, which often required a mediator to talk to a higher power and promised damnation at every turn. Instead, it was a religion stressing a connection to those who had passed before you and the reward of becoming a part of the universe if your soul could find its way to the light. As the movement gained momentum, the Civil War broke out, and while the men in the field still wore crosses, those left behind were drawn to a new religion that allowed them to help their recently departed cross over and find peace.

It also helped to mold the shift of America's idea of a good death and how the moment of one's demise controlled the manner of his afterlife, perhaps unsettling the souls of those who died enough to make them return after death.

It also gave rise to the séance. With the help of a trained professional, any dinner party could lead to a spiritual awakening in the parlor. The upper class made it a regular event at their social occasions, bringing spirit communication into the mainstream. There was a surge in the use of spirit boards and tarot cards and crystals, allowing these things to be forever connected to successful ghost hunting.

The effect of the Spiritualist movement is still being felt today. There are still churches where talking to the dead is the centerpiece of a belief system. In addition to the exposure of old methods of talking to ghosts, it established a protocol for how to conduct an investigation. The vigil so many investigators use now is much like a séance. The questions are very similar, and our idea of the disrupted souls and of concepts such as moving into the light are all based in those parties. The reenactment we'll discuss in Chapter 6 is a modern word for the older spiritualist idea of a trigger object. Even the use of mediums and psychics can be traced back to the work laid down by the followers of the Foxes.

Figure 3.7
The psychic Jackie Barrett getting ready for a séance.

This Is a Science?: Parapsychology in Context

BEING A GOOD LISTENER and discovering the cause and effect of the world around us are two of the most important skills a student can learn. As a high school teacher, I feel it is my job to train my students to master these concepts before they can understand literature or become good writers. With this in mind, I have come up with an exercise I go through with my freshmen every year in school. I sit them in a circle and tell them I have a power that I consider both a blessing and a curse. I can talk to the dead, and as we sit, I give them messages from loved ones who have passed, sometimes going so far as to make some of them cry thinking their deceased grandmother is sitting next to them. One year, three students said they could feel their hands being held.

Now, I'm as psychic as a rock. The lesson, while considered cruel to some, is designed to show how a little knowledge of human nature mixed with observing people's reactions can convince people of just about anything. When my students see how many questions I have actually answered incorrectly, they are embarrassed at how easily they fell for it. While I use it as a lesson in my class, mediumship and psychic ability are big business today, from inspiring television shows to bringing in the dollars out of someone's living room. There are no less than three on my way to work before I hit the highway, and it all points to the belief that our human mind is capable of things we do not understand. The experiment I conducted was pure psychology, but the idea the mind can control the outside world is the battlefield of a different branch of science known as parapsychology.

It is cliché to talk about what a small percentage of our mind we actually use, but like all good clichés, it is based in truth. There is so much we don't understand about it, and unlocking some of this mystery might help to solve some of the larger questions posed by paranormal investigators. Brain study is the field of science, sometimes far removed from the idea of demons or spirit energy, but the potential of the mind extends far beyond the parts of the brain or how information is sent to our hands. Science gives way to something more difficult to define, but the people charged with getting their hands dirty doing this are not ghost hunters but highly trained researchers who know more about laboratories than cemeteries.

The parapsychologist received training in psychology, but what they do is seated firmly in science and the scientific method. They are not known for using a spirit board but for creating a controlled environment to study the psychic ability a subject might have. Then they analyze and repeat, all in an attempt to understand. They have been doing their work for more than a century, and while acceptance by the general scientific community was slow in coming, producing evidence the general public will listen to has been slower.

Paranormal Infancy

People can debate whether modern day ghost hunters use science when they are out in the field. Part of this is based on a lack of scientific proof, which can be repeated and isolated. The evidence is there, but with no organization and standards, not to mention people with no actual science background doing the research, most of the data gets dismissed. There is an aspect of the work that is based in science, and while the word is thrown around without a real understanding of what it entails, parapsychology is the "real" side of looking for ghosts.

Try to remember your old science classes. First you have an idea, a hypothesis. You test it under the best controlled environment, judge the results, and then rework your hypothesis. You repeat this to carve out all that is not true and hopefully you are left with a truth that can be repeated under different conditions. This is what the parapsychologist does, and the better paranormal groups strive for in their investigations. While most can't create a controlled environment, using the same techniques and trying to create a standard all ghost hunters should use helps to create some level of legitimacy.

Parapsychology has not always been honest, and this has helped to promote the idea that what they do is more science fiction that scientific research. There have been times where evidence has been faked or results exaggerated. At its best it offers a model for nonprofessional researchers to use. Ghost research is a byproduct of what the science is about. Its primary focus has always been the natural, unexplained, psychic force within each person and what people might be able to do with their minds. For more than 100 years, scientists have tested a human's ability to move objects with thought, predict the future, and manipulate the world around you with nothing but your brain.

The work really began with the formation of the Society for Psychical Research (SPR) in 1882. Back then, it consisted of Englishmen under the direction of Henry Sidgwick, a professor of moral philosophy at Cambridge University, and was dedicated to the idea that science and philosophy could understand the questions religion had been dancing around. The Society was formed to, "examine without prejudice or prepossession, and in a scientific spirit, those faculties of man, real or supposed, which appear to be inexplicable on any generally recognized hypothesis." They gathered scientists, writers, and doctors in an attempt to approach the paranormal from different angles. Some of the smartest men in the country found their way to the group over next few decades, and by the early 1900s the movement had spread to the United States.

The Basic Research

Rather than measuring the amount of energy in a haunted place, the SPR and the ASPR (American Society for Psychical Research) worked on the question of our human ability to create unexplained phenomena. They focused on things the advancing sciences had yet to approach in a meaningful way, such as near-death experiences, seeing the future, and the appearance of ghosts. It was organized and did more than merely document things that happened. Instead, they characterized things and classified experiences and encounters. It wasn't enough to say things happened. They needed to be labeled and connected.

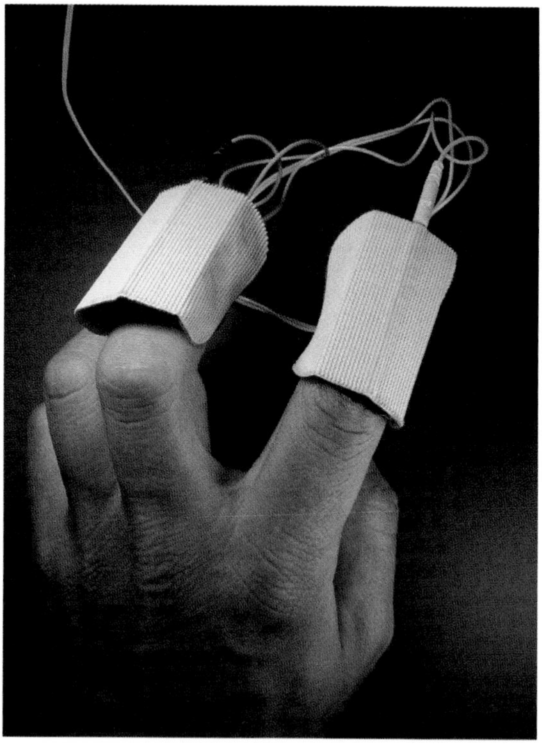

Figure 3.8
©istockphoto.com/Dan Brandenburg

Modern times have seen a shift in which the investigator tries to recreate the haunting in order to find natural explanations for it, but there is not enough work being done to expose people who are faking evidence or manipulating information. One of the early purposes of the Society, and the one often lost to modern ghost hunters, was to expose frauds who were using Spiritualism as a way to make money. It was another step in the process of taking away what was not paranormal from the mass of cases they received.

Sometimes science is confused with experimentation. When Darwin began his work, he did not dissect animals to see how natural selection worked. Instead, he observed and put things in columns. It is not as active as some of the work we do today, but it may be more important. The SPR gave the community this kind of organization and the basics for a methodical approach to looking at the unexplained, which it had been lacking to that point. When information is processed in this way, trends and truths come to light.

Then They Hit the Lab

Due to the influence of the academics who were embracing parapsychology and becoming members of the community, the idea of psychic energy and the existence of ghosts gained momentum and credibility. This was finally confirmed when universities began to open themselves up to research, including Stanford in 1911 and Duke in 1930. Things took on a new significance with the rise of Joseph Banks Rhine, a traditionally educated man who turned to parapsychology and who worked out of Duke for 40 years. He began to test people for their psychic ability, perfecting the analysis for the tests researchers still use today, including the Zener cards. These cards have simple pictures on them, such as circles or sets of lines, and are used to test a subject's ability to read the tester's mind. His idea was not that parapsychology was an entirely new field but rather an offshoot of psychology that could be understood and experimented with.

You can't force a ghost to haunt a room and measure the results, so the official work of parapsychology dedicated more of its time to psychic experimentation. This also allowed it to rise as a science because it could be approached in a consistent manner with controls and direct results. You either could perform tasks such as seeing the picture on a card or a number that had been drawn or you couldn't.

Rhine's experiments were duplicated across the country, although the majority of universities shied away from the field. Results were a mixed bag and seemed to prove not that we all had the ability to tap into our own psychic ability, but rather that some people could. All this really did was add to the concept that the unexplained was the unexplained, although the template of how to move the field into the accepted scientific community was forming. The results in the lab were also brought under fire for the next 70 years, and every instance of fraud was exalted. When exploring the unaccepted, it is easier to prove a negative than a positive. Nevertheless, parapsychology was officially recognized as a science in 1969 when the American Association for the Advancement of Science finally put its stamp of approval on it.

Some say psychic ability is not needed in the paranormal field, and many groups downright dismiss anything not found on their equipment.

Figure 3.9
Zener cards.
Picture used courtesy of Umbrax from tinWiki.org.

If you want to be the best investigator possible, evaluate all ideas. Maybe even try to tap into your own ability. Find a set of Zener cards and test yourself. Better yet, get a deck of playing cards and start that way. If you decide to use mediums on an investigation, test them as well. Anyone wanting to truly advance the field will not be offended.

Are They Even Connected?

For a minimal fee, you can join the Society for Psychic Research, get their newsletter and journal, and have full access to their online library of research and book titles. Like so many of the paranormal degrees you can now get online, becoming a member does not make a ghost hunter a parapsychologist. People throw the name around, often claiming to be an amateur parapsychologist or something very formal sounding, but calling yourself an amateur neurosurgeon doesn't mean you can scrub in to an operation.

True members of the SPR, the ASPR, and other similar organizations are highly trained and educated individuals, many of whom have doctorates in more traditional sciences. Although there have been scandals throughout its history, parapsychologist is not just a word to place in front of your name because you have devoted yourself to looking for ghosts, the same way reading books on demons does not make you a true demonologist. It is a highly disciplined science with strict guidelines and a ruling body, as well as several scientific organizations, to answer to.

The question still has to be asked whether there is any connection between these people in labs and the paranormal investigator in the field. The distinction, or lack of one, comes from the outside. People who do not understand the work paint them both with a broad brush, but the disciplines are very different. Internally, it may be time for the investigators to admit they are not parapsychologists and recognize that while the two may be running in the same circles and looking closely at the same questions, using the terms interchangeably may be like calling an archeologist and a treasure hunter the same thing. They both may find the tomb, but they took different paths and will get different things from it.

And Then Came the Show

IT HAPPENED OVERNIGHT. On day I was looking in cemeteries for ghosts and recording stories about the paranormal, and the next I was being called by newspapers and magazines looking for a new angle on the paranormal. The show had that kind of impact on what we do. It's the same as reality shows about dancing making people around the country put on tap shoes or a character on a sitcom changing her hair and starting a revolution. In October 2004 the ground rules changed.

In that month, *Ghost Hunters* premiered on the SciFi Channel and chronicled the caseload of the Atlantic Paranormal Society, or TAPS. It was akin to the old paranormal shows like *In Search of* and *Sightings*, but it also showed the members of the team as real people who had wives and problems, especially with each other. At times, the show's focus was on the haunting they were investigating, but it can quickly jump to explore the dynamics between team members. It was part ghost story, part soap opera.

People loved it. They tuned in for the drama and the scare. Polls had been claiming the number of people who were interested in the paranormal for years, and the success of the show proved it.

It was more than that though. The show became interactive for some. When the public watches a crime drama, they turn off the television when it's over and wish they could be a detective putting the pieces together. They can't put on a badge and start solving crimes. *Ghost Hunters* allowed people to take that moment of illusion and carry it outside the house when the show ended. People hit the streets and cemeteries.

Paranormal Role Models

Using the same theories and methods the people in the show did, investigators started to spring up everywhere. Some were people inspired by what they had seen on the show, but most were people who had always felt connected to ghosts and finally found a means to express what they had been feeling. *Ghost Hunters* gave them the words to use, the equipment to buy, and the acceptance of society. Of course, the public on the whole does not put much weight into ghost stories, although they like them enough to listen. Instead, it is the same theory as a successful lottery winner. Although you have little chance to win, seeing people on television holding up big checks makes you feel it could happen to you. Those who investigate gave the public the impression that what investigators do is strictly scientific and that all people take them seriously.

To many, paranormal investigating is what they see on the show. They use a heavy scientific approach with expensive equipment and a group with a clear hierarchy and rules. People mirrored this and began looking for ghosts the way they had seen it done on television. Not only were people clamoring to get into the haunted sites they went to, they started to move and speak like the members of TAPS. Whatever they did, the people did. The ideas they held as truths, people followed without question.

So often I get the question of whether or not *Ghost Hunters* has a negative or positive effect on the paranormal community. The answer is not a simple one. The show has opened up more people to ask questions and look for answers. The cream rises to the top, and with so many people now out there doing it, new innovations and ideas have come from people who might never have found investigating without the show. Many are taking up the good fight and finding more haunted places to expose.

Not all of the reaction has been positive. Paranormal investigating is a discipline involving research into different fields and practices honed through trial and error. Hitting the field after only watching a highly edited television show doesn't provide the investigator with enough information to do the job the right way. Instead, many run through cemeteries and abandoned buildings with no regard for themselves or property. By following one group's ideas without a foundation in ghost hunting, people not only do not learn to question what TAPS does, but few know that what the *Ghost Hunters* do can be questioned.

What the show offers is a starting point. As a group to model, there are worse people out there than the TAPS crew. They are consistent, offer explanations for what they are doing, and provide some of the best reasons for why a haunting is not a ghost. Their down-to-earth nature makes them more accessible than a university parapsychologist, so think of them as a source to pay attention to. Then look for other people so you can learn different ideas. You'll find many well established groups follow the same rules, but the variation is where your education will be tighten up.

And the Hits Keep Coming

The show has created an unreal expectation for those who watch and then mimic the actions of the group. Posting evidence and racking up hits on their websites, many feel ghost hunting is the key to fame and fortune, and to some degree they are not wrong. The paranormal media is exploding, and many who would never have the chance to publish a book or be on television are now being called.

Using *Ghost Hunters* as a model, more networks began broadcasting paranormal programs, some reality shows like the original and others paranormal dramas. With each new show, the way it was covered became specialized to the audience the networks wanted to target, and each new show became a bit more diluted. Now, no matter what you are looking for, there is a ghost show out there for you, and with so many appetites to satisfy and so many shows to choose from, the drama is stressed as opposed to the ideas or techniques.

People watching take these shows as the right way to do things, which is not always the case. While people have issues with the members of TAPS, they are somewhat consistent and have been in the field for several years. Other groups on television flap in the wind, creating situations ripe for the best drama, not necessarily the best true results. Bizarre ideas have become commonplace, such as three in the morning being the best time for paranormal activity or invasion of demons. One person actually asked me if you could get a rid of a ghost by shooting a shotgun filled with salt.

The Future

What will happen to the field when the ratings drop? It is hard to tell, but these things move in cycles. The new hot trend will shift and the show will be off the air someday. It may mean the end of the meteoric rise of ghost hunters, but not the end of paranormal investigating. Those who do the work out of the love of it will press on. The new ideas will move it forward, and the old ideas will be reevaluated and looked over. Many of us will be doing this for the rest of our lives, and hopefully you will be one of them. No matter what is on television, you still determine how much you want to do, and that is okay. Your level of interest will ebb and flow as well, and if you find yourself taking it more seriously in a few years, you might find the cemeteries less crowded.

NIGHT STALKS THE MANSION
GHOST STORIES
Miller
10,000 Dreams Interpreted
THE BERMUDA TRIANGLE
PSYCHIC!
INVESTIGATING THE PARANORMAL
The Complete Prophecies
ROSSLYN
HOLY GRAIL
MONSTERS
Dark Woods
RIMAX

4

The Equipment

I HAD MY MOST VIVID AND AFFIRMING paranormal experience late one night after coming out of a deep sleep. I was preparing to move from a haunted apartment to a city across the country, and with most of my things packed into a moving van outside, I slept on the couch. I was awakened at two in the morning by a pressure on my cheek, a kiss. Thinking it was my female roommate, I opened my eyes to tell her I would miss her too. The young woman in the room was crouched over me and slightly resembled my friend, but as she stood up, I saw it was not her. She stared at me for a few seconds, smiled, and turned to leave. As her shoulder hid her face, she dissolved. I could hear my roommates snoring in the other room.

It's easy to say this never happened. Perhaps it was a dream or one of those sleep moments that slip into the real world for a brief moment. But I don't think so. I was awake and could hear the sounds in the room and feel the couch underneath me. I believe beyond any doubt that the young woman was the one we had felt and heard in our apartment for over a year, and she was telling me goodbye in her own way.

Of course, this is not enough for a ghost hunter, and it really should not be the end of the story if your goal is to generate evidence. I saw her and I consider myself a reliable witness, but with the right equipment, I would've been able to present something physical to the community. It would have reinforced the story and provided a real leg to stand on. Instead, it's just a story.

A Picture Is Worth a Thousand Words

GHOST HUNTING IS ABOUT trying to capture evidence, for whatever ends, that can be seen or heard by other people. This is impossible without the right tools and the right training. Get to know what you can do and all the little nuances of the equipment. Experiment and try different things to bring new ideas into your investigations.

Always try to bring the equipment you need for the job. I received a remote control power outlet as a grab gift at a Christmas party and quickly added it to my toolbox. Then the more I thought about it, the less I could find a good reason to use it in the field. Don't bring a motion detector along on a cemetery investigation or a thermos to a haunted residence. Instead, buy two toolboxes and fill one with what you need for the investigation and the other with things you may need; leave the second toolbox in your car. Of course, have plenty of batteries in each.

The most compelling proof you can get comes from some kind of visual evidence. You can explain what the reading of any equipment tells the world, but seeing something makes them feel it. It is something concrete rather than some abstract idea based on a science people might not believe to begin with. Seeing is believing, or at least coming one-step closer to believing, so attention must be paid to getting as much visual information as possible.

Remember That Old Thing Known as Film?

The first ghosts were caught on film, and they were a total fraud. The first cameras took time to produce a photograph, and a person could come from behind, stay a brief moment, and then appear like a ghost lurking around the original target. Today we can snap pictures and edit them in one device thanks to digital technology. Somewhere in between lays an advanced version of our old film-based cameras. As people have gobbled up better resolution and more pixels, companies have been making the old-fashioned camera better as well.

Figure 4.1
The old-fashioned camera is still in fashion.

Why It Works

First and foremost, a picture captures what is seen by the human eye. A picture is used to save all those classic moments that you want to last forever. It may be a child's birthday or your first car or a full-bodied apparition that appears to you in an abandoned asylum. If you can see it with your eyes, a camera should be able to capture the image. There are very rare times when a ghost hunter comes face to face with a phantom that manifests itself physically. Imagine not having a camera to save the moment.

Cameras of all kinds pick up things our eyes can't or that happen too quickly for our brain to process. Think of them like the pause button on a VCR or DVD player. They not only save the moment, they freeze quick moving objects. The better the camera, the more likely it is to get details the eyes may miss, especially if the added features don't focus on the power of the zoom or other non-paranormal extras. This chance is increased when you have the ability to use Nightvision, not available on many cameras, which uses all of the light in an area and magnifies it, or infrared film, which picks up heat and displays it as an image.

How to Get It

The good news is, cameras are the easiest of all your equipment to get. They even sell film and disposable cameras at the checkout lines of most grocery stores. I've gotten good evidence using just about everything. The bad news is, the better evidence comes from the better cameras, and they cost money. Then there is the added cost of the film and the processing.

How to Use It

Everyone knows how to point and click, and you can feel free to leave it at that. For more advanced investigators, however, the normal methods might not work. The best ones will mix and match their camera settings to try to hit a haunted spot with different eyes. Experiment with camera speeds and film speeds and play with the f/stop. Use the flash and then take it off and take the same picture, even in low light. If you have the money, you can invest in infrared film and filters. Rarely use autofocus; instead, try to focus manually to get the widest range on film. If you have a camera that allows it, take multiple pictures in a matter of seconds, especially when something is happening or you see something with your eyes. This allows you to understand the anomaly by capturing how it moves or comes in and out of the scene.

One of the benefits of using a traditional camera is that any evidence you get will be seen on the negative, adding another level of credibility. You may want to learn to develop your own film, although this can be an expensive and time-consuming hobby, which, considering the low cost of film developing these days, does not really add much to the process. It might be better to invest the money into better equipment across the board.

When getting film developed, you can save money by purchasing the pictures on disc only. You still get the negatives if you need them later, and evidence can be evaluated more easily in a digital format.

The Downfall

Price and mobility are the biggest drawbacks to using traditional film. Add the price of film with the right accessories to take the best picture, and the hit on your pocketbook is significant. There is also an issue with switching out film during an investigation. Especially if you are mobile, it is hard to load and unload as you shoot and keep your film organized. Many cameras can do more than the average person knows, and when you get to the more advanced cameras, this becomes even more complicated.

Odds and Ends

Take pictures at an angle rather than straight on. Unless you are trying to get the perfect picture for a book or a contest, the way it looks is secondary. Try to get something stable and solid in the frame that offers perspective for anything that appears there.

Digital

Digital cameras are the preferred equipment to use during an investigation but that may be more out of ease than quality. A digital camera is a self-contained picture studio, so they reduce further processing and allow you to begin evaluating the evidence as you investigate. You should incorporate both digital and traditional film cameras to get the full range. Picking something up on only one medium may be a problem with the camera, an explainable light source, or another reasonable issue. If you pick it up on two cameras that process the information differently, pointed at different angles, something paranormal may be happening. Consider the digital camera to be the frontline of the paranormal investigation. You need more for a complete picture, but few hit the field without one.

Why It Works

The basic premise of the digital camera is the same as the traditional camera, but the newer cameras actually pick up a wider range of the world than the older models. Imagine a film camera as working with blinders on. What you see might be clearer for the price, but digital picks up more along the higher and lower ends of the spectrum, including dipping into the infrared and ultraviolet spectrums. It sees things your eyes can't and quicker than they can as well.

You can test how far out of visible light your camera goes. Paranormal expert, Jeff Belanger, offers this advice. "To find out if your camera can do this, take a picture of your TV remote while you press a button on that remote. If you see the light bulb in the front light up in your photo, your camera is peeking into infrared."

How to Get It

Again, digital cameras are popping up everywhere, from major department stores to convenience stores. They even have disposable digitals these days. Look for the highest number of pixels you can afford and read the manual.

Figure 4.2
One of many types of digital camera on the market.

Then read the manual again. There are more features to master on these devices, and many were not made to do what you want. The more money you have, the more of these features the camera can come with. I suggest you sacrifice the size of your preview screen for resolution. You can look at the picture you just took, but don't spend so much time observing the captured image that you forget about the real world.

How to Use It

The same rules apply to the use of both kinds of cameras. Different pictures, different settings, and all that. Leave the autofocus settings alone and instead try to toggle between portrait and scenic type settings.

The Downfall

Digital cameras are too good at their job. Back in the day, investigators had to worry about camera straps and leaving the cap on. Now we have to worry about the digital image making every drop of rain in the air and fly buzzing by a phantom. The speed it works at captures too much, and when you add a flash, dust becomes orbs that can fool most people. We'll spend more time in Chapter 5 talking about how to evaluate the evidence you get, but keep in mind the majority of pictures you take with a digital camera will reveal a need to clean the house and not life after death.

Digital cameras can also snip at your ghost-hunting budget because of the batteries they consume. You always think you have enough, but they run dry quickly, especially when you zoom in and out or play with the features. Rechargeables help with the problem, but they are unreliable and seem to drain more quickly, although drained batteries is often a sign of something ghostly (see the residential investigation in Acushnet, Massachusetts on the DVD for a live demonstration of this).

Odds and Ends

Spend money on a good camera. You can always use it in your everyday life. Can't say that about an ion counter. Don't waste time and money using the camera as a video camera. It is an added feature, but it uses too much of the battery and usually has a hiccup in the playback that makes it useless. Buy a few memory cards. They are getting cheaper by the day and allow you to snap dozens if not hundreds of pictures without having to erase evidence. Never delete a picture once you have taken it, especially while the investigation is going on.

Video Killed...Something

If cameras catch a moment in time, video cameras capture the whole process and string those moments together. You can also keep them running for the duration of the investigation and capture everything. There are a few people who still record on analog video, but these cameras are harder to find now and seem as outdated as the cameras from days before "talkies." If you must use an older camera, make it a stationary one. Other than that, go digital.

Why It Works

Like a camera, video sees a scene in its eye and burns a record of it. Digital cameras then convert this to a digital image, although it is often transferred automatically to a video. Some new cameras leave the last step out and only create a file. Either way, we still call it video, which is a bit archaic. Video cameras work better than the human eye and can record things we might dismiss or pass by too quickly. And many have Nightvision capabilities as well. Almost all are affordable, so they are accessible to all.

Figure 4.3
Several cameras needed for the job.
Picture courtesy of the Texas Paranormal Society.

How to Get It

You can get these cameras just about anywhere, but I would caution against getting something too expensive. Unless you are planning some documentary filmmaking, the quality plateaus at a certain point. You are then paying for things like size, memory, and added features. Given the odds of getting really solid visual evidence on tape, I suggest spending more money on a camera with more powerful Nightvision and then taking some money and investing it in microphones that are compatible.

How to Use It

I'll get into some more specifics when we hit the field, but as traditional photography goes, so does video. You should try to make the camera stationary and then have another to go mobile. You have a better shot of catching something when you stay in one place than trying to position it at just the right time.

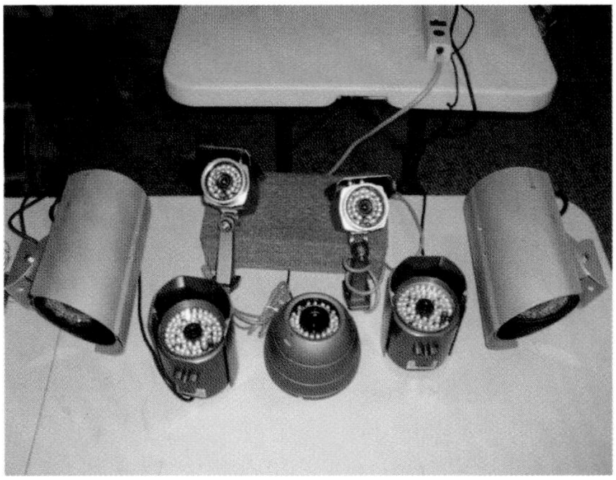

Figure 4.4

Security cameras, some equipped with Nightvision, which can be set up and then hooked up to a computer or monitor.

Picture courtesy of the Texas Paranormal Society.

The Downfall

Time slips away on video. Here is where the investigation evaluation really comes into its own. An hour of video needs time for review, and you must look at every inch of the screen to try to catch anything. If you focus on the middle, you miss the sides. If you focus on one side, you miss the other side. You need time to develop video eyes to take it all in at once. There is no way to do it justice by watching it in fast forward, unless you are watching a stationary camera shot. Remember that each time you take footage and transfer it to a new medium, from digital video to VHS or computer editing software, you lose some of the quality and increase the risk of creating your own anomaly.

Odds and Ends

Buy an external microphone for your video camera or try to use the camera as another microphone out in the field. When you run the video through filmmaking software, you can see an independent audio track. You can focus on this and look for ghostly sounds known as electronic voice phenomena or EVPs. There have been times I thought an investigation came up empty only to find something in that track .

Looking Through Different Eyes

DON'T JUST TRUST what you see with your eyes. Pictures are a good add-on, but much of the evidence you may get in the field does not come from any visual means. Instead, you have to look through different eyes, which sometimes means your ears, and bring in some equipment you might not be as familiar with.

Audio Recorders

Imagine that you have to put together a swing set. There is a big slide, two swings set at different heights, some monkey bars, and a little tree house with a search scope to look into the next yard. Your child is next to you crying to have it up in time for him to play before his nap. In your hand, you grip a screwdriver and a hammer. Then it hits you. You have to get this thing together and place it in the ground far enough and tighten all the bolts well enough to avoid accidental injuries and a lawsuit from the parents of all the neighborhood kids who will be playing on it. Good luck.

The best rule for audio equipment is getting the right tool for the job. Investigating puts the investigator in a wide range of situations, so to think one type of recording device can be right for each job is a bit nearsighted. Before you consider which recorder you need, try to think of all the possible reasons you might need one.

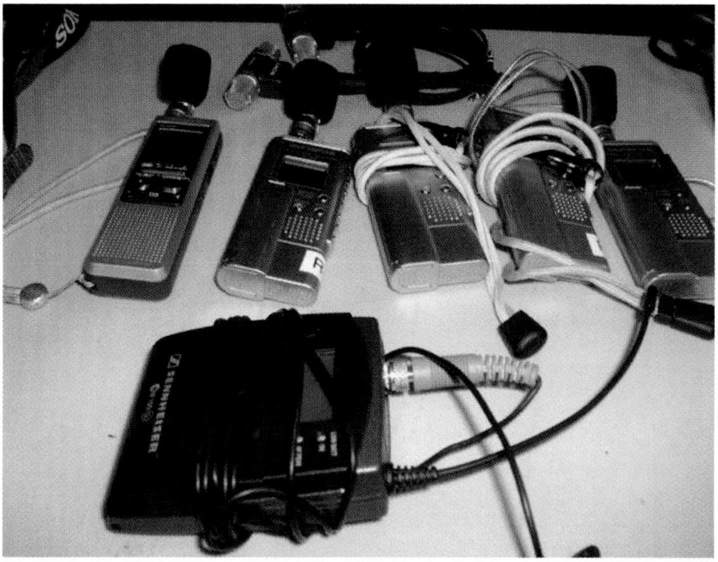

Figure 4.5

The more different types of recording equipment you can bring to an investigation the better.
Picture courtesy of the Texas Paranormal Society.

There are endless rows of recording equipment out there to choose from and you could spend a year's pay getting the highest end microphones and audio software, but why? I recorded all the interviews for my first three books on a tape recorder my roommate received from her mother to record lectures in law school in the mid-'70s, long before the expression *micro* came into common usage. Mike Markowicz, EVP specialist and host of the webcast *East Bridgewater's Most Haunted*, uses at least a dozen highly sensitive microphones linked to a computer to gather audio evidence from a haunted location. Somewhere in the middle is where you will start your investment.

Figure 4.6
A Panasonic digital tape recorder.
Picture courtesy of ghost-mart.com and Panasonic.

I suggest buying a cheaper tape recorder for interviews and thoughts you might have on investigations. With today's technology, most will still be of high enough quality to do an evaluation for EVPs after you have taken notes. It will run you between 20 and 50 dollars and hold up for years. You can use the popular microrecorder used in classrooms around the country or the even more traditional tape recorder. The smaller one is easier to keep in your pocket to pull out at the slightest hint of a story, but many of them lack the proper outlets to connect to a computer or other equipment you might need. The more conventional tapes are often cheaper and run longer.

The digital tape recorder is the staple of the ghost hunter, and it is worth it to spend a little more money on one. Look for a digital tape recorder with good sound quality and an internal microphone. Some investigators will say the more internal noise a device has, the easier it is for spirits to use the energy to talk, but most prefer a better quality and clearer baseline recording.

Digital is good for evidence but hard to work with when taking notes from an interview, and it is somewhat time-consuming to archive. I suggest leaving them for the actual evidence gathering. We'll talk about how to gather EVP later, so I'll cut it short for now.

The real fun, and the expensive side of audio equipment, comes in the accessories. Here is a list of things that will add to your arsenal. Always keep in mind the amount you pay for these should be proportionate to your emotional investment in ghost hunting and the quality you need for the job.

Infrared Motion Detector

Think of conducting a hunt as you would setting up a base camp and then setting a perimeter. Ghosts move in and out of hotspots and like to check out the electronics people are using. Finding a way to monitor an invisible presence moving in and out of your work area, maybe even hunting you, can prove very valuable.

Why It Works

We have all seen the movies where the thieves must move in and out of infrared beams to get to the treasure. Same idea works with these detectors. They send out a beam of light, and if anything blocks it from coming back, an alarm goes off.

How to Get It

Thanks to a general distrust of nannies and neighbors, these devices can now be found in any department or hardware store. They are also fairly cheap, and there is not much of an upgrade the more you pay. Some cover a wider range and offer more sensitivity. Some are designed to be used in conjunction with an alert system that can be connected to your computer, but I would save that for the last piece of equipment you buy.

How to Use It

Motion detectors should be located in places where people are not going to be. Don't paint yourself into a corner by placing them in places you are going to cross through during the hunt. Instead, place them around the primary active area. Turn them off when you conduct your investigation of that area and then back on as you leave it. Having a few motion detectors will help you cover multiple areas, just know where they are and come up with a word to say when you know you have tripped it yourself. I have seen the twinkle in an investigator's eyes when a motion detector goes off, only to see one of his teammates walk through the door a moment later.

The Downfall

Motion detectors can only be used in a limited area and in limited types of investigations. They can't be used outside because anything can set them off, and they limit a group's mobility in a smaller house. They might work best in an abandoned building where they act to warn of an approaching spirit or someone you don't want nearby coming up the stairs.

They might do their job a bit too well. My house shakes when a large truck goes by, activating all of my son's motion activated toys, and that same motion is enough to set off an alarm. Ultimately, we don't know if spirits can even trigger them, so they might be altogether useless anyway. Like so much of the new technology, you have to buy into a certain set of rules to believe the equipment will help you.

Temperature Reading Equipment

Cold spots are the calling card of the paranormal, especially poltergeist activity. Even before people began investigating and tried to explain what was going on, they associated temperature changes with ghosts. There are few reports by witnesses who don't say at some point they felt a cold come through the room or the room got very hot when something was about to happen.

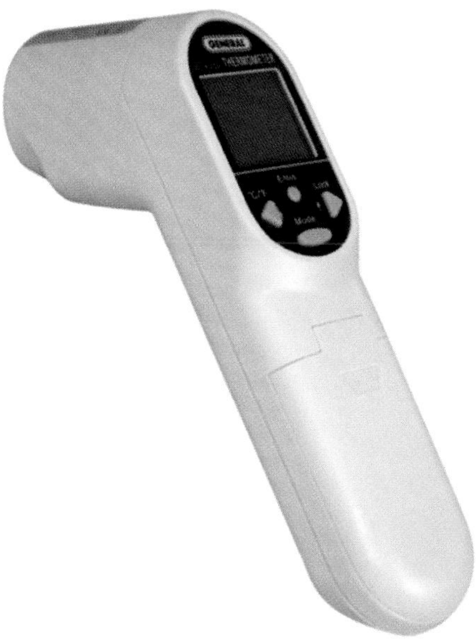

Figure 4.7
A General Tools Gun Style Infrared digital thermometer.
Picture courtesy of ghost-mart.com and General Tools.

Why It Works

Trying to explain cold spots or temperature changes is like trying to explain lightning to someone three thousand years ago. There is an immediate crossover between story and science. It is the foundation of much of the science of ghost hunting, which is to say it is the theoretical science of an unaccepted field of study. The fact is, people feel temperature changes in conjunction with happenings, so people have put forth possible reasons why.

The most widely accepted idea is that ghosts absorb energy when they are present. They use the energy in the room around them, making it colder. It does not make total sense, but there is an exchange between objects of different temperatures. For example, the release of energy is used to explain why it might get hot. It may never be agreed upon or standardized, but the fact of the matter is those drops and rises are often felt when ghostly activity has been reported, so it is one of those things worth measuring.

How to Get It

Thermometers can be found anywhere and for just about any price. A rise in the cost means more sensitivity or size, neither of which is all that important. A temperature change of only a few degrees can be easily explained away, so measurement to the tenth of a degree is overkill.

Figure 4.8
A stationary and a mobile digital thermometer.

Instead, think of reaction time. It takes your normal thermometer a while to show a change, so do not take your average home thermometer on an investigation with you. An infrared or laser thermometer is accurate and fast, and they are cheaper than they were just a few years ago. Anything more sophisticated is a waste of money.

You should also have something that keeps a constant measure of the room and registers with a digital readout. These cost fewer than 10 dollars and can be set to different levels of reaction. In other words, they take a reading every minute or 30 seconds. This can be used to note prolonged change but also to give an ambient or baseline reading that may be in conflict with the digital, which offers an immediate reading to note when something is different in the room.

How to Use It

The standard thermometer should be set in the center of the room and then the area should be swept with the infrared. Any change of more than 10 degrees should be recorded and anything more than five should be noted. I had an experience where someone was intentionally aggravating a spirit, and the more he talked, the more the temperature went up in the room. I thought it important to note out loud each degree change. This is a good idea when you are doing something intentional or when other activity is noticed.

The Downfall

Cold spots are almost as easy to explain away as creaking floors or banging on walls. There are too many natural reasons for it to get colder in a room. An inexperienced ghost hunter jumps too quickly when the infrared changes, while an experienced ghost hunter looks for reasons for a draft instead. This is an important step during the interview and tour. Note where drafts might be coming from.

Also, remember the temperature follows the beam. If you feel a cold spot and click the trigger, you are not measuring in front of you but the wall beyond, which may naturally be colder. Experiments have been conducted with the equipment, and it was found that what the beam goes through does not register, so never think you are getting the area in front of you.

Odds and Ends

Then there is the granddaddy of thermometers. Infrared thermal imaging is technology not available to everyone, but it takes the measuring of the room to a visual level. There are infrared scopes, film, and cameras, but this is something different. Infrared thermal imaging uses the same technology, but it allows you to see objects that have different temperatures, and it displays different levels with different colors. The results are amazing, although it does not explain what you are seeing. It means something though when you see a cold spot in the shape of a person when there is no one in front of you.

The price for an infrared camera can run from a few hundred dollars for a good used model to thousands for a better, industrial model. Thermal imaging will run you quite a bit more. A used commercial infrared camera is a few thousand dollars, but a new industrial model might cost more than ten thousand dollars. The commercial cameras have added features, such as built-in connectors to recording equipment or a mobile screen. Industrial cameras, like the ones firefighters or HVAC technicians use, are more accurate and durable but do not allow you to record easily, and never during a mobile investigation.

I suggest you make friends with some people who have access to a professional thermal imager and invite them to join your team. I'd go for the firefighter because they have the equipment, and it is always good to have a person like that around when you are in a jam.

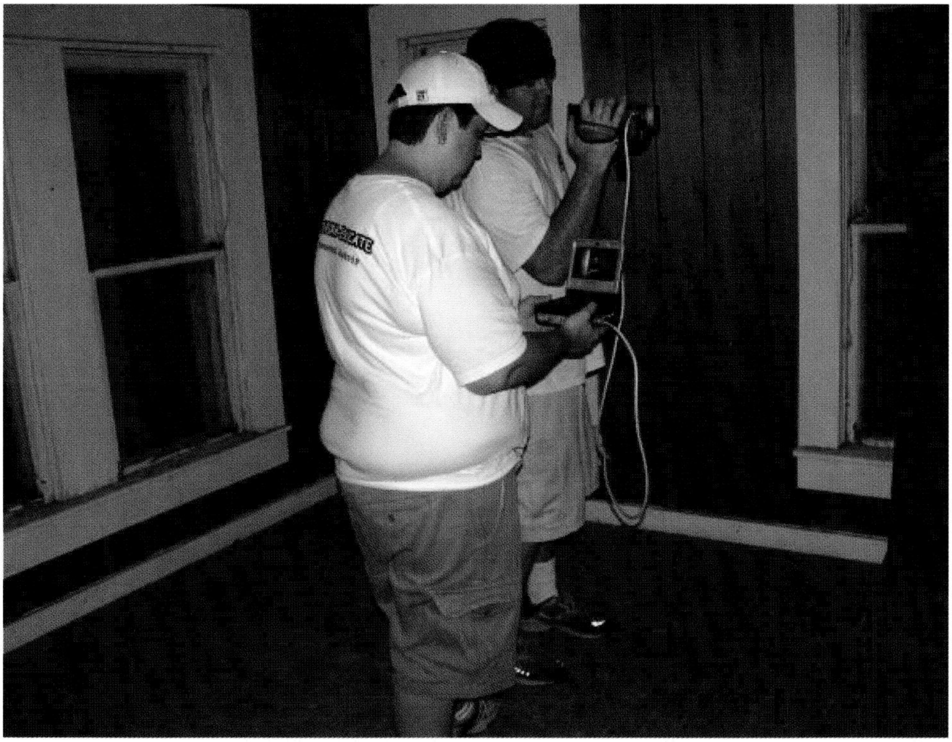

Figure 4.9
A thermal imager in use.
Picture courtesy of the Texas Paranormal Society.

Measuring the Soul

I WAS SPEAKING AT A TOWN meeting talking about an extremely haunted location (see the third investigation on the DVD). I was explaining how the many suicides in the location, as well as other acts of violence, may have somehow trapped negative energy there. Many reported having depressing thoughts hit them quickly, and several even had thoughts of suicide. A man raised his hand and asked me if I had gotten any electromagnet reading. I shook my head. He asked if I had checked for possible radiation using a Geiger counter. I said no. He whispered something to the man next to him and they giggled. I felt like I had just said I believed in the Tooth Fairy.

It was all easy before we created new ways to measure energy. You took a few pictures, maybe used a spirit board to try to communicate, and then maybe took out a tape recorder and captured a voice. Now you are expected to have readings from a meter to be taken seriously by some investigators. While they may be based in a science that is not a complete science, using them has advantages, especially in the eyes of the paranormal community as a whole.

Figure 4.10
An array of meters and counters.
Picture courtesy of the Texas Paranormal Society.

Air Ion Counter and the Radiation Detector or Geiger Counter

Here is where the science gets a bit thin, but anecdotal evidence backs up what people sometimes find in an area. The air ion counter looks to measure ions in the air, most of which are naturally present due to radioactive decay, radon, lightning, or water changing into a gas form. Radiation may be due to natural reasons as well, although the equipment was designed to measure dangerous levels.

Why It Works

Think of a ghost as a hiccup in normal energy. These meters all measure this kind of force in an environment. People have gotten strong readings in haunted places, so the technology has been attached to finding a ghost. The science is sketchy, and it might be worth your time to read more and see if it makes sense to you. Media outlets with budgets use them, so they have become very popular, and in response, new Geiger meters have been designed to provide the ghost hunter with what he needs.

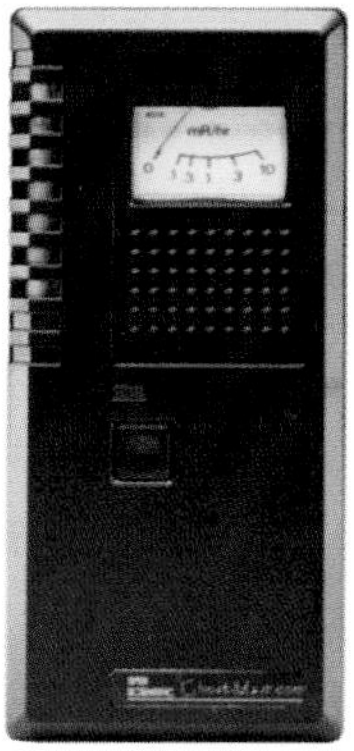

Figure 4.11
Sper Scientific Radiation Leakage Detector.
Picture courtesy of ghost-mart.com and Sper.

How to Get It

Forget the industrial strength versions and go with the meters designed for ghost hunters. The major sites, such as Ghostvillage.com and Paranormal Investigation Outfitters, all offer them.

How to Use It

All of these should be used in a sweeping manner after you have established levels already present in the room. Once an area has been swept, place the meter somewhere close and try to use other, more immediate pieces of equipment. When a reading on another tool indicates that something has changed or something has been seen or heard, take the meter back out and see if the levels in the room have changed. One mistake many investigators make is to focus their attention on the little needles and ignore what is going on in front of them. If you are looking down at a meter, what is happening slightly off in the distance that you're not seeing?

The Downfall

People have fallen in love with these meters, and television is partly to blame. It looks good to walk around with these in your hand, and moreover, it makes you feel as if what you are doing is solid and not akin to trying to catch mist in a bottle. They force you to ignore your senses for a science just this side of making sense. Oh, they are also really expensive.

Odds and Ends

Science is based on theory tested in the field. The idea behind these tools does make sense, or at least is parallel to stories told, so using them pushes the envelope. Just remember, the Earth was once flat, and the sun revolved around the Earth. You might be able to help advance the field by using them.

Electromagnetic Field (EMF) Detector

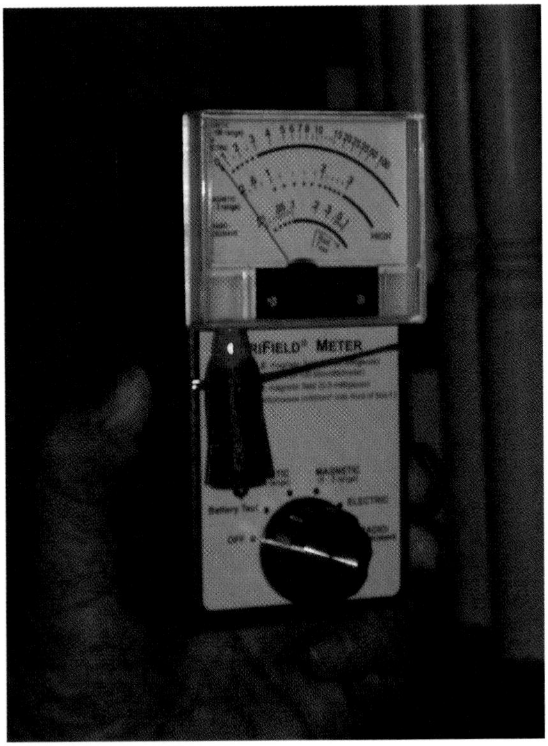

Figure 4.12
A higher-end tri-field EMF meter equipped with a red LED light so it can be read easily.

Jeff Belanger, paranormal writer and creator of Ghostvillage.com, has a small bit he gives during speeches. Playing on the "You know you're a red-neck when," routine, he presents his, "You know you're a ghost hunter when" bit. One of the last jokes is, "You know you're a ghost hunter if you have ever brought an EMF detector to a relative's funeral." It always gets a laugh from the group, usually made up of investigators. Most of them have an EMF detector in their pocket as he speaks.

There is no device so tied to paranormal enthusiasts' sides as the one used to measure the elusive electromagnetic field.

Why It Works

As a scientific concept, the electromagnetic field makes more sense or is easier to hold onto than some of the other energy measured by meters. Any electrically charged object has a magnetic field around it, the measure of which increases with the amount of energy. Tracking that field in an environment tells you the amount of energy in the room, and when that changes suddenly in a room with no visible source, that is an area of concern. If ghosts are energy, they might be the source of the rise.

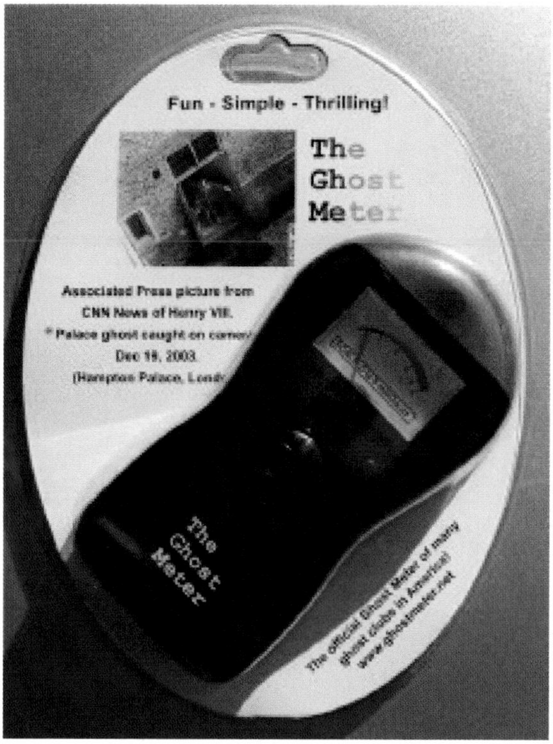

Figure 4.13
A classic cell sensor EMF detector, the Ghost Meter by Alternative Technologies. *Picture courtesy of ghost-mart.com and Alternative Technologies.*

How to Get It

When in doubt, ask another investigator. Chances are they have two or three extra in their pocket. Like all the equipment mentioned, the more money you spend the more exact reading you will get. You can get an EMF detector for less than 20 dollars, but they only measure extreme changes. For 50 dollars, you can buy the ghost hunter special, which is good for anything you might need. There are models that run much more, and it might be worth the money to invest in one of the more expensive models, especially if it comes with an audio alarm.

How to Use It

If you are setting up a vigil, set it down somewhere in the middle of the room or near an object that is the focus of activity. If on the move, keep it in your hand and make gentle sweeps. Most are too sensitive to movement and will go off if you swing it around. Other than that, it should be used much like the other meters. I like to have one that measures only extremes and does not react to motion. I tape it to another piece of equipment and use it as an early warning tool.

The Downfall

These too, are relied upon too much. Don't sacrifice your own vision. I also see too many investigators spending time sweeping as far as their arm can reach to try to get a reading in the corner of a room. If the ghosts are up that high, chances are they can get away from you.

These meters also pick up energy from everyday things, so the results can be tricky. Computers, vacuums, and refrigerators will make them go off in a house. Some radios and common devices can also trigger them. Outside, power lines read as ghosts, so be careful to know where you are in the world.

Odds and Ends

There have been links in the medical field between EMF and the physiology of the human body. The presence of a high amount of EMF energy might mean the witness is suffering from something causing hallucinations. A constant high level means danger for the family and not from a phantom. It sounds like science fiction, but extremely low frequencies (ELF) that are picked up by EMF meters have been linked to personality changes and, in conspiracy theories, mind control.

The infamous K-II Meter has been the subject of much debate. It looks really good because it has flashing colors, and some have claimed to get strong results from it. Much of this might be due to human error because the measuring button has to be pushed down by the thumb. Any movement produces a result. Ghost hunters have overcome this in ingenious ways. Many use a coin to hold down the button, but I have seen people use a poker chip and a key. One television host I investigated with used a stirring straw.

Then there is the tri-field meter. This reads EMF energy, natural and artificial electric waves, and radio and microwaves. They usually run around 150 dollars for a standard issue but can run into the thousands. It is the next evolution of EMF meters, so it might be worth saving your pennies.

And Don't Leave Without...

THINK OF AN INVESTIGATION, even one inside, as a camping trip. Pack the same way, minus the tent, and you will most likely be prepared. Now imagine you are a professional musician on a camping trip and your toolbox will be complete.

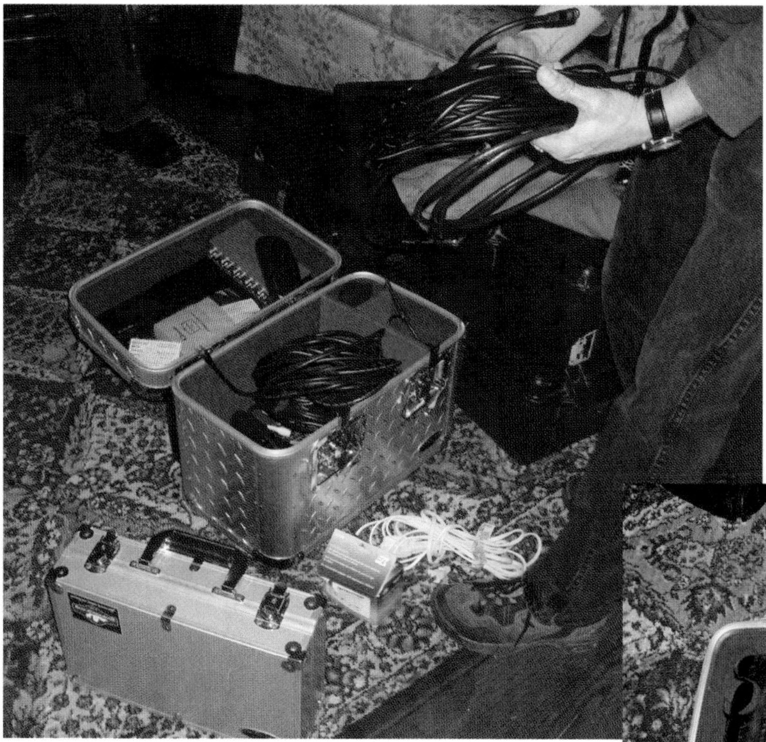

Figure 4.14
Equipment all packed up.

Figure 4.15
Another angle of the paranormal toolbox.

Here are a few good ideas:

- **Batteries and more batteries**
- **Power cables and adaptors**
- **Connectors of all shapes and sizes**
- **Measuring tape**
- **A lighter**
- **Some more batteries**
- **A whistle, especially during an outside investigation**
- **Your cellphone**
- **Your driver's license or another form of identification**
- **Water or something else to drink**
- **Gum or hard candy (see Chapters 7 and 8)**
- **A first aid kit**

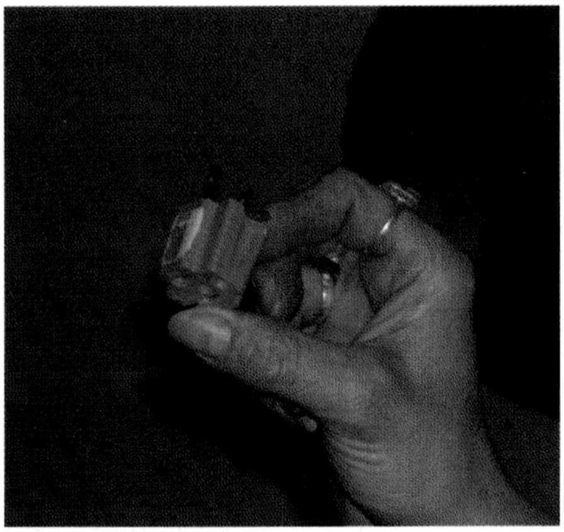

Figure 4.16
One of the most useful tools: an electrical adaptor.

Talking with the Unseen

There are other things you will need or that might come in handy. (In Chapter 5, we'll discuss trying to communicate with the dead, but it is worth mentioning here.) In addition to recorders to try to get EVP, there are other communication devices used to attempt to reach the other side. The most common, or at least the most recognizable, is a Ouija Board, or spirit board. This is the subject of much controversy, but it is a tried and true tool that has been used for generations. We'll look at these and other older tools in Chapter 5. There are other devices gaining notoriety, such as Frank's Box and the Shack Hack. Try to bring along something to allow ghosts to say hello.

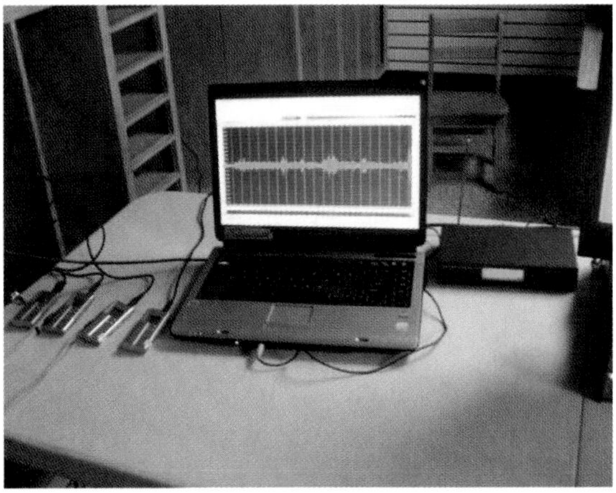

Figure 4.17
An EVP audio "real time" analysis.
Picture courtesy of the Texas Paranormal Society.

Figure 4.18
Walkie-talkies are a good way to stay in touch in the field.

I like an old radio with headphones. Sounds simple, but many believe spirits can use anything to communicate. It is all about the intention. I set it to the AM band to a frequency no one is transmitting on and just plug in one ear. Anyone who has tried to use the radio in the kitchen with the microwave on knows there will be an audible disruption when the two waves clash. It might be a station coming in very faintly in the field, but it offers another way to detect and talk.

Talking to the Living

A cellphone is good when there is an emergency, but something else might be needed for regular communication between team members when investigating a larger area. Invest in some walkie-talkies and keep everyone in the loop. They usually work with certain mobile phones as well.

Seeing Them Both

Let there be light. Investigators look to shed light on the paranormal, but before they can, they need to have light. Never leave for an investigation without several different kinds of flashlights. They are the reason you need so many batteries and the most likely tool to malfunction in the field. Even if you conduct investigations during the day or in a lighted environment, you usually end up straying into places where the light can't reach. Try going into a crawl space without one.

Many investigators purchase headlights like the ones miners use. Those are not my cup of tea, but I always have at least three on me when things get dark. Have a small one for looking at equipment in the dark or invest in a small red LED light. I always carry a large flashlight, like a

Mag-Lite, to cut through any form of darkness and offer some protection in case you run into something you can't control. There is also the shake light, which runs on a current you create and is nearly impossible for any spirit to drain. Some investigators bring along glow sticks or flares just in case.

Safety should always come first, so be sure to visit an environment you are going to look into during the day if you can. Learn the nooks and crannies so at night you can move around better. Then make sure you have a constant light source.

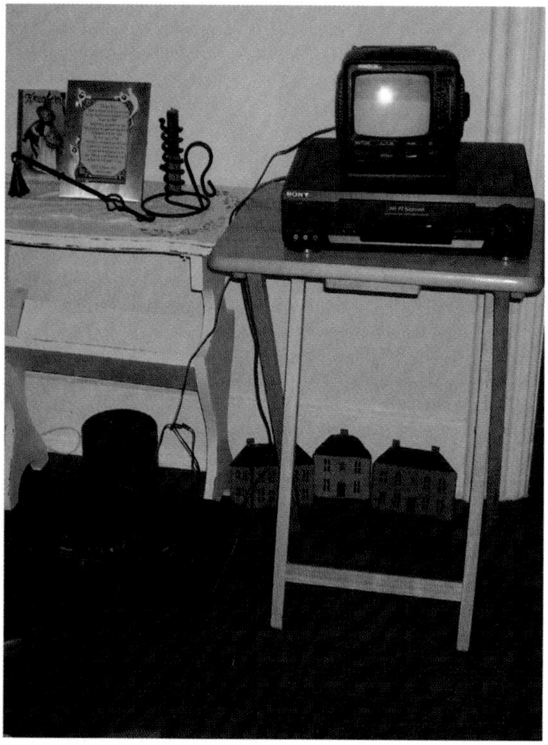

Figure 4.19
Equipment hooked up to a monitor and VHS recorder.

Bringing It All Together

They sell cases to put all of the equipment in these days, but you might be better suited to get yourself a good toolbox. For 20 or 30 dollars, you can buy a two-level toolbox with space for all of your equipment and small compartments in the lid for your small bits and pieces, such as extra tapes, adaptors, and wires. You might not look like the guys on television going into a house, but you'll be able to get to what you need quicker.

Then there is the bringing together of evidence. Many investigators have the funds to invest in television monitors and mobile DVD players that can be hooked into other equipment. Others scour yard sales looking for old, small televisions. Either way, you will need something to view what you are looking at, even if it is only to see if everything is recording the right area.

The alternative to this is a laptop computer, which you can also attach to a webcam. This can provide multiple recordings with different mediums. In other words, you can hook a microphone into one jack for EVPs and a video camera into another jack for the visual. Investigators with real funds can set up several Nightvision cameras and connect those as well. You can also use a laptop to record the same notes you would with a pen and paper.

Of course, all of this has to be scrapped when you go mobile. You can't carry around a television when you are in a cemetery or leave it alone when you are in a place someone might steal it.

The Old Guard: Old Tricks and Tried and True Methods

THERE IS A REASON THE OLD methods of the ghost hunter were used for so long. Some actually work. Science has replaced superstition, so many of these have been pushed out of the paranormal toolbox. These tried and true techniques and equipment can still find their way into your investigations, however. Some are reminders of a day long past while others are just everyday objects and tools that have been left out too often.

Compass

Figure 4.20
A good example of a compass.

Cheap and available everywhere, a compass can be your best friend on an investigation. It does the same job as an EMF meter for much less, although it is hard to get specific readings. When it comes down to it, what does a small reading mean anyway? All you need to know is that there is something amiss. Everything else just tells you something is there in a more precise way. A compass has the added feature of helping you know where you are when you are outside the house. It works if you get lost, but also to understand the environment of a haunting.

The Old-Fashioned All Tool

These small and useful little devices can be a lifesaver, although there are very few instances where that has been literal. They have a built-in screwdriver, can opener, knife, and file. They also usually have pliers of some kind.

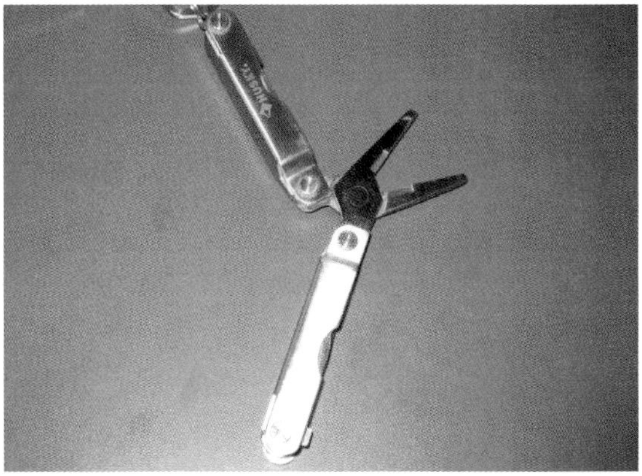

Figure 4.21
An all tool.

Notebook and Something to Write With

Too many times, I have been with someone who wanted to write down a reading or an observation, but they had nothing to write with. So much happens on an investigation, from little bits offered by witnesses to something very subtle you will forget the next day. As an investigator, you are a chronicler of events, and how can you chronicle something without a pen and paper? So much is based in the moment, and that moment is gone before you know it. Writing down readings, thoughts, and observations becomes more important. I have often found myself using some sort of communication device, such as a Ouija Board or an audio device and struggled to remember what it had said later.

I suggest carrying a few pens and a small notebook that fits into your back pocket. You don't need to write a novel. Fragments and shorthand are fine, and you are not marked down for bad grammar.

Stopwatch

One of the most common phrases you hear from witnesses is, "It seemed to be a lifetime, but I think it was more like ten seconds." This is not good enough for an investigator. A stopwatch not only tells you what time it is but offers you the chance to measure how long something happens.

Something White and Powdery

This is a classic investigation technique. Place some powder on the floor and leave an area alone. Go back later to see if anything has been disturbed. It is cheap, if not specific, but there are times when it works. One house I investigated several times always had something left behind in white and once the word yes appeared in response to the resident's question. Powder will also tell you whether that weird noise you hear behind the wall is small with four clawed feet. Something to note, leaving sugar for a ghost to mark is a bad idea in case you do have mice or rats or insects that like that kind of thing.

Diving or Dowsing Rods and Pendulums

Figure 4.22
Thomas D'Agostino using dowsing rods.

Water company trucks in Rhode Island all have dowsing rods placed on the front of their trucks, although few are looking for ghosts. They are natural and accurate waterfinders and have been used for centuries to learn where to dig for wells. The same may be true for ghosts, although they are primarily used for communication. Instead of pointing to where a ghost may be, dowsing rods are used to get simple yes or no answers from a spirit.

The same is true for pendulums, but not many electric company workers have them. They are used to get answers to questions and to give directions to a specific location.

Both of these will be covered in more detail when we talk about communicating with a ghost in the next chapter.

Incense

Forget chanting, or at least place it to one side for now. Incense not only smells nice, it is said to create energy in the air some ghosts can use to manifest. If some spirits can be sensed by their odor, a logical leap tells us they can be drawn in or repelled by smell. You can consult a book on natural magic to get a more detailed breakdown, but it might be more science than mysticism.

Of Course, You Also Need That Sense of Adventure

You have the equipment, now tap into the sense of discovery. All of these tools are not just props. They bring a new level of exploration to your paranormal trip. You should not only be looking for ghosts, but you should be experimenting to try to make the most of the toys you have collected. You now know the basics, but the best way to use what you have is to get out there. All the technology is useless if it never leaves the case, just like an investigator with the gear is useless on the couch. Use it, learn about it, and get a move on.

And, bring batteries.

Figure 4.23
Packed up and ready to hit the field.
Picture courtesy of the Texas Paranormal Society.

©istockphoto.com/1joe

5

Talking to the Dead

WE WOULD BE ABLE TO SYMPATHIZE with the dead if they would just be nice enough to talk to us. It would clear up so many things and make this world better for us both. It might even make it a better afterlife for them. Imagine the lack of fear of the unknown if it no longer became unknown. The dead are not so considerate or cannot always be straightforward with us, so it becomes our responsibility to seek them out and try to open the lines of communication.

The world of ghost hunting is very much centered on making conversation with someone who has passed. Most people would believe in ghosts if one were to appear in their living room and say hello. The evidence would be so overwhelming to that individual, he would have no choice but to allow at least the smallest opening to the belief that spirits may exist. This happens all the time, and even most investigators admit they began their journey after having their own experience. This makes reaching out to ghosts, and trying to hear what they have to say, the cornerstone of paranormal investigating.

Look at someone across the street for a moment. Now walk up and try talking to them. They are two very different experiences, and introducing yourself invites a relationship. This connection might work out for both of you, but there are dangers as well. As you read and learn about different ways to reach out, think of them like someone you might meet at a party. Saying hello does not mean the person can be trusted or that he is a nice guy waiting to drive you to the airport. Add the element of darker, often demonic entities, and talking becomes more dangerous. You never know until you introduce yourself, so remain open but guarded.

Their Eagerness to Talk

THERE IS A CLASSIC STORY about the true believer and the flood. After hearing a report that water levels in his town were getting high, a man took comfort in knowing he would be saved because he was a believer. As the water levels got higher, a boat comes along, but the man refuses rescue, claiming he knows he will be saved because of his strong faith. He retreats to the roof where a helicopter comes by, but he refuses again, saying his devotion will come through in the end. The man eventually dies, and when he meets his god, he asks him why he was allowed to die.

"You idiot," he is told, "I sent you a radio broadcast, a boat, and a helicopter."

The story rings true for ghosts as well. When something unexplainable happens, we naturally fear it and try to remove it from our life. We wish they would just tell us what they want and move on, but the disturbance itself is a message, a way of trying to break through and get something across. The idea that communication should be simple and take the form the living wants is silly and part of the reason for the tension between the living and the dead.

What Is Getting in the Way?

Think about how hard it is to get your ideas across to your coworkers, your parents, or your children. We assume talking to the living would be easy, but it may be nearly impossible for a spirit to do. There may be several reasons for this, but even the basic premise is flawed. We have been conditioned to think that there is always a reason for a haunting, that the dead need something from us. This is usually not the case, and in the circumstance of a residual haunting, it is never the case. Ghosts may live parallel lives with us, but do not assume there is a symbiotic relationship between the two. Here are some other reasons spirits seem hesitant to talk.

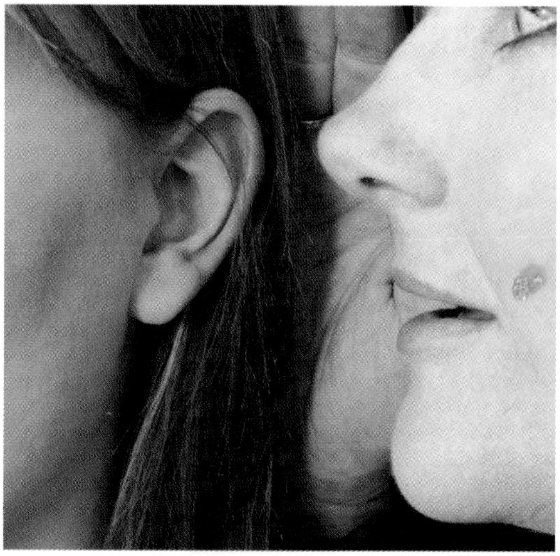

Figure 5.1
©istockphoto.com/Amanda Rohde

Mood

We assume people somehow become enlightened when they die. In reality, most people believe you maintain your personality in death. If you were a jerk when you were alive, you will be a jerk in death. If you didn't like to talk to people, that is not going to change. You might stay silent just because you like to mess with people or to play practical jokes. The mood of a spirit in general on any given day can be the most dominant factor in trying to bridge the gap between the living and the dead. Don't feel the dead want to talk just because you do, and don't feel they want to remain silent just because you don't feel like talking.

Knowledge

A ghost might not know it is dead, so it wouldn't even think about making contact. They may also have no idea how to get in touch with you. Don't think that just because some ghosts can communicate, all can. If this were true, every ghost would manifest itself the same way. It might not understand the technology you are trying to use to talk. If someone died 100 years ago, how would he know how to work a digital tape recorder? Spirit communication might involve teaching spirits how to use a radio or another communication device.

The Rules

During an investigation with Mike Markowicz, we set up almost a dozen high-end microphones in the house, and the results were amazing. We picked up almost constant chatter from the different spirits in the house, but the most enlightening aspect was their interactions with each other. Some knew what we were there for and were able to communicate it to us. Others could not see us but sensed us there somehow. There were several times when one spirit was talking to another and a third came through and told them to be quiet because they were being recorded.

There seem to be rules in the afterlife, and some of them might govern what spirits can and can't do to the living.

It's weird to think that even after we die, we are held to some standard and must follow some order, but there is evidence to back it up, or at least stories that seem to bear it out. Traditionally, the spirits of children are the most active and, some report, more commonly seen. If there were rules to be broken, the most likely offenders would be children who would have trouble understanding and following a system set. This also might be the reason negative spirits or tricksters are more likely to come through, explaining why so much of spirit communication initiated by the living results in getting unconstructive spirits.

Figure 5.2
Child ghosts don't know the rule about not talking.
©burningwell.com/Jim Smith

Enlightenment and Soul Development

There is a belief system that speaks of two kinds of ghosts. The first would be the energy of a person somehow trapped and making contact. The other would be the soul of a person who has died, paid some kind of cosmic dues, and can choose to come back to speak with the living. The theory is they do this to help people and to facilitate another soul's growth. This is a common idea among several very popular mediums and one possible explanation for guardian angels.

Under this system, spirits can and will talk to people, most times without the help of any equipment, old or new. It also means they are open to helping someone get in touch with someone else, like caller assistance for the dead. Spirits who have not reached this stage in their development are forced to remain silent or do not have the ability to talk.

You might try developing a relationship with this kind of person on the other side when you become comfortable with your own psychic abilities or if it calls into your belief system. At the very least, you can introduce yourself to spirits in the room when you arrive and call on messengers to help them along. If you have good intentions, a good spirit might be willing to help.

The Famous Talking Board

WANT TO GET A PARANORMAL investigator really upset with you? Ask if a Ouija Board is a good thing to use during an investigation and then disagree with whatever stance he takes. The result will be more frightening than actually seeing a demon in an insane asylum. Boards are the great magnet. They either pull people in and force them to sit down or repel them to the opposite wall.

Figure 5.3
A classic Ouija Board.
Picture courtesy of Justin Mycofsky.

There are few aspects of the paranormal that have as strong a galvanizing effect on investigators as the Ouija Board, and the reason might be more reflective of the media's influence and the religious passion of people than any actual science or rational idea. There is not much of a science to the use of one in the first place, so superstition can fill the void and make a piece of wood and a piece of plastic a glimpse into the other side or a one-way ticket to damnation.

How to Work It and How It Works

There are few people who haven't seen someone using a talking board on television, in the movies, or in person. The basics are pretty simple. Place the planchette on the board, ask a few questions, and talk to the dead. There are ways to get better results, most of which are based on ideas and nothing too solid.

The basis for the board is that the energy of the users attracts and then is channeled by the consciousness of the spirit contacted. They then create a kind of field on the board and can push the marker and point to letters or symbols on the board. Success then depends on the people involved. The number of people and their intentions are important. The ideal number of users is four or five, and everyone should be focused on the task of communicating.

There are different techniques people have used over the years to try to generate more accurate information. For example, some claim having all the members move the planchette in a circle while asking the questions provokes better responses. This seems to do more to focus the energy of the user and not to directly affect any ghosts.

Here are some basic methods that might work and some things to avoid:

- **Beware of oddly phrased questions, especially couching a question in the negative. For example, do not ask, "Do you not like candy?" Instead ask, "Do you like candy."**
- **Keep a pen and paper with you to write responses down. This might make it easier to understand what is being said, and it helps when you try to track down confirming information later.**
- **Don't all talk at once. Communication with a Ouija Board seems to work best when one person does the talking.**
- **Try to get information only the spirit would know or something that can be confirmed later.**
- **If you ask the spirit to make itself known in the room and it doesn't, don't get discouraged. Communicating and manifesting are two different skills.**

Figure 5.4
Another board used during a séance.

Is It Effective?

Let's start with an explanation of why you are not talking to ghosts. Small muscle spasms or the unconscious mind can move to letters as easily as a ghost can, and this might be the reason for the swiftness of the spirit and the clarity of the message. In other words, the living people on the board are intentionally or unintentionally spelling things out. The subconscious can be a powerful enemy to the ghost hunter, ruining evidence and making natural shadows proof of an afterlife. Nowhere is this more evident than when using a board.

Now let's assume you are talking to a ghost. There are very few spirits who come on that have not died a tragic death, usually a murder or suicide, and need your help. Reference the section above about why they might not communicate. The lower, trickster spirits who are not reliable have a habit of finding their way on. Their goal is to keep you talking, perhaps because they feed off your energy or because they are lonely. They are lying, and they are not buried in your backyard. This is one of the reasons they spell slowly or are confusing in their answers. People often report using the board for an extended period of time and look up to see it is the middle of the night and they have not gotten a real answer to any of their questions.

Here are some things to look for with trickster spirits:

- **Don't trust the cause of death they tell you.**
- **Get off if the spirit begins to threaten you or manipulates the environment around you.**
- **Stop using the board if you start to have bad dreams or find yourself thinking about when you can use it again.**
- **Get off if the spirit claims to be your spirit guide. If this person is real, they would be able to talk to you in a different way, and it is a classic way for them to get you to keep talking.**
- **Beware of false prophecy. If the ghost claims to be able to tell you your future or know things that come from a mystic place, do not trust what it says. Again, they use this to keep you talking to them.**
- **Those little pictures in the top corners of a Ouija Board represent channeling, meaning they want to talk directly through you. This means they want to take you over to make chatting easier. That's bad.**

There are some successes from the board as well, and despite the bad press, it might be a useful tool if used the right way and with a healthy bit of skepticism. Many use some kind of protection when using the board. I knew a Wicca who would cast a circle, bless everyone who entered, perform a ritual when closing it again, and washed the board with a mixture of salt and water before and after we used it. I remember her getting very upset when my roommate crossed the circle to get to his computer. This was not extreme, but her belief system, and I encourage you to get protection from wherever you can. Remember, many places you might get protection from are strictly against the use of a board and you may be at it alone.

Figure 5.5
A different type of board used during table-tipping ceremonies.
Picture courtesy of Elizabeth Russell.

Okay, but Is It Evil?

The Exorcist, the popular book by William Peter Blatty that was made into an even more popular movie, changed the way people thought about demons and possessions. Reports of dark attacks increased after the release of the movie and created an upward trend that has reached a critical climax today. Everything that happened to that little girl can be traced back to her playing with a Ouija Board by herself. Sales of the board increased the more pea soup she threw up, the same way accidental death by gunshot did after *The Deer Hunter* was released in 1978. It also became the whipping boy for anyone looking for a reason for possession. A quick SAT analogy; ghosts are to ancient Indian burial grounds as demons are to Ouija Boards.

Seven Old Wives' Tales about Talking Boards

1. Using the board alone will increase the chance of getting a demon.
2. Not moving the planchette to "goodbye" will trap a spirit in the board.
3. Destroying a board with a trapped spirit will release it and cause a full-blown haunting.
4. Fire or burial is the only way to get rid of one.
5. Only a wood board will work because of wood's spirit conductive nature.
6. Never move into a new house or apartment with an old board. Leave it when you move.
7. Sleeping in a bed with a board underneath it will cause bad dreams.

Automatic Writers and Pendulums

PEOPLE HAVE USED JUST ABOUT anything to try to talk to the other side, and before the invention of electricity, people used traditions handed down through the generations. It was a mix of distorted religious ideas and rural superstition, but it formed the beginnings of ghost hunting. Modern investigators who rely on electronic equipment too heavily might look down upon the older methods, but they have never gone away. In fact, many of them are making a comeback in the field.

Automatic Writers

There is a waiting period with talking boards that becomes too tedious for some. Waiting for the pointer to move and trying to decide where it is pointing can be removed by the use of an automatic writer. In the early days of Spiritualism, a medium would allow a spirit to talk through them and that spirit would take control of the medium's hand and write down the message. Entire books have been written using this method. This type of communication is still being used today, but many choose to have a tool to help them. This old-fashioned device, now modernized but with very few improvements needed, consists of a planchette type device with a place to insert a pencil or other writing device. As the session starts, the pointer moves and literally writes down the communication between you and the spirit. The results are a written document from a ghost.

Usually the written results are a combination of circles and words, some of which make sense and some that are as abstract as messages gotten from a talking board.

While this method of talking has recently regained some popularity, it is as flawed as a talking board, although it does not have the stigma attached to it. The subconscious is still blamed for many of the messages one gets, and the argument is stronger because one person uses it. There are no filters. Automatic writers also do not produce any better results that Ouija Boards, and you may find yourself trying to make random angles and loops into letters that might make sense.

Pendulums

I know investigators who will not go anywhere without their Geiger counter and their pendulum.

Figure 5.6
©istockphoto.com/Jonny Kristoffersson

It seems like a contradiction in many ways. One is a tool of pure science, or at least ghost hunter science, and the other is something used by followers of New Age philosophy. In reality, spirits can use anything to talk to us, and there might be something scientific about the movement they cause in the pendulum.

Most are made from some rock or crystal that may have a special conductivity, which spirits can manipulate, but there are some made of metal. The choice is up to the user, and its effectiveness might have more to do with intention than material. This weight is placed on a chain of some kind, the user asks questions, and the movement of the crystal gives the answer. This dates back centuries, and is used in the superstitions of different cultures. For example, if you hang one over a pregnant woman, it will tell you the sex of the baby. The method and how to read the results vary from culture to culture, but it is an example of folklore still being practiced today. A firm hand is needed to practice this way of talking, and there might be a bit of the user in the answers you get.

For the paranormal investigator, the technique is much the same. The pendulum, and you can make your own out of a string and a weight to start, is held out. Try concentrating on a need to talk or clearing your mind. Begin asking questions, telling the spirit how to signal "yes" and "no." There is a limitation similar to knocks and bangs given in the early days of contact because of the code you need to establish with them, but it might be effective for answering questions and even pointing things out. In a recent investigation, a spirit directed our group to where something was in the woods by swinging in that direction.

Pendulums can be made of anything and seem to work more on the intention of the user and the power of the spirit. The rocks and crystals gather that energy easier, but people have also used their gold or silver chain with something on the end, and some psychics doing police investigations involving missing people go so far as to place an object from the missing at the end.

Very similar to this are the dowsing rods we discussed in Chapter 4. They also answer simple questions by movement, usually with a crossing meaning yes and a separating meaning no. They also can point to specific places and are often used to talk to the dead during an investigation.

EVP: Voices from Beyond

IT IS THREE DAYS AFTER an investigation, and you're alone in your house. You are a typical ghost hunter, which means you have at least one full time job that has nothing to do with ghosts, and you need to fit investigating in at night when the family is asleep. You are going over the evidence from the cemetery, closing your eyes and remembering what the temperature was and how you felt while you walked among the headstones. You hear your voice asking if any spirits would like to speak when you hear it. It is soft at first, a whisper almost by definition, and you know it only because you hear a scratch. You isolate the sound, filter out some background noise and turn the volume up. Someone not seen that night, someone not with your group and maybe not even from your time or plane, comes through with a simple sentence. "I'm cold."

It is the moment that makes the investigation, and without it, all you have to remember the night are some easily disputed orbs and a few bug bites. This is real, or at least something you can listen to over and over again. There are reasons why it might be there, but it's as solid as things get in the paranormal world. This might be why ghost hunters focus so hard on trying to record the voices of the dead. More than anything in the paranormal, it makes tilting at windmills feel worthwhile.

Figure 5.7
An EVP session accompanied by some explainable lights and some not so easily dismissed.
Picture courtesy of the Texas Paranormal Society.

The Investigation Standard

Most people who work extensively with electronic voice phenomena, or EVP, have a certain look about them. They are a bit paler, hold onto their equipment a bit more tightly, and have a more serious look to them. These are traits molded by hours spent working alone, listening to tapes and bent over a computer, playing and replaying the same moments over and over again. EVP work has become the standard of paranormal investigating because it is the hardest evidence to dispute. There are levels of quality and situations where the noises on tape can be explained away, but a solid EVP has to make even the skeptic scramble to find a reason for it to be anything but a ghost.

All investigations should have someone doing audio work. With all of the new equipment out there, and the old equipment having a revival, a tape recorder might be the one item that makes the difference. Something relevant said can confirm the stories people have told about the haunting or make a reading mean something profound. For example, if there is an EMF or Geiger spike at the moment something is heard on tape, you have hard evidence to quarrel with. Temperature drops or even that gut feeling you have during a hunt can be explained away, but not if a voice comes with it.

Any kind of ghost can be trapped on tape. The spirit might want to talk to you or you might get something unintelligent left behind in the air. You might get the sounds of someone intelligent but who doesn't know he is being recorded. Some have even captured the sound of unseen pets or gunshots and cars that are not there. The whole rainbow of what you can capture inspires the EVP investigator, and wondering what the noises could be and what they mean for the field keeps the practice fresh.

The Reason You Can Hear

Voices of the dead can be heard with the right equipment. The why is a bit harder to nail down, but the ideas seem to fall into two major camps, which are both really the same answer said in different words. It all comes down to energy.
If a ghost is energy, and that energy can exist on several different levels of the energy spectrum, then the ghost might be able to use the electrical equipment to record its own voice. After all, the machine itself does not know it is recording sound, it just takes one kind of force and transforms it to another.

Figure 5.8
©istockphoto.com/Rolf Bodmer

The largest group of believers put faith in the direct electrical energy theory. In other words, the energy the ghost creates or gives off can be recorded. Without a voice box or mouth, this is all it can possibly be. You might be recording residual energy left over in a location or an intelligent spirit, but the energy is being recorded.

Others feel the spirit can manipulate energy, like the ghost who uses the spirit board does, and make their presence known that way. They use the energy of the machine itself to create the voices. Unlike other investigators, people who fall into this camp usually prefer analog tape recorders that are somewhat loud.

Then there are other ideas that change the angle of ideas slightly. Some believe the spirits manipulate the tape itself, using their abilities to change the little metal filings to create syllables. These same people feel they can play with digital in much the same way. One idea outside the lines involves spiritual energy, which is not the same as our world's physical energies. This comes from the soul, can't be measured, but can be transformed into acoustic energy and left on tape.

The Best Methods and Equipment

When the word "tape" is used in reference to EVP work the term is rather loose. Most recorders are digital and have no tape, but hunters still say, "left on tape." It is an expression carried over from the old days but still significant today. Some people like working with tape while others prefer to use only digital. We discussed the differences in Chapter 4, so I'll leave it to you to decide what you will work with. I will again say, however, getting the same evidence on two different kinds of mediums is one step closer to having rock solid proof.

Figure 5.9
An older microcassette used for analog EVP.

How people conduct EVP work is as selective as anything else in the paranormal. People have their tried and true methods, usually molded by what they think a ghost is and what they believe an EVP is. There are some basic techniques that are good for any investigation. Audio work is best done while standing still or with the recorder on a solid surface. Too much movement makes it too easy to get scratching or odd bumps. An active style of questioning is best, as opposed to leaving it somewhere. There seems to be an added power given to spirits when someone is speaking to them. They respond instead of being caught.

Always be silent when you first turn a recorder on, and wait at least ten seconds before you begin speaking. There is a curiosity factor to the other side, and often times they start talking before you have anything to say. Some of the best evidence is gained in those first seconds. Some have even showed wonder at what the investigator is doing or ignorance as to the tools being used. Voices have been heard saying things like, "What is that?" or "Who are you?"

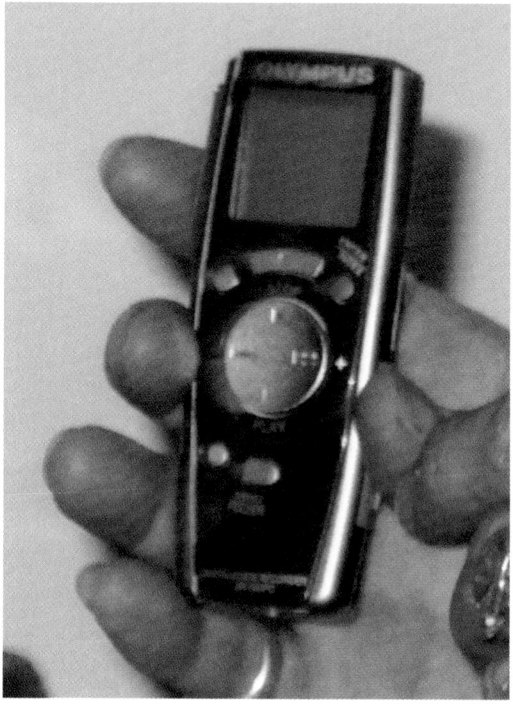

Figure 5.10
A digital recorder for EVP work.

Once you've created that buffer, begin your line of questions. Find your method and go with it. Some prefer the gentle approach and ask simple questions that the spirit might know the answer to, such as their favorite food or what color they like. Have some respect and don't ask them what it is like to be dead or how they died. You might be able to get to it eventually, but would you like someone to introduce themselves and then ask you about the worst day of your life?

Continue asking questions for a limited time, preferably five to ten minutes. There are different places in the location to look into, so there are plenty of other opportunities to have them talk. Always leave some time to allow for an answer. Twenty seconds or so is probably enough time, but you need to account for what they say and how long it might take for them to be able to communicate. When you are done, you should give them a warning, telling them you are going to end and asking if they have anything else they want to say. Move on and repeat.

Like we discussed in Chapter 4, some investigators like noisier machines because they believe the internal noise can be used by the spirits to talk. Many also provide some background noise like running water or a metronome to facilitate this. Remember, different ghosts might talk in different ways, so try it with this kind of white noise and without.

Much of EVP work is done after the fact, so we'll go over some of the pitfalls later, but for now, here are some of the dos and don'ts of EVP work:

- **Don't spend a fortune on an expensive setup to capture EVPs. Older machines have a better chance of catching evidence.**
- **Alternate sessions using an external microphone and the one built into the machine.**
- **Always leave time after asking a question.**
- **Make note of external noises during a session. This might help you to explain a voice on the tape or it might be used by a spirit to communicate.**

Much of the work of EVP comes in the evaluation after the investigation is over, so we'll leave out a closer examination until Chapter 9, but keep this in mind. Good results are usually the result of experience. Many quality EVPs are left on tape without ever being heard twice. As you practice more, and as you start to listen to them later, you will realize questions you should have asked or times you should have turned the tape on. There is time to collect the perfect EVP, so take your time and stick with it.

ITC and the New Ways of Looking

INSTRUMENTAL Transcommunication, or ITC, is a wide range communication, and the field really extends to any communication using an electronic device. Some of ITC happens on its own, like the sudden possession of your computer, the turning off of your television, or even the crisis ghost that calls to announce they are dead but okay on the other side. Several of the devices we have mentioned fall into this category, such as any tape recorder used for EVP, but there are other devices being created that look to open up a direct line of communication between the living and the dead. Some are manipulations or variations of existing, everyday devices, while others are constructed specifically for this kind of talking. Others have just been stumbled on, like finding diamonds while looking for gold.

Figure 5.11
A television set to white noise.

The Talking Television

We live in a visual world, and pictures are worth more than a thousand words when it comes to the paranormal. Naturally explainable orbs make investigators go crazy with glee, so imagine if there were a way to tape a ghost talking to you on the television. It can be easily faked, but if a genuine television broadcast could be taped and passed to the public, it might mean a huge step forward for the paranormal field.

The simple way to start would be to turn to a station with no signal or use a television with no cable connected. The static produced creates a palette, which spirits might be able to use to talk or even appear. It is much like a CB that no one else is tuned to. With quality television programming on every other channel blocking out potential contact, these white noise stations might be enough to offer a free conduit for ghosts looking to break through.

The best method to use with this method is to set the television to a channel with no signal and start a session similar to one used to gather EVPs. Ask questions and wait for responses and note any disturbances in the picture or sound.

It would be ideal if you set up a VCR or other television recording device to record the conversation. The problem with this is most modern VCRs have a habit of blocking out channels that do not come in by turning the screen blue or black. It might be worth the investment to buy an older model at a yard sale. This kind of communication is always done with the widest net possible, so better results might come if you merely tell the spirits they can talk if they would like and inform them they may speak through the television. This technique can take a long time to conduct and review, and getting any results is a long shot, so don't spend too much time on it and don't get frustrated if you get no results.

Figure 5.12
Into the camera...

Figure 5.13
...And into the VCR.

The improved method involves creating a theoretical disturbance in the energy of a room by creating a loop. All you need is a television and a video camera to punch a hole in our dimension. Connect the camera to the television by plugging into the auxiliary jack or a VCR. The latter is better because you would also want to record the results. Aim the camera directly at the television. What you should get is a seemingly infinite picture of the picture of the television. This is thought to disturb things, like creating visual feedback.

Figure 5.14
The loop.

Ghosts have been known to use this loop to communicate. Begin taping from the VCR to save your camera's film and ask questions of any spirits that want to make contact. This is another method requiring a broad intention; be careful when reviewing the evidence later. Evidence in this type of ITC might be more subtle than with EVP work and might be either visual or auditory. It is sometimes best to view the evidence frame by frame to try to catch an image or a voice.

Two-Way Communication: The Wave of the Future

VERY EARLY ON IN MY investigation career, I had an idea in my head that my radio could be used to hear the dead. I used to scan through stations as a teenager, thinking some force would offer inspiration or the answer to a question I had about life by giving me the right song at the right time. The same was true for ghosts willing to talk. I knew nothing of the science or that I had stolen the idea from people who had been doing it for decades. I just used to turn the radio to a frequency on the AM band that did not come in and notice when the sound changed.

Figure 5.15
©istockphoto.com/Matthew Hertel

Once in a cemetery I was using this method while trying to track down the ghost of a woman who appeared all in white. As I walked past the headstones, one of the investigators I was with began to get wobbly and sat down, finally placing her head on the ground because she was overcome with the desire to sleep right at that moment. While the entire episode was going on, my headphones picked up a slow breathing, like a gentle snoring.

I had touched upon something already popular with ghost hunters, and since then the practice of using radios to try to tune into the other side has grown in popularity. While visual advances are slow moving, there are new products and ideas coming out every month to try to get something that can be heard.

The Spiricom

Media may have kept interest in the paranormal alive and inspired people to start, but it is the innovators who keep the fight alive and move the field forward. One such visionary is George Meek. He created a device known as the Spiricom, and since his death in 1999, people have taken his original idea and schematics and tried to make improvements on his design. The machine acts as a type of universal translator. Human speech is played through a series of tone and frequency generators and broken down. The spirit in turn uses its energy to activate the same mechanisms on its end and transform whatever that might be into a human voice.

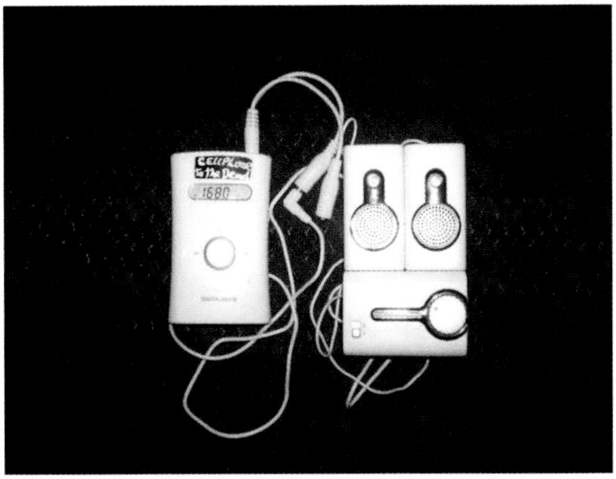

Figure 5.16
An example of the spirit phone.
Picture Courtesy of Tim Weisberg and Spooky Southcoast.

Meek found the machine worked and made contact with people from the other side, including a scientist who had died a decade earlier who helped him make the device more effective. They talked for years. Clips of the conversations, as well as plans for the machine, are all over the Internet, and people continue to build their own machines with varying levels of success.

More information and designs can be found at www.njghostresearch.org and MP3s of Meek's original recordings can be found at www.worlditc.org.

Frank Sumption and His Legacy

When Frank Sumption decided to invent a new way to try to talk to aliens, he accidentally set the paranormal world on its ear. Thomas Edison had set the groundwork years before, but Sumption brought it to the world. His invention, first called a Frank's Box, has been the newest innovation in the world of the paranormal and has sparked debate among investigators and drama in the community.

The idea behind the box is simple, and like many things in the ghost hunting world, it is amazing people didn't come up with the idea before. Using an older radio, Sumption found a way to remove the radio's ability to stop during its scan mode. The result was a machine that ran up and down the band of a radio, stopping randomly based on no set of rules. When a question is asked, the radio begins to run down the dial and stop at stations where words are spoken.

In other words, an answer is received by arbitrary words spoken over several stations. You ask, "How are you?" and the answer comes out, "I am cold," but it may come out over three different radio stations. The longer the sentence and the more frequencies it talks over determines the quality of the evidence. Getting, "no," has almost no meaning because the odds of hearing that on any station at any time are pretty good.

Figure 5.17
A picture taken during a box session with Chris Moon.

Frank eventually ran into conflict with his distribution of the box and others have taken his idea and run with it. It can now be made with directions from the Internet or purchased as a Minibox from different sites.

Mike Markowicz tells of being alone in a room reviewing evidence after an EVP session. It had occurred a few hours earlier, and as he listened, he heard a voice say, "I'll be talking to you later." It hit him the spirit was right, the spirit was talking to him later. Markowicz credit this night as the one that made him devote so much time to gathering evidence, and most people who work with EVP tell of the same experience of the one voice that drew them in.

All spirit communication has this effect. A picture might be worth a thousand words, but when the board tells you something you can prove or you hear the low, drawn out voice on tape, the hairs on the back of your neck rise. For most ghost hunters, investigating is not just about capturing a moment in time but rather making contact with whatever might be out there. It is a sign of some form of intelligence after we die and your ability to make their world part of yours.

The "Ghost Box Hack" By Tim Weisberg, investigator and host of "Spooky Southcoast"

With the proliferation of "Frank's Box" among the paranormal community, there has been more and more call for electronic devices that supposedly communicate directly with those who have passed on. While Frank Sumption himself does support the use of these devices to speak directly with the deceased, he does recommend to those who seek that purpose a few of the modifications to his original designs.

One such device is known as the "Ghost Box Hack" or the "Radio Shack Hack." By making a simple modification to a Radio Shack-brand AM/FM radio with digital tuner, any paranormal investigator can have an inexpensive and effective ghost box of their own.

These digital radios have a scan option that sweeps either the AM or FM dial, depending on which you select. When a signal is strong enough to register, the sweep automatically stops on that station.

Essentially, by removing the mute pin from the radio's circuit board, you can eliminate automatic stop when a signal is received. So instead, the radio continues to sweep the channels. The theory behind it as an ITC device is that the spirits can pull whatever words they need out of the great vastness of radio waves. Sometimes, words may come through in the spirit's own voice, but much of the time they just utilize what is already being broadcast. The important thing to remember when using this device is that even though you may be able to easily identify where the words come from—a popular commercial jingle, a station ID, baseball play-by-play—you can't dismiss it for that reason. Worry not about where the words are coming from, but what words are being said. For that reason, these devices are considered most effective when used in a question-and-answer format; it is important to keep asking the same questions, or to ask for a repetition of answers, in order to verify that it is not just a random event.

Figure 5.18
Tim Weisberg using the Box.
Picture courtesy of Tim Weisberg and "Spooky Southcoast."

The device has been tested and recommended by those in Sumption's ITC-EVP group on Yahoo!, and the popular blog site http://www.ufogeek.com contains videos, instructions, and the latest modifications to these Radio Shack devices. It also has recommendations for how to connect external speakers, recording devices, echo chambers, and more.

The two devices used are the RS 12-469 (retailing for $24.99) or the RS 12-470 (retailing for $39.99). The 12-470 features TV and weather bands for additional scanning options. Both run simply on three AAA batteries, giving paranormal investigators a cheap, effective, and highly portable device for speaking to the dead.

6

Hitting the Field

IT'S ALL ABOUT THE JOB. Before you buy your first digital thermometer, you'll be tempted to hit the field, and you should live a bit of the paranormal life before you invest any more time and money. There will come a time when looking for ghosts in your basement becomes boring and you'll be tempted to suit up and investigate a real site. Here are some things you need to know as you prepare for your first hunt.

Before You Start

BEFORE I SEND YOU OUT THERE, let me share some advice that remains the same for all the types of investigations that you'll go on. There are some elements unique to the setting you are in, but there are some generalizations, some things that fit no matter what the situation. Think of these as helpful hints, not rules set in stone. As you go, you'll develop your own technique and your own way of viewing things, but have a baseline first. Ultimately, your best option is to find a more seasoned ghost hunter or a local group and learn more by working with them, but the advice I'm about to give you is a great second choice.

Patience Is a Virtue

As I have stressed many times before, there is very little about investigating the paranormal that is immediate or quick. Think of it as being a right fielder in Little League baseball. There are long stretches of time when you do nothing but chase mosquitoes, but that can change very quickly. You are looking for a moment, and that moment might not come, but if you do not have your eyes open and your glove up, you might miss it when it does.

Figure 6.1
Investigator Thomas D'Agostino preparing for a quiet session of ghost hunting.

At no time is this more relevant than during the actual investigation. You want that moment where you turn your head and ask what that noise was, but it likely won't happen that way. Things are a long time coming, and sometimes they come when you do not expect them and in unanticipated ways. I once did an investigation with some people, and despite the thousands of dollars of equipment we had, almost all of us missed a flashing of lights in response to our question because we were too busy making sure the setup was right.

Wait. People ask me if I like the term "ghost hunter," which I usually do not. So often, it is less about hunting and more about being still and letting things come to you. Remember, the evidence you are looking for might not make itself known until days later when you are going through the data you collected.

Protecting Yourself

Many investigators call upon different religious sources to shield them from anything physical or psychic during an investigation. They also believe it may prevent anything from going home with them. You may believe in these methods or discard them completely. I know an investigator who has created his own paranormal mix, mostly made from holy water, that he applies to his equipment and investigators before they begin their hunt. I'm not sure it works, but I always let him dowse me with it. It's better to be safe than sorry.

Holy Water, or plain water blessed by a priest or minister, is one of the most common forms of protection. Some people cast circles with spells or spread salt around them before starting or pray for protection. Incense is good too. Many investigators carry amulets which are said to ward off bad spirits or carry crystals they feel will form a shell around them. It really comes down to personal belief and intention.

Be Still

One of the attractions to paranormal investigating is actively looking for something unexplained. The best ghost hunter, however, might be an inactive one. Spending all your time running from room to room or waving equipment around focuses you too much on tasks and not enough on the environment. Set up equipment, scan, and then be still. Think of yourself less as a hunter trying to shoot an animal and more as a photographer trying to get a picture of it. You would wait for it to appear and then try to capture it with something other than your hands. Keep the same philosophy during an investigation. I like to bring along some gum or candy I can put in my mouth to pass the time.

Getting Active

THINK OF IT KIND OF LIKE playing good cop and bad cop. There are ghosts out there that might be willing to pop their heads up and say hello, but chances are you'll spend many nights looking at Nightvision shots you have taken without seeing a dark shadow. You might have to get your hands a bit dirty and try to get something to come to you. There is no real bait, but there are ways to wake up the dead and get them to make contact.

For better results, become comfortable in your paranormal shoes and try to stir up some activity. There are good and bad ways to conduct an active investigation, but those words might be relative. If your goal is to gather evidence, you might be more willing to go over the line. Remember that causing waves may mean waking a tiger.

Figure 6.2
NAGS being active during an investigation.
Picture courtesy of the Native American Ghost Society.

Call Things Out

There is, of course, a kinder, gentler way to engage the spirits. Once equipment is set up, you might want to call out whatever is there. Introduce yourself and say why you are there. It might feel funny talking to the air, but remember, part of the reason you are there is because you believe an invisible presence is with you in the room. How would you like someone to start poking and prodding you without introducing themselves first? Invite the spirit to make itself known, and as you use each piece of equipment, tell it what the equipment does and how they can affect it. Karen Mossey, an EVP specialist and a woman whose recordings have appeared in movies and television shows, often speaks of the knowledge we think ghosts have. "When we're out there, we expect them to talk to us. They may never have seen a tape recorder or know they can communicate with us. Tell them how they can." Ask them to get involved in your experiments or activities.

Let the ghosts know you mean them no harm and ask them if they are in need of anything. Many hauntings are the result of a tension between the living and the dead. For example, renovating a building or disturbing a resting place may be the root of a haunting. The ghosts might be able to talk to you about how to resolve the tension. Imagine yourself upset with someone asking if you can see the light. You just want to complain and let someone know how you feel. Give them a place to do this, and they might just take you up on it.

Some investigators, especially demonologists, may think there is a danger in this, and to some degree, they're right. There is always a chance of something negative answering your call or gaining some power from being acknowledged. Be careful not to invite anything into the location as you interact with whatever might be there. Frame your questions and comments to whatever might be there, and if things seem to get worse after you're gone or you think there might be something darker there, refer the case to someone who might be more qualified to handle it, like a more experienced investigator or a demonologist.

Relive the Moment

Many hauntings are a part of a family's everyday life or are connected to known events that happened long ago. There was something about that moment in time that made a ghost sit up and try to be counted. It may be what the living did gave the spirit the energy it needed or caused an emotional response from an intelligence in the house. Battlefield reenactors, like the ones at Gettysburg, find their activities cause a rise in paranormal experiences.

Try and relive these moments. They are your best road map to what the entity might respond to. If the haunting involves the television always being shut off, turn the television on and ask the ghost to turn it off. If people see a ball roll across the floor, put the same ball in the same spot. A clock in the Lizzie Borden Bed and Breakfast, a notoriously haunted location, has a habit of slowing down for one group who investigates there. They make a habit of not winding it and noticing how it moves when they ask for something to happen.

Figure 6.3
Investigator Matt Moniz reenacting a moment in the Lizzie Borden Bed and Breakfast.

There was an old television show called *Fear* on MTV. It was one of the first paranormal reality shows, and it worked on the premise of putting really scared people in scary places and forcing them to do creepy things designed to make them scream. Don't dramatize the haunting as you go through. There is a certain level of respect that should be there. If you are investigating an old jail, don't sit in the electric chair; don't strap yourself to an old gurney in an abandoned hospital. It is in bad taste, and might do little more than make your adrenaline rise.

Conversely, bring props that might help you draw something out. If a childless couple has been hearing little kids giggle, bring some toys with you. I keep a xylophone in my truck just in case I need it on an investigation. Child ghosts may be anxious to play with something, or they may not know they are dead and be drawn to it. Tools are always good, in part because they have universal appeal, and partly because they are metal.

Figure 6.4
This bell was the focus of paranormal activity. During an investigation we rang the bell and invited whatever was in the house to use it to contact us.

Don't ever bring food or drink for a ghost with you. This opinion might not be popular with some investigators, but I believe it draws unwanted things to the scene. There are things out there that are very hungry, be they animal or not.

Don't Get Angry, Unless You Want To

Then, of course, there are the not-so-polite ways to call ghosts out. There is a new method of gathering information that has been steamrolling into ghost hunters' repertoire recently. Many people have their own approach, and the evidence they get is reflected by how they handle themselves. It is now very popular to antagonize a spirit in an effort to get something to manifest. Yelling makes the ghosts come out. This may be true, and I know many ghost hunters who employ this when looking into a location. If you know some history of the place, or even know who the ghost may be, yelling at them or insulting them may be enough to get them to come forward.

I don't do this myself. If you start a relationship on the wrong foot, you set the mood for all of your interactions. Is this how you would like someone to introduce himself to you? You also have to consider the type of spirit who would respond. Ghosts are the leftover bits of people, and being angry during an investigation may draw angry people to you. It also might invite something from the demonic realm. You might start a conversation with the wrong person.

Common and Uncommon Sense

THE E-MAILS I RECEIVE every day fall into four categories. Some ask if I know about a ghost story from their area and what is the best way to get there. Others want to share stories about spirits they've seen or legends they have heard about from their towns. Some people take the time to e-mail to tell me I'm crazy, but the fourth type is the one that always takes me aback. People want to know how to investigate the paranormal, and some of the specific things they ask about seem like things everyone should know. Things are not that simple and some things that feel like common sense are not all that common.

Get Some Sleep and Put the Drink Down

It might go without saying, but I'm going to say it. Never conduct an investigation under the influence of illegal drugs or heavy prescription drugs. Never drink alcohol before an investigation and try to get a good night's sleep the night before. A drunk investigator is unprofessional when you are in somebody's house, and it's a liability in the woods, a cemetery, or an abandoned building. The same is true for someone too high to know what is happening. Investigating is about observing, and being under the influence or half asleep makes you miss activity that is going on. If you are going to go in late at night, take a nap in the afternoon. Leave the beer until the next day when you're sitting around talking about what happened.

There is another more imperative reason to have your wits about you. If something intense happens, you want to be able to react. You also do not want to leave yourself open to anything that might be trying to attack or feed on you. Many paranormal elements feed off of human energy, even mundane human ghosts, and your best defense is a strong mind. You are already applying energy to the situation, something akin to putting the flame to gunpowder, so do not allow anything in. These kinds of feeders look for the weakest link and then seek an opening. You don't want to create a neon sign for them to follow.

Mark As You Go

Load all of your recording equipment before you get to the scene, including audio and video tapes and camera film. They have a habit of being dumped and replaced quickly when the event is on, so start with fresh recording equipment so you can find it and organize it after the investigation. Label each with the date and location and try to label as you go when you can. If not, mark each tape or roll of film as you pack up or when you get home. There is nothing worse than having to sort through 20 tapes a week after you recorded on them, trying to find what you are looking for. If using the timestamp function of your video recorder or camera works for you, do it.

You should also try and state what is going on, where you are, and the time as often as you can. State as many factors (time, temperature, odd sounds, etc.) as often as possible. In the excitement and rush of everything, something can get missed or forgotten if it is not noted in the moment. You also might not know what is important until after you leave.

Verbalize anything natural when it happens. You coughing or your camera beeping might be translated later as an EVP if it isn't explained. Before you click a camera, say something like, "Flash," so other investigators can explain away something they get on their camera. Even a click on a recording should be mentioned. While evaluating the evidence you will be asked to pay attention to every detail, and these things get in the way.

Going Dark

Why do ghosts only come out at night? The first answer is that they don't. There are many reported hauntings during the day, even in places where there are crowds of people. There is, however, something to be said for working in the dark. People say the sun spreads so much energy it overpowers other sources of energy and so night is a better time to combat that overflow. According to Jeff Belanger, " If you look at a graphic depicting the earth's electromagnetic field, you'll see that on the sunny side of the planet, the field is concentrated to help ward off the sun's deadly radiation. On the dark side, the field is not nearly as concentrated because it doesn't have to be."

The same basic theory concerns lights in a house. Much of the paranormal toolbox works better in the dark, perhaps because the equipment uses waves on the spectrum, like ultraviolet, that are affected by light, or possibly because they measure energy that lights interfere with. This can be combated by taking baseline readings with the lights on for most of the equipment.

They say a person who has lost his sight has his other senses strengthened to compensate. There might be something to this while looking for ghosts. Without lights, your other senses, including your natural night vision, are called upon to help out. Going dark may focus you and help you to become one with your environment. It also helps to reduce shadows or tricks of light that may be mistaken for spirits.

Most of the "going dark" rule has to do with the mood of investigators. There is something romantic about turning the lights off and walking around with your paraphernalia in the dark. Most television shows work this way, and it adds to the drama for the audience. Don't be tempted to think all investigations have to be done under these conditions. Some of the best proof of a haunting I have gotten has come from a ghost's manipulation of lights.

When You're There, The Mics Are Live

A friend was setting up his equipment in a haunted location when his eyes saw something race across the screen he was setting up. He was waiting for the perfect angle before he turned the tape on and missed getting whatever it was. He now starts recording as soon as he arrives and sets up with audio and video tape rolling.

Ghosts do not wait until you say, "Cheese," to make their presence known. They manifest at their convenience, so stay sharp from the moment you arrive. There is something to be said for their interest in you as you arrive and unload, and ghosts have been known to flee one part of the house for another. This might be recorded if you are live with your equipment as soon as you arrive.

Figure 6.5
Taking a photo of investigator Tom D'Agostino while he sets up in an attempt to get evidence.

Clothes Make the Hunter

I already discussed looking professional when conducting an interview and during initial investigations, but there is something to be said for useful attire. One of the hardest things for me to get used to when I started, and many people who I have worked with will tell you I still struggle with, is organizing myself. You want to be comfortable and functional when you investigate. Think of what the environment and the challenges will be before you get there, and if possible what you will be doing, whether you'll be working alone or as part of a team. Dress to get the job done.

I used to sell sausages outside Fenway Park in Boston. Good work if you didn't mind the street brawls and the drunk customers. One thing I learned was to be organized with the money, especially when it got busy. I still remember it. Singles in the pouch, fives on the outside. Tens in the left back pocket and twenties in the back right. Never accept a fifty.

Use the same kind of method when you suit up. Wear cargo pants for added pockets and come up with a system for where things are kept.

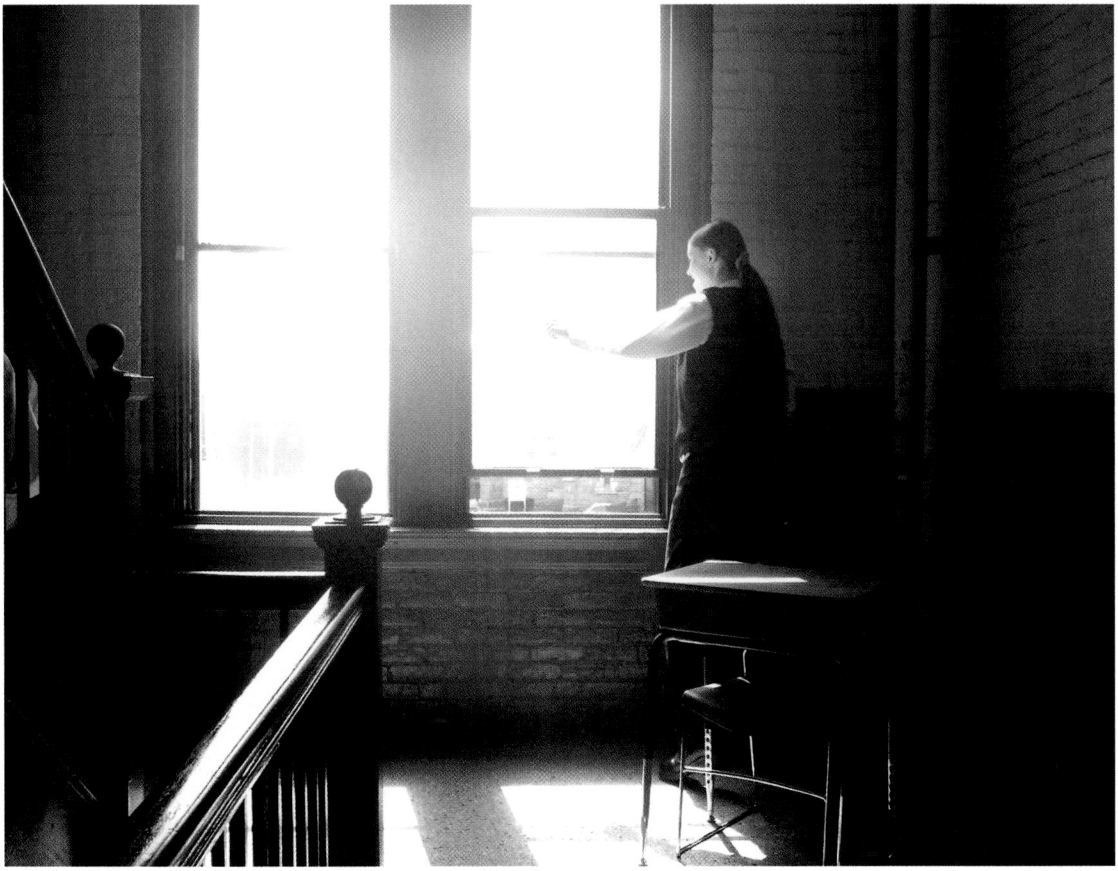

Figure 6.6
A Catholic school uniform does not make for great ghost hunting gear.

Then stick to it and modify it as you develop what kind of investigator you are. It helps you not lose anything or miss an opportunity to record something. Now I know: big flashlight left side, small on the right. Thermometer hooked on the left and EMF in the back right. Camera in the pouch or shirt pocket.

Not All That Glitters Is Gold

You find the missing link, the one perfect instant where the spirit world opens up and touches you on the shoulder. This is what the investigation is about, and capturing it will mean proving the existence of ghosts and make all those hours in cemeteries worthwhile. The figure gets closer as you raise your camera. You snap a picture and get a perfect shot of Fido, the family dog.

Adrenaline and hope can be a dangerous mix when you are in the field. How do you remain even-keeled and be observant at the same time? There is no easy answer, but it is something you have to develop. The majority of the time you spend on an investigation will produce nothing and seem like a waste of time. This is never true. Don't let every creak from the floorboards mean a phantom is coming toward you. Be careful not to over analyze the moment, but rather take it all in stride. There will be a time later, when it is quiet and you are not face to face with the situation, when you can think about all you saw and recorded. It's better to do it then.

Don't be quick to jump when you experience something. Nine times out of ten, it is something natural or explainable. Always be critical, even when you don't want to be.

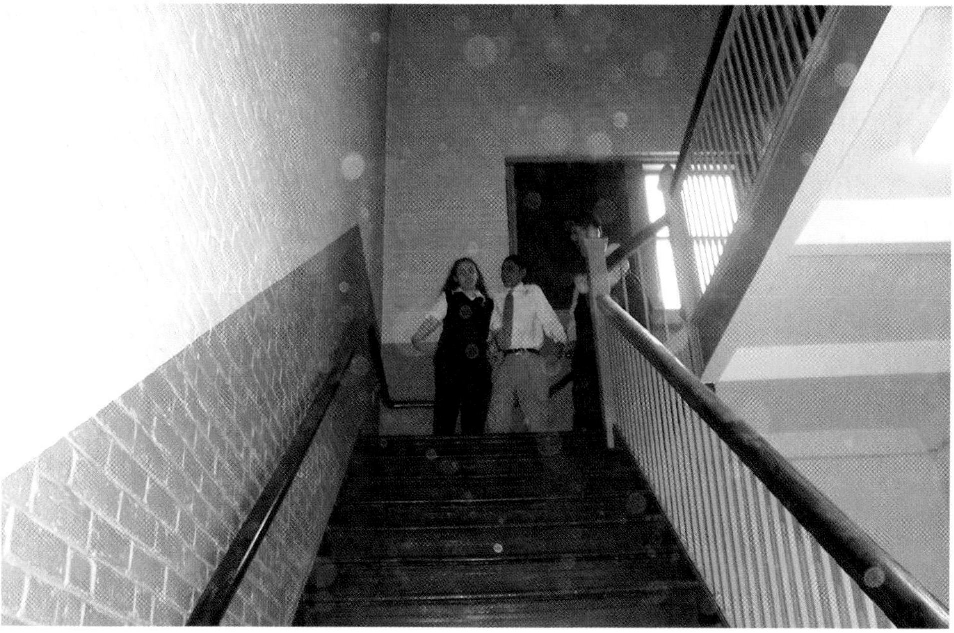

Figure 6.7
False evidence gathered during an investigation in a school. These ghosts are actually dust.

Psi Versus Science

THE NUMBER OF INVESTIGATORS who refer to themselves as parapsychologists has increased in the past few years, which is astounding given many of them do not allow psychics to accompany them into the field. It is a basic misunderstanding of the term, and although we covered the science in Chapter 3, it's worth looking at one of the terms they have adopted and how people in the field use it.

Psi, in its simplest form, is the power of the mind to see things without using eyes or manipulating the world around it. Think of it like the Force from *Star Wars*. That really covers everything from telekinetic ability, or moving things using your mind, and bending spoons, to predicting random numbers and sensing the dead. To the ghost hunter, predicting pictures on cards may not be useful, but the ability to talk to the dead or feel a ghost is appealing. If you are trying to get solid evidence that might prove to others that ghosts exist, this might not be enough, so many who consider themselves based 100% scientific avoid mediums or psychics like the plague.

Science and Psi. They are not exclusive, but people sometimes find they can only investigate on one end of the spectrum. Science and mystic ability are not always friends, and your approach has much to do with why you are investigating. Can you be a slave to two masters? When it comes down to it, you have to be comfortable with who you are as a person. Either way, you need to know both sides to make an informed decision.

Trust Your Stomach

There is a confusing place between science and Psi that makes many investigators uneasy. Think of it as low level ESP, or sensing from the pit of your stomach. Some religions consider the solar plexus as a highly psychic sensitive area, a gateway to feeling things you can't see. Think of how you cross your arms to protect yourself in a highly emotional moment. Drop the religion part of it if you want, but don't dismiss the power it might have. We have all felt uneasy when something bad is about to happen, or we've experienced that sinking feeling in the pit in our stomachs when we know we've just done something wrong. You can explain it away as the acid in your belly, but leave yourself open to the possibility that something might be working there.

Enter the chicken and the egg. Does the feeling in your solar plexus result from hormones and adrenaline based on the intensity of the situation? It's difficult to say, but think of situations where there is no heightened level of chemicals in your body. Often the feeling comes out of nowhere, and is pushed out unless it gets too strong to ignore. We would have to believe our body is more sensitive to our environment than we thought before, and I'm comfortable with that. Perhaps the only thing that can be said about it is that you should embrace the feeling, but understand it might be coming from you and not a ghostly invader.

Often during an investigation you'll feel something you can't explain. You may just sense something or feel uneasy. Don't let those moments go by without saying something or documenting it somehow. It may spit in the face of the science side of ghost hunting, but you can't leave yourself open to the idea that we exist after we die and then deny an experience that may support that idea. Too many investigators complain how the world doesn't accept what they do and then scoff at the idea of psychic abilities. These windows briefly open when you're in the field, and it's a shame to let them go. Later you can apply logic to them, but when they happen, say what you feel and try to go where the impulse takes you.

Psychics: Third Eye or Third Wheel

One of the most controversial facets of investigating ghosts is the use of psychics or mediums in your work or whether your equipment should tell the whole story. It is an important decision and helps mold what you believe about the other side. Purely science-based investigators shun the use of psychics and believe they add an element of showmanship to an investigation and provide information too easily dismissed and faked. People still have the old gypsy in a tent picture of a medium, one hand on their head and the other in your wallet. It's true that many are frauds. Their use might also confine you to a particular set of ideas about what ghosts are.

Don't judge all psychics by the worst of them. Used correctly, they may offer a view of a case that isn't apparent to science. They might also offer the best way to communicate and resolve a haunting. I had a case where we were able to confirm with evidence that something was there. We tried different things to talk and communicate with it and ask it to move on or stop intimidating the family, but nothing could break through. We brought a medium in and he went into the house alone. He emerged a few minutes later and nothing has happened in the house since. He never told us what happened in the house, and when it came down to it the family didn't care. That becomes one of the frustrating aspects of working with people with psychic abilities. Some just don't share their secrets.

You should encourage the development of your own abilities. Even if there is no such thing as psi, or intelligent energy, many of the training methods of the psychic enhance your other five senses and make you more aware of your environment.

Figure 6.8
A setup used by psychic Jackie Barrett during a ceremony in the haunted Lizzie Borden Bed and Breakfast.

Home Is Where the Haunt Is

THE HARDEST AND MOST INVOLVED paranormal investigation is the one that takes place in a private home. While most ghost hunters start with the bone yards and famous haunts in their area, the ideal condition for an investigation is a house. It is a live area with solid stories attached to it. You are forced to deal with the living, but they are open to you because they approached you and allowed you to come in. That means you don't have to worry about getting permission from the police or getting in the way of something else going on.

Understand What Is Happening

For the family to agree to seek out an investigator, they must be in a pretty desperate state. They may be into ghosts and want to get involved, but most have a hands-off approach and initiate things because they are scared or intimidated by what might be in their home. Understand this and proceed with delicacy.

Figure 6.9
A haunted house.
Picture courtesy of Arlene Nicholson.

Figure 6.10
Never avoid the basement.

Then it is time to get your hands dirty with what is wrong with the house. Learn where the activity is centralized and what has happened in each spot. I try to set up my equipment in two places at once, usually one stationary and one with me as I go from room to room. If the house has been known to have footsteps down the hall on the second floor, don't spend an hour in the basement because you think it looks haunted.

The Tour

You should always begin the investigation with a tour of the house, even if you have been there before. You need to know where things are and what has happened in each location. If an interview was conducted in another location or in a room of the house where no activity has taken place, this will be your first chance to see the setting for the experiences. Walk around, ask as many questions as possible, snap pictures, and tape the entire tour. You'll need it for a baseline later and to catch any evidence, especially spirits fleeing or showing curiosity.

Here are some other things to look for:

- **Electrical Outlets: This is the power source for the equipment and also where the juice is flowing in the house.**
- **How air moves in the house: This can help explain cold spots. Keep in mind, sound moves the same way as air does in a house. It absorbs and pours out in the same place, so testing it by calling to each other will give you double the information.**
- **Where large electrical items in the house that produce EMF readings are located: Note where they are and what is behind them. A high reading actually might be coming from a computer in the next room.**
- **Where pipes are located: Pipes are great for banging and rapping.**
- **Whether there are any pets and signs of how they travel through the house.**
- **Presence of an attic and whether or not it is isolated from the rest of the house. These are places cold air enters the house or little critters might be staying.**
- **Location of windows and mirrors and how the normal light of the house hits them: This helps explain some of the "corner of my eye" sightings people have.**
- **Religious artifacts: Try to determine whether the places they are located are more active or less.**

Figure 6.11
Stairs are often an area of high activity.

Setting Up

Once you have established the area of the house with the most activity, set up stationary equipment there. I usually like to have a video camera placed in the room or hallway that has been identified as a problem spot. I use my webcam, attached to a computer, and let it run while I set everything else up. Don't use autofocus on the camera. Try to get the widest possible shot of the area. I like to have a mirror or window in the shot, but not straight on. There are many who use the mirror as a way to talk to spirits and believe the surface is a perfect conductor for paranormal waves. I am not sure about the science, but ghosts are often caught only as reflections, which may be why they appear in pictures. In the primary room, you should also leave a recording device. It may seem like duplicating your efforts, but whenever possible, try to catch activity on two different devices. If you have motion detectors, place them at the door of the room. You may get something trying to avoid the cameras or trying to get back to a place of comfort.

Figure 6.12
A team setting up for the investigation.
Picture courtesy of Arlene Nicholson.

A second camera should be placed in the second most active spot in the house. The reasoning is the same as the first. You may not have enough equipment to place audio recording devices everywhere, but if possible, you should place one here as well. These rooms will be left alone when you conduct the rest of the investigation, and the rest of the equipment will go with you, so the basic stationary setup is finished.

If you have more cameras and motion detectors, place them spreading out from the primary spot. Focus on the rooms where people have reported things, but also on hallways and high traffic areas for the living, such as stairs. Many ghosts travel the way they would have when they were alive, so these spaces become highways to them. Always leave some equipment for other floors and set it up in a similar fashion.

Room to Room and Wall to Wall

You're now ready to start. If you are going dark, this is a good time to do it. Start from the primary room, carrying an audio or video recorder and another piece of equipment. Another investigator should have a third piece of equipment and a still camera. Set up a stationary thermometer to get an ambient reading for the room, taking it from room to room as you travel. Introduce yourself and ask the spirit to make itself known. While you talk, start an EMF sweep of the room, going from one end of the room to the other, along the walls and up and down. If you're not eight feet tall, don't worry about getting the high corners or the ceiling, unless of course, there has been some story relating to those areas.

Figure 6.13
Sweeping the location where a camera is recording.
Picture courtesy of Arlene Nicholson.

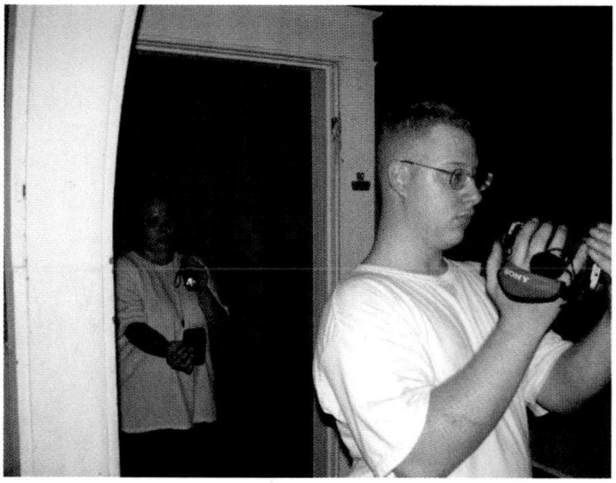

Figure 6.14
Investigators scanning the room.
Picture courtesy of Jamie Chesterson and the Texas Paranormal Society.

Once you have done an initial sweep of the room, try an experiment with the activity that has happened. Relive a moment or try to recreate something the family has told you. Remember, there are many reasons a normal occurrence can be mistaken for a haunting, so this is also a time to evaluate pragmatic explanations. Look for drafts, doors or floorboards that make noise, or traffic from the street. Whatever the haunting involves, try to find anything that could duplicate it. On the other hand, an investigator consumed with debunking may miss something right in front of him that is genuine. Try to be as exhaustive as possible without spending all your time looking for the natural explanation. Alternatively, have another investigator or team focus on that while you look for the supernatural.

Investigate the same way, moving from rooms of activity to ones nearby. The natural reason may be located in another room, such as a faulty wire or noisy pipe, so even if nothing is reported, scan each room fully. Pay special attention to vents that carry sound. I once had a family who reported hearing voices at night. The voices were too low to understand what was being said, but they were there. We discovered that their son, whose bedroom was on another floor, would fall asleep listening to music on his radio. Late at night, the station he listened to switched formats to a talk radio show and the voices of the guests would get louder as they argued. The sound was carried to the parents' room through the heating vents.

When you have hit all the rooms, make your way back to the main room and conduct another quick sweep. Try to collect EVPs, and then be still. You have stirred up the house and should now wait for everything to settle. Now that you have a small handle on what the house is like, or even what sounds it makes, you can dispel them when you hear them. Be still and hope the ghosts come to you.

Owner Knows Best

Investigator and writer Tom D'Agostino talks about moving into a new house. He and his wife were convinced it was haunted because they heard an odd breathing sound late at night.

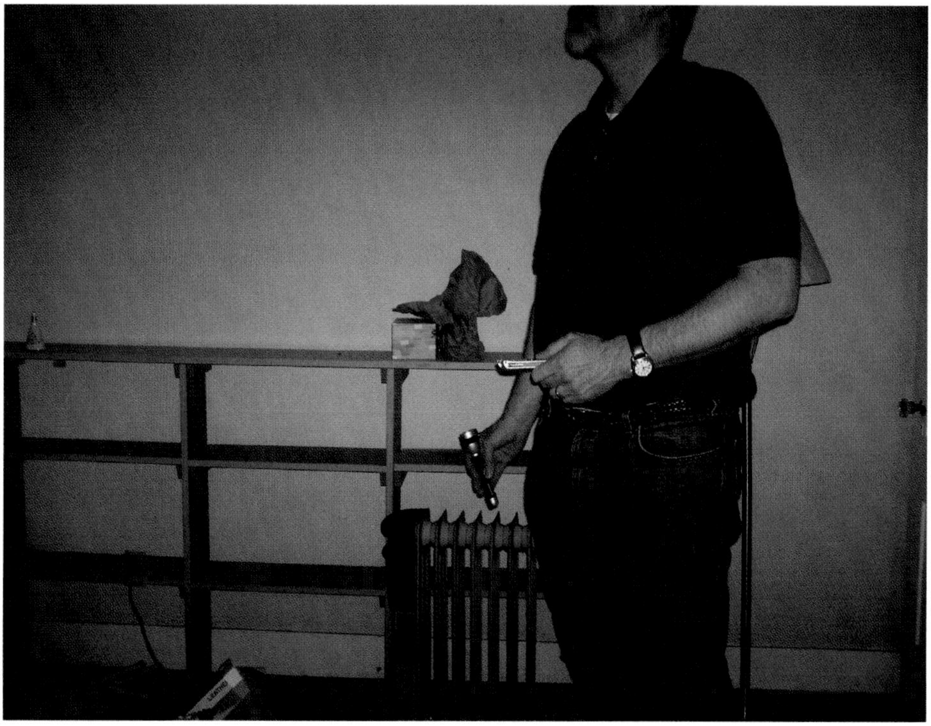

Figure 6.15
Investigator Mike Markowicz doing an EVP session during a private investigation.

Figure 6.16
A dining room the owners said had activity in it.

They both knew it was clearly breathing. One night he got out of bed, determined to capture something and discovered he had a dog with a horrid snoring habit. The dog slept in another room, and they have never heard the snoring before because their old house was so noisy.

Homeowners know their houses better than anyone. They spend years there, learning what step on the stairs creaks and how the window rattles in the bathroom on the second floor. Residents can be an overlooked resource when you are investigating. If you get something you can't explain, tell them about it. They may be able to tell you all about the door that opens because the hinge is loose. You may want to ask them a question after you have swept the house or wait until you have had a chance to look at the evidence.

Some Dos and Don'ts

- **Don't overreact.**
- **Don't be tempted to explain what has happened to you that night to the owners. Until you evaluate the evidence, you may have experienced something you don't understand.**
- **Keep at least one piece of equipment running while you take down the rest. It is best to use a video camera or audio recorder.**
- **Don't let the owners participate in the investigation. They are too close to the situation and may have called you only to get involved. Besides, you'll spend half your time explaining to them what you are doing. Keep questions about the house until after the investigation.**
- **Don't scream or yell. It just scares everyone and ruins your credibility.**
- **Be thorough. Answers often come when you least expect them.**
- **Don't be so interested in looking like a ghost hunter that you forget to *be* a ghost hunter.**
- **Bring all of your equipment, but try to specialize when you start. You'll want your walkie-talkies in the box, but if the house is small leave them in the car or at least don't take them room to room.**
- **Even in the light, bring a flashlight.**
- **Take pictures at an angle and not always straight on. Changing your perspective might change your results. This is not so much to explain away something you might see, although it can do that, but rather to train yourself to stop looking straight at things all the time.**

If you want to make a good marinara sauce, start by frying some garlic and onions in olive oil. Add some canned tomatoes and some spices, and when the pasta is ready, pour some on top. Simple, but so incomplete. The key is the trial and error, finding what spices you like in what amounts and learning the secrets your family or friends use. In my family, a sauce is never set in stone but is rather an evolving experiment that lasts until you die.

The chances of encountering a genuine ghost on any investigation is fairly slim. They have a habit of not wanting to be photographed and keeping quiet when the tape is rolling. Go out enough and something will happen, and during each investigation you refine your own methods. You will learn the best way to get what you are looking for and the best way to evaluate it once you have it. Refer back to this chapter once you have been out there a few times and you might completely disagree with what you have read, and that is okay. You now have the template, and what you do with it is limited only by your imagination.

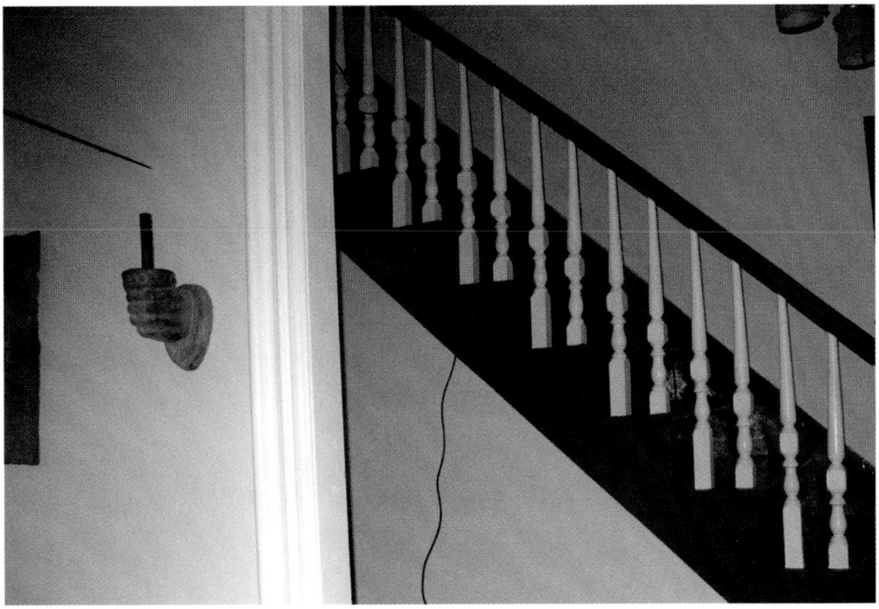

Figure 6.17
A picture taken straight on.

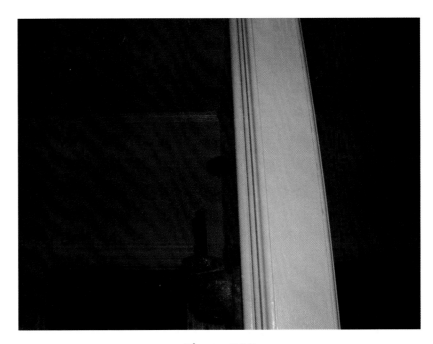

Figure 6.18
The same area taken at a different angle.

The notoriously haunted Charlesgate Hotel.

7

Different Places, Different Approaches

IF GHOST HUNTERS SPENT ALL of their time in private homes, there would be more brownies and cups of coffee served and no need to ever buy a poncho. Private homes are the ideal in many cases, but ghosts don't limit their activities to a warm, safe place. The majority of an investigator's time is spent sifting through dust and getting his shoes wet. There is a romantic side to the job, but some other haunted places are harder to work in and present new challenges. Each site is unique, but there are things that can be said about the kinds of places you'll look into. The rules of a home investigation are a good foundation, but you'll need to learn the regulations of each type of site to get the best evidence you can.

The Place Where the Dead Sleep

PEOPLE ASSUME CEMETERIES have to be haunted, although there are few good reasons for this. If a spirit is trapped energy, like a residual haunting, the manifestation would be at the release point and not where the body was buried. If a soul has unfinished business, it will be in contact with the living, not hanging around with the dead. One of the reasons cemeteries might be active is because the spirit itself is lost so it returns to its body or wakes up from a dead sleep to find itself in one. It might feel compelled to return to where its body is.

There might even be a deeper reason for the haunting. One cemetery I investigated was known to contain a spirit of a father who had buried his daughter before he died. When he passed, his son-in-law dug up his diseased wife and moved her to his own family plot across town. The father now walks the rows looking for his daughter's headstone. There are also reports of people wandering the afterlife behind graveyard gates because their graves have been disturbed (think of the ancient Indian burial ground) or because they were not buried according to their wishes.

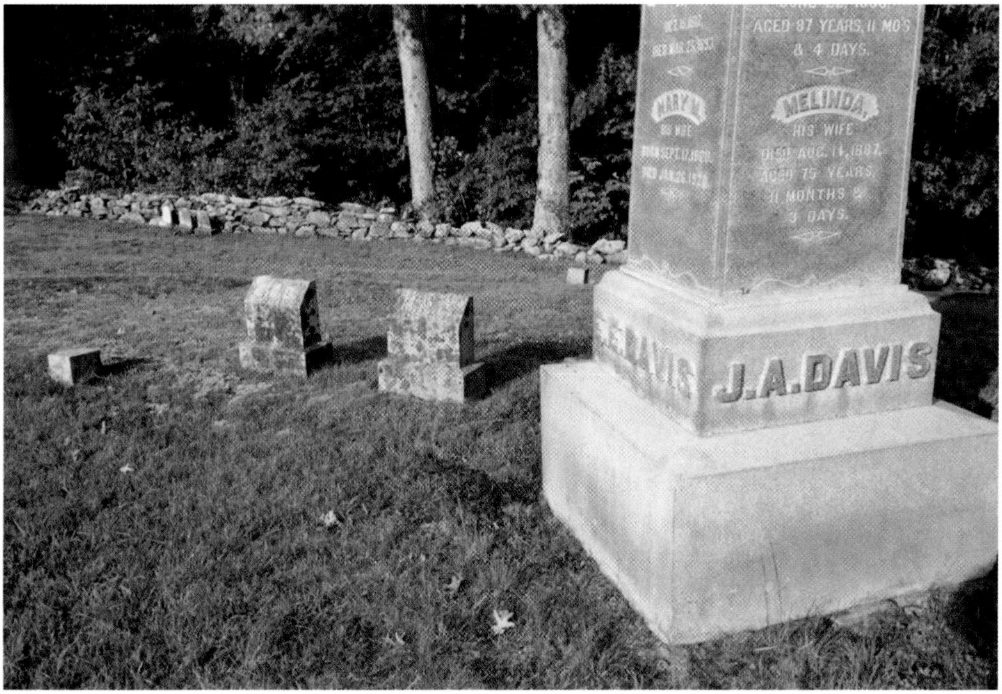

Figure 7.1
A haunted cemetery at a peaceful time.

Many of these reasons ask you to make the leap into believing all ghostly activity is connected to a story. Ghosts stay in or go to cemeteries because investigators go there looking for them. Desperate to connect to something, they find any way to communicate. The investigator, whose heightened senses might be due to fear or some type of psychic connection, is more likely to hear the call. This is an idea that comes up throughout this book, and over time you will have to decide if it sounds like a catchall excuse or valid reasoning.

Difference and Similarities

Graveyards come in all shapes and sizes, but all of them are outside. There may be mausoleums or some kind of indoor structure, but for the most part you are at one with the elements. The first thing you need to understand is that you have to dress for the weather. Sneakers, even in winter, are a good idea, but boots are better. You don't want to be so focused on being cold that you lose valuable time or evidence. Dress appropriately. Make sure you have enough batteries and then buy some more. There is nothing worse than getting there and having your supply tapped in the first half hour.

Figure 7.2
Evidence found in an older cemetery.
Picture courtesy of Bree Pouliot.

Cemeteries are a place of great reverence, and you should show respect while you are there. In a home, you are using the history of the place and people to try to explain the present, but you don't need to look for a reason for a graveyard to be haunted. Dead people are there. Knowing this, focus on the moment and not on trying to figure out the "why" of what you might find until you are gone and looking at the evidence later.

Understand that you will be outside and you will come face to face with nature in all its manifestations, so you should prepare yourself for this. In a house, you have a controlled environment. There may be a car picked up on an EVP, but if you see a shadowy figure, you can be sure you have seen something. In a graveyard, it could be anything, and it most likely is something natural.

You should take the same basic approach you do with a house investigation. If odd things have been reported in a specific area of the cemetery, use that place as your center. Set up some stationary equipment, keeping in mind that you have limited battery power and must make good use of your time. Span out and EMF sweep, taking some audio and video recordings. Your thermometers are basically useless, but you may want to record any extreme changes in the temperature, especially if the fluctuations seem to be concentrated in one area.

Figure 7.3
A haunted cemetery in Massachusetts.

A good way to gather EVP evidence is to place a recorder on a headstone and walk away. Do this in five-minute intervals, marking the times you switch and reciting the information of the headstones nearby. If you get evidence later, you might be able to confirm information based on this.

In and Out

There is also a greater area to cover outside, so a larger group and some way to communicate, such as walkie-talkies, is a good idea. Stay within line of sight with the people you go out with. This allows all of you to know where everyone is, in case something happens, positive or negative. It also prevents your misinterpreting their flash or movements with activity. I prefer to not talk during a cemetery investigation unless necessary. You should try to visit the cemetery during the day to get the layout and find some of the odds and ends that add to the personality of the place. When you go back at night, you may be able to explain away much of what happens. Plan ahead where you are going to go. The land can vary in size, but for the most part don't bite off more than you can chew.

Figure 7.4
Mysterious fog seen in a famously haunted cemetery in New Hampshire.

In a cemetery, staying still becomes very important. Unlike in a house, you may be able to get more evidence by allowing the activity to come to you. Most stories connected to graveyards are urban legends, so rather than trying to recite the person's name three times because you heard that makes them come out, find a spot and try to get a feel for the place. I suggest taking turns, with other members of the team spanning out while you stay in one place and then going out yourself and letting them stay.

Don't overstay your welcome. Unlike a private house, there is an unlimited amount of time you can be in a cemetery. It can drain you though. Chances are, if something is going to manifest, it will do so in the first hour and a half. Try not to spend more time than that in there. It might make you feel funny to do this, but I always thank the spirits when I leave. I make a habit of inviting spirits to make themselves known and saying goodbye whenever I am in a haunted location, but a cemetery is a different beast all together. You know some of the people had difficult lives and perhaps aren't at rest. Thanking them is a sign of respect and a bidding of good luck on their journey.

I Fought the Law

Know the laws of your state and town when it comes to graveyards. Most don't allow people in after dark and some don't care. Some have laws governing this sort of thing and others don't. Always try to get permission, but if there is no gate and you get caught inside, plead ignorance and don't bring up my name.

Figure 7.5
Another odd sight found in a cemetery.
Picture courtesy of Bree Pouliot.

My cousin works for a local police department in Massachusetts, and the saying is that if you are on duty and need to catch up on your sleep, park in the cemetery. This may be true, but even if it isn't, police do make regular trips to cemeteries, especially in this age of increased interest in the paranormal. If you are caught in a cemetery, permission or not, don't run. Fleeing implies guilt. Usually, they are on the lookout for partiers, and you should be aware of them as well. If the area has a reputation, locals find out and try to scare investigators. If you are stopped, explain why you are there. More than once I have been forced to pull out my driver's license and by the end of the conversation had another local haunt to look into and permission to do so from law enforcement.

The Ghost Lights

We conducted an investigation in a graveyard well know for its paranormal activity and thought we were on to something big. As we moved, we saw small flashes of light and began moving toward the source, getting more excited with every step. Then we spotted another one a short distance away and split up to follow both. We arrived at basically the same time to discover the secret to eternal life. If you want to live forever, have your relative set an eternal fire at your grave. These small candles are fed by a gas line, much like the one set to honor President Kennedy at Arlington National Cemetery. Great for remembrance; bad for investigating.

Figure 7.6
A ghost, or light reflecting off of natural fog?
Picture courtesy of Native American Ghost Society.

Cemeteries are like this. At night, walking into one can be like flashing a light into a mirror, and the resulting ghost lights can have you walking in circles. The headstones are made of granite and other rock that has small deposits of other stones with reflective properties. Many are now polished and finished so that even moonlight hits them and bounces back looking like phantoms. Many of the glowing graves people report are just that. The stones themselves reflect light at night and give the surroundings an eerie feel.

The designs for burial grounds have changed over the years, and the shift offers another impediment to investigators. Originally, the dead were buried away from the center of the town, close enough to visit but far enough away so the smell of the dead and the reality you will soon be one of them is only a memory. In time, as the towns got larger, they built closer to established cemeteries. Now graveyards are more prominent in towns, many even being a place where people go because of their beauty. Most are surrounded by trees, at least along the outer edge, and bordered on all sides by roads. This means cars traveling on the road at a distance have headlights that will disappear behind trees and then reappear, much like a ghost.

Depending on how long a person has been dead, there may still be a significant amount of decomposition going on. I know we do not like to think about it, but we are not just ashes to ashes, but ashes to ashes and gas. As our bodies lay six feet under, they release these gases into the air through the soil. This has the ability under the right lighting conditions to create what looks like flashes of light. It is a classic explanation for the government to say a UFO was swamp gas, but in the case of bone yards, it might just have some validity.

Figure 7.7
Another "ghost" seen in a cemetery.
Picture courtesy of the New England Regional Paranormal Society.

Keep all this in mind when you go looking for ghost lights, and then remember that other members of your team are wandering around in the cemetery taking flash pictures. There are other things you can do in there, but take your pictures with a big grain of salt. If you get something convincing, you might have gold, but if you take 20 pictures showing orbs, don't think you have slipped beyond the veil that separates the living from the dead.

Try to recreate the way certain light may play itself out in the graveyard. Next time you are driving down the highway at night, pay closer attention to the cars behind you. Don't get into an accident, but notice how the lights flicker in and out as they move over slight bumps. Some seem to go from high beams to low while others go out for a brief moment before returning. Light does strange things with all of its refracting and reflecting. Usually, no matter how odd they appear, the shadows and flashes you see can be explained and recreated.

Move your flashlights around and move throughout the graveyard to see if you can make the lights appear. Take the same picture and then take it again, especially if you have a digital camera and can erase any you don't want. Go so far as to have an investigator get in his car and drive around the edge of the cemetery to see if headlights could have caused it. It sounds exhaustive, but think of how much more authentic your evidence will be. It still will not explain all of the possible natural causes, but it takes you one step closer.

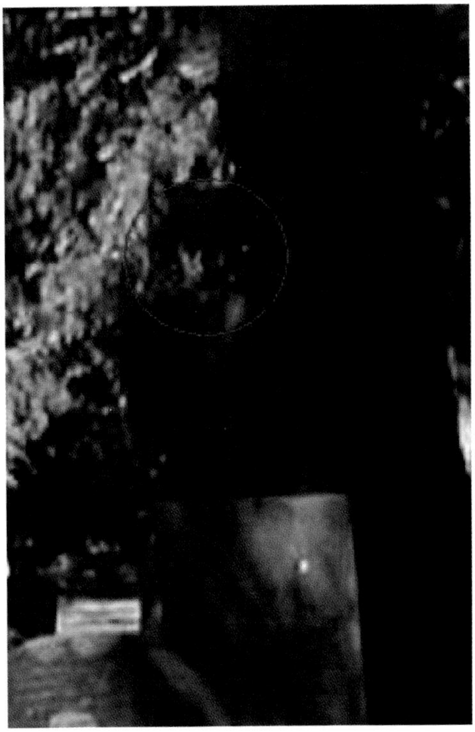

Figure 7.8
An unexplained face seen in a cemetery.
Picture courtesy of Carrie Shimkus and M.A.G.I.C.

Old Versus New

Romance within the cemetery gates. It sounds like a bad trashy novel, but grave rubbings are a very popular hobby and a way for people to connect with history. When picking sites for the best rubs, people usually prefer the older headstones because they are drawn by a romantic appeal. There is just something about those old time graveyards that stir us, as if there is something antique about the souls laid to rest there.

Can the same be said for investigating in one? There has been a long debate over whether older or newer cemeteries are the most active, but it seems to come down to the people buried and the kind of evidence you are trying to get. If you believe a soul can move on if they were once a ghost, a Revolutionary cemetery might be like trying to get water from a dried up well. The juice might have left. If ghosts are nothing more than energy, that energy might have dissipated over time, leaving no old souls to roam. It might be hard to find records or information about the people buried there if you are looking to back up information you get during an EVP session.

However, there are some reasons to pick old graveyards over new ones. The gas I mentioned would have been released long ago, leaving any odd fogs or orbs a little less explainable. They are usually easier to get into and many have no gates and are accessible to the public. The best reason might be the one you can least get your hands around. In an abstract way, the ghosts might be more lonely. Older spirits might be eager and willing to hear from someone, like someone in a nursing home wondering why the kids don't come and visit anymore. You might be able to take advantage of this to get some good evidence.

Old Buildings: Dust or Demons

WHEN YOU ARE MAKING a creepy television show you need some base elements, something to fall back on to scare people just with the look or feel of it. People will always be scared when children are involved in a haunting, for example. The audience loves psychics whose faces distort when the spirit is near. Most of all, people love old abandoned buildings.

Old buildings have inherent activity in them. Whether the building is an asylum or an old hospital, there is always a half fictional history used to draw you in. Different paranormal folklore themes sweep in and out, but there are also the very real cases of neglect or torment or death that happen in these buildings. Many are more famous after they close, but in part because we know a bit of the negative activities that happened there. Here is a case where the stories that develop might have a bit of truth in them.

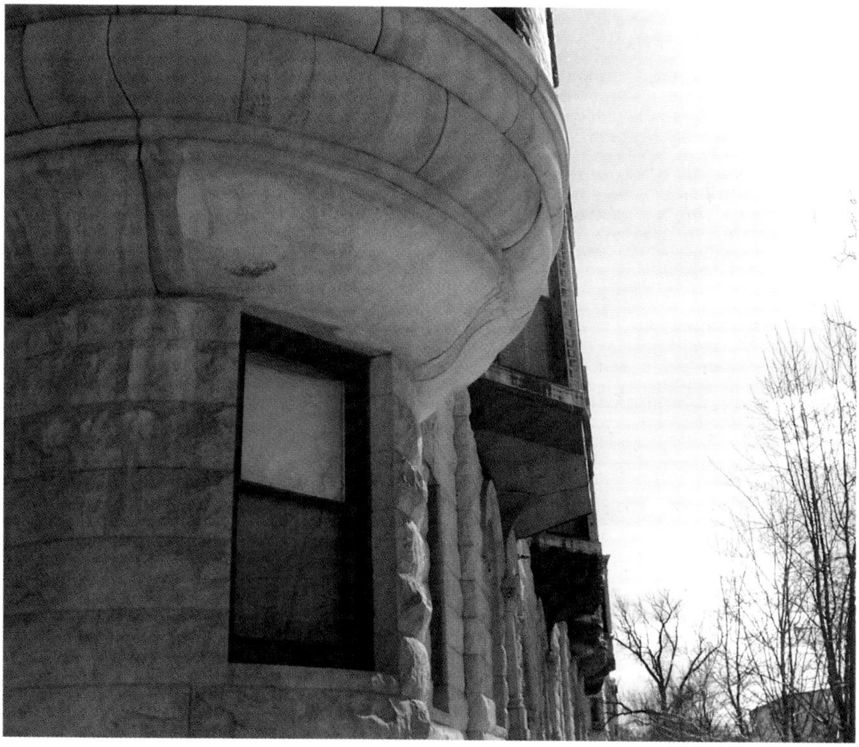

Figure 7.9
Another shot of the Charlesgate Hotel, one of the most haunted buildings in Boston.

Regardless of how nice it may have been in its day, at some point the staff there were overworked, there were too many people trying to get help, and someone there was neglected. This is obviously less true for old schools or buildings, but if they were successful and didn't have times of tragedy, they would most likely still be open today.

Figure 7.10
An old hospital with a rumor of ghosts.
Picture courtesy of Brandon Paulson and the Eidolic Paranormal Research Association.

We are also drawn in by the romantic nature of the buildings themselves. Like cemeteries, these places feel haunted because they look the part. Many that are now closed have been getting on in years, which usually means some interesting architecture and design accents that add to the Gothic feel. That may be mixed with shattered windows and crooked doors that make the building seem lost to the world. The juxtaposition of the two, towering buildings made to be bigger than life with broken stairs and bent metal, are unsettling and appealing at the same time.

They are the perfect place for a residual haunting. In addition to any building materials that may trap energy, you also have the potential release of high amounts of energy during intense episodes. So many of the distractions that may be there in a residential setting, such as busy streets or noisy neighbors, are gone. The tranquility may be your chance to tune into whatever might be left behind.

The Major Suspects

Any of these places, with permission, of course, are great places to look into. Most will have some local history connected to them and you may even find some people alive who either worked or stayed in them. Here are some places to consider:

- **Hospitals**
- **Asylums**
- **Old buildings like warehouses or mills**
- **Schools (both college and primary)**
- **Churches**
- **Jails**

How to Start

In the early part of the 21st century, a new mall opened near Fenway Park in Boston. It was on the grounds of an old mall that had been abandoned years before, leaving an entire city block in a major city empty and desolate. When the new mall was opened to the public with a major ribbon cutting ceremony, it was believed that this was the first time the public had seen the inside in years. Obviously, homeless people had wandered in and out over the years, even going so far as to make it home for a while, but they didn't know if had been a must-see place for some people for years. Urban explorers had been breaking in as part of their adventures and research.

Urban explorers make these kinds of places the object of their hobby. They find abandoned buildings, break into them in the same way they would climb a mountain, and map the insides just as you might a hidden cave. Some are looking for ghosts, but most enjoy the challenge for its own sake. Even if they don't look for the unknown, ghosts and other oddities of the night find them, making believers out them. They know something many of us have only assumed in the marrow of our bones. Ghosts are alive and well inside the abandoned buildings of the world.

Figure 7.11
The view from the top of Waverly Hills Sanatorium.
Picture courtesy of Matt Moniz.

Drawn in by old stories and a great store front, paranormal investigators know the halls of their local structures better than the people who designed them. They look good and provide a testing ground for their skills, much like a police academy field house for ghost hunters. It often provides much the same access as a cemetery, almost like a boneyard with a ceiling. If done the wrong way, you have a wasted night, but touching what might be in these structures can be well worth the trip.

Ask before You Hunt

It all starts with asking permission. Whether it is an old hospital or an empty school, remember that even if no one is there, someone owns it. Getting into these places legally is hard, but the consequences could be drastic if you don't ask for permission. In 2005, two young men were found on the grounds of the famous Danvers State Hospital and arrested for trespassing.

Figure 7.12
A picture from the haunted Metropolitan State Hospital in Massachusetts.
Picture courtesy of Carrie Shimkus and the M.A.G.I.C.

It happened to all go down in the month of October, so it made all the papers and was picked up by the national media. Being in the area, I was asked to comment by all the local media, and eventually I received a call from someone claiming to be from Avalon Bay, the owners of the land who were working on building condominiums there. I was politely asked to discourage people from stepping foot on the grounds and my refusal could prove to be a headache for me..

Even if they hadn't asked me nicely, I would suggest always asking for permission first. You are a representative of all investigators when you are out there, and anything illegal you do ruins it for everyone and makes owners less inclined to allow any of us in.

Figure 7.13
Another picture from Met State.
Picture courtesy of Carrie Shimkus and the M.A.G.I.C.

It also means that your evidence might be taken more seriously, and you do not have to worry about releasing it and subsequently having owners come down on you for legal reasons.

Researching

If you consider yourself strictly an investigator, get over it. You have to be a researcher before you ever set foot in the building. This does not stop with finding out what people have seen there or the history of the place; you need to do some nuts and bolts time in the library or hall of records. Unless you are looking into a one-room schoolhouse (and there are good haunted one-room schoolhouses out there to look into), the place you are going to investigate is much like a maze. The larger it is, the greater chance you have of getting lost or being useless once you are in there. You will need to know the layout of the land and what is connected to what. More recent information might be helpful in finding areas that are more dangerous or closed off. Maps might also help in finding the construction history to know if some areas are additions or changed their use. That kind of shift can confuse ghosts and make them more active.

Some groups prefer to go into a haunting knowing nothing about the location. I can see the benefit of this. It removes the specific lore about a building or importance of a space in that location. It removes a level of the observer tainting the evidence. I don't work that way. I don't like doing anything blind, and there may be a missed chance to catch evidence where someone else has reported something. If you decide to do any investigation cold, research after and try to line it up with evidence you get or experiences you had.

Figure 7.14
The basement of an abandoned building.

More than you would in other investigations, plan out what to do before you arrive. Instead of just using your planning to determine the best places to look into, it also helps you know the building before you get there. A large asylum can be intimidating, and you will be eager to get to every room. Know ahead of time which areas you will be looking into, and understand the activity there may shift when you actually get to the location, but it will help you stay focused.

Beware the Living

Rats almost took down all of Europe with the Plague, and they can find their way into a broken down jail. Animals are always a part of a building hunt no matter how well boarded up the place may be. Raccoons, rodents, and birds are the worst enemy of the investigator. Not only do they make looking into the building hard, they taint the evidence and force people to waste time on a wild goose chase, although it usually is not a goose you'll be chasing. They also make the place dangerous. Animals can be mean or diseased and coming across one may make you fear rabies more than demonic possession.

Figure 7.15
An abandoned wheelchair found in an empty hospital.
Picture courtesy of Carrie Shimkus and the M.A.G.I.C.

Then there are the living humans. Any investigation is made more complicated by the presence of other people, but in an old building, there is another level of difficulty that can be outright dangerous. Squatters and sketchy people come to these buildings to get away or to find shelter. They may be involved in things they do not want to see the light of day, so someone with a video camera is not really welcome. You may be walking into a situation where your life and property are at risk. You can buy a lot of drugs with a pawned camera. They may also be there, depending on the reputation of the place, to scare you. Always be more afraid of the living than the dead.

Going Mobile

Given all the elements involved, a building investigation is a mobile one. Even with permission and a guarantee that you are alone, there are too many chances for outsiders to play with your equipment. There is also so much square footage to cover that the odds of picking up something in a small monitored area will be slim to none. Be ready to investigate as soon as you get there, and carry your extra equipment in something that can be slung over your shoulder. Leave the cases at home. The best equipment to use would be your recording devices, your digital thermometer, and an energy detector.

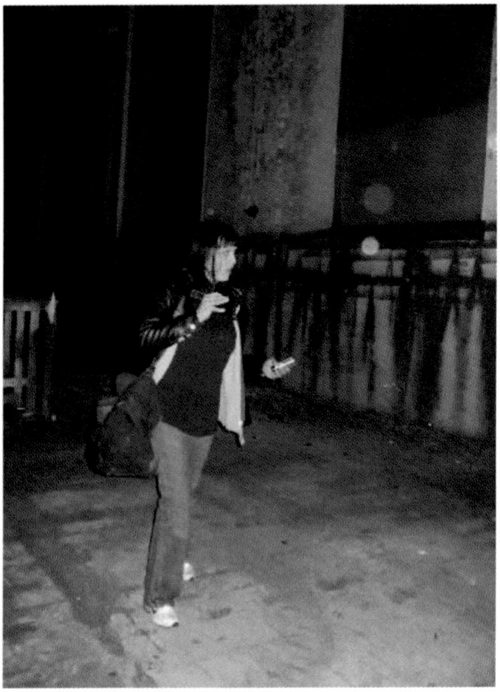

Figure 7.16
A hospital investigation.
Picture courtesy of Carrie Shimkus and the M.A.G.I.C.

Believe what you see with your eyes. Anything could be wrong with the building, from bad piping and heating to animals and creaky boards. You can never know the terrain as well as you can that of a house, so focus on the area you are in. Don't run around to every noise you hear because you will find yourself turned around and tilting at windmills.

Consider each room or hallway a separate investigation. I suggest labeling a map before you start and clearly signifying what room you are in with your tape or video recorder. Sweep, take pictures, try to draw out, and move on. There is a large area to cover, so being still will force you to miss activity that might be happening in another wing. Take your time, but investigate and move to the next location.

Figure 7.17
Waverly Hills.
Picture courtesy of Matt Moniz.

Most of all, stay together. You may feel this is the perfect chance for you to try out those new walkie-talkies you bought, but there is strength in numbers and these types of buildings wreak havoc on communication devices.

Hotspots

Depending on what kind of building you are in, the hot spots will vary. Any place where people have reported paranormal activity is a start, but there are other places with potential. Any place with a negative history is a good place to look as well. At Richardson High School, a student shot himself during school hours. The story was made famous by the band Pearl Jam in their song "Jeremy." Since the suicide, that part of the high school has reported strange banging and even gunshots.

Figure 7.19
A haunted school.

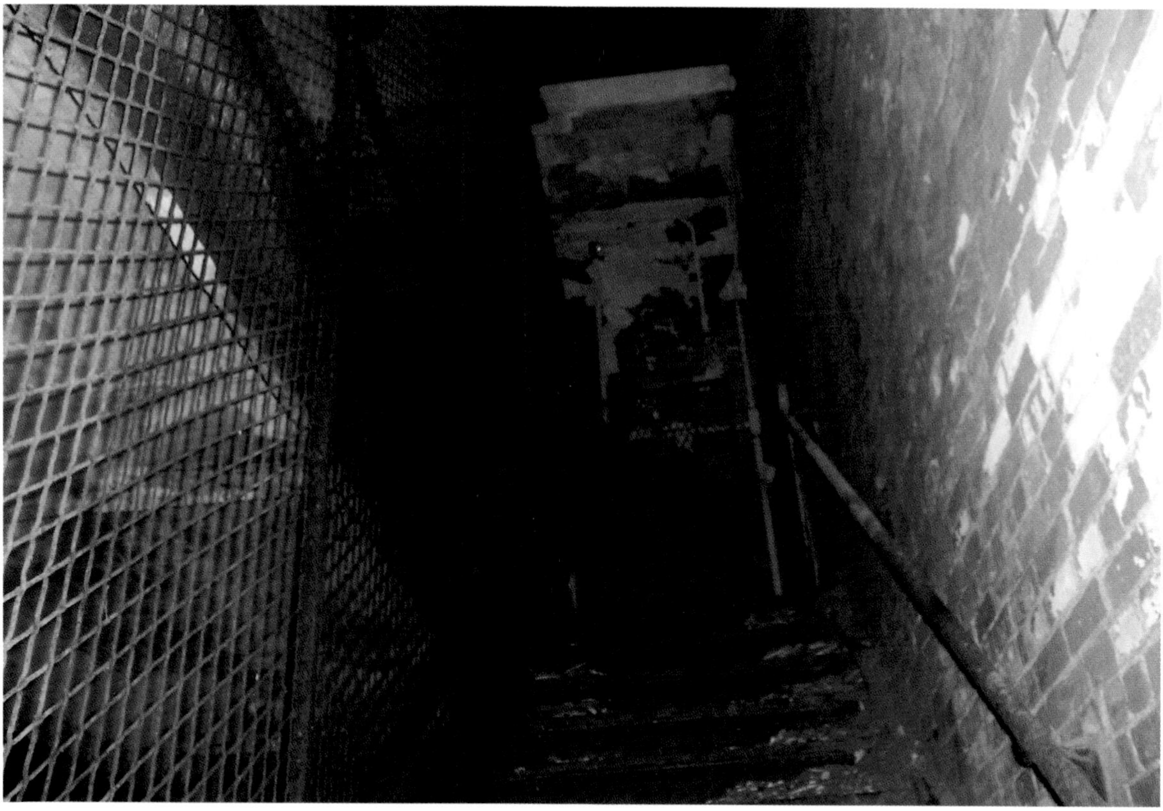

Figure 7.18
The haunted basement of an asylum.
Picture courtesy of Brian Paulson and the Eidolic Paranormal Research Association.

Think of what a normal day in the building was like. Any place where people were, people can still be. Look for high traffic areas like lobbies and bathrooms. Avoid smaller places like closets and out of the way rooms unless there are stories attached to them. Try finding the location in old newspaper accounts, especially anything associated with trauma. This can then be used during the investigation. For example, you may want to try to talk directly to someone who died there during an EVP session.

Figure 7.20
Another haunted school where desks have fallen over with no one around.

Think of places that might have been the site of high emotional activity or mental anguish. The morgue of a hospital may be scary, but the emergency room has a better chance of being haunted. The basement of a school is dark and dank, but there are more haunted theaters in schools than murderers in the cellar. Always visit the main office, and remember in these kinds of places, the hallways are as suspect as the rooms. Anyone who has seen the halls of the school when the bell rings or the passageways of an asylum before lights out knows they are not just ways to get from point A to B.

Looking Down Below

There is an old Catholic school tradition. If there is an underground passageway from the school or seminary to a church there will always be stories of torrid affairs between priests and nuns and usually some reference to a midnight abortion. Even outside this environment, such as an asylum, these subterranean hallways always have a story attached to them. They are usually built to get people quickly from one building to another in bad weather, although many are also said to be part of the Underground Railroad or Prohibition smuggling. Be careful of these areas. They are the stuff legends are made from but also very dangerous to investigate. Anything might be hiding in them, so use your best judgment.

Figure 7.21
An old tunnel connecting a haunted school to a nearby church.

Dust and Asbestos

Despite their history and aura, old buildings may be the hardest type of investigation to get evidence from. While an outside hunt is the most challenging, indoors you have too many things that can taint what you get. Take your results with more than just a grain of salt. These places are havens for dust, asbestos, and mold. When using a digital camera, these kinds of irritants can do more than jump start your allergies. On film, they look just like spirits. Many of these places closed due to poor living conditions or because parts of them were falling apart. These are not ghosts, but they will pretend to be.

It is also a matter of credibility. Someone will always say a picture from inside an asylum is merely dust, even if there is a ghost in the middle of the shot holding a sign. Knowing this going in, use traditional film and make notes on the video camera of conditions in the room. Never get too excited about what you get there until a second person looks at it.

Figure 7.22
The belly of an asylum.
Picture courtesy of Carrie Shimkus and the M.A.G.I.C.

Look at what the building is made from. Certain materials and the design of a place can cause random radio frequencies to find their way into your audio equipment and are better conductors of energy that can give you false readings on your other equipment. Some older buildings were thought to be built to intentionally harness and draw in paranormal power for some dark purpose. This is a great plot for a movie and a common urban legend, but there is still some truth to building materials attracting energy in different ways.

Drawing Things In

I hate to finish each section I write with an obligatory warning of something evil. The truth is, there are more positive paranormal experiences than negative ones, but the bad ones are frequent enough that I have to stress them. Nowhere is this more the case than in an abandoned building. It may have been a hospital or an asylum with enough horror during its day to wallpaper the place. There are things out there that are drawn to these kinds of places, so just remember to always protect yourself and be aware that danger comes in all forms.

Wide Open Spaces: Looking for Ghosts in the Wilderness

IN MY FIRST BOOK, I COVERED the hauntings of a state forest, and when it was released, I was contacted by people who wanted to go out and find the ghosts. They asked if I had investigated it myself and where to get the best results. I had been out to the forest on numerous occasions to get a feel for it and to fish for people who had seen the supernatural there, but I had never conducted an investigation there. I knew the best places to go, and of the 15 square miles of trees, I knew where people had seen the unknown like the back of my hand. However, I never took a piece of equipment out in the three years I spent researching it, unless you include a camera and a sound recorder.

Haunted outside locations can get you the evidence you are looking for, but the odds of getting anything you can use there are very slim. Know it going in and realize that when you are out in the field, you are looking for a needle in a haystack, and the haystack can be miles long and filled with many things that look like needles. Done the right way, there is a chance of something positive, but those finds are rare.

Figure 7.23
A haunted area on the campus of a college.

Figure 7.24
The haunted Horn Pond.

Some of the best places to look for ghosts outside are:

- **Battlefields**
- **Haunted woods**
- **Cliffs and rock formations**
- **Bodies of water**
- **Mountains or hiking trails**
- **Old villages**
- **Roads, especially ones off the beaten path**
- **Haunted tours**

Of these choices, your best bet would be to look into a good battlefield or old village.

Following the Tale

Places where people died are a great start for any investigation. You know there is a reason for the dead to return or be trapped, and there is instant backstory to reinforce any findings you get. The trouble is when the only driving force to a haunting is the stories you have heard, especially when they fall into the realm of urban legend, which we'll cover in Chapter 11. Outside investigations are, by their very nature, prone to this. Unlike a home where people make a life for themselves and have some hint at what a normal day should be like, people do not live on a haunted pond. When something odd happens, they have nothing to compare it to. Many of these stories are tales of days gone by repeated through the years, so the original witnesses are hard to track down.

Figure 7.25
A known spot for cult and ghostly activity.

The Good, the Bad, and the Alive

I'm going to get the bad out of the way first. Outside hauntings can be some of the most productive and exciting places to look into, and many reach the status of famous or infamous. There are many obstacles to overcome, or at least things to make your evidence irrelevant, so let's tackle them.

Animals

Any time you are outside, the chances of running into an animal increases. The further you are off the path, the more likely you are to cross paths with small critters. Some people like this, especially if they are nature lovers, but wild animals make that rustle of leaves harder to take seriously. Chances are you won't run into an animal that will harm you, but know what kinds of animals have been seen where you are going. This is not as important on a haunted tour, but a hike into the woods in the right season is a different story. There have been reports of haunted animals, such as those we discussed in Chapter 2, but I am referring to real animals that might be mistaken for ghost movement.

There was recently a new television show that showed an investigator going deep into the most remote places in the world looking for legendary beasts. At two in the morning, he always found something to run after because he heard a noise or saw something stir a ways away from him. It sounds silly when you say it, but I was drawn in for several episodes before I realized I could replay the same scene in my backyard on the right night.

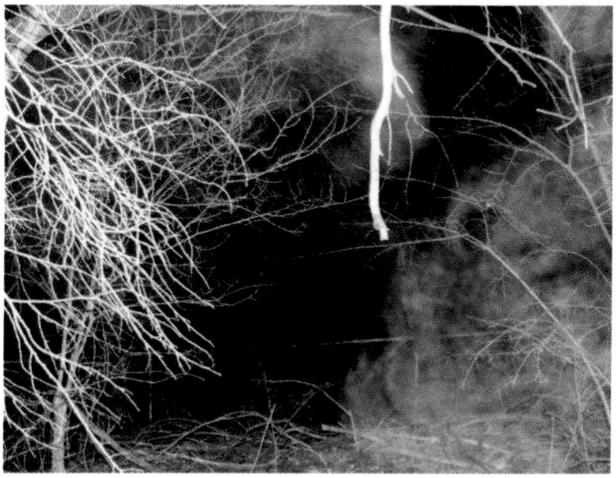

Figure 7.26
An unexplained mist.
Picture courtesy of the Native American Ghost Society.

The Weather

I had been looking into exploring an old abandoned village for years. I had heard all the great stories about it and was looking forward to getting some images to go with the tales. I made a plan to meet with some of the top investigators from the area, but I had to cancel for one reason or another. When they called me the next day, they told me the rain had started as soon as they were away from the car and well on the path. It continued until they got back into the car. They had a few laughs, but the evidence they had hoped would prove the existence of ghosts was nowhere to be found.

The weather is a main factor when you're planning an outside investigation. It goes without saying that you should probably not go out in a blizzard, but there are more subtle reasons why Mother Nature does not like the ghost hunter.

Figure 7.27
Inside Dungeon Rock with investigators Ron Kolek and Maureen Wood from the New England Ghost Project. Weather and ghostly interference stopped this investigation moments later.

Any moisture, rain, or even fog, can provide you with false results. This is easy to understand when you consider going out in the rain, but remember, when the rain stops, the water is still in the air and on the leaves you disturb with your feet. Rain also brings mosquitoes, which look a lot like a ghost when you snap a photo. In a very different way, heat and cold can shift results.

Figure 7.28
Another view of the entrance to Dungeon Rock.

Extreme changes in the weather make for pockets of cold and hot air that register on a thermometer and can even play with infrared scanning.

I Have the Power

If you are deep in the woods, you know what to be careful of, but the closer you are to civilization, the more you will need to be aware of external power supplies. Electricity travels through wires that are no real danger to you but that wreak havoc on your EMF meters. Power lines can also alter sound waves and create oddities in recordings. Keep track of where you are and make note of the power supplies near you, especially wires that cross over where you are and the location of the transformers they travel to.

Figure 7.29
The edge of the infamous Bridgewater Triangle. Activity there seems to follow the power lines, making some of the evidence inconclusive.

Before You Leave

Before you enter the location, interview as many people as possible about their experiences there, even if they are normal, everyday situations. It will help you get a feel for the ambience of the place. Also try to find the maps or trail maps and plan where you are going to go. With limited time and resources, you can't visit every place and still give each the attention it might deserve. The location may be inside another larger area, and you will be tempted to focus on only the most active part. Keep in mind our rules of ghostly travel. If it is seen in one place, it might be seen in another as it tries to get away. We don't think of them like this, but it makes sense and has borne itself out on more than one investigation.

Figure 7.30
A pond at Stonehill College where a mysterious mist floats over the water on the anniversary of a plane crash.

Figure 7.31
A bridge where a ghost has been seen.
Picture courtesy of the Native America Ghost Society.

You may also want to check and double-check all of your equipment, especially anything that helps you stay in touch with your fellow investigators, and you should not be out without fellow investigators. When a battery dies in a house, it is a nuisance, but when it goes and you are a mile away from the car with limited power on you, it can ruin a night of work. Batteries will drain at the worst possible time, but fortune favors the prepared, and assuming it will happen and packing even more will help counteract this.

The most important aspect of your preparation in this circumstance will be coming up with a game plan for the location. I was planning to visit an old battleground and went with some people I had never been out with before.

When we got there, they began splitting up, trying to hit all the locations that had some story attached to it. I trailed along, but the investigation was so disorganized, no one could agree where to go, and we took dozens of photos of each other's flashes. It sounds like common sense, but have a short meeting with the people you are going out with to talk about goals for the investigation and ways to approach the site. You might find they have a completely different view from your own; if so, all those issues can be worked out while you're safe at home. Midnight in the woods is not the place for a power struggle.

Figure 7.32
Buie Park in Stamford, Texas. There have been reports of paranormal activity there for years. *Picture courtesy of the Texas Paranormal Society.*

Take It All In

Finding a ghost is like trying to trap lightning in a bottle. The paranormal is about experience, and you may never experience what a witness did because the perfect set of circumstances may never repeat itself. It is somewhat easier in a house because you can duplicate what happened. As the witness went through this door, she saw a man climbing the stairs. This is much harder in an open space. The perspective the witness had is hard to recreate, so the chances of jump starting the same event is very slim.

Instead, think of an outdoor investigation as observing. Instead of being the active hunter, you are the one who is sitting at your post, waiting for something to go by. You do not need to be passive, but allow your natural senses to do the majority of the work. This is good advice no matter where you are, but in these kinds of environments, it does more good than harm to have the equipment by your side.

Figure 7.33
The view from the top of haunted Anawan Rock in Massachusetts.

Figure 7.34
A welcome center where the ghost of a Native American has been seen.

If you have two sets of investigators, which is ideal, have one stationed with equipment in some part of the location that has a history or some story attached to it. The other team should split up, in twos if possible, and maintain some visual contact with each other, although this does not have to be as strict as it is in a building. There is a larger area to sweep, so you can allow yourself more room. The two things I always have with me on this type of investigation are a whistle and a flashlight, even during the day. Call me overly cautious, but I like to see where I am at all times and have a way to signal when electrical equipment fails. Thermometers are basically useless, as are other types of meters, and should be considered secondary. When something is seen, or every few minutes, these should be used to check the area you are in, but it only looks good to have them out at all times and might not be functional.

Figure 7.35
Haunted woods.

Make a baseline amount of time to stay in each spot in the location, say 30 minutes, and stop every 5 to wait, observe, take a few readings and try to do some EVP work. When you reach your 30-minute point, turn around and make your way back to the central location, taking a slightly different route to get home. When the whole team is back, discuss anything that happened and then send the team that was at base out while the other team stays at home base.

While staying back, don't use the time to go over your evidence. You are still in the field and should be doing the same thing you were active in when you were walking, only this time you are in a stationary place. You would be surprised how much can happen while you are still and just paying attention. The people at home gain the overall perspective while those out in the field are close to the action. You can confirm or explain something that happened.

When the second sweep is done, meet to compare notes again. If one or two places seem like they might have had something going on, abandon home base and go out in groups to visit those places again, only this time take more readings along the way and stay in one spot longer. As you pack up and go, shut your video cameras off last and then head back for the safety of a nice roof over your head.

8

Other Things You Need to Know

YEARS AGO, I WAS ON A FRIEND'S RADIO show talking about what I do, emphasizing some of my work with hauntings and urban legends. I was surprised when he asked me, "So, do you consider yourself more of a researcher than an investigator?" I was taken aback. I didn't know there was a difference, but as the field became more diverse, people felt the need to specialize in things. I was just into ghosts. Whatever it took to get closer to them and report other people's experiences was good with me.

Equipment, with all its bells and whistles, brings investigators into the field. They see it used on television shows, watching hours of footage shown through Nightvision, and they feel that is all ghost hunting is about. It makes sense though. It feels real to look for something most people feel can't be seen with something that might just capture it. The trick is to understand that the equipment is only part of the picture. Much of an investigation happens before anything is taken out of your toolbox or turned on. There is another side of looking into ghosts, much less romantic, but necessary to approaching a case from all sides. Mastering these techniques will give the researcher and investigator the most complete set of skills.

The Interview: What to Ask and What to Avoid

"I usually try to find out about the history of the location and the person's relation to that spot as well as background. Have they lived there a long time? Were they raised in a religious atmosphere? Under what conditions did they have their experience? How do they feel about it—is it a topic of fear or revelation? Has the experience been repeated?"

—Brian J. Cano, The SCARED! Crew

"We prefer to have people tell their stories in their own words without asking 'leading' questions. This way, people don't tend to sensationalize their stories. However, we do have a regular sheet that divides the phenomena into sounds, sights, feelings, and smells."

—Dale Kaczmarek, Ghost Research Society

Figure 8.1
A haunted house where children have been heard running up and down the stairs.

I WAS SPEAKING AT a conference once about the famous killer clown urban legend, which began in Massachusetts, and went outside to gather my thoughts. A woman was smoking a cigarette and asked me if I believed all the stuff I had just said. I told her there were different ideas out there and let the conversation go where she obviously wanted it to. I knew she had experienced something, and pretty soon she described a roadside ghost story for me to add to my collection, but I knew there was something more. The drags on her cigarette become harder, and she looked at me less and less.

We started out with her making up a name for me to call her, and an hour and a half later she revealed her real name and told me the amazing story of what was going on in her house. It was one of the most unique cases I have come across, and I owed the information not to my expertise in science but to my abilities as a journalist. A good investigator has both, and to let one completely dominate you means something is going to get overlooked.

What Is an Interview?

An interview is a general term for gaining secondhand knowledge about a haunting. As we already discussed, you will undertake different kinds of investigations, so the interview will mean different things. In its simplest form, the interview is nothing more than someone telling you what they have heard about that cemetery down the street. Everyone knows it's haunted and have you heard this story. Most times, the interview ends there and you merely file it under the general sense of a haunted place.

Other times, the interview is an emotional telling of someone's personal experience. These should not be left alone because you can't investigate them. If the haunting is from years ago, interviewees might just want someone to tell or to have someone explain a weird time in their life. That is part of the job. Even though you may never investigate it, the haunting is important to know about because it builds your knowledge in the field.

Ideally, the interview is the first step in the process of investigating a possible ghost and should be treated as a vital first step in the information gathering stage. It should be handled with the utmost professionalism and care and have the same attention as going into the house or the location with equipment. Different groups conduct interviews in different ways, and the situation obviously dictates how you handle the questioning, but there are some basic things to remember. When someone comes to you, he is placing a certain trust in you, and it is your job to hear that story first and foremost. Take your need out of the equation for a while, and more information will come out. Some people jump on their agenda too quickly, asking if it might be a demon after 5 minutes or asking to go in and investigate after the first 20. Don't be so eager to suit up. Let the story play itself out.

The Sometimes Long Process: Gathering the Details in Everything

While the more well known and established groups have set up active phone services with possible clients, the first contact will almost always be an e-mail. Most people who experience the paranormal have no frame of reference for it and are not looking to be touched by the other side. There might not be fear or intimidation, but there is an anxiety about coming across something that should not be there. Understand this and sympathize with it. The e-mail allows them to put the feelers out to people as they try to come to terms with what has happened. Read it carefully and respond as soon as possible. It might not come to anything, but I always try to get them on the phone after that.

A paranormal investigator is many things, and one of the most uncomfortable roles we play is that of psychologist. Chances are you have no training in it, but it can't be separated from what you do. Inexperienced people who contact you are looking to come to some meaning behind what happened to them. A paranormal occurrence can be the most emotional experience of someone's life, especially if the person comes into contact with someone they know or miss. That person then finds their way to you. Most want nothing more than to pass on what has happened to them and to have someone tell them they are not crazy. Do not jump into investigator mode immediately, but allow them to tell their story in their own words.

From the first day you decide to investigate the paranormal, you are an observer of the world. Things may come to you, or a simple conversation might start an investigation, so buy yourself a tape recorder so you are sure not to miss anything. I carry both an analog (which is another way to say old-fashioned) and a digital tape recorder so I can switch into research mode at a moment's notice. I like the analog to conduct interviews because I find it easier to play over and over again once I've finished the interview and while I take notes. I can then catalogue it and store it away until I need it. It might be more expensive in the long run, but when you begin gathering hours of information, it becomes harder to save a digital format for archiving. I also think there is something romantic about the old school recorders.

Figure 8.2
A Wireless Microphone, Transmitter, and Receiver Kit.
Picture courtesy of ghost-mart.com.

I keep the digital around in case anything happens to the analog (and things will always go wrong with your equipment once you start investigating) and because it's easy to use but also to record phone conversations. Invest in a system to get recordings off of a phone because most people will prefer to talk on the phone and not in person. That makes it too real for them initially. Always make sure they know they are being taped and agree to it, and go so far as to get their agreeing to it on the tape. Respect them if they say no and settle for written notes. A digital interview also has an added bonus. The tape can be reviewed later for EVPs. I have gathered a surprising amount of them this way, and they help me to determine what cases to take or follow-up on.

Ideally, an interview should be done in person and on video, although don't suggest this until you are comfortable with it yourself and the witness is beyond comfortable with you. This can be very intimidating for them. For the interviewer, it allows you catch subtle things you might miss, such as the person's body language. It also allows you to review how you conducted the interview and how the person reacted to you. You should always be looking to do your job better.

Getting Down to Brass Tacks

I teach a journalism class in a high school in Massachusetts, and the first thing I teach my students is to focus on the six Ws. I'm not too keen on the how, but I love who, what, where, when, why. I also add, "who cares," because I think that is the most important part. There is a school of thought that feels people experience the paranormal when they need to, when it is important for some kind of growth or connection. It is important why the person feels they were contacted or what they think about what happened. Just the facts are not enough.

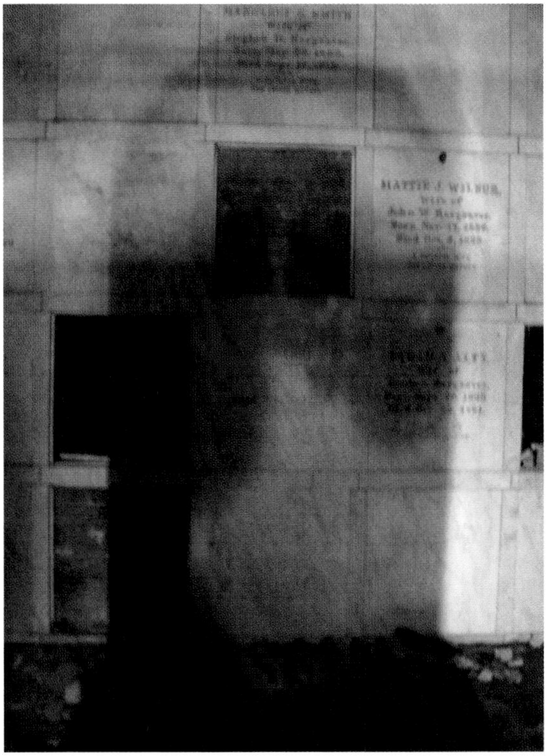

Figure 8.3
A haunted part of a cemetery.
Picture courtesy of Luanne Joly, Whaling City Ghosts.

Keep these types of questions in your pocket though. Just listen at first. Let them get it off their chests and vent their experience. Comment in a general way so they know you are listening and to keep the conversation moving, but don't talk over them. They will tell you when the story is done, and then you can begin dissecting what they have just said.

Take notes as they talk. We all think our memories are impeccable, and the entire interview should be recorded somehow, with their permission of course. Still, there are ideas you have as they talk, follow-up questions you'll want to ask later, and they can fly out of your mind as other ideas come in. It also adds an air of credibility, as odd as that might sound. You look professional doing it, and that might be enough to put them at ease.

Try and get all the people involved in the experience to talk, even when they won't all go on the record. It helps to establish the truth versus someone's perception of an event. It also gives the same occurrence from different angles, and some people pay more attention to sound or smell and others to what was seen. The more people who have information, the clearer the picture is of what might be going on.

Some Great Questions

Develop your own style, but there are some things that are important to cover as the interview goes on. If they don't volunteer any of this, you'll want to know it. It might seem basic, but you'd be surprised what gets left out. Ask all your questions more than once to try to get the clearest picture, and always ask questions about the natural setting of the house to get information that might result in finding a non-ghost explanation for any activity. Here are some things you should always cover:

- **What time did the experience occur?**
- **Is there any area of the location that has more activity than others?**
- **Did you notice any odd smells?**
- **Did you notice any changes in temperature or energy in the air?**
- **Have any of the animals nearby reacted to things in the house?**
- **Has there been a sudden increase in the electric bill?**
- **Has the mood of any individuals been affected by the haunting?**
- **Has there been any change in sleep patterns?**
- **Has there been any added stress in the house right before the haunting happened?**

Some Questions You Might Not Have Thought Of

Some other questions might be uncomfortable for people to answer, or they might be uncomfortable to ask, but they point at some of the other elements in the paranormal world. You should always look at the root of a haunting, although not at the expense of the haunting itself. Some of these ideas are connected to other types of supernatural elements in a haunting, specifically the possibility for a demonic infestation. Many in the field feel most hauntings are either hidden demons or invitations for demons to attach themselves to a location. Take it for what you will, but the other elements in the supernatural are a part of the large picture. Try to get the best picture by finding out this information:

- **Are there children in the house or children who are familiar with the location? This question hits on three different ideas. The first is to make an accurate record of the people living in the house. The second is to open the door to asking about the child's experiences, mainly because children seem to experience the paranormal more deeply. The final reason to find out about children is to explore the potential of a poltergeist, usually connected with children in a house.**
- **Has anyone in the house played with a Ouija Board, used Tarot cards, or used any other form of spirit communication? It might seem obvious, but someone asking for communication might get it even after they stop trying. This is also a classic invitation to demons.**
- **Have you ever felt threatened by the spirit in your house? The question indicates the presence of something that might be getting stronger, but it also gauges how comfortable the homeowners are with what is going on.**
- **Have there been any renovations recently in the location? It is one of those reasons that may be more myth than reality, but changing the physical environment of a location is known to bring out angry spirits confused at their new surroundings.**
- **Is there any history of mental disease, medications, or drug use? These are very sensitive questions, but any of these things can alter someone's perception of events. It also might be a signal of a barrier removed, which allows the paranormal to make itself known.**
- **What are your religious beliefs? Again, this is a very touchy area, but it might offer some link to the nature of the haunting or how best to help the residents.**

Figure 8.4
A haunted grave in Boston.

Other Interview Odds and Ends

Here are some things that might best be applied at the end of the chapter under professionalism, but they are closely related to the interview, so we'll address them here.

- **Always ask a few follow-up questions. It keeps both of your minds going.**
- **When you finish the interview, write a quick summary of your impressions, or add them to the end of the tape to review later. It will help you work through things at the moment when the ideas are fresh and give you something to think about when you take notes later.**
- **If you are conducting an interview with one of your fellow investigators in the room, avoid looking at your colleague or overreacting to something he says. It might seem clear to you what the signal means, but the witness might feel as if he is the butt of an inside joke.**
- **Unless there is an immediate need, wait at least a day before going over the notes so you can take what is said at face value.**
- **Always ask a follow-up question a few days later. It will make the witness see that you were listening and took the interview seriously, and it will get him to remember other details.**
- **Always try to interview a witness at least twice.**
- **Never conduct the initial interview on the day you conduct the investigation. They are two separate beasts, and trying to do both will force you to sacrifice one. Even if you have to conduct a short interview over the phone ahead of time, talk to the witnesses before you pull any other equipment out.**
- **Buy two different types of recorders and have them both accessible during the interview. Talking is spontaneous, and you do not want to lose anything.**
- **Always accept whatever is offered you in terms of food or drink graciously, and eat or drink it in the kitchen. There is something about a kitchen that makes people open up.**
- **Much like an investigation, never conduct an interview drunk or under the influence of anything that impairs your judgment.**
- **Don't leave the witness in a lurch. Once the interview is over, you may feel the need to council them on your initial thoughts. Beware of making generalizations about what might be and ask them how they would like you to proceed.**

The Witness Motif

THE FIRST LEVEL OF PARANORMAL investigation is always the witness, even if you yourself are the witness. The paranormal event and the emotion it releases are the spark for whatever comes after it, and as an investigator, it will most likely be the basis for the work you do. Before there can be an investigation or a follow-up, there has to be a reason to go there in the first place. The earliest evidence was what someone said had happened to them, and for years that was enough.

So much of modern ghost hunting involves debunking what someone has experienced, so there is a clash between the two camps. There is no way to truly understand what has happened in a location without putting heavy weight into someone's first-hand experience. If there is evidence that completely goes against what they have said, you can evaluate the situation as possibly being nature and not supernatural. For example, they hear a banging on the wall in February and you discover frozen pipes in the walls behind the bedroom. If there is no solid evidence against what they have said, their words have to be part of the larger story.

With that being said, witnesses are human and might be influenced by outside factors when they believe something has happened to them. If the investigation is conducted in their house, don't just look for a ghost. Notice other things about the environment, like a bookcase filled with titles on ghosts or a movie case filled with horror DVDs. This does not make them a liar.

Figure 8.5
The witness who took this picture swore it was a ghost, but it ended up being a bleed in the film.

It might just mean they are more likely to mistake something common for something ghostly.

Allow prejudice to slip in, but don't let it overwrite what is being said. Teenagers are not the most reliable witnesses. A blind man might have trouble seeing. A Christian woman might describe a vision as an angel whereas someone else might say it was a ghost dressed in white. Trying to understand where a person is coming from, their background and frame of reference, is as important as gathering an EMF reading.

Years ago, a woman contacted me about a ghost she thought she had in her backroom. She was an older woman and started the conversation by asking me if she was being punished by God and if that was why her house was haunted. I took everything she said after that at face value because here was a woman who not only didn't want her ghost, but thought she was cursed by God because of it. She was not looking for attention or publicity. She wasn't making her story up. In the same way, when my father, as hard-boiled as they come and a retired private investigator, approached me years ago to talk about a ghost we had in the house I grew up in, I listened with both ears.

Figure 8.6
The entrance to a haunted locale.
Picture courtesy of Luanne Joly, Whaling City Ghosts.

What's in a Word

I also look for buzzwords that tell me the person may be too ready to have a haunting in their house or they may be too eager to interpret something they have seen in a known haunted area. How do you know something they say is real? Assume it is all real unless there is something about them you don't trust. Evaluate the person as well as the ghost. Are they trustworthy or do they seem to be searching for the answers to things. Conduct more than one interview and see if their answers stay the same. The best evidence they can give you is something that falls outside of the known vocabulary of the ghost hunter. In other words, the more unique their experience, the more odd the words used to describe it, the closer to being truth it is.

Some words tip me off the other way. When I hear them, I know a person has been watching a lot of television about ghosts. Again, this doesn't mean they are lying or exaggerating the truth, it just means their minds were thinking ghost even before they experienced anything.

This becomes harder because the mainstreaming of the paranormal makes some words part of everyday conversation. Here are some that might tip you off, however:

- **Orb:** This is a term used by paranormal investigators and adopted only by people who look into ghosts. Everyone else will describe it, usually, as a ball of light.
- **Activity:** No one uses this to talk about a ghostly encounter other than ghost hunters.
- **3:00 as an important time:** It can be debated whether the supposed witching hour is in fact a time of heightened paranormal activity, but unless the person is into the paranormal, this won't even cross their minds.
- **Entity or apparition:** Again, these are ghost hunting terms. Most people will just say figure or person.

Forms: Red Tape and Formality

THERE ARE NO RULES TO conducting an investigation, and the only rule to any ghost hunt is to not break a law in the process of getting your information. This usually means not entering a cemetery after dark without permission or entering private property to find that haunted third floor of an asylum. There really is no governing body that approves and certifies the paranormal investigator, so much of what happens in the field is more of a lesson in best practices. Other than common sense and things you might not have thought of, much of the life is a free for all.

And yet there are those pesky little things known as torts to worry about. For those who do not have a law degree, let me explain the basis for tort action. A man walks up your front steps and slips on some ice. He hurts himself due to your lack of skill with a shovel and salt and then sues you. You settle out of court and your insurance picks up the bill and passes the loss on to you. That's a pretty hairy situation to have to deal with as a homeowner, even if there is no direct payout from you for the man's injuries.

Investigating the paranormal has all kinds of opportunities for lawsuits, and it has become increasingly more important to protect yourself from any kind of danger. I am not saying wolves are waiting around the corner in sheep's clothing to take your money from you, but we live in an age of litigation, and you can never be too careful. It might be an uncomfortable subject to breach when you are entering a person's house. Keep in mind, there is no insurance to take up the slack for any damages they might come after you for. There is no, "They made my house more haunted," law, but there can be other damages associated with an investigation. The most obvious is damage to the house, be it structural, electrical, or cosmetic. There is also a chance any publicity from the investigation can impact real estate sales. In colonial times, a man once sued another for defamation of character on behalf of his house because his tenants put forward the idea it was haunted. He did not win the case, but there is at least a precedent.

The best way to handle the situation is to deal with it before you start. Write out exactly how you are going to investigate and have the homeowner sign that they understand it. Don't deviate from it without their permission, and try to get any changes in writing as well. The forms in Appendix C of this book may help you design one for your group, but they are not legal documents. Make sure the homeowners understand what you intend to do with the evidence and assure them in writing your release of information will be what they want. Either everything is anonymous, they agree to have their names changed in any publishing of your findings, or they agree to have full disclosure. Also make it clear to them from the beginning that no results can be guaranteed. You can't remove anything from the house or even tell beyond a shadow of a doubt whether something is in the house. Just be upfront, and then get everything in writing or on tape or both. And be careful when you go up the stairs.

To Charge or Not to Charge

MONEY IS THE ROOT OF ALL EVIL, and there is something to be said about the person out for nothing more than the truth. At some point you have to decide whether or not you will charge for an investigation, and your decision on this will determine more than just how much is in your bank account. Charging money, and what you charge for, says a lot about your level of commitment to the field and your status in it.

If you charge for an investigation, the majority of people who investigate will shun you and think you are a fraud. I hate to be blunt, but there is a real backlash against those who ask for money. Most people do this in their spare time and feel that charging a fee taints the evidence they get. It encourages people out to make a quick buck to become paranormal investigators and invites fraud. Most people who approach an investigator have had some kind of emotional experience that compels them to come forward, and this makes them ripe for the sheering.

Figure 8.7
JFK Prep, a haunted school in Wisconsin.
Picture courtesy of Jaeson Jrakman.

Charging makes it a business, and if ghost hunting becomes a business for you, your approach has to change. There is a stronger need to find something, making evidence your currency and giving the investigator more of an incentive to interpret the evidence to prove something is there. There is also a need to make it more dramatic and to make the ramifications for not doing anything about the haunting more dramatic. If the exterminator says you have ants, you shrug. If he tells you there are ten million ants in your foundation that are slowly burrowing through and having children, you hand over the money without question.

What are you charging them for and what makes you worthy to accept their money? What makes you more qualified than someone else? Doctors and lawyers and other professionals have some certification process, some means by which they can prove their expertise. There is none of that in this field, and as a consumer of paranormal equipment and classes, beware of anyone who offers you a certification or an honorary degree. It is not worth the paper it is printed on.

Some groups will say they are offering peace of mind by telling people what exactly is in their home. Be careful of this. If we could say what was in someone's home, we would have proof ghosts exist and then we'd all be rich.

Be careful about assuming that you have enough information or expertise to remove a ghost from a location, but be doubly sure if you want to charge for this. There is very little to prove you have removed the ghost, or that a ghost can even be removed, and how do you handle a refund or exchange plan if the house is still haunted?

On the other side, this is an expensive venture for you. Equipment can run thousands of dollars depending on your level of commitment, and gas money alone can be a heavy bill. There is also something to be said for the time you invested learning about ghosts and the time you spend conducting the interview and investigation and then reviewing the evidence. A financial planner might charge you for the advice they give you, and if you never take it, you might be out some money. You still have to pay for their perspective and their knowledge. Just because you might not be able to solve a paranormal problem, doesn't mean you didn't perform a service.

Here is where I fall. I don't charge anything for what I do because I am dealing with an unestablished subject and doing something based only on theory. No matter what anyone tells you, there is no proof the science of ghost hunting is anything other than a pseudoscience based on anecdotal evidence and connections made. I can't prove anything or produce something that is not wrapped in maybes, so I don't ask for anything. Some groups believe it is okay to charge for gas or equipment used, like batteries or film development, but I feel it should go no further than that.

The Elements of Professionalism

During my first investigation, I was hot on the trail of a famous ghostly hitchhiker. It was a well known legend in the town, and there were enough people who had supposedly seen him that I believed I could track down someone who had experienced something. I started talking to an older woman who worked the counter at the gas station, basically telling her why I was in town and hinting I was looking for people who had seen something.

"Well, people really keep to themselves about that kind of thing," she said with disinterest. "Most people are in their beds here by nine at night."

Not meaning any harm, I said, "Typical Puritan town in New England." The woman was offended at the religious slight and asked me to leave the store before I could pay for my soda.

Figure 8.8
A haunted military fort in Rhode Island. The evidence of the activity exists only as stories.

When you enter a person's house or talk to them about a haunting, you are representing yourself or your group to someone on the outside. This person may not share your ideas politically, socially, or religiously. They may be in an emotional place where they are feeling vulnerable or defensive. You are probably not making money doing this, but you are still a professional and must conduct yourself that way. You do not need to take an etiquette class to hold a Geiger counter, but just keep these things in mind:

- **Dress appropriately:** There should be some balance between comfort, functionality, and presentable. I prefer jeans or cargo pants, a button-down shirt, and a pair of brown or black shoes. Jeans and sweatshirts are great for an outside investigation but might put the client on guard. Many groups like to wear a t-shirt with their group's logo. As long as it's tasteful and respectful, feel free.
- **Be clean:** These people are trusting you with their house and, at times, their emotional well being. They might not be as open to someone who comes in with dirty pants or a sweat-stained hat. I am not saying you need to get a shave and a haircut to go look for ghosts, but imagine if you went to the bank and the man behind the counter looked like he hadn't slept in a few days. Not so quick to turn over your savings, are you?
- **Don't swear:** Damn and hell are probably fine, but think before you speak. If something happens and there is a sudden outburst, I am sure they'll understand, but try to keep it PG.
- **Keep them informed:** Don't disappear into the basement and come up two hours later and say you'll get back to them. Tell them what you are doing, although you might want to keep results close to the vest until you can get a full picture of the place.
- **Pick up after yourself:** I recently heard a countertop installation commercial on the radio that praised itself for picking up after themselves. I always thought it was common sense.
- **Look organized:** The more you look like you know what you are doing, the more trust you'll build. When in doubt, fake it until you make it. Always seem in control.

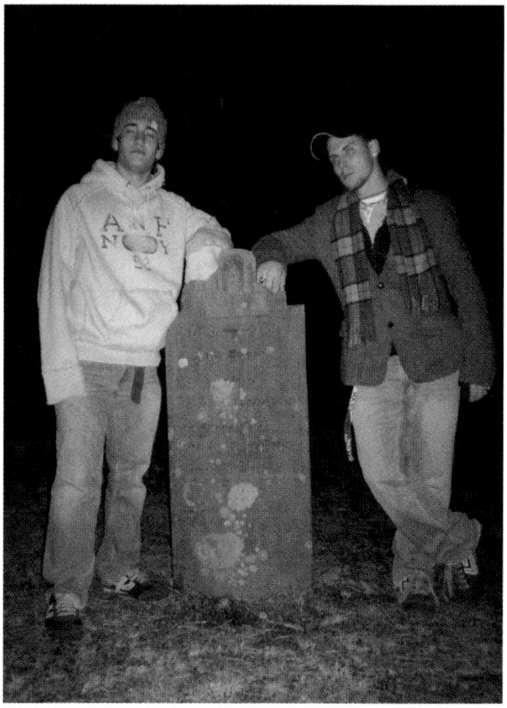

Figure 8.9
Ultimate professionals.
Picture courtesy of Brian Paulson, EPRA.

Buy a Library Card and Use the Internet

AN INVESTIGATOR IS SOMEONE who hears about a haunting and approaches the site looking for evidence of a haunting. A researcher is someone who tries to discover the origin of the activity through techniques that involve something other than observation and equipment. The two should not only be friends, they should be different sides of the same person. Many paranormal groups online will feature a member who they consider to be the researcher, or the expert in history. A good ghost hunter finds a balance between being in the field and being in front of a book or a computer screen. Never let anyone put you down for being a researcher. They add context to the haunting, and sometimes they provide the necessary link to what might be in the location.

Figure 8.10
Two birds with one stone.
This library is known to be haunted.
Picture courtesy of Tim Weisberg and Spooky Southcoast.

The Library Is Your Friend

The library should always be a crucial step in an investigation. Get a library card. You can borrow movies for free, but it also opens up a whole new world of information, not all of which can be found on the Internet. Many investigators find it a hassle to take the time to crack a book, but your local library can offer you things you don't even realize you need.

There are thousands of books about the paranormal available, most of which you can purchase online or from a book vendor or book store. That's too much money for my taste, and some out of print books are no longer offered. You can get just about any book ever published with enough patience and effort through the smallest branch of a local library. If the title is not part of their catalogue, they can get it from another library anywhere in the country. I recently held a lesson on interlibrary loan in one of my freshman English classes. We were looking for a book about John Updike from a random search we ran. Within ten minutes over the phone, the book was on order and the student picked it up four days later and finished her paper on time.

A well-rounded ghost hunter has a little bit of knowledge about everything from brain chemistry to local history. That can mean spending so much on research materials you might need a second mortgage on your house. However, books can be researched for free with the right direction. There can also be useful resources from the local paper, a national directory, or even an obscure genealogy book. As you go back further in history, you are more likely to run into self-published pamphlets not found anywhere on the web. They may have something to do with the archives or special collections and you might have missed it. I was researching a haunting at a college when I came across a copy of the school paper that had never been archived digitally. It spoke of the ghost being seen over a hundred years ago and referenced the journal of a student who wrote about seeing it. A little more digging and I found the journal as part of the same collection.

Access to the library also gives you the key to dozens of academic websites you might not be able to get into from your house. At the very least, a library card will get you into some of them from a remote location. These sites offer tens of thousands of articles from papers, magazines, and journals. There is so much information, you might get lost before the trail gets cold, but many are cross-referenced, and the websites offer organizational tools and abstracts to help you sift through everything.

Librarian are the gatekeepers of knowledge, and what's better, they're bored. Having worked as one for four years, I can tell you the highlight of my day was when someone needed me to find the impossible. Librarians get paid to know how to get information you need and are often historians of the town in their own right. They might know the best place to look or the right person to talk to. They know where that little yellowed book is deep within the special collection room. They also have the lowdown on other patrons and will bring your name up if something develops.

I was investigating a haunted schoolhouse in a nearby town and called the librarian from that town two days in advance. She asked me to arrive a little after ten so she could have time to set me up, and when I got there she had pulled three books and four old folders from different file cabinets, had placed a reading lamp on the table, and had provided two sharpened pencils and a pad of paper. The only thing missing was a brandy and a pipe. I was well into my research when I noticed two more folders had been placed at the end of the table. When I asked her if they related to the haunting, she smiled and told me they were about another haunting in the town I might want to look into. About a week later, a woman called and asked me to investigate her house. The librarian had told her about me when the subject of ghosts had come up. I wasn't even a member of that library.

That might be an extreme example, but there is something about the town library that makes me work better. Whether it is the employee or putting my mind in a focused mindset, I always get something connected and unexpected by the time I leave. Did I mention you can borrow movies for free?

The Other Sources

There are other sources within a community that may provide the information you need. All of them provide the dual purpose of uncovering something hidden connected to your case and of getting you out and in the public eye. This may give you media coverage that allows you to get more cases or it may just put your name out there for when you need information from someone. Sometimes the best ghost hunter is the one people have heard of.

- **The local paper:** Most larger papers have decades' worth of archived editions, but smaller towns and more obscure papers might not have everything on computer. Going to the source allows you to look at everything, and oftentimes puts you in contact with the person who wrote the article.

- **Town Record:** Depending on the size of the city or town, it might be a one shot deal to visit the town hall and the town collector. They have all the information you need on the history of the house, changes made to it physically over the years, tax information, and sometimes obscure details about it. Most of the information is a matter of public record and usually the information can be retrieved for free.

- **Town historical societies or "friend" organizations:** These are the people who have the real town story, and visiting them will allow you to see many forgotten books about the area and even personal journals and little town secrets. I was speaking at a historical society's monthly meeting as I was finishing a book about the town. One old timer stood up and corrected some information I discovered. I made the correction and got two more stories from people as the meeting ended. It might be best to tell them you are not looking for ghosts but rather just doing research. After that, judge their mood and try to wiggle in the real reason for getting in touch with them.

The Internet: Friend or Foe

THERE HAS NEVER BEEN MORE information at the fingertips of the common man in any time in history. The Internet has allowed people to gather information and communicate ideas on a scale that almost seems inconceivable. There is a large paranormal community out there, and the access to information and archives allows an investigator to put his fingers in so much. Is it a good thing though? Much has come out about having too much information and the quality of the information out there. I love an old-fashioned jukebox, but the downfall of having one at the pool hall down the street is that you put your entertainment in the hands of people you might not trust. Information on the web is sometimes like that.

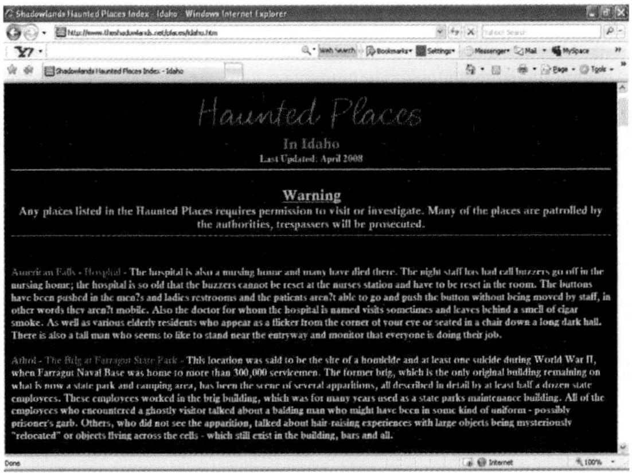

Figure 8.11
The Shadowland, one of the most extensive lists of haunted locations on the Internet. Due to public postings, not all the locations are accurate.

On one hand, people who need help can find you and connect. On the other, information that will get in your way is out there and ready to connect. Depending on what you are looking for, signing on can be your best friend or your biggest obstacle. It all depends on how you look and where you go.

When You Are Looking

I read about a haunted location online and went out to research it for myself. I drove the hour and a half and got to the haunted restaurant to find it closed. I asked someone at a gas station what had happened to it, and he looked at me like I had two heads. He told me that restaurant hadn't been open for more than five years. I asked if it had anything to do with the ghost who supposedly lived there, and he laughed. "Ten years ago someone made that up," he told me. "There was a contest to come up with a ghost story and the guy who owned it made up this story and won. It didn't even take place in the restaurant, but someone got the story messed up."

The flow of misinformation sometimes feels like the Mississippi. Too many times, I have tried to follow up on a haunted location only to find the website I got the story from was completely wrong. At times, the wrong town is identified, or the street comes into question, and often a rumor becomes a full-blown cursed neighborhood.

Some sites are better than others, but many cut and paste information and present it as research, perhaps with a bit of commentary or details from another site. We'll discuss later how this helps to create urban legends out of hauntings, but for now we only need to see this as a landmine to dodge.

Ghost hunters gain experience and satisfy their need to investigate by finding these locations. They are some of the most interesting settings to look for a ghost, and they should be explored in the right way. The trouble is so many have nothing to confirm their activity but a story that makes it on a website that then gets mirrored by seven others. Many sites and message boards give posting privileges to anyone, so the genesis of the story might be an unreliable person. Most of these are not done with malicious intent but are rather the product of overzealous researchers wanting to fill pages with content. Proceed with caution.

Here is how I go about things. Search for places in your community to investigate. Look for local groups who may have been there before or old news articles that might mention it. For fun, look in your paper's archives and just type the word ghost or paranormal. There is plenty of information from these sources. Then try to find a second group or reference that is completely independent from the first. Watch the words used to describe the spot and the occurrences there. If they say the same thing, one copied off the other and you need another source. I go so far as to copy a fragment of wording and put it in a search engine. If I get seventeen sites who all say the same thing, I am less likely to consider it genuine. I also use town message boards where people who are not ghost obsessed might share a story or offer some information you need.

Avoid national sites that publish long lists of ghosts found in each state. If you want to follow up, try to find the same location from a local source to confirm it. If you see a long list on a local site, they cheated on their information and lifted it from the national site. Also, read the tone of the website and the kind of information it has on it. Consider who you want to listen to, the same way you would if someone were trying to sell you something. How many years has the group been investigating? How clear is their evidence? On the other hand, be careful not to discredit a website where there are spelling mistakes or one that does not look as neat and clean as another. A good investigator is not necessarily the best writer or a good webmaster.

If you can, try to contact someone who might be familiar with the location. The web allows you to do this even though you might be intimidated at first. As someone who doesn't have a group, I find freedom in being able to get in touch with people from all around my area. It has allowed me to see different techniques and come into contact with different ideas. Most groups are more than happy to hook up for a joint investigation. You now have someone with more knowledge and you've just made friends with a peer.

When You Have a Case

The Internet becomes a whole new beast when you already have a case, and using it becomes more about gathering as much information as you can. I was researching an area known to be haunted by the spirits of Native Americans. Using the web, I was able to get information about the tribe, e-mail addresses and phone numbers of representatives of the tribe, and several witnesses to the odd occurrences. Everything I found helped me investigate, and the representatives and witnesses had other stories to share.

Connecting leads to more connecting, which is the lofty goal of the Internet in the first place.

Figure 8.12
A well-written-about haunted schoolhouse whose popularity has grown because of the Internet.

There is also information to be found in old newspaper articles or historical websites. Much of what you can do at the library, you can do online, although it is sometimes limited by how much the source can get into a digital format. Other websites can offer circumstantial information about the place you are looking into. If you go to some, they offer satellite views of the area. I once was disturbed by a haunting where one of the signs of activity was a strong smell of garbage at odd times. The satellite view allowed me to see a town dump positioned in such a way to the house that the wind would blow the smell their way.

Again, consider your source. Online databases are often edited by people who have an agenda or not enough information to be considered an authority. Use these sites as a springboard but not as the ultimate truth.

Use the web as a way to find people who might be resources for you. My cell phone is filled with local authorities on the paranormal because I approached them to help with a case. I use them when I need a new perspective, and they call me with ideas or questions. This kind of sharing leads to finding the best information gained by experience. When I need advice on a case involving a possible inhuman or demonic case, I call one person, and when I am getting evidence I don't understand, I go to another. Having these people in your life makes things easier and helps find the best person for the job.

9

Looking at the Evidence

THE INVESTIGATION IS OVER and you're back in the real world. You continue your day as a police officer, a garbage collector, or a CEO, and everything seems a bit slowed down. The adrenaline has stopped, and, depending on your personality or the people you work with, you push that ghost hunter part of yourself down into your gut for a while. You know it's there though, waiting near your computer. The investigation is over, but your job has just begun.

The hunt is the drama, but evaluating the evidence is your best chance of touching the other side of the veil. Spending time in front of a video monitor or a computer screen is the part that gets edited out of the television shows. Instead, they speed to the part where the investigator's face changes. It is that moment where a rumble on tape holds meaning or a quick movement of a shadow may be a household pet or a ghost saying hello. The adrenaline comes back, and your mind holds that moment, thinking about how, only a few days ago, there was a ghost looking over your shoulder.

Did You Hear That?

CLOSE YOUR EYES FOR A MOMENT and listen to the world around you. First, you'll hear your inner voice talking about bills and work tomorrow, but even that falls away and you're left with the sound of your breathing and the room you're sitting in. The clock ticking might as well be a drum solo, and you can hear the electricity running through your computer.

Figure 9.1
A good set of headphones may be all you need.

Most of us live in a world of ignored sound. Our mind has been trained to shut it out and process only what we need for survival. Listening for audio evidence is like retraining yourself to hear. Your filters are different, more advanced. Watch two experts listening to an EVP in a noise recording. They'll smile and nod at each other while you struggle to just hear the recording. You'll develop a more fine-tuned listening ability. It only takes time and effort.

Traditional Hearing

You do not need to have expensive equipment or even a computer to look for EVPs. Today it helps to have something to run your recordings through and format them for others to hear, but for decades investigators heard the dead without anything other than a tape recorder and a well trained ear.

You must learn to turn off your other senses. It sounds odd, but your hearing will improve if you allow everything else to be dulled. You don't need to smell, or even see, to get the results you want. Find a quiet room and earphones that cover your whole ear. Turn off the lights and hold your hands over your ears. Remember, you're alone so it is okay if you look silly. Besides, if you squint and lean your head in, it improves your hearing.

What to Listen For

When you have nothing but sound, you are listening for anything that can't be accounted for. At this point, you are doing a general listening, like observing a foundation for obvious cracks. Once something stands out, isolate it and get in closer. With no outside equipment, this means listening to it repeatedly at a high volume. Each time, notice how the sound comes in and what it does at its peak, which may be for only a quick second; then notice how it exits.

Think of a chair scraping across a hardwood floor. You hear the initial squeal followed by the drag. At the end there is a sudden stop and a bit of an echo as the sound moves past the physical act. To hear any of these by themselves might sound unusual and be mistaken for something paranormal. Together, they are obvious.

Take this approach to all random sounds on the recording. Pay close attention to rustlings, scrapes, and whispery noises.

Take your time evaluating in this way. It may be a while before you start to be able to pull pieces out of evidence and isolate them. I was conducting a Frank's Box session with a group that included a cynic, two television hosts, cameramen, and some trained investigators. As we heard the bits of sound come through, everyone heard the obvious, but only the investigators heard the quiet voices hidden within the other messages. We call them EVP ears, and they become more precise with each session you listen to.

Critics will say you fool yourself into hearing what you want. As a parent, my mind has been trained to hear my son crying or falling from his bed at night. I am even skilled at hearing him laughing from three rooms away. The downfall of this is I hear kids laughing all the time, even when there is no one there. High parts of songs on the radio sound like him crying. The same might be true for EVP work. All this listening makes you a bit punchy. Add in a desire to make order out of chaos, and ghosts come out of the woodwork. There is no way to fight this except to keep a check on yourself and challenge your own results. Always account for what a sound may be and consult notes you made during the session to exclude anything that might not be paranormal.

Technology Steps In

You don't need to settle for your own ears, however. Running your recordings through computer software allows you to focus on something that might be out of the usual, drop outside noise levels to hear it clearly, and clean up or manipulate the track to bring out what is there.

Figure 9.2
©istockphoto.com/Fabio Bianchini

Most also allow you to play a recording backwards and add effects such as reverb to clarify what is being heard.

Most investigators prefer a program like Audacity, which can be downloaded for free off the net at http://audacity.sourceforge.net/, or Adobe Audition, but there are many on the market, and with the popularity of ghost hunting today, new ones are marketing themselves as investigator-friendly. There are two things to remember when buying a program. First, you have a limited amount of time to spend on ghosts. Many powerful programs have more bells and whistles than you'll ever need. You could spend months trying to figure out how to work everything, and that means less time in the field and less time actually listening to the evidence. It might be worth it to get a free or less expensive program, learn how to use it, and then upgrade.

You also have to look at the nature of the evidence you create when you allow a computer to manipulate the recording. There is a point where it becomes too much. The further you get away from the original recording, the less effective and genuine your evidence is. If you add echo, reverse it, and then loop it, you run the risk of taking sound and creating a voice.

I use Nero Burning Room. The program is easy to use and gives me all the features I need. I run it simple. Recording takes the actual running time to fully process, and I take this time to listen to the recording for the first time. Make notes as it plays for sections to review and look at more closely. The first listen sometimes brings the best evidence to the surface, so it should not be skipped. It also serves to refresh the session, bringing it back to mind and filling in the holes in your memory.

Once the recording is in, cut it into segments for easier evaluation. It can be daunting to sit and listen to hours of EVP sessions, especially at the beginning, but playing them ten minutes at a time lessens the load. Break it up visually, meaning you need to note times where there are drastic bumps in audio readout. These may be due to background noise or a cough, but it may be something different. Many EVP technicians notice a precursor noise before a particularly strong communication. Before the voice appears a loud noise is heard which acts as a heralding of sorts. Some feel it might be the spirit breaking a dimension border while others feel the ghosts might use the resonance itself to gain energy to talk.

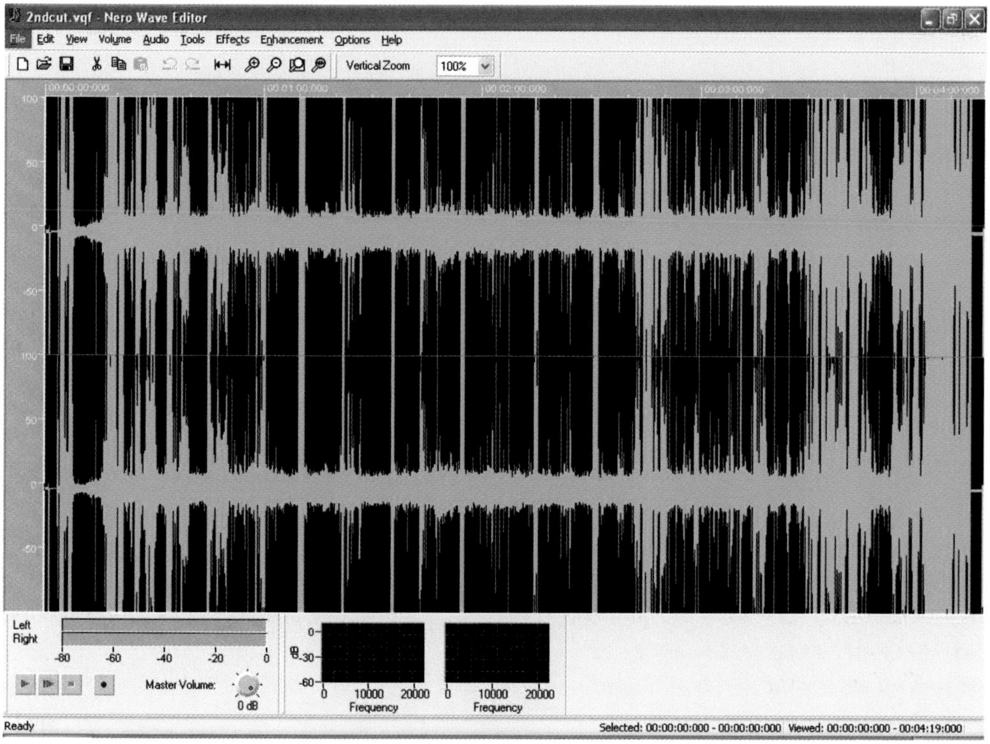

Figure 9.3
Nero Burning Room.

The Audio Made Visual

Audio playback software can do more than help you manipulate and edit your recordings. It also shows the recorded sound visually, allowing you to focus on snips of the sound for closer evaluation. Trust your ears, but use your eyes as well. They can notice subtle changes in the track your ears might miss. Ultimately, using both together gives you the best chance of catching something.

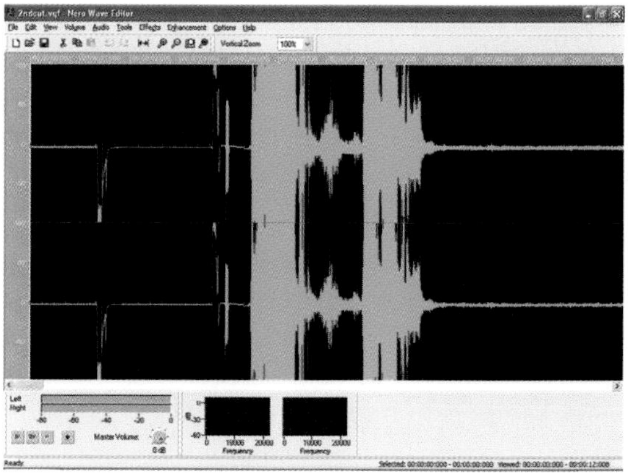

Figure 9.4
A visual readout of a recorded sound.

Once the recording has been processed by the software, play it, listening but also pulling up the visual that shows the sound levels in the room. It will look like the monitor in those old science fiction shows where computers tried to take over the world. You'll want to zoom in so that approximately 15 to 20 seconds show on the screen at a time. You can adjust this to your liking, but it gives you enough to evaluate and not so much that the screen changes too quickly to focus on anything.

Be aware of how your voice appears visually and what your fellow investigators voices look like in the recording. Shut out sounds that can be explained away. What you're left with are little anomalous lines. They are your signposts. Stop the recording, isolate it, and then run it through all the filters and processing you feel comfortable with.

Continue in this manner until the recording is over. This will not help you find voices inside of louder noises, but it does give you a handle on those little whispers. It also helps distinguish voices within the normal human voice register from those that fall outside of it.

All in Good Time

Without practice, all the little wiggles on the screen will look the same, and they should for a while. EVP work is work of the ears and then supplemented by the new software. The more you work with it, the more the two will be in sync, but it should come from recognizing sounds first and then seeing how they look on the screen. Eventually, you'll see patterns in the way you talk and know where to go fishing for possible EVPs.

Where to Look

The most obvious place to find an EVP is in the quiet times after you ask a question. If there is a sound in the lull, check that area for something, especially if there is something visual that implies possible speech. This should come fairly quickly for most, but this is only the beginning. You should also search for times when there is a loud or abrupt sound, such as a cough or a furnace being turned on. These are natural sounds, but many times a spirit uses these to talk, as if they are riding the sound waves. It is similar to the idea of them using the noise within an older recorder to gather enough juice to talk.

There are less obvious places investigators often miss. Think of these as the gold in the diamond ring. They are valuable but are often overlooked for the flashy, more noticeable evidence. If you get a voice that says, "Take me home," after you ask, "Can I help you with something?" that's the solid, flashy EVP, and there are many times when you can get that. Imagine though if you miss the voice that asks what you are doing while you set up your equipment because you never bother to check that time on the track or assume any noise during that time is only you plugging everything in. Always start the tape before you start investigating and look those times over carefully.

You also want to spend time looking at the recordings where other equipment showed the possible presence of a spirit, and you would be surprised how much time you spend going over those details. Once I was in an old home and the temperature dropped. The difference was so dramatic, we pulled out more equipment, trying to get an EMF reading and snapping pictures.

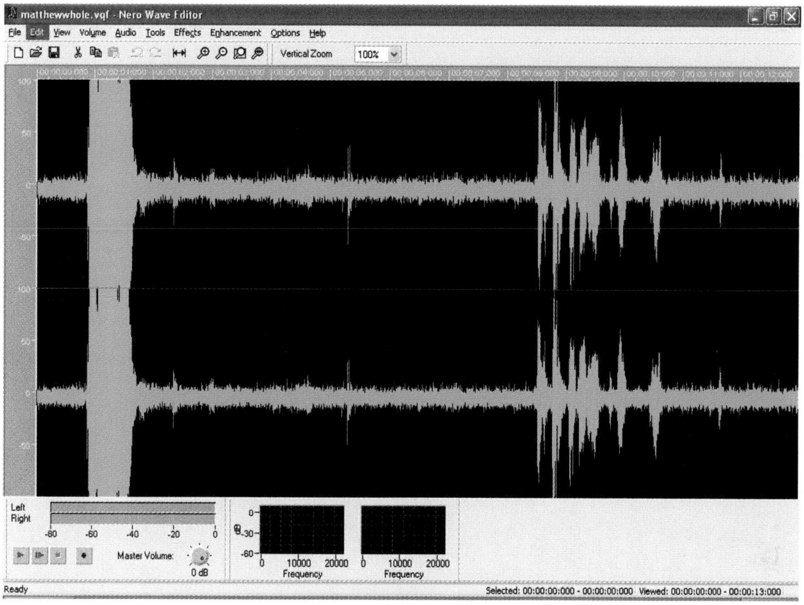

Figure 9.5

A computer readout of a short EVP session.

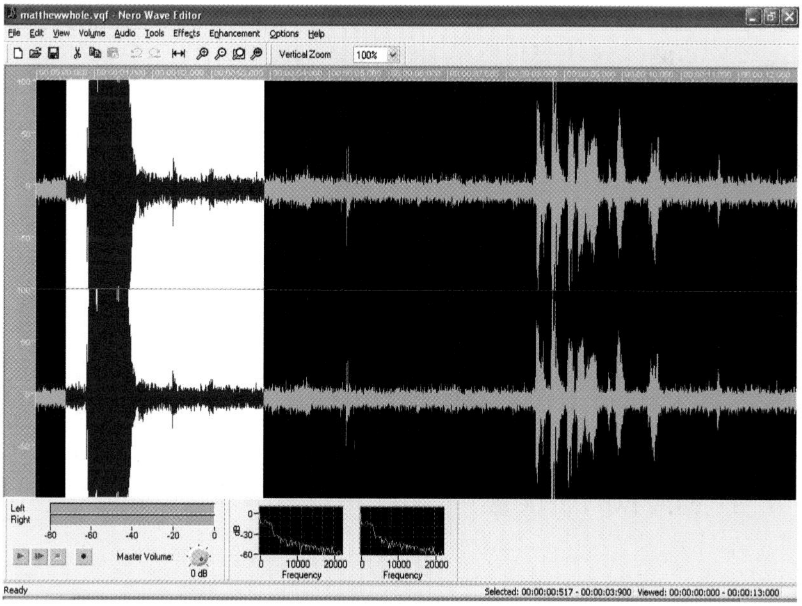

Figure 9.6

The same readout with a segment isolated.
The large wave is my voice and the small one to the right is an unknown sound.

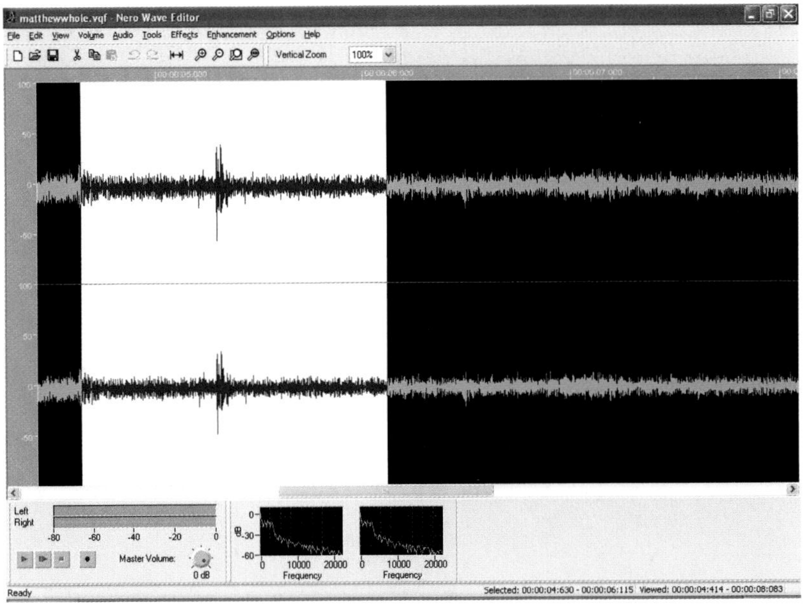

Figure 9.7
The close-up of an EVP hidden inside the segment.

Nothing else showed up, but when I checked the tape, somebody not with our group could be heard saying, "I'm cold too." Whether the cold spirit was making the room cooler or reacting to something else is impossible to say, but our conversation almost caused us to lose the evidence.

They're Talking to Me

EVP technicians sometimes play in holes for too long. The first conference I spoke at had a speaker presenting his EVP results. Some of the tracks he played baffled me with their clarity and frequency, and what I was amazed with was how often the dead were ready to talk. He played several that were not as clear, or what investigators call Class B, and the room erupted. One person raised his hand and said he clearly heard, "This is the one." Another became almost violent, saying it said, "This is my son." The room was split, and as the presenter got more annoyed, his breathing became heavy. "No," he finally said. "It says, 'Those I have sung.' We got the EVP at Jim Morrison's grave and we had just asked him what he thought about his life."

While I enjoy a good paranormal showdown, I have to admit I have seen this scene played out too many times when good listeners get together. There should be discussion about what an EVP says when you evaluate the information you get, but too often people lose sight of the fact that they just talked to a dead person. Perhaps they have become desensitized to this fact, but there should always be an element of wonder when exploring the unknown.

The Effect of Effects

Doing anything to alter the recording changes the message. Here is where you have to compromise and even challenge your ideas about what an EVP is. Many technicians who spend time running their recordings through every whistle their software has also say any device can capture an EVP and that the spirits work on intention. It would seem with all the hoops you have to go through to get the voice clear, they are playing a bit hard to get.

Instead, think of an EVP as their best attempt to talk, or perhaps even a bit like eavesdropping. They do not have the ability to gift-wrap it for you, but they make their best attempt.

Use some effect then, but be careful not to create an EVP in your attempts to discover one. The primary feature of your software should be a noise reducer to clean up your recordings. This may be the least intrusive. In theory, all you are doing is removing everything that is not the message. If your software has it, the next best option is to slow the track down. A quick bang can sometimes be a few words strung together that might be missed at faster speeds.

Reverb and other pitch altering routes are a mixed bag. They can sometimes stress the difference in audio tones, making something easier to hear. For example, reverb can make a quick syllable stick around long enough to have it form a word. You have to wonder when you go this far whether the EVP is worth the effort. The resulting track will be of poorer quality and open to criticism, and with limited resources, you have to wonder what you are not listening to, or hearing, elsewhere on the tape by spending so much time and effort on one little moment.

Being a big fan of rock and roll and heavy metal, I understand the value of hidden and backwards messages. I ruined more than one record needle looking for them in some of my favorite songs. With so much unknowing happening between the world of the living and the dead, something might get twisted. Therefore, spending some time reversing sounds might produce a valid EVP. As you get more experience listening, you will notice human speech has a certain quality to it, and you will come to recognize this pattern. When debating whether to reverse a sound, use this skill to weed out which ones you should go to the effort for.

The Best and Worst of the Voices

Unlike many things in the paranormal, there is a formal ranking for the quality of an EVP. Unfortunately, there is a disagreement over what falls into those ranks and whether the current standard might be too limiting. Voices of the dead are placed into classes, with a Class A EVP being a clear voice whose words can be understood and make sense together. It slides from there, but most recognize only a Class B and a Class C below that. Places like the American Association of Electronic Voice Phenomena at www.aaevp.com can help you grade any EVP you get.

Classification A: This is a clear voice where anyone who hears it can accept what it says without being told what you think it says. It also can be heard without the use of headphones or extraordinary amplification.

Classification B: A voice can be heard but it is slightly muffled or soft. It might require EVP ears to understand or some prompting from you. Headphones might have to be used.

Classification C: Something is there but the voice can't be fully heard or understood. Headphones would most likely have to be used, and what is said becomes dependant on who hears it.

The problem with the current system is that it does not take into account the relevance of what is said. For example, during his work in a haunted house, Mike Markowicz picked up a Class A EVP that said, "Once you try crack you never go back." Clearly this was very strong and understandable, and the odds of those random words being placed together or heard together without a conscious being in the house are very low, but it did not pertain to the investigation and made no sense when compared to the other evidence he received. Can this really be ranked as the best evidence out there?

What might be better, and something to consider when you take a look at your EVPs, is how the communication relates to a question asked or the stories that exist in the home. For example, if you ask, "Are you the one who keeps knocking on the door?" and you get a voice that says, "My mother likes flowers," that might not rank too high. Think of a ranking system more as a chart. On the bottom would be the three current classes of EVPs, but on the side would be a ranking of one to four on its relevance. At the crossroads would be its new classification. A Class A ranked a four represents the best possible proof. Running it through this kind of process might also help eliminate random radio transmissions or other non-ghost information picked up via your recorder.

Take that same question and run a clear EVP through it:

Are you the one knocking on the door?

1. **Tigers like to eat ice cream.** This has no relevance to the question asked and does not even make sense.

2. **I like to eat ice cream.** This makes a bit more sense and might convey the reason why the ghost is knocking. It wants ice cream.

3. **They won't give me ice cream.** This has a stronger feel as to why there might be knocking.

4. **Yes. I want some ice cream.** This response has answered the question and given a reason.

Is This an Orb?

JEFF BELANGER, the Mayor of Ghostvillage, often gets e-mails from people looking to have their evidence verified. They send him everything they can get, sometimes giving him scans of photos taken decades ago. Most have a glowing dot somewhere, and people are convinced this means there is something in their house watching their children and creeping into their rooms at night. Knowing there is a weight to his words, Belanger thinks before answering, but always answers the same way. What the person has captured is 100% an orb. Of course, that doesn't mean it's a ghost. Let me rephrase. Almost never does it mean there is a ghost.

Figure 9.8
Orbs?

These little balls of light are the gold standard, but too often people are panning for fool's gold. They spend time hoping they get them and then scanning pictures looking for them, and finding one explains everything away. They place significance on their location in a picture and their size and color, and people even see faces in them. There is a good reason people who do not believe in ghosts are not cramping their necks to see these pictures, or most spirit photography. There just is no telling what is a ghost and what might be a bug stopping in to say hello.

The Anti-Orb Movement

Orb: A sphere.

The pendulum has swung, and it is not in response to a question asked by a medium. Much of the late '90s and the early part of the 21st century was a race to get the best orb in a picture. Ghostly pictures have always been the cornerstone of evidence, but the classic ghostly figure was replaced by eerie spheres of spirit energy. No one was quite sure at the time what made the best orb, and usually the argument had to do with someone defending why their ghost was best.

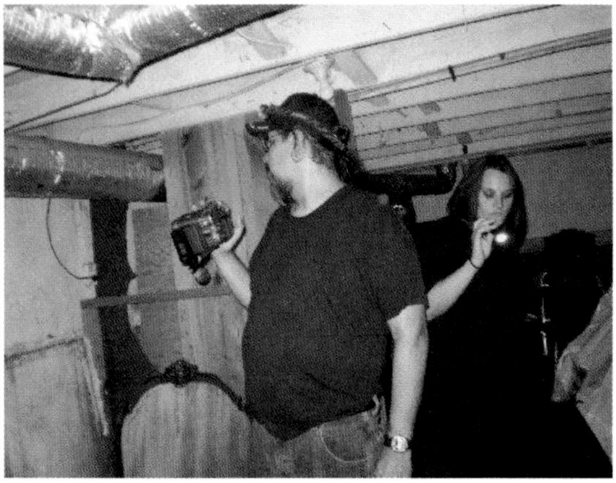

Figure 9.9
Notice how easily another investigator's light, or the light from another source, can become an orb. *Picture courtesy of the Native American Ghost Society.*

Orbs have always been a part of the paranormal, even before the chase was on. Native Americans sometimes called them Tei Pai Wankas and believed seeing them was like coming upon dead relatives. The term Will-o-the-Wisp was used by Europeans later, but the idea was basically the same. Railroad tracks and bridges, as well as cemeteries, were sometimes home to them, creating legends and folklore about the dead in those locations. These ghost lights were thought to be the spirits who had enough energy to be made partly whole and were mainly seen with the naked eye. Detractors saw them as either semi-explosive natural gases or the imagination. They have also existed in pictures, but the rise of better noncommercial cameras and digital photography has increased their number, making people believe we finally have the technology to see the dead. Being able to control the exposure and advances in flash are partly to blame, as well as the sensitivity of these tools and the ability to take multiple pictures in a short period of time. The field became flooded with pictures of orbs, and the debate began.

Many ghost hunters who have been in the field for a while don't put much weight in these photos. There are too many things that can show up on a camera. My uncle was famous for having the best collection of pictures of his thumb, with a few camera straps thrown in. Once you can account for these things, the hurdles get a bit more complicated.

Figure 9.10
A bit obvious, but notice how the flash reflects off the glass in the picture.

I have a glass globe that looks creepy when I take pictures of my son playing with his indoor basketball hoop, but other reflective surfaces in a location might surprise you. While not an orb, white walls can glow orange under the right conditions. Any surface with glass or even a shiny metal object can become otherworldly. These can be identified, but some orbs float in the air with nothing visible causing a glare. Dust and moisture are the most common reasons for these to show up. The flash of a camera hits these specks and reflects back, and because most of these exist as somewhat circular objects, they come back looking round. Kick up some dust in your house, snap a picture and see the dead rise. There are also bugs and pollen to deal with. Actually, 99 percent of orb photos can be dismissed just by looking at the evidence.

Figure 9.11
A ghostly appearance intentionally made by Josh Mantello to show his investigators what not to look for. He kicked up dust to create this.
Picture courtesy of Josh Mantello and the Berkshire Paranormal Group.

But There Is That One Percent, Right?

Then there is the other one percent. Investigating the paranormal is usually about cutting away all that can be explained naturally and dealing with the fraction of information left over. If a 2×4 is the amount of perceived ghostly activity, imagine the really baffling stuff to be a splinter. After the settling of houses and bad pipes, dismissed spirit photography takes the biggest chunk.

That annoying little one percent is still there though and has to be dealt with. There are two ways to start figuring out whether or not your picture might be genuine. Consider the conditions and the location first. Were you in a dusty location, such as an abandoned asylum or a basement? Were you outside right after a rain storm or where bugs were biting at your neck? Were there two other investigators in the area snapping pictures and walking around with equipment that could be reflective or with small lights?

Figure 9.12
The haunted room before he kicked up the dust.
Picture courtesy of Josh Mantello and the Berkshire Paranormal Group.

If you have made it through the first stage and ruled out more pragmatic possibilities, look at the picture itself. It's not enough that you got one. You now have to take a hard look at how it shows up, and this is where the debate continues. Orbs that have that transparent look to them are dust, and those that seem to have faces inside them are probably moisture. The lines of the face are actually the crystallization of the water. Spheres with tails or that have a solid center and then get softer toward the edges are harder to explain away. Really solid balls with no known light source and perceived density are the best.

Figure 9.13
A picture taken during the baby shower.

Here is an alarm for the really science-based investigators out there. If you get an EVP of a man saying to put the gun down and there is a history in the location of a man being shot, that history gives the EVP weight. In much the same way, the story behind a haunting might lend credibility to a ghost photo. I captured one during the baby shower for my son. It was in a known haunted location where the ghost of a woman was said to roam the hall. She was murdered by her husband when it was discovered she was pregnant with another man's baby. Mom and the unborn child were killed and buried on the property. The orb was discovered next to my son's godmother, right level with where her stomach, a possible bleed point for spirit energy was. If this ghost was going to manifest, it would be at a baby shower, and her location was near a vital family member. The picture itself is unexplainable, and when you factor in the back story with the quality of the photo, it makes for strong evidence.

Figure 9.14
A close-up of Elizabeth.

The best advice is to cut the flash if you can. If light allows, go solo. Remember, you're not trying to capture a picture your girlfriend can use to springboard her modeling career. Out of focus, low light pictures might not look pretty, but they can show a ghost just as well as a perfectly lit one. Take dirty pictures and if they still come out, you might have something there.

Beauty Is in the Eye

I remember an old episode of the show *Thirtysomething* where an artist was on a date with one of the main characters. He asked her to draw a picture he showed her, and when she balked at the offer, he turned the picture upside down. He told her to ignore the picture and just draw the lines. She took the pen and when he showed her the result when it was over, it was almost exact. He said a very romantic line about changing her perspective and making the impossible possible.

Working with pictures, while not nearly as romantic, benefits from the same advice. While taking the pictures, try to get things skewed by snapping the camera different ways, but the same can be said for looking at it when you're done. It is not enough just to scan for orbs and then move on to the next photo.

Evaluate each picture in different ways, especially if you have a prompt for doing so, such as a reading or an odd feeling. A basic photo editor that comes with your computer will do the trick, but there are more advanced programs on the market. In addition to flipping a picture upside down and on its side, you can change the color features of the image itself. The most readily available adjustments are the contrast and the brightness. By running the picture up and down the scale, you can bring out slight differences between objects in the picture. Not only does this give you a new perspective on the image, it also might offer you some aspect of size and texture.

Photo editors can also make you feel a bit like Sherlock Holmes. Take out your virtual magnifying glass and zoom into places where there are anomalies. Something might be hidden in the corner of the photo, or taking a closer look at something, such as an orb, might reveal the natural cause.

Figure 9.15
An odd figure caught in the window.

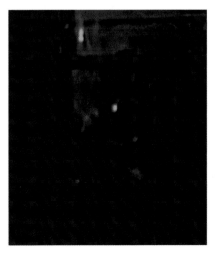

Figure 9.16
The same picture with some manipulation to try to bring it out.

I was documenting my wife's pregnancy for her mother who lived in another state. Every few weeks, we would take the obligatory side shot to document how big her belly was getting. I was looking at one of these photos one day and saw a strange shadow in the window. I zoomed in and caught a shot of someone looking in who would have to be floating to reach our second floor. I then ran it through some image changers. I looked over the room, trying to recreate the ghost with things in our apartment, but I finally had to label it unexplained.

Other Things to Look For

Whether looking at unaltered photos or using some form of manipulation, here are some things that may also be of interest.

Ghostly Mists: These are probably the most natural unnatural objects you can catch. If you find one in a house, you either have a ghost or the house is on fire. If you are outside, there are more explanations, the most common being actual fog. Document the temperature where you are, but also think about what it was during the hours leading up the investigation. It is also said a good digital camera can capture the carbon dioxide being released from trees, and many swampy areas, even if they appear dry, do release the cliché gas. Don't make too much of faces you see in any mist, but note it changing its density or following you around.

Figure 9.17
©istockphoto.com/Stan Rohrer

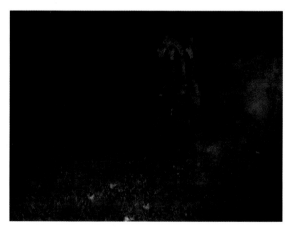

Figure 9.18
A mist caused by the investigator's breath.
Picture courtesy of Josh Mantello and the Berkshire Paranormal Group.

Figure 9.19
A mist caught at a party that is a little harder to explain away.
Picture courtesy of Brooke Hutchel.

Rods: There was a rod craze a few years ago where people believed ghosts had reached a critical mass and were in danger of coming to get us. People found streaks of light through their pictures and placed more weight on them than orbs. Treat them both the same way. Most are objects caught in flight or captured due to over-exposure.

Figure 9.20
Rod intentionally made for a group's training.
Picture courtesy of Josh Mantello and the Berkshire Paranormal Group.

Figures and Shadows: If only they would stop and smile for the camera. Sometimes a picture picks up a face, shadow, or full body apparition. These are the jackpot and need careful examination to account for anything that may have caused them. Back in the day, a traditional camera may have suffered from a double exposure or some damage to the film, but with digital, you do not get the same interference.

Glowing Lights: These are a bit more solid, although not literally, than orbs but suffer from the same downfall as our spheres of light. They are usually the result of bad photography and powerful flashes. Be careful if they are coming from under doors, and always try to recreate the light. This makes them easier to dismiss but harder to explain when you can't.

Figure 9.21
A unexplained dark figure seen in the picture that was not visible when it was snapped.
Picture courtesy of Kathleen Popola, Blue Moon Paranormal Investigations.

Classifying Paranormal Photographs

Contributed by Josh Mantello, founder of the Berkshire Paranormal Group.

Over the past few years, the people in the electronic voice phenomena field have been placing their recordings into classifications based on the clarity and ease of understanding, assigning them a rank from Class A to C. This system has worked well for them, but I wonder why other aspects of the paranormal investigating field have not adopted a similar grading system.

Recently, I was preparing a presentation based on photographs and the paranormal, which would show a series of pictures ranging from a fake picture to some that I thought had a ghost in them. While preparing this presentation, I wanted an easier way to explain and categorize the pictures for the attendees and a method to explain why I thought they were ghost pictures or why I thought they were fake and misleading based on known natural causes or picture anomalies. I then developed a grading system not unlike what the people in the EVP field use, putting the pictures in a ranking from A to C.

These pictures classifications were as follows:

Class C: Natural causes can immediately be contributed as the cause of the anomaly in the photograph. In other words, not a ghost picture.

- **Orbs in a picture that was taken in a dusty room or when raining.**
- **Fogs, mists, and ectos (physical residue of a ghost) in pictures when someone was smoking nearby or it was foggy outside.**
- **Apparition in window when someone was standing behind window with sheet over his head.**

Class B: Natural causes cannot be ruled out as the cause of the anomaly in the picture, but other documented paranormal activity was occurring at the time of the picture being taken.

- **An orb the looks similar to dust orbs, but its placement coincides with someone's personal experience or high EMF reading and/or temperature variations.**
- **Matrixing cannot be ruled out as the cause of an apparition, but someone else present during the picture might have seen or experienced something.**

Class A: Natural causes cannot be found as the cause of the anomaly in the photograph.

- **A smoke or mist in the pictures when it is known that no one was smoking at the time of the picture and it was too warm for breath to show up.**
- **Light streaks when shutter speed on camera was set to a fast speed or a tripod was used.**

It is possible to mix these using a + /– along with each classification. These can come in handy and work well when we as investigators start trying to present our pictures as evidence to other investigators or the public. Obviously, we won't be showing our class C pictures to either the public or other investigators as evidence. Class B might be something worth showing to other investigators because they will respect and understand the personal experience and events surrounding the pictures whereas the public may not understand. But maybe a good Class B+ picture would still be appropriate for the public with good explanations. Obviously, a Class A is what you want to show to the public and let the skeptics and naysayers try to pick apart. Offer it up, knowing you can't find a logical and reasonable explanation for the anomalies.

Even if you do choose to use all the classes of pictures as presentable evidence, at least putting them into classes for the public to see will help people to better understand the picture and what they may be looking at.

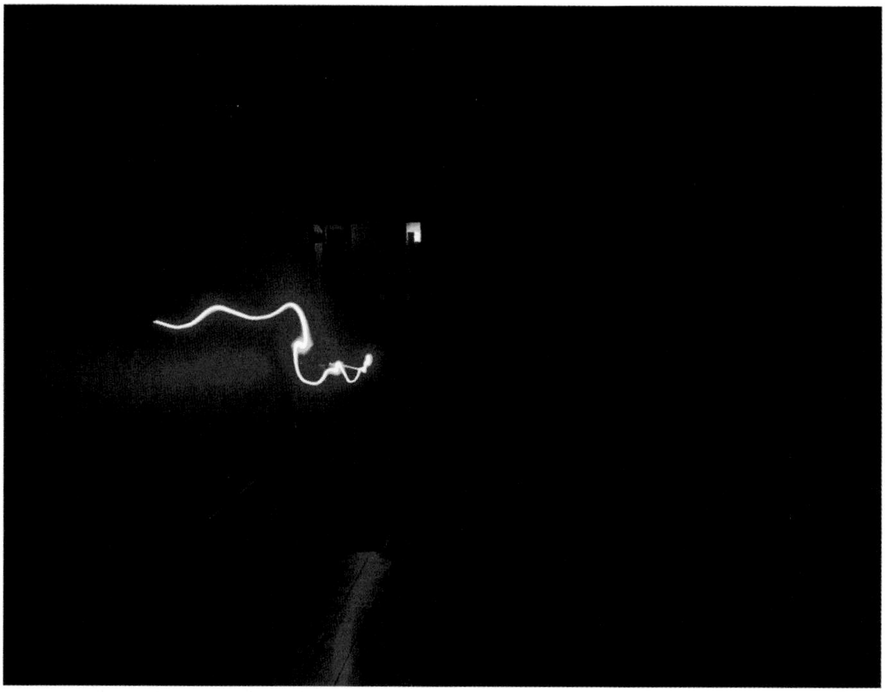

Figure 9.22
A moving orb created by shutter speed and an LED light.
Picture courtesy of Josh Mantello and the Berkshire Paranormal Group.

Just because we give the label of Class A to a picture doesn't necessarily mean it is the final proof of the paranormal we need and are all looking for. I would only say that this may fall under being 70 to 90 percent proof or documentation of a haunting; I surely wouldn't say a house is haunted based on one Class A picture. This is mostly based on the fact that there are a lot of natural causes out there and environmental effects that sometimes even the most scientifically controlled investigation can't control or document.

I offer this up to the paranormal investigating and ghost hunting community as maybe a future guideline to help present or document their photographs during investigations. I tried to keep it simple so that it can be adopted easily without large explanations or hours of teaching, but obviously, a good general knowledge of photography and cameras does help. If we start using this on our web pages and as evidence it might help the public and new investigators looking to our pictures to see them as guidelines to base their future evidence on. They might better understand what a really good ghost picture is and what isn't.

Natural Pictures

Remember, you are not only evaluating every picture for signs of a haunting. You are also looking for the natural causes of what you see. If you see something unexplained, try to explain it. Look around the rest of the picture for what might be leading to the bright light or the rod streaking down the middle. To some degree this means becoming well versed in what things look like under the influence of light or paying attention to sources of light to try to predict where shadows should appear, but when you begin to enhance your awareness of these factors, it becomes a part of your inner skeptic.

Figure 9.23
Another ghostly mist, but this one was caused by cigar smoke.
Picture courtesy of Josh Mantello and the Berkshire Paranormal Group.

What Do All These Readings Mean?

YOU SPEND MONEY ON ALL the right equipment and then find the perfect place to keep it on you while you search and scan the location looking for a ghost. You write everything down and document changes that happen on multiple pieces of equipment at the same time. At the end of the night, you are left standing with a notebook full of numbers and a sense of accomplishment. Do all of these readings really mean anything though?

There's a short answer to the question and a long one, and I usually like to take the short answer. For a moment, assume the science of ghost hunting makes sense, that there really is a science to it. It would still be such an imperfect field that any readings would be lost in a haze of uncertainty. What did all of those beeps and flickering lights mean? Your needle moved, but what made it move? How much of a change in electromagnetic energy constitutes a ghost?

More than any other evidence you get, these field meter readings can't exist in a vacuum. There might be a reason for that quick figure you captured in the mirror, but you can note things and then try and explain them away. It is different for energy readings. There is too much we don't know about the natural EMF or radiation around us or how much our furnace or refrigerator might give off. Severe spikes can be explained away, but investigators who rely on equipment also take pride in the small movements they get. This can't be explained away as easily; some we label unexplained and theorize about it being a ghost.

That was a short answer. The longer answer points to the role an investigator might play in the development of ghost hunting as a science. All the information you gather on an investigation gives you a more complete picture of the haunting. Meters are a part of this, and while it might be hard to establish a standard for how much of any one thing points at a spirit, collecting this information might give you a context for the evidence.

Think of yourself as a scientist for a moment. You are trying to explain for the first time how much time it takes to boil water. At some point, the rolling boil happens and the answer is clear, but there were steps along the way. At what temperature did the first bubble appear and when did the first bubble in the middle of the pan flare up. These would give you the best picture of the relationship between heat and boiling.

Now transfer that to the field. Alone, the numbers mean nothing. Side by side and compared to others and then shared with fellow investigators, patterns start to come to the surface. There is no reading that can prove the existence of a ghost by itself, but enough of the bits and pieces can provide a baseline for the future.

Here are some important things to document when investigating:

- **Time**
- **Date**
- **Weather and temperature (outside the house, inside, and in each room)**
- **Activity seen in the location**
- **What the room is used for**
- **EMF baseline**
- **Who was in the room and what equipment they had**

Shadows and the Wind

IT IS SAID THAT WHEN John Carpenter shot the original *Halloween*, he made sure there was movement in the corners of each shot, such as the wind blowing a tree or a car driving by. The intended mood made people feel something could jump out at any moment. It fed our fear of that which we see only out of the corner of our eye. The ghosts are preparing to jump out any time now.

Moving pictures can be seductive. There is something very cool about walking around shooting with Nightvision or some other kind of light-enhancing equipment. Whether it is the glowing eyes, the idea of making light out of dark, or just because the guys on television do it, it makes you feel you are a bit more invested than the next group. Shooting video is important to any investigation, so make looking at the world through that eerie greenish-gray light part of your life. A well shot video showing something unexplained might be dramatic enough to convince someone there is something to this ghost thing.

Watching the Stillness

Looking at video for a phantom can be a time-consuming venture. Imagine watching a home movie your aunt has shot. The subject might be interesting, but she keeps pausing it to point out the details. You smile for a while but notice the minutes ticking away. Video might shoot a wider range than the human eye can see with Nightvision or infrared, so assume the first thing you are looking for is something walking across the frame. After that, it's all about finding that shadow that does not belong or that small ball of light moving in a way it shouldn't.

Your first exposure is important, so you have to make a decision about how to handle the evidence. You can run it through your television and leave it like that or make a file using a film editor on your computer. The latter allows you to archive it and makes the footage accessible to other features, such as zooming or converting it to pictures for manipulation. You should take the same approach as an EVP evaluation, cutting the footage into segments and viewing them for just a few minutes at a time. If you stare too long, everything becomes important or your own boredom after 10 minutes might cause you to miss something.

Figure 9.24
The problem with a solitary webcam picture.
The resolution and the delay in the image don't always make for good evidence.

I remember when I was 10 and took karate classes. I don't remember how to do a high kick, but I remember the 16-year-old sensei telling me to always look at my opponent's belly button. If he moved any part of his body, I could see it. I take the same perspective on looking for ghosts. Movements can be small, and if you focus on the right side, you'll have to spend an equal amount of time paying attention to the middle and the left. I choose to focus on everything all at once by not zeroing in on one part. I intentionally allow my vision to zone out, and when there is something there to see, I am more likely to notice it.

The good thing about video is, it exists as a moment in time but running, so you can pause your memories. When you see movement, pause, rewind to 10 seconds before the movement, and track it. What caused it? Account for every light and every person in the location to make sure someone has not moved in front of the camera and caused a shadow. Look for every natural reason before you even consider the paranormal, including wind if you are outside or drafts if you are inside. Notice other things in the area. If you see a shadow move quickly or a rustle of something, see if other things in that vicinity also move. The wind takes predicable but unfamiliar trips through areas.

When you have determined that a movement is unexplained, examine the object itself. Pause the frame and zoom to get a better look at it. Did you see the movement when the shot was taken and make note of it in the audio track? Does it have density to it, or is it more like shadow or light? How large is it, and where does it appear? It is not enough to just see something; you have to see it in the context of the scene. If you zoom in on anything, it takes on weight, but how large or solid is it in comparison to the objects around it?

When I was on an investigation at a famous hot dog restaurant, we filmed a room where people had experienced odd sounds and other activity in a residence above the restaurant. We captured a few sketchy orbs and noticed some odd things about the place, but ultimately came away with little evidence. That is until we got home... .
I noticed something unexplained in some of the footage shot of the bed in the room. A clear object appeared on the bed in only a small fraction of connected scans of the room. It was there and then not. It was solid enough that we would have noticed it on the bed while we shot in there, but nothing was said about it. It was not until the investigation was over that I noticed it move slightly and then was able to see it and then have it disappear in the next shot.

Figure 9.25
The unexplained object seen at the hot dog restaurant.

The Movement of Bugs

No matter what you have captured, be it an orb or a shadow, the most important part of the evaluation is to determine how it moves. How does it enter the shot and leave, but more importantly, how does it interact with the world around it? When it passes something, does it obstruct it or can you still see it? This not only gives you a handle on where it was in the room but also indicates how opaque it is. If you see a shadow come in quick and then disappear, it might be something moving in front of the light, but something that moves across the room and then vanishes might be something more. Although it is hard to break it down mathematically, think of it in those terms to some degree. The longer something is seen and the more it moves, the higher the probability it might be something ghostly. It might be better to think of it in the reverse terms. If the odds of it being natural or something that can be explained are 100 percent, that percentage goes down with every frame it remains.

A full body ghost holding a sign might be the best evidence you can get, but there are other things to look for. Orbs and shadows are the most common, but if you look too closely for those, you might miss other manifestations. Mists may often be dismissed when you experience them in the field, but on camera after the fact you might notice parts that are unnaturally thick or movement that might be irregular. If you are outside and the wind is blowing one way but the mist is following you, that might be a hit. The companion to the mist is what I like to call the shimmer. More and more people are describing apparitions they see as looking like heat rising off the pavement or a refraction of light roughly in human form. They notice it in conjunction with other activity, so it is something worth looking for.

You can be fooled by the same things in moving pictures as you can by still pictures. One of the most common mistakes people can make is to track orbs coming in and out of the frame only to discover that they have been focusing on the movement of bugs. They can glow off Nightvision or flashlights and can mimic what we think a ghost moves like. The best way to get around this is to understand how a bug flies. They take straight paths but change direction quickly. They don't make slow turns. If something moves, floats, and then slowly changes direction, that is most likely not a bug. If there is a trail behind it, examine it more closely because you have not seen a bug.

On the Go

Matt Moniz, a scientist and radio host for "Spooky Southcoast," was investigating Waverly Hill Sanitarium, a well known haunted location in Kentucky. As he filmed his movements with military grade Nightvision, a dark figure appeared behind him, seeming to peek its head out from around the corner. It looked for a moment, seemed to notice it was being filmed, and then ducked back out. The entire encounter lasted only a few seconds, but it may have been captured better had the crew not been on the move.

Much of an investigation is captured while the investigators are moving through a haunted location. This makes it harder to evaluate the evidence after the fact because it becomes more difficult to account for other team members and the moments are shorter. Evidence may also be contaminated by how quickly the camera goes by it. Think of sitting in a stationary car and having the car next to you pull away. For at least a moment, it seems as if your car is moving and the other is still. Conduct the evaluation the same way as you would with a still camera, but take this into consideration. Think of our probability equation earlier and move the percentage back toward 100 percent explainable.

While a still assessment can be done at high speed, a moving assessment benefits from slowing the tape down. It might take more time, but you can't focus on one spot and notice movement because the shot is moving. Instead, you need to take everything in and compare it. This means more time on each frame to see if anything changes.

A Few More Bits

The audio track of a video recording should not be ignored. When you run the raw film into a film editor, it will automatically create a running field of the audio captured. This can be examined for EVPs in the same way you look for them when using a sound program. Zoom the audio track as much as you can and look for unexplained jumps. It might be a footstep, but it might be something more. It may also give you a marker for visual activity.

Remember that not all paranormal activity is visual in the same way. Everyone wants to see a ghost on film, but the spirit might have manifested in a different way. During the same investigation where we caught the clear object, we found another clue indicating we were not alone in the restaurant. As we left, the owner began to tell a story of how he passed by one night to check on the place and found the light in the same weird bedroom on. No one ever went in there, and he got angry with the person on the second floor for going up and not shutting the light off. The next day, he found the man had never entered the third floor. As he was telling the story, we noticed the light was on in the room we had just left. We had made sure to shut it off, even making note of it on camera, and no one was left in the closed restaurant.

These are the kinds of things you need to notice when looking for flying orbs. Has something changed in the room? Are doors locked or lights on? It might go unnoticed during the investigation, but you can see it clearly on tape. It also might help to clear up arguments over whether the toy was on the floor when you left the room.

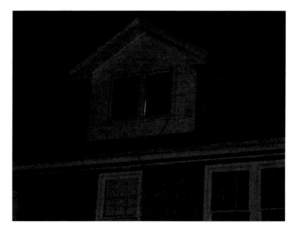

Figure 9.26
The light was off when we left the room.

Measure Twice, Cut Once

MY FATHER LOVES BOOKSTORES. He shops online for books more than I do today, but he still loves to go into the store and walk around looking at titles. He used to take me out every weekend while he looked for books. He would thumb through them, pass them through his hands, observe other people in the store. He would do this week after week, but as a small boy, I was annoyed because he never bought anything. Why look if you had no intention of buying? I asked him why one day. "The book didn't move since last week," he told me. "It must not be good if no one bought it."

He had the same trait the first time we went to buy a computer. We went to three stores and asked the same questions about the same computers, leaving empty-handed each time. The next week, the same thing happened until we purchased the first one we had looked at in the beginning. "I had to see if people would say the same things about it." I never understood what he meant until my father-in-law, a former contractor, explained it to me one day. Measure twice, cut once.

In the paranormal field, we want to leap to conclusions. So much of field work has to do with what happens in the moment, which you hope is then backed up by looking at the evidence later. We look because we hope to find, but we sometimes put the cart before the horse.

Duplicity

One day you may get an EVP that says, "Hello. I am the ghost of John Johnson, and I would just like to tell you I am dead. Tell my wife I love her." Until that day comes, your evidence should be beyond reproach and backed up by other evidence. This means there is a need for doubling up on what you bring in, or duplicity as the military calls it, in all phases of the investigation. Assign a number to the quality of the evidence you get, rating it from one to five with five being the best. Be honest when you do this, even overly critical, and then see where different pieces of equipment overlap in quality. A well-defined orb with the presence of an EVP and a radiation spike would be better proof than any of these individually. Most investigators carry an analog and a digital recorder with them and compare the audio evidence. When they get something on both, it might mean something natural. The opposite can be said of evidence that crosses mediums.

Don't Be a Stranger

I never share evidence with the owner of a suspected haunted house until I have been there three times. The first time, I tour the house and interview the members of the family who have had something happen to them. The next time, I conduct a full investigation, like a clean sweep of the whole location. I then look into all the evidence, but here a crucial step is left out by many investigators. I call it a ghost hunt wish list. Imagine you could conduct the investigation again.

What would you do differently, or what would you devote more time to? This should be based on the evidence you get. If you got an EVP in the kitchen and none in the basement, you would want to spend more time where the family eats.

This wish list also should come as you find out more about the location or do research into similar activity. Say you get a picture of a figure that looks like an old man. You then find out there was an old man who died on the second floor. You might want to take another trip and make contact with this man using information you found out about him. This is also true for messages you receive. I once recorded an EVP of someone saying, "look at the dog." When I went back to the same location, I asked questions about the dog and got responses.

If you investigate a house, make that third trip essential. An odd shadow might be explained away now that you know what to look for. A temperature drop might have been a wind that night.

Leave the Demon Out, Will You?

One of the biggest leaps I see investigators making is assigning demonic causes to potential ghostly encounters. It makes sense with the media exposure to these dark forces, and so much of demon lore is ambiguous at best. There are no confirmed meter readings for them, and one would imagine they would not need energy in the same way as spirits, so all an investigator is left with is this lore. The signs are well known: the smell of garbage or sewer, dark figures, things moving around the house. These could really be signs of just about any type of haunting.

Some demonologist say the vast majority of hauntings have a demonic root, but the estimate might be high. The real number might be closer to nothing, so do not be so quick to call a bad smell a demon.

A Sample Investigation

In Figure 9.27, you'll see some of the notes I took during an investigation. By the time I entered the basement of the private residence, I had been investigating for over an hour. The size of the house allowed us to all stay together while we swept, so the names and equipment information are with the notes from the previous room. When I went outside before entering the room, it felt cooler to me, so I noted the outside temperature again.

I began by noting the temperature in the basement as well as a baseline EMF reading. The temperature changed several times, but the EMF remained the same so I only noted the difference once. I was careful to note the temperature changes during the EVP session because of the dramatic swing, especially during a certain question. I also made a note of having to stop the session and start another track as well as the furnace turning on when we ended the session.

I also found it important to describe the figure the family had seen on the stairs, but what I want you to also see is how I wrote down how many pictures I took and how many used flash. This helps to relate other evidence to when the picture was taken and evaluate the picture knowing if the flash might have caused light in the picture. I also wrote down when we heard a noise on the stairs and its relative time during the EVP session.

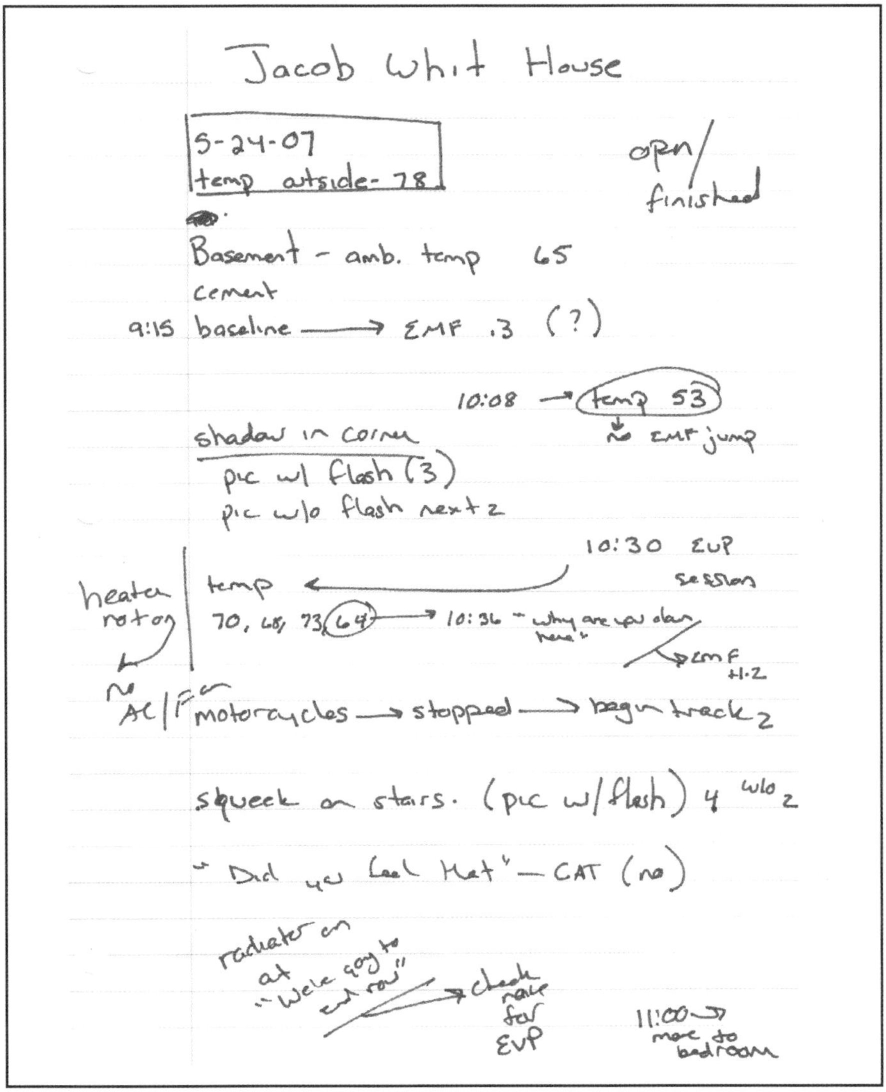

Figure 9.27

Like all of the evidence I gather, the information from that night was transferred to a digital format and stored together. This allowed me to ask other experienced investigators to look at what I recorded and makes the information I got that night safe and sound should I need it again. Unlike other investigations, the family did not want me to come back because the activity stopped after I investigated and they were a bit spooked by the whole thing. Usually this information would have made it to a typed format without my horrible handwriting for the family and my own files, but with the investigation reaching a stonewall, I spent my time on another investigation. Perhaps they'll call again (ghosts have a habit of going away and then coming back) and I'll have the chance to show them what I found.

10

Connecting with Others

I OPENED AN E-MAIL FROM A MAN NAMED KEITH. He knew of some haunted areas around where he lived and had been out in the field looking for ghosts for several years. There was evidence and experience, but the group he had been involved with had just disbanded, and he was looking to hook up with another one to keep the spirit alive. Having viewed my site, he was hoping we had a field investigator position that needed to be filled. I wrote him back telling him I did not have a group but rather worked with other investigators and organizations when I went out. It allowed me to choose the best hunter for the job and not worry about any of the internal conflicts of working with a group.

He e-mailed me back that he didn't understand. How could I have a site with no group? Who was I affiliated with? I composed and then deleted the e-mail I had written him that I aligned myself with my wife, but sometimes my sister took priority too.

The nature of the paranormal beast is to establish and then join, although not always in that order. It is a smart idea in some ways. Not only are you automatically a part of a community, but there is something to be said for safety in numbers when you are out in the field. Whether you join a team or form one of your own, the paranormal is about making a connection to others.

Finding a Group and Founding a Group

THERE IS A PARANORMAL dating site on the Internet. When you sign up, you give your age and sex, the area you live in, and your thoughts on the paranormal. You can meet online and discuss your ideas on ghosts, and then maybe meet and go looking for them together. There is a romantic side and people use this as a way to date, but the site also offers a chance to meet people in your area looking for a haunted friendship.

The site is just another evolution of a basic principle of investigating. Ghost hunters look for one another as much as they go out looking for apparitions. As you continue your ghostly journey, one of the next steps is to look for people to investigate with.

Figure 10.1
©istockphoto.com/JailFree

The Internet Revolution

The want ads are dead. It is almost impossible to find like-minded people down the street without the help of a computer. You might be able to meet someone at a conference or a book signing somewhere, but the easiest way to see people from your area who are investigating is to go online. Chances are you have seen these groups because your interest has drawn you to find hauntings in your town. Now it is time to stop viewing their pages, e-mail them, and see if they are looking for another person to go out.

Hit the information superhighway and find some investigators. The age we live in has provided us with as much diversity and specialization as you will ever need as an investigator. You may be an 80-year-old man who believes the best approach to the paranormal is a Christian one. There is a group for you. You may be a teenager looking for a junior group that practices Wicca as a way to connect to the other side. Someone is out in cyberspace trying to find you. There is someone near you; it just might take some time to find them.

At first, it might be best to join an established group rather than form your own. Sometimes it happens quite naturally with people you know. You and your friends all decide to start a group, and the only thing left to do is come up with a name. Other times you need to find people in your state or your town and make yourself known. Hopefully, there are several to choose from, but keep in mind the significance of not only where a group is but where they investigate.

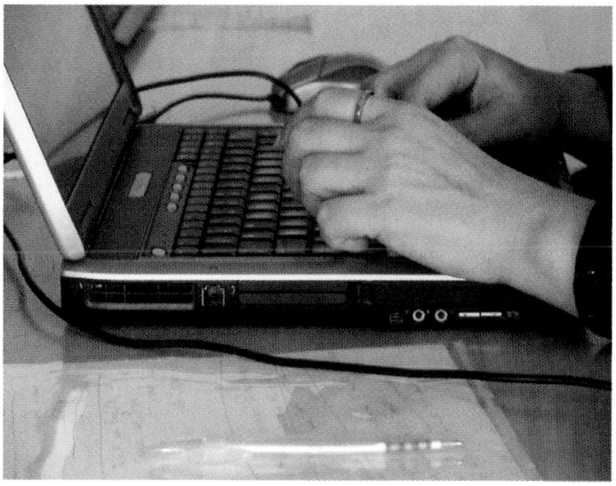

Figure 10.2
©istockphoto.com/JailFree

Most ghost hunters have a bit of an ego, so they most likely have photos of themselves and what they think about the paranormal on their site. Don't leave anyone out, but you might be more comfortable with people who are your own age. You can see who they are and what kind of work they are doing, but it might take a few meetings to find people who will work well with you. Send out some e-mails and see what happens. Here are some things to consider when looking and writing:

- **The way you write is a reflection of who you are.**
- **Some groups are tight knit, so don't take it personally if they deny you.**
- **Size does matter to some, so they might not want to take more people on.**
- **Avoid groups where multiple family members are involved, especially husbands and wives. Personal conflicts find their way into the group.**
- **Don't overstate what you have done on your own, but feel free to brag about equipment you have. Remember, Ozzy Osbourne was accepted into Black Sabbath because he had his own amp.**
- **Be leery of people who charge to have you in the group or whose time requirements are beyond what you are willing to give. Many groups do charge something for membership, but if the price becomes too high, start to ask where your money is going.**
- **Don't be eager to join a group when there is an uneven level of power among members. It's a fight waiting to happen.**
- **Don't join a group that worships another one, even a very popular one, but one who seeks to establish themselves.**
- **Remember predators of all kinds can hide in the paranormal community. It says something about you that you are interested in ghosts and someone might be up to no good. Never meet anyone alone or in a remote location.**

A quick check around the net will show you the odd requirements some groups have. Overall, this is done to ensure the best investigators and not just someone looking for fame. As you search, the more established a group, the more it may require. Several groups I know will make you buy a certain book and learn its techniques to become involved, and one even goes so far as to provide a written test, which you must pass before they consider you part of the official group. Until the passing score comes, you have an "in-training" tag attached to your name. More established groups will often force you to apprentice for a while before you get your t-shirt and business cards.

Are They Serious

Much of this implies that paranormal investigators take themselves a bit too seriously. There are dangers to working with ghosts, but many groups take it one step too far. With a limited number of haunted areas and only so many media outlets to get their name in, many are tight with their evidence and guard membership like the Skull and Bones. This may be for you and may be a complete turn off. The good news is there are people out there who have the same level of seriousness and commitment you do, no matter what that might be. Hold out for the best fit.

Figure 10.3
A website promoting paranormal unity.

There is bad news though, and it is twofold. Many of the groups doing the best work and being taken seriously in the community have strict guidelines and take themselves too seriously, which might be one of the reasons they have gotten so far. As the new person in, you might have to play the game in order to be accepted. As in any group, the newcomers are always having to prove themselves. The other bad news is that you will probably never enter a group that doesn't have some kind of hierarchy and plenty of drama. It is in the ghost hunter's nature.

Remember that membership with a group doesn't tie you into all they do. They might require too much from you, or personalities might not mesh well. Never sign a contract, although it probably wouldn't be legally binding, and know you are always free to go. You might get out in the field or attend some meeting with them and realize your ideas are far from where they are. You are always free to go and the only thing you might sacrifice is a relationship with someone you might not like anyway.

Don't get me wrong and decide to push away the idea of being in a group. There is a social aspect to being part of a paranormal group, often stemming from a desire to know you are not alone in your passion. Being in a group means bouncing around ideas and even safety on investigations. Finding the right group will help you and give you a compass in what you do. The trick is to find the one that best fits what you are looking for.

Meetings

I was recently out in the field with a well organized group. Small talk sparked up and they began to tell me about a recent trip they had made to a haunted restaurant. One started talking about something he had picked up on the stairs, something like a shadow moving down towards the group and then running back up. He had snapped a picture and was waiting to see what it might be. "Oh, that was Kelly in the upstairs bedroom moving out of the room into the hall," said another member of the group. He produced a computer printed close-up photograph of the shadow and a sneaker clearly visible in the upper corner. The first man asked why he hadn't been told about it because he had been waiting for the evidence to be evaluated. "You weren't at last week's meeting."

Getting together, even without a place to investigate, might be a vital part of a group's success. Every aspect of the professional world has some level of meeting you must go to, and often suffer through, to maintain relationships and keep everyone on the same page. Ghost hunters are no different. You may have signed up for going into cemeteries at night, but you might have to deal with sitting in someone's living room before you can go out. It may be the best time to show how new equipment works or to discuss how things are going with a case.

The best meetings are informal and mainly used to discuss evidence that has been gathered and new places to investigate. Many will deal with cases, or people who have sought the group's help.

This is when they become a productive part of the process, and some kind of organization is needed to ensure that everyone knows everything he needs to know. It also means more eyes and ears looking at evidence (remember the investigation equation) so it's good to have people to challenge what you find and evaluate evidence of their own.

Be careful of groups who have weekly meetings or have too much structure. These tend to degrade very quickly and offer too much opportunity for personalities to clash, especially over power in the group. Many organizations will have a limit to how many meetings you can miss before being asked to leave, I know one group that puts people on probation, although they are unclear about how you get out of trouble.

Think of meetings as people assembling to talk about something they have in common. That is how they should be. There is business, but there should be more time to tell stories about what has happened, share ideas, and just get to know each other.

Creating Your Own Group

You're in a job interview, and you know the question is coming. What are three things you don't do well or need to work on? The key is to make yourself sound self-aware and humble while still describing your best attributes. I always say, "I have a hard time delegating. I have high standards and want things to be done with that level of attention." What it really means is that I'm a controlling person, which might not be a bad thing when it comes to paranormal groups.

If you want it done right, at least by your standards, it might be best to form your own group. It is always recommended to investigate with others, so it is only a small leap to find people who want to do what you like to do. You maintain the organization of the ghost hunt and can hand-pick talented people you want to work with.

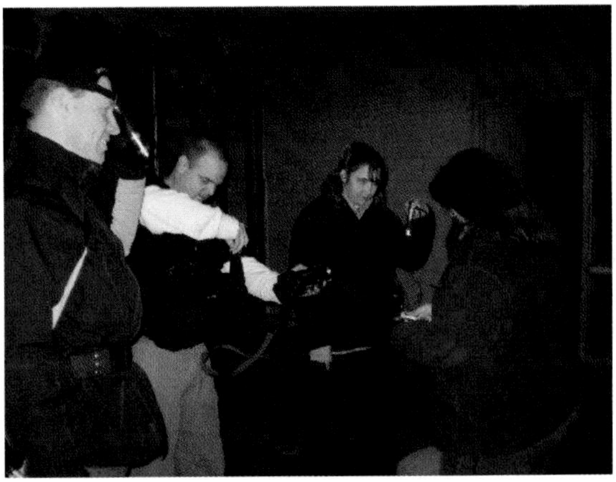

Figure 10.4
An investigation group just starting their hunt.
Picture courtesy of the Native American Ghost Society.

It is best to start with your friends because they're the ones you like spending time with anyway. Chances are, you know someone who shares your love of ghosts and he has a friend who shares your love. Pretty soon, you have four or five people all willing to work together. Stay at that number for a while. Learn to work together and establish what you do before you give yourself a name. After a while, come up with a name, create a website, and reach out to others. Five is a good number to stay at, but you might want to work with other groups from the area or connect with one from someplace you don't know very well when you plan to investigate there. There is always someone who knows more, and finding them will only help you.

Here are some helpful ideas when starting your own group:

- **Look for people with talents and use those talents rather than finding people who all think and act the same.**
- **Concentrate more on learning and investigating rather than titles.**
- **Have realistic standards and stick to them.**
- **Embrace the psi, spiritual, and scientific side and don't rely too heavily on one or the other.**
- **Choose people you would go out to dinner with or play a round of something (golf, Risk, darts) with. It is always a good measure of personalities that mesh well.**

There are some don'ts as well:

- **Don't come up with an acronym to represent your group just because it sounds good.**
- **Don't spend time attacking other groups. It makes everyone look bad.**
- **Don't publish the name of people who have been forced to leave the group on your website. The relationship didn't work. Move on.**
- **Don't be quick to leave out someone you don't like at first. They may challenge you in amazing ways.**
- **Don't fill your group with all like-minded people who always agree with you.**
- **Remember the reason you're out there in the first place.**

You Have to Have a Site

It is not enough today to just gather evidence and tell people what you do. In the modern world, people take you more seriously if you have your own website, and establishing one can be done so easily that it makes sense to invest the time and energy, and even the money, in one. It gets your name out there, as well as the name of your group if you have one, and allows people with cases and haunted areas to find you. Consider it a requirement. People in your town are already online, and no one will be able to get to you if you don't keep up.

There is good news for those with little computer knowledge. Most websites can be established for a small monthly fee, and some are free but force you to post advertisements. Sites such as MySpace offer you the opportunity to run a site through them, reaching people and allowing you to post videos and pictures from investigations. Add free blog space, and you have a presence on the net.

Figure10.5
©istockphoto.com/Ed Hidden

Most sites come with free software to edit and post your pages, so you never have to even learn what HTML stands for. Designing a page is no more difficult than putting together a digital collage, so establishing yourself is easier than ever. Here are a few pointers once you have created a website and you're waiting for connections to be made:

- **Go on as many message boards as possible and comment on stories or ideas posted. Always leave your web address.**
- **Add your site to your e-mail signature.**
- **Take advantage of any and all free search engine lists offered by your server.**
- **Create a links page and exchange with as many people as possible.**
- **Find popular keywords and add them to your site. I posted a story about a case near me investigated by the famous Ed and Lorraine Warren and found people were finding my site by searching for them. I added them to the hidden keywords of my site and included them in the writing on pages.**
- **Keep things fresh. It makes people come back and look through all of your pages.**
- **Mention known cases and people and then get very specific to where you are. You might be surprised how many people in your town are looking for local stories.**
- **Add a blog where you present and comment on what is new in the field or things you have heard or seen that interest you. It may even be a place where you or other group members can put up your own ideas or articles.**

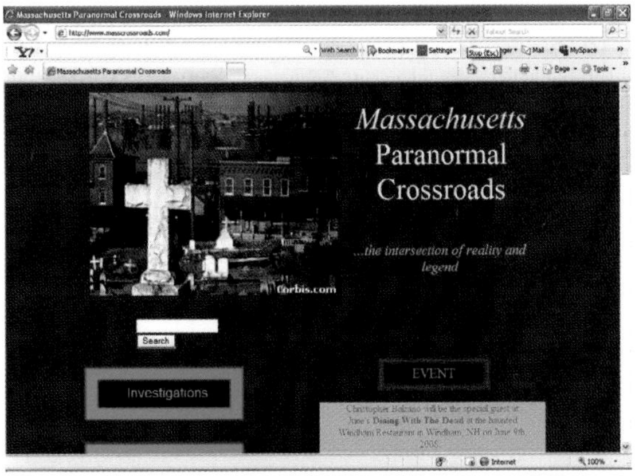

Figure 10.6
An example of a paranormal website.

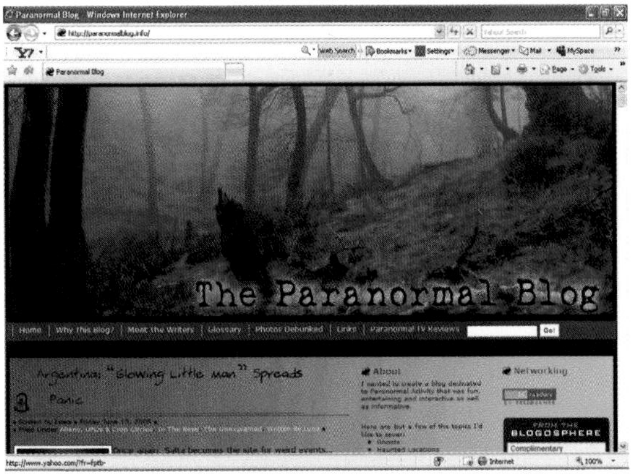

Figure 10.7
Another site that's more like a blog.

Roles and the Hierarchy

I WAS OFFERED A RAISE MY second year working in a library. I was asked to be the Senior Acquisitions Librarian, which in theory meant I had been the Junior Acquisitions Librarian without knowing it. It sparked an interesting exchange with my supervisor.

"Will I make more money?"

"Yes, but it is the same money you'd get in your yearly raise."

"Will I be in charge of others?"

"No, they still report to me."

"Will I have more of a say in what goes on here?"

"No, but you will have more responsibility. It also looks good on your resume and a business card."

I took the position because I had never been a Senior anything, but as the work piled up, I began to wonder just how my place on the company flow chart had changed.

It was bound to happen. When you get people together, there is a natural tendency for some to rise to the top as leaders and some to step back as followers. Encouraged by the model presented on the television show *Ghost Hunters*, paranormal groups do this very quickly. As soon as they form, they get job titles and responsibility, and they take them very seriously. They have everything in place, from lead investigator to member-in-training and oftentimes have a standardized way to move up the ladder, although I am not sure how many lead investigators you can have before the title loses power.

There is a positive side to all of this. During an investigation, an air of responsibility is needed. Organization provided by a leader helps to make the most out of a limited amount of time and resources. It also provides some accountability to members to mentor people who are less experienced.

The danger is when these roles become a bone of contention within the group. They spend more time fighting over leadership than looking for ghosts. I have seen this happen, and many times their roles in life are reflected in the group. Fights become frequent and are about more than you see on the surface. It also becomes concerning if any investigator becomes limited by the job title they have.

Figure 10.8
©istockphoto.com/TommL

Here are some of the popular titles and responsibilities being doled out:

- **Lead Investigator:** This is usually the title reserved for the founder of the group or someone who has been in the group for a certain amount of time.
- **Investigator:** This person did not found the group, but he has put his time in out there looking.
- **Investigator-in-Training:** One who has not paid his dues yet.
- **Case Manager:** This is the person who acts as the face of the group to the public. He gets the phone calls from the people in need and arranges the investigations. I find it troubling that this person is often a woman, like the only thing women are qualified to do is be a paranormal secretary.
- **Tech Manager:** This person is responsible for the handling of the equipment and the training of other members in how to use it. There are subtitles to this position, such as EVP specialist.
- **Field Analyst:** This member is responsible for the bulk of the evidence evaluation.
- **Demonologist:** This person is responsible for tracking and dealing with any demonic aspects of a case. This is the most dangerous position because many groups feel they must have one and few have the training to deal with what might be out there.
- **Occultist:** This person knows everything there is to know about the occult.
- **Historical Researcher, or just plain Researcher:** In most cases, this is the person who finds the context of the haunting. They research town records and old newspapers looking for the origin of the haunting.
- **Medium/Psychic/Sensitive:** This is the person in the group with a third eye, or one who is in touch with his psi. Many groups do not like to have one.
- **Cryptozoologist:** This person is responsible for knowing all there is to know about the creatures of the night. This is another growing trend in the paranormal, and many groups also have a UFOlogist.

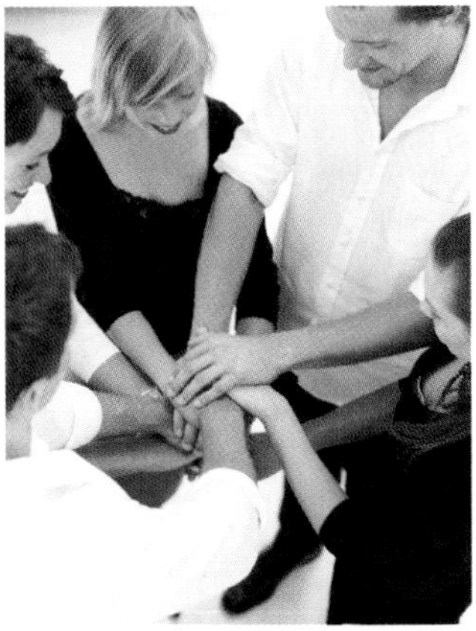

Figure 10.9
©istockphoto.com/Jacob Wackerhausen

There are other people involved whose responsibilities are unclear or a bit makeshift depending on the needs of the group: Case Profiler, Media Specialist, PR Manager, Secretary, Treasurer, Skeptical Advisor. All of these roles, except for the founder/lead investigator role, have their in-training or assistant positions as well.

Mentors and Maniacs

I LEARNED HOW TO TEACH BY FIRE. I entered my first classroom having taken no courses and knowing nothing about how the brain learns or how to engage a student. I did what came naturally, and it worked long enough for me to develop an edge about what I did. The Educational Director came up to me once and asked to see my lesson plan. I laughed and said I went with the tone of the class and made it up as I went. He giggled and told me, "Failing to prepare is preparing to fail." I rolled my eyes, and the next week I was stuck with a room full of pupils with nothing to do.

Seeing other people do what they do or just getting your hands dirty is only good to a point. Eventually, you will need to find people you respect who know more than you and who are willing to share. You are only as good as what is inside your head. Think of learning as a game of poker. When you rake it in, you have all of your information and knowledge you gained from other people who put something in the pot. Admit you don't know everything or that someone else might have a different approach that might work.

The best mentor is someone who can communicate what they do and who doesn't hold their knowledge too close to their vest. There might be an uneven power structure in it, but the best thing you can do for your paranormal learning is to realize you do not know everything. A good teacher will have years in the field, and a solid feel for why things work. They want to spread their knowledge and see it as a chance to bring someone who might have something to contribute into the field.

The best approach is to find several people who do certain things well. I was working on investigations for years before I met Matt Moniz, a scientist, investigator, and radio personality. I could have forced what I do on him, but instead I yielded to what he did well and learned some new methods of investigating and some old-fashioned tried and true techniques. A week later, I was working with a psychic and the next, a news reporter who had never been out in the field. I still learn with each new person I work with because everyone brings something to the table. The worst thing you can do is read this book and think you know everything there is to know.

Then there is the other end of the spectrum. I saw a group once refuse to unpack their equipment until the Lead Investigator got to the site. They did nothing without him and saw nothing wrong with this, as if the ghosts stayed hidden until he made the scene. I have seen new members of groups having to carry all of the equipment. This is a bit more than having to pay your dues. This establishes a relationship where one or several people tell others what to do, and it becomes harder to express yourself or learn in this environment.

The mentoring process might be part of a training method when you join a group. Take advantage of this, but remember you have something to add to what they have already established.

What Do You Stand For?

STANDARDS ARE SOMETIMES the only thing you can hold onto. If you don't stand for something, you will fall for everything. Until you know the good and bad sides of the paranormal community, or more accurately, until you know what you think about things, it might be hard to establish who you want to be. Some things may be common sense, but there are people who go against it. Some people might seem to have the paranormal world by the tale, but you do not say anything because they are the established one and you are the newcomer. You might not even be able to say why you don't like it. It just gives you an unsettled feeling in the pit of your stomach. In this field, follow those kinds of feeling.

Over time you will learn to prefer equipment and methods of investigation, but this is not really what is meant by standards. Instead, think of standards as things you will not do, like break into a supposed haunted building or bless your equipment with holy water before you start. I always thank a spirit when I am done with an investigation and apologize and say a short intention of good will for those who have passed when I leave a cemetery. If anyone made fun of me or said I could not do this, I would never work with that team again.

When you experience something, or someone, decide how you feel about it. You may feel anywhere from excited to disgusted, but most moments fall somewhere between the extremes. Judge each experience with how uncomfortable it makes you feel. If you disagree but don't feel offended, leave it alone. I have worked with groups who are angry and aggressive in their investigations. Not my cup of tea, but I still work with them. They might be on to something, and I do not feel strongly enough about it for it to get in my way.

Associations, Standardizations, and Coalitions

THE PARANORMAL HAS MOVED to a new level in the past few years. It is not enough for some to look for ghosts and tell others what they have found. Sparked by a need to prove that ghosts exist or a desire to crush out juvenile personalities in the community, many have found the need to unify for a common good or against a perceived bad. You have a group, you have a site, and now you need to think about whether or not you want to join an association or coalition.

Figure 10.10
©istockphoto.com/Geoffrey Holman

The Need for Standardization

There is a reason for investigators from groups in different parts of the world to unite. Different people look at the paranormal in unique ways, and no way can be defined as right or wrong, but this makes the evidence uneven. With no definite handle on what a ghost is, how evidence was gathered is as important as what the evidence says. A picture in an attic might be full of glowing orbs, but dust is the most obvious cause, not a visitor from the other side. Some of it might be more subtle than that. How an EVP was obtained tells what other potential reason there might be for the voices. If being a ghost hunter is about carving out all the natural reasons for a disturbance to look closely at what is left, we should all use the same knife. This does not mean all investigators have to use all the same equipment or take readings the same way, but it more focuses on best practices and invites the hunter to take into account his environment while forcing some accountability on the release of information.

Much like the established sciences endured, paranormal investigating is in its infancy, a stage where everything is theoretical and not entirely reproducible. This makes it seem like the furthest thing from science and makes professionals laugh. In actuality, it suffers from the same downfall of all new ideas. Standardization will help with this. You may never be able to reproduce results in a lab or eliminate all variables and natural explanations, but if different people can conduct the same experiments and get the same results and then report it in the same way, the amount of data gathered might convince someone to fund further research. If anything, this kind of homogeny will at least force investigators to do the right thing when out in the field and may encourage some outside of the paranormal circle to investigate what we have only just heard stories about before.

These standardizations run the gamut, which is part of the difficulty in creating a standard for all. Some ask you to pay attention to lunar cycles while others focus only on the equipment used. Most exist as standard operating procedures within a particular group, and this may be a baseline for the future of a creation of some type of sweeping rules of thumb. Begin within your own group by viewing other investigators' rules and following a basic scientific method.

Rings and Lists

In the early days of the Internet, paranormal rings were the fad. Once you created a website, you found someone else who had one. They had a ring, or a group of different sites that all promoted the same ideas, and you joined. You added a link to the ring and a community was started. Most often, you never really read what a group stood for, you just wanted to reach more people. This has died down as of late, but there are still a few out there. They have instead been replaced by things like MySpace communities and organizations. If you can still find them, they are a great way to get your name and site in front of people.

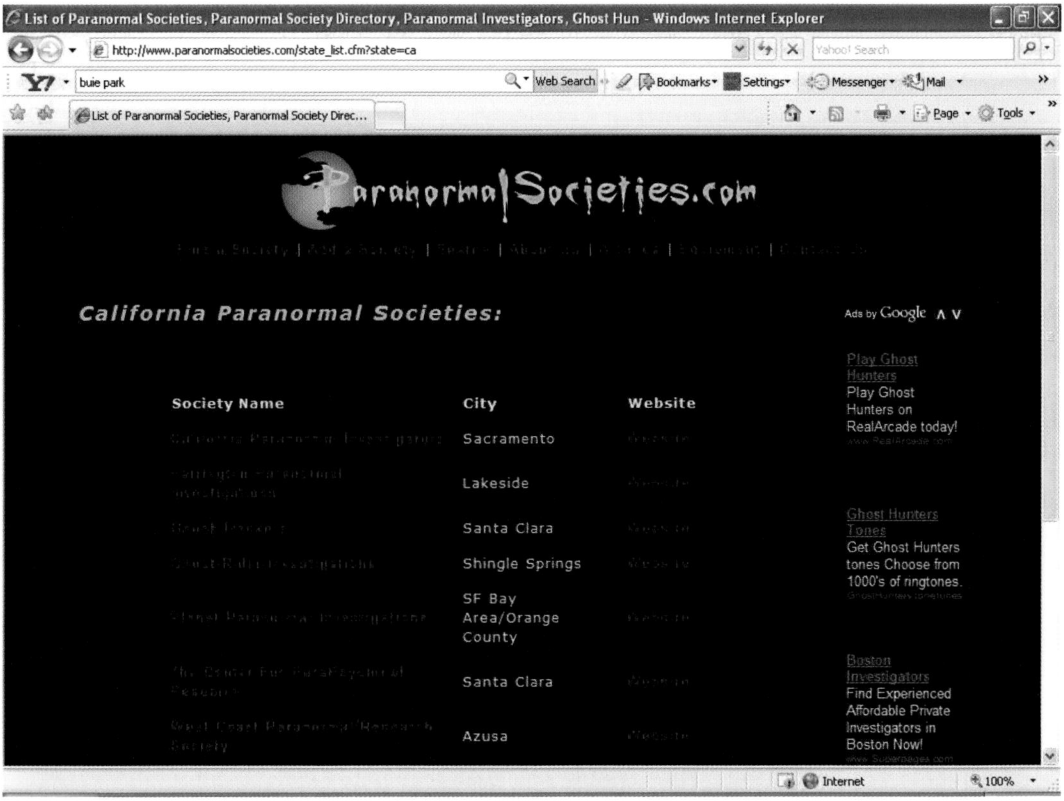

Figure 10.11
The Paranormal Societies website.

Lists are also an effective way to build up associations. Joining one is not a commitment to marriage and might expose you to other groups you can learn from and share evidence with. Most have no really strict rules for who is allowed in, and most merely talk about unity for the sake of trying to get along. One of the largest is Paranormal Societies at www.paranormalsocieties.com. They offer a state-by-state listing of groups and articles on the paranormal while promoting accurate investigating and reporting. According to founder Bill Wilkens, "I created ParanormalSocieties.com hoping that it would become the most comprehensive directory of paranormal societies from around the country. The site is meant to assist people who are in need of help or advice to find it quickly. With all the nation's paranormal societies scattered across the internet, I thought that it would be helpful to create a centralized list. Every society that is listed is screened before they are included, so users can feel comfortable about the groups they find on the site."

A group with a different take on uniting the paranormal is ParaNexus, founded by Doug Kelly and Jari Mikkola. They believe not only in getting together, but working toward the common goal of advancing the scientific aspects of the field through standardization and offering a list of best practices. "ParaNexus' vision is to become a primary resource recognized worldwide as a frontrunner in the paranormal field by providing training, a forum, and database of credible paranormal evidence." They believe in the sharing of all evidence with other members from around the world and collect dues, which they invest back into the paranormal community. They also offer classes and certifications on what they have established as the right way to do things.

Figure 10.12
The ParaNexus website.

The IPP

International Paranormal Investigators at www.international-paranormal-investigators.com satisfies another need in the paranormal community and looks to move the process of standardization forward. Think of them as a collection of people looking to separate honest investigators from dishonest ones. More importantly, they believe in support and technical help and have established ways to get information to groups in need. It is like an online help for the ghost world and a place to bounce ideas. Providing positive motives, they currently boast more than 200 groups and 600 members and provide a staff comprised of investigators from different areas.

The Paranormal Petition

Think of it as "We Are the World" for ghost hunters. The Paranormal Petition at http://www.petitiononline.com/studies/petition.html is a way for investigators to have their voices heard. It looks to have colleges and universities establish official and accredited degrees in parapsychology and paranormal research while promoting the paranormal as a way to better society and individuals. There are more than 200 current signers.

The Alliance for Professional Paranormal Investigation

Some groups, such as M.A.G.I.C., are looking to make standards for behavior, conduct, and training. According to their founder, Carrie Shimkus, the actions of a few groups are tainting the image of all. There are licenses for almost everything, but there is no certification and no governing body protecting the practices or the values of paranormal investigators. She proposes something that does not regulate but rather brings together like-minded people who agree to protect the reputation of those in the field and, by extension, protect the client and make them more willing to come forward with their experiences. "This alliance would be mutually formed to ensure that there are reputable groups out there who have training, experience, high standards, and professionalism," says Shimkus. "We recognize that we cannot control every negative thing that happens in the paranormal field, but we can give our clients and those looking for help some security in knowing they are not being taken for a ride. Ultimately, the goal of forming this alliance is to unify those that want to study and learn about the paranormal without placing restrictions, commitments, and dues upon the individual groups."

In addition to bringing people together, she calls for a certain level of professionalism and some standard practices. This would also help to create a platform for discussion and evidence evaluation where everyone can say they did things the same way. The ideas are not perfect, but even the fact it is out there shows a growing need within the field.

Her proposal is still a work in progress, but some of her ideas are:

1. Each participating group must not charge a fee for any investigation. Fees can be accepted for:

   Conferences and public speaking.

   Events such as trips.

   Books or public writings.

   Movie or media.

2. Each participating group must have at least two years' experience in the field as a team or independent researcher.

3. Each participating group must uphold the highest professionalism standards.

   Each participant will not trespass.

   Each participant will abide by a strict protocol when investigating.

   Each participant will have a dress code of sorts.

   Each participant will uphold a high confidential standard when investigating.

   Each participant will not claim to be an expert in this field.

   Each participant will teach and educate those who are willing to learn.

4. Each group will participate in yearly meetings with other groups in the same locations.

5. Each group must have a web presence. Standard website preferred.

6. Each group must have at least one member of the team active in their community.

7. Each group must provide five references, not per individual but as a team.

   As stated: One reference from community. Anyone can state that they are active in their community. We want to know for certain that you are definitely active.

   One personal reference not associated with the group.

   Two references of other groups that you have worked with. We want to make sure that you work well with other teams as well as confirming your standards while you investigate. If you have shared your findings with other groups for their opinions, these groups can also be used.

   One reference from an investigation that has been performed. (Please note that we understand confidentiality to cases and we will consider another reference in the case. This will be on a case-by-case basis.)

8. Each group will be responsible for its members' conduct. Remember, one sour grape can ruin the whole bunch, but I am sure you are aware of that.

The Haunting as Bonding

I WAS DOING A SÉANCE in the Lizzie Borden Bed and Breakfast when I was approached by someone who wanted to share her experiences there. She told me her story and then called her son over to fill in the holes. He put one arm around her and told me his side of the story. They told me they were there with her best friend and her son and they came here once a year to check out the activity and hear the stories of other people's moments with ghosts. They did it together, and as the son walked away, the mother talked in a more hushed tone. "The rest of the time we don't get along. We share nothing with each other, I mean nothing. Except this. This lets me talk to my son."

Figure 10.13
An odd glare at the Lizzie Borden Bed and Breakfast.

I was touched by the idea but had started to notice it was a growing trend. I've heard of ghost books being passed between the members of a family. More e-mails referred to a cross-generational bonding happening over the souls of the dead. I was seeing more children in the audiences of conferences, and many times it was the older generation encouraging the younger to share their experiences. Now it feels commonplace to be approached by a mother and her two daughters or a father and his son (although this is seen much less). I even received an e-mail from a woman in another state. She and her boyfriend were planning a trip to my area for his birthday and she thought a trip out with a real ghost hunter would be the ultimate gift for him.

She told me they watch all the shows on television together and wanted something for them to share. "I want him to be able to have the experience of a lifetime. We understand we could see nothing, but I think the experience would be enough for him."

It is not always passive. One of the most successful groups in Massachusetts, the Berkshire Paranormal Group, is multi-generational. This is happening more and more, with older members of paranormal groups forming junior groups to include their kids. I also know of individuals who hunt ghosts without a group but who bring their father along for the ride and then spend time together talking about what they found and where to go to next.

It is understandable when a family comes together because they are sharing a haunting. I have seen isolation happen in these cases, especially when something darker is involved, but for the most part, it unites them. They even plan family rituals around the activity. I see why this happens. They want it to be real, and if they can talk to someone who is going through the same thing, it makes them feel less crazy. They are not alone.

This new trend is different from that. People unable to talk to each other are finding their ways to television sets on Wednesdays and then paying money to go out together. Maybe it has something to do with the popularity of the genre itself. In other words, if shows about plants were popular, there would be scores of families bonding over their gardens. For the first time in a long time, it is acceptable for people to be into ghosts, and the field touches people of all ages, some of whom are allowed to admit it for the first time. If they can take a vacation to a haunted battlefield instead of an amusement park, they'll take it. They hunt a few ghosts together and then talk about their lives. Think of it like the old radio programs that called for families to gather around to listen.

There might be something deeper than that. In the past, religious ideas were passed down through the generations and ideas about the eternal soul were easier to teach. Not so much now. Religion has been watered down, and many feel the American family has suffered from it. It was not only a glue, but it offered a spark to other conversations, something constant that didn't change like fashion in clothes or music. A belief in ghosts, and trying to experience the paranormal, has replaced this for some. Not that investigating has replaced worship. Instead, it offers a touch of something unseen, which leads to a discussion on who we are and where we are going. While methods of trying to get evidence change, those bigger questions remain.

I don't believe this happens on a conscious level. It is in the background. When it comes down to it, they are having a good time together, and that is the main motivation. They might be bringing something to the table though. Perhaps some hauntings are stronger when a family is using it to come together. If the ghost is able to see our world or use our energy, the unique mix of a family doing something together might help it manifest better.

I hope the trend continues. It not only brings more people to the field who may generate new evidence and come up with new ideas, but it brings people together. There are so many reasons people have to not connect with their loved ones, it makes me feel good to bring them together. Many people have reported feeling alone when they have something paranormal happen to them. The tide has turned. Families are starting to turn sitting around a fire and hearing ghost stories into a family destination, and looking for apparitions is turning into a family affair. It's not easy or safe to be out there alone in the paranormal world, but some people have become discouraged and frustrated with the dynamics of a group. It's a tough choice, especially if you do not have people in your life who want to investigate with you. There is a group out there for anyone, or at least enough people out there to help you through everything you need. Connect. It really is the best way to find out about the haunts near you and how people are investigating. Most importantly, it shows you are not alone. There are people out there looking to find the answer to the questions you have, and as communities grow and get in touch with each other, the paranormal community as a whole benefits.

ON AIR
ON AIR

11

The Paranormal Media

MY THREE-YEAR-OLD SON WAS GIVEN a pouch of colorful dinosaurs as a gift. He opened it up, pulled one out, and said, "Dad, look. A peri-tackle." I beamed as only a father could and retold the story to everyone I saw. A few weeks later, we were speaking to a teacher at his new daycare and I thought it was a good opportunity to share his brilliance. I told the story and she tousled his hair and said, "Someone watches too much television." After I got over the fact my son was not headed to Mensa before preschool, I had to admit she was probably right. There is not a lot of prehistoric creature talk in my house.

Despite those who fight with all their breath, saying the media does not have an effect on people, the point seems so obvious as to not even warrant an argument. Growing up, I thought everyone but us had a maid named Alice, dogs could talk if you could get them alone, and I could become a superhero if I spun around in circles fast enough. The shows change, and our filters get stronger, but the weight we put in what the media feeds us is still felt on our shoulders. The media can't make us do something against our morals. It just helps to mold what those morals are.

The paranormal is not exempt from this. From books to movies and television to radio, much of what we think about ghosts is born of what we are told by the media. Like all art, it both reflects our ideas and helps to create them. As an investigator, you have probably been inspired by a television show, or you have at least watched one. You have maybe even read some other books, usually with conflicting information. Think of this chapter as a guide through the best sources of information and a way to see some of the flaws in what you may have already been presented with. By the end of the chapter, it should be clear that the best media advice is to make sure you look twice and try to find as many ideas out there as possible.

I Saw It on Television

I HAVE A THEORY. If three or more paranormal investigators are in a room, the conversation will turn at some point to the SciFi television program *Ghost Hunters*. If they talk about it long enough, it will develop that one person hates them, the other used to investigate with them before they went corporate, and one will admit he has heard of them but has never watched the show. Like any success story, the men and women of The Atlantic Paranormal Society (TAPS) have those who love them and those who hate them and others who are just waiting for them to be knocked down a peg.

Figure 11.1
©istockphoto.com/Shaun Lowe

Like them or not, the group and the television show are responsible for much of the paranormal boom and for much of what modern day ghost hunters know about the paranormal and how to track ghosts. I am frequently asked on radio shows what I think of them, and I know the host usually has an agenda. The fact of the matter is, TAPS do what they do very well. They are not, however, the first group to investigate ghosts and not the only authority on the subject. Paranormal investigating attracts people who are searching for truth or reasons, so don't close yourself off to other ways to go about things.

The Paranormal Narrative

I was shooting a television show for a British production company, trying to contact the spirit of Albert DeSalvo, otherwise known as the Boston Strangler. We had brought a communication device known as Frank's Box, or a "phone to the dead," and as we struggled to understand the messages coming through, I caught a glimpse of the director. He had flown across an ocean, had filmed in several cities, and was now waiting for the final bit to make the show complete. He had envisioned a typical scene with people around a Ouija Board or holding hands, and there we were sitting around a small radio with tiny speakers, trying to contact a serial killer. He was getting more and more frustrated, looking for a visual to go with the intriguing evidence we were getting from the box. We finally agreed to finish, and I could tell he had not gotten all he wanted.

There was money for the flights and the talents and the people who lived in the location, and this was not how his mind's eye had seen it. Always the professional, he looked at me as we packed up and said, "We'll get it in the edit."

As a high school English teacher, I spend much of my time having students recognize and draw out the plot diagram Aristotle formalized hundreds of years ago. He came up with it after spending years plowing through the ancient stories until he saw trends in what all good stories have. It is the best way to understand the story, and it gives students segments they can break down and analyze. For those some years removed from freshman English, they are:

1. **Exposition:** You learn who the characters are.

2. **Trigger:** Something happens, setting the wheel of the story in motion.

3. **Rising action:** Things begin to happen, usually at a faster pace.

4. **Point of no return:** At some point, the characters can't turn back. They must push forward to an end.

5. **Climax:** This is the point of highest interest. It is the final fight scene or the point when the man jumps three cars to get to the woman he loves who is leaving on the bus.

6. **Resolution:** The hero comes through in the end, everything is changed but for the better, and the good guys ride off into the sunset.

Good ghost stories follow the same pattern, although it is usually not until after the fact that people can look back and see it. There is a contrast to how the paranormal invades a family and how it is portrayed on television. People have experiences with things they do not understand all the time, and most times it is a single experience that never repeats itself. Many are more like full-blown hauntings, and they play themselves out like a story. It obviously varies, but most look something like this:

1. A family moves into a new house with the best intentions.

2. Someone, usually the mother or a child, notices something odd and begins to think something might be with them in the house.

3. The whole family experiences things. Usually it begins with something simple and then escalates.

4. The family might call someone in to investigate, or they might decide to confront whatever is in the house on their own. It is the moment the family fights back.

5. There is a final conflict between the family and the spirit or spirits in the house.

6. The living win, and the family come out the other side, stronger and more in love with each other than ever. Often there is a moment where some aspect of the case makes sense for the first time, like the man who kept appearing in the closet holding his neck was the man who owned it years ago who hung himself there.

It is important to remember that paranormal shows often feel they must present a well-organized plot for the audience because that is how stories work. They offer neat and clean packaging so they can be understood by the viewer and offer the most drama at the moments those watching expect it, as well as when the most commercials will show. All of the pegs fit in the holes.

Investigating is not always like this. The background of the case comes in flashes where one story reminds the witnesses of another. They do not remember what came first, and the importance of a moment might not make sense until months after you think the case has come to an end. Beware of thinking you are on a television show when you begin to ghost hunt. Do not try to have the evidence fit what you think will make a good story, but rather follow the clues where they lead you. Too many investigators believe they are staring face-to-face with a demon as soon as the clues look like they might be headed there. Much of this has to do with television building the need for the story to lean this way.

Not So Real

The TV show, *Ghost Hunters,* is also guilty of creating a false sense of narrative on their show. TAPS was well known in the paranormal community before the show ever aired and were known as good investigators, so the issue is not with their techniques or their methods. Instead, the issue is more about the show's presentation of their cases.

If the average paranormal show has a preset and predictable story line, you can set your clock by *Ghost Hunters.*

1. The investigators give a rundown of the history of the case.

2. The team arrives at the scene and begins setting up their equipment, usually with some drama as something technical or personal goes wrong.

3. The team begins to investigate, running through the most haunted areas of the location and gathering evidence.

4. The team reacts to something and there is that, "What was that?" moment. This is accompanied by a commercial.

5. The evidence is evaluated, and there is some measure of proof provided to back up a claim, or the team decides the location is not haunted based on their evidence.

6. The homeowner or manager of the location is told the results and the end credits leave us wanting more.

The show works because we know what is going on and the subject matter draws us in. It is a product of good editing, and this is something the audience often overlooks. The investigation and the evaluation of evidence takes many hours, but the magic of television makes it as compressed as an episode of your favorite sitcom. There is also a resolution and the house is either haunted or not, even though they leave any negative findings as open but inconclusive. Most investigations are not like this, and the first time you are there might only give you a baseline of the house to compare activity with inactivity.

The Buzzwords

Working with different investigation groups can expose you to different techniques and ideas, not all of which you may agree with. With so many groups influenced and inspired by the television they see, certain words have entered into the investigating field. People feel they need to use them to be a good investigator, but they rarely understand what they mean. When you investigate a house, chances are the people have watched paranormal television shows, if for no other reason than to try to find out what is happening to them. Avoid sounding like the people on television and just try to be yourself.

Avoid using such words as:

- **Debunk:** To tell someone what they have experienced didn't happen. Don't look to prove or disprove when you enter a house. Just collect information and try to find the truest reason for it happening.
- **Reveal:** To sit and explain the evidence you received. Reveal is a verb and not a noun.
- **Manifestation:** To glamorize or dramatize something a client has experienced. There is something to be said for connotation or the feeling certain words create. *Fuzzy bunny manifestation.* See, still sounds bad.
- **Client:** Someone who you serve and who usually pays for services rendered. You are dealing with people, most often people with some emotional investment in your being there. Don't be so clinical. They are real people and not just cases.
- **"Dude, Run" Moment:** A reference to a television moment where an investigator ran because of a possible ghost. If you don't know what I am referring to, ignore this. If you do, don't reference it during a ghost hunt.
- **Go Dark:** The idea that an investigation needs to set up and then every light source needs to be extinguished. As we addressed in Chapter 6, there is something to be said for going dark, but it does not have to be a part of every investigation.
- **Dead Time:** A reference to the witching hour, or between 3 and 4 am when ghostly activity experiences a spike. Several television shows promote this as the best time to get evidence, but more ghostly reports from this time are probably more a result of the quiet of the time and people being woken up and not any actual paranormal standard.

Education and Entertainment

Watch plenty of television. It does not hurt your eyes like your mother told you. When people ask me what I think of the increase of interest in ghosts because of the television shows that are on, I smile and remember watching the old documentaries about UFOs and ghosts. They're what helped to spark my interest, and just because there are more of them now and the presentation has shifted doesn't mean I am ready to say they are as bad for you as sitting too close to the television.

Just remember, there is a difference between the reality and what you see when you tune in. Making that distinction is easy when you are watching a movie or a docudrama. It becomes more clouded when it is presented as a true story. It is different when the word "reality" is attached to it. The television should be used for entertainment first and education second. Just be careful not to think you understand it all just because you watch a few hours of an entertaining show. I like to tune into *This Old House*, but I can't even hang a picture straight.

Have You Read Any Good Books Lately?

MY MOTHER USED TO WORK a bit late and the local library was only a few blocks from my middle school. I used to walk there and wait for her, losing myself in the stacks while I waited for her to show up. I remember two books I took out so often I don't think anyone else was ever able to read them. One was a book on how to be a good private detective, and it showed things like how to sneak up stairs and move through a house without making a sound. I still use these ideas when I am trying not to wake up my young son.

The other book was a collection of odd and unexplained stories. I remember the tales of Daniel Webster and the Devil, a grave where the flowers always grew in a cross, and the tale of a song that made people commit suicide. They ran the gamut of local legend, urban folklore, and true hauntings. I always had the book under my arm and would take it out at family functions and explain how the dancer in the Mexican bar knew it was the Devil because of the cloven hooves.

Even today with so much on the Internet and television producing both quality and mediocre programs, there is still something about a ghost story told from a book that warms the heart while chilling the bone. Today, it's one of the few nonfiction genres that are growing. Of course, this is a product of the paranormal boom caused by the television media attention, but there has always been something about the written word and the unexplained that seem made for each other. Good ghost books were written before the millennium and good books will continue to be released well after the television shows have stopped and the investigators stop being rock stars.

Figure 11.2
A paranormal collection.

The Old Guard

Do you remember the first time you couldn't go to sleep because the movie you saw was so scary you spent the night checking and rechecking your closet? I grew up in a strange time. My parents let me watch *The Exorcist* from the backseat in a drive-in and then didn't stop me from watching it on late night television where the swearing was taken out but the terror remained. It was like that for many of us. It takes a lot for us to be affected by something, but there is something about the old guard, those who laid the groundwork for the work being done today, that still molded decades of people and scared the pants off us.

Some of the best books can be found at yard sales, library sales, and the discount racks in bookstores. They may be somewhat outdated given the advances in paranormal investigating, but they offer some of the foundation work today's ideas are based on. They have not been tainted by new ideas and are almost always written by people who know what they are talking about and can also write. Remember, the two things are not related and today's authors don't always have to pay their dues before they publish. You can also get these older titles for next to nothing, and buying them means you are usually getting the cream that has risen to the top.

Many of these people are still writing, and their ideas on the new trends are just as insightful as their older work. Some of the better and more well known of the old guard are:

- **Hans Holzer:** **In many ways, he is the grandfather of modern ghost hunting. His work is strong, but his ideas are very specific, and his use of psychics may turn off some readers.**
- **Brad Steiger:** **Prolific and timeless. With dozens of books in print in different languages and editions, Steiger balances the heart of the paranormal with a clear explanation of some tricky subjects.**
- **The Warrens:** **Although they do not always write all of their own material, Ed, who died in 2006, and Lorraine were on the frontlines of some of the first big cases that brought the paranormal into the mainstream.**
- **Brad Scott:** **Just the facts. As a coauthor and author, his works paved the way for the modern ghost story. His research and narrative make his books a necessity.**

There are also many who have had only one or two titles to their name because of the changing tastes of book buyers. The best way to find them is to discover an author you like and flip to the back. In all that stuff after the last chapter, you'll find a bibliography or a section on further reading. Use this as a general rule of thumb. If the book is still in print after more than ten years, chances are it has something good inside. If it is worn and well read at a yard sale, someone read it and wore it out. It might just be a keeper.

Just remember, older books are filled with old ideas about everything, not just ghosts. Many involve strong ideas about religion and the use of psychics, which you might be uncomfortable with.

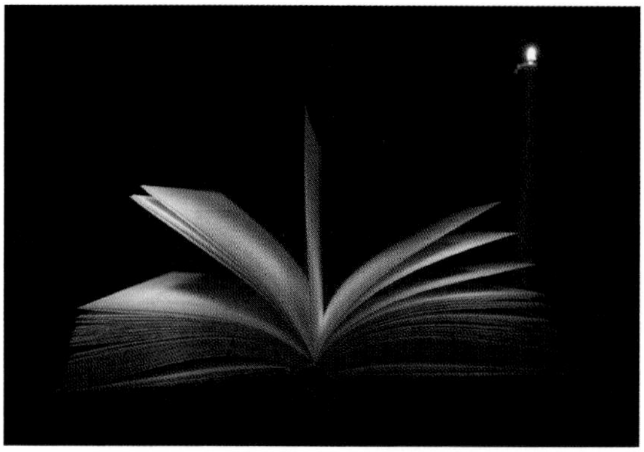

Figure 11.3
©istockphoto.com/Alina Solovyova-Vincent

But That Old?

In Massachusetts, you can't say you know the local paranormal scene and not know who Cotton Mather is. For those who have not studied Colonial New England or the Salem Witch Trials, he was a minister in the early days before the Revolution. He has some of the earliest writings on the supernatural in this country, and if you can sort through the religion, there are some very interesting ideas.

Here comes that commitment thing again. There are 400-year-old books out there that can open your mind to dizzying ideas, but they take time to read and understand. Some interesting work was done in other languages and is still being translated and updated with modern perspectives on the old words. Alternate them with more current books and widen your understanding. One of the most interesting things you'll find is that old ideas seem silly and the latest breakthrough will go the way of the horse and buggy someday.

Figure 11.4
©istockphoto.com/Duncan Walker

The New Guys in Town

The torch has been passed, and a new way of looking at ghosts and a new way to ghost hunt has produced a fresh generation of writers who are bringing the other side into your living room. They are artists born of the Internet and influenced by the current flow of information. A few have separated themselves from the pack, and you may even know them by their names or have visited their websites.

The Four Horsemen today are:

- **Troy Taylor**—www.ghostsofthepraire.com Taylor is probably the most prolific of the new breed. When you visit his site or buy one of his books, you know you'll get a well-researched and well-presented story.
- **Rosemary Ellen Guiley**—www.visionary living.com—Guiley's research hits upon subjects other authors avoid, such as fairies and monsters, but her writing and research is sound and entertaining.
- **Jeff Belanger**—www.ghostvillage.com—Belanger created Ghostvillage almost ten years ago and has ushered in the paranormal boom. His work approaches the paranormal through the eyes of a reporter, and he walks the delicate line of being entertaining and humorous without losing integrity.
- **Loyd Auerbach**—www.mindreader.com—Auerbach is the face of the modern ghost hunter, and his title is well founded. He also brings the Harry Price spirit back alive by bringing the parapsychological angle to his work.

What's Going on in Your Town

When I published my first book, I sat around waiting for a flood of people to phone me and e-mail me telling me how much of an impact it had on their lives. I carefully checked the best-seller list waiting for my name to appear, but, alas, it was not to be. A few months in, a stark realization came to me. My book, my pride and joy that I had spent so much of my time and energy on, would be read by a few hundred people. I would be lucky to sell a thousand copies.

For years, the shelves of bookstores have been filled and refilled with books on ghosts, but until recent times you had to settle for a national book that might mention your town in it. There were titles about the larger cites, or at least places that had reputations as being more haunted than others, but the closest thing to a regional book about the haunts around you came from ones about your general area, like a ghosts of the Pacific Northeast, or Midwestern ghosts book. This all changed when traffic on the Internet proved there were ghosts everywhere, everyone had a story, and people cared about the phantoms in their town.

It is a perfect storm really. Smaller publishers want a taste of the money ghost books can bring in, people are willing to buy them, and new writers, trying to get their feet in the door and dying to write a book that is almost guaranteed to not make money, all collided. The result is a new canon of paranormal titles by previously unknown writers about every locale in the United States and beyond. If you're looking for it, it is out there, like a haunted tour from Maine to Washington to Hawaii.

You might think these books have nothing to offer you. If live in Bethesda, why do you care about the ghosts of San Diego? There are some good writers out there, and they may not come from your city. Also, there is something to be gained by reading tales from other parts of the country. I can see patterns of hauntings, or at least reactions to hauntings, by exploring other parts of the country. They also offer a great resource for your own work and have authors who are usually so happy someone has read their book they are willing to talk about how they got their stories and mentor you in your paranormal journey.

All is not bright in Denmark, however. There are many new authors who spend more time on websites than out in the field talking to people or gathering evidence. I feel it is okay to write a book without ever having been on an investigation, but too many of the new writers are also retelling the tales of places they have never been. This is made worse when they present material as if they have been in those places. Imagine that your level of interest in a local book is placed on a scale and balanced out by twelve pounds. For every state between the author and the place written about, add another pound. As soon as the balance hits the table, put the book down. Chances are it was written from the comfort of the author's house and offers no new information or insight. Save your money and get the stories where they most likely did; the Internet.

Big Books with Big Ideas

Major publishers want to release a book and have it appeal to a large audience. They can't make their money back from a title that sells well in only one region, and they have enough name recognition and can provide a big enough push that they want to have everyone open it up. These books are good for all time zones, meaning they try not to offend and offer a little of this and a little of that. The best can become a reference book on your shelf and give some new perspective on approaching the supernatural.

When you buy a national book, think of what you want to know and find a book to suit you. It might be a challenging twist that draws you in, like all ghosts are actually aliens testing our reaction to death, or that demons are human time travelers. Choose carefully, reading online reviews and even running the writer's name through a search engine. You can probably listen to the author talk about the book somewhere online, so you can look before you buy.

Figure 11.5
National books for national interests.
©istockphoto.com/Alina Solovyova-Vincent.

Remember, a book in the nonfiction section does not always mean that what is inside the book is true. For many years, true ghost encounters existed only as chapters in books about the unknown. Times have changed but not that much. Think about where you find a ghost book in your local store. Stretch one arm and you'll find how to improve your love life using astrology; wiggle the other and take out a book about dreams. These things might be connected to the paranormal, but because ghost hunting is not a religion or a science, people find the need to classify it with anything known as New Age. There might be books that seem appealing until you find they have too much of something you don't want. At a local metaphysical store, I once bought a book that I thought would help with my understanding of talking with spirits. Instead, it demanded a knowledge of magic I did not have and instructed how to conjure and capture spirits to do your bidding.

You will need to decide if you believe in aliens and Bigfoot and whether you want to read runes. There are still many titles that include these ideas alongside volumes of hauntings. Be picky. We live in a time where we don't have to look for true ghost stories as if we were attacking a salad bar. There are enough great titles that talk only of ghosts for you to spend many hours by the fire reading.

Some Good Reads

Here are a few of the old guard books you might want to look into.

Ashley, Leonard R.N. *Complete Book of Ghosts and Poltergeists.* New York, NY; Barricole Books, Inc, 2000.

Cohen, Daniel. *Encyclopedia of Ghosts.* New York, NY; Dorset Press, 1984.

Mack, Carol K. and Mack, Dinah. *A Field Guide to Demons, Fairies, Fallen Angels and Other Subversive Spirits.* New York, NY; Henry Holt and Company, 1988.

Hauck, Dennis William. *Haunted Places National Directory.* New York, NY; Penguin Books, 1996.

Mitchell, John and Rickard, Bob. *Rough Guide to Unexplained Phenomenon.* London, England; Rough Guides Ltd., 2000.

White, Michael. *Weird Science.* New York, NY; Avon Books, Inc., 1999.

Evans, Hilary and Huyghe, Patrick. *Field Guide to Ghosts and Other Apparitions.* New York, NY; Quill, 2000.

North, Anthony. *Paranormal: A Guide to the Unexplained.* London, England; Blanford, 1997.

Denning, Hazel M. *True Hauntings: Spirits with a Purpose.* Philadelphia, PA; Llewellyn, 2000.

Buckland, Raymond. *Ghosts, Hauntings and Possession: The Best of Hans Holzer.* Philadelphia, PA: Llewellyn, 1995.

Creighton, Helen. *Bluenose Ghosts.* Halifax, NS; Nimbus Publishing, 1994.

Davies, Owen. *Omni Book of the Paranormal and the Mind.* New York, NY; Zebra Books, 1983.

Greer, John Michael. *Monsters.* Philadelphia, PA; Llewellyn, 2002.

Visions of Ghost Armies. New York, NY; Galde Press Inc., 2003.

Coleman, Martin. *Communing with the Spirits.* York Beach, ME; Samuel Weiser Inc., 1998.

Steiger, Brad. *Out of the Dark.* New York, NY; Kenington, 2001.

Bell, Michael. *Food for the Dead: On the Trail of New England Vampires.* New York, NY; Carroll and Graf Pub., 2001.

Rao, K. Ramakrishna. *Basic Experiments in Parapsychology.* Jefferson, NC; McFarland and Co., Inc. Pub., 1984.

Martin, Malachi. *Hostage to the Devil.* San Francisco, CA; Harper, 1976.

Robinson, Charles Turek. *True New England Mysteries, Ghost, Crimes and Oddities.* North Attleboro, MA, 1997.

Magazines

THE PRINTED PARANORMAL world is not limited to books only. There has been a rash of new magazines dedicated to the supernatural. Cryptozoologists have a dedicated, literate audience, so magazines having to do with monsters and odd animals sell fairly well. Ghosts, however, have a much harder time. Many have popped up, and many have fallen, and there doesn't seem to be any new, innovative titles that remain consistent. It is a problem of numbers. To draw more people in, the editors choose stories they know will attract crowds. What you get are the same stories told over and over again about the same topics. They also deal at times with an identity crisis. Some are so investigation focused they do not take on other aspects of the paranormal.

Figure 11.6
When a paranormal story hits a mainstream magazine.

There are a few solid titles that have been around for years. *Fate* is at the top of the heap, but the *Fortean Times* is close behind. On the other end of the spectrum is the *Skeptical Inquirer*, which targets paranormal ideas and tries to knock them down. Other titles can be found by searching the Internet or asking your local bookseller, but don't expect to find many on the shelves. Even the heavy hitters are not sold in stores that feel their demographic won't buy them in large numbers.

Another option is to peruse the pages of some of the more mainstream titles. *Scientific American, Omni, Discover, National Geographic,* and others sometimes print interesting articles about the more science-based aspects of the paranormal. There are also old articles in magazines that can be found in online archives or your local library.

On the Air without the Air

I REMEMBER SPENDING HOURS in my grandfather's basement listening to talk radio. I don't think he ever stopped to pay attention to what they were saying. He just liked something in the background. I, however, soaked it up and it helped to mold my politics and view of the world. I loved to hear the hosts yelling at guests, but I more enjoyed the confidence that came from their mouths. They knew everything about everything, and I longed to have that kind of information in my head to shoot out when challenged. With modern technology, radio is becoming less and less influential. Sports talk and politics will always be there, but the number of shows dedicated to the unknown is still strong and evolving as the world evolves.

Here is a word right out of the SAT: *terrestrial.* It is a fancy word that means of or from the earth, but its effect on modern paranormal media is being felt exponentially, which is another good SAT word. Many of the current paranormal radio shows are terrestrial, meaning the people on the show sit in a little room and the signal is sent out by antennae. It may then be syndicated all over the country and in some instances over the world. Some of these shows are on the AM dial and have a small local listenership.

The bigger trend is to get the word out by having the show picked up by stations outside the normal vicinity or to modernize the process by having it recorded and broadcast on the Internet.

The larger, more established, shows can be found in different formats, the most popular by far being *Coast to Coast AM* and its offspring show *Somewhere in Time.* Once hosted by the revolutionary Art Bell, the program still presents four hours a night of odd radio, hitting on paranormal issues enough to make it worth listening to.

After the *Coast to Coast* show, there is a significant drop off, and the Internet becomes the major vehicle for ghostly talk. Most are focused in an area of the country, and hosts split time talking about regional supernatural issues and national trends presented by guests. There are a few recorded in the studio, such as *Beyond Reality* from the TAPS founders and *Spooky Southcoast* located in Massachusetts.

Many are instead broadcast as Internet shows only. Guests call into a virtual studio. These are a mixed bag. People want to find any corner of the world to own, and there is not much of an investment of money to get one. The result is a whole catalogue of people with little experience, and like most of the overflow of paranormal, there are some hosts using the computer airwaves to promote themselves. If you search for one in your area, you may be disappointed or you may find a hidden gem.

The Internet

AGAIN, THE INTERNET STEPS IN and becomes the driving force behind the growth of the paranormal. You can find everything from John Zaffis speaking at a community college to footage of a ghost trying to sneak a peak at investigators at the famous Waverly Hills. Like all media, there are some really poor examples of the web as a way to communicate, but some material out there is produced by professionals for a variety of reasons.

The web is used to share ideas and connect to hauntings, but it is also a way for investigators to present information to be scrutinized and spread. A proposed ghost is shot up online before the group can say ectoplasm. It is then out to a community starved for anything paranormal. People view it without a critical eye and the rumor of a ghost is now out there. Not that all that is uploaded is fake, be it through intent or investigator error, but it takes training to see the real from the staged. The same standards you apply to watching your own evidence should be applied to seeing others. Try to track each instance to its original source, and if possible, contact that group. Over time, most evidence gets altered, usually for length or in an attempt to clarify the picture, but the original group will have the untouched video.

This kind of distribution also gives life to media thought lost or being produced in nontraditional ways. Old documentaries are given new life, and many of the low budget productions of years past have their chance to influence a new generation. It also has allowed documentary filmmakers to film, edit, and publish their craft, and many of these documentaries cover paranormal topics. Perhaps the most popular use of Internet television is the uploading of local public access shows. What once was seen by only a few dozen people can be viewed by interested parties across the world. Some even film for the Internet audience using the resources of public access. Some of these shows bypass the terrestrial route altogether and film with their own cameras.

The 'net also offers online instruction for ghost hunting or online EVP sessions. Some of this is interactive where you can ask questions and see results as they happen. Take advantage of these when you can, but always look at the source and price, and measure whether it is worth it. The best is probably Loyd Auerbech's out of Ghostvillage.com.

Figure 11.7
Demonologist Keith Johnson on Spooky Southcoast.
Picture courtesy of Spooky Southcoast.

Beware the Snake Charmer

LIKE ANY STRANGER WHO approaches you with something to offer, the best defense against being scammed is a critical eye and a critical mind. People who are interested in the paranormal devour anything about ghosts, so people who want to make money place their sharks in the water. The result is multiple media outlets vying for the dollar to be made. Much of it has advanced the discussion about ghosts and is wholly positive for the field. Investigators are fans too.

Use your best judgment when taking in any kind of paranormal media. What are people trying to sell you and who is the source? Anything is dangerous when you allow it to be your only source of knowledge. Delve deeply when a magazine promotes an idea or a television show tells you there is only one way to investigate. Read as many different books as you can, old and new, and keep your mind open. Make your knowledge a puzzle created from the different pieces out there, but leave one piece out for the information you have not learned yet.

This chapter has been about the media, but think of it as a danger in single source thinking. In other words, don't just listen to one podcast or read one book or watch one show and think you have seen all that paranormal is. I am exposed to new ideas all the time, and some are advancing the field. When you find an internet source, look for one that collects information from other sites, such as Ghostvillage or Haunted America Tours at http://www.hauntedamericatours.com. These give you what they view as the best of the best, so your net can catch new ideas. Add these ideas to what you are already learning in the field, and you will be a more complete investigator.

Students looking for the ghost of Maria.

12

Legend Tripping

ONE OF THE MOST INTERESTING CASES I ever investigated was in a school in Lawrence, Massachusetts. It had opened on the site of a rundown Catholic girls' school turned adult education center, and the new tenants lived in the building for two years without any problems. A story started to circulate from one of the teachers who often worked late at night, and it was supported by another who found himself in the building after school hours one week during midterms.

The story began to flesh itself out. Maria was a 15-year-old from the Dominican Republic, like 80 percent of Lawrence and 95 percent of the school's population. She had come to America only a few years before and had fallen in love with the sister who ran the school and lived in the convent in the attached building. She did not get along with her classmates, and her parents wanted nothing to do with her, so when she started to spend more time with the nuns, no one really took notice. One week when the school was on vacation, she slipped off to the building and found the nuns had left on retreat. She had the whole school to herself without anyone to bother her or pick on her. She even slept there overnight, but one night she strayed onto the roof during a storm to watch the lightning. As she was gazing at the lights over the city, she lost her balance, slipped and fell, avoiding falling to the ground only because of her long, black hair, which got tangled in the ironwork of the roof. She hung there, screaming, until she eventually died of asphyxiation. The doctors who performed the autopsy said she must have suffered for at least 12 hours, gasping for air and using every last bit to cry for help.

The tragedy was enough to close the school, and it was not until a new batch of teens arrived on the same spot that Maria chose to make herself known.

She was reported to be seen on the roof from the street below, as well as heard around the neighborhood screaming for help. People inside the building came into contact with her as well. She had made a pencil travel from the stairs leading to the roof to the second floor with unseen hands. She was known to open and close the door outside on the fourth floor, and one faculty member even claimed to have seen her walking the halls and disappearing.

As a teacher at the school instructing a whole class of scared teens in the techniques of paranormal investigation, I decided it was best to check out the story for myself. Bringing along all of my equipment and 15 teens trained in how to use it, I conducted three separate investigations of the school. We got several EVPs and a shot of a young girl with long black hair in a doorway. We had solved the case.

The trouble was the ghost did not exist. Another English teacher at the school, wanting to make the new students feel like real students, invented a ghost for them because, "all high schools have to have some kind of haunting, right?" My investigation, although I knew there was nothing there all along, had produced a convincing girl-like smear of dirt and a few trickles of the teen investigators' conversations, which sounded enough like they came from the other side to convince the kids she was there, even after I told them the story was not true.

The English teacher was not trying to be cruel or lie to her students but trying to connect them with a history and trying to make them feel they were part of a bigger picture. In fact, she merely tapped into a very powerful urge we have to belong to our surroundings. When we have a common bond, something that ties the initiated together, we are stronger. The paranormal does that to us. A shared ghost, one passed down from senior to freshman and added onto every year, creates a sense of community felt more intensely than singing the school song or fundraising.

Why a chapter on folklore in a book about ghost hunting? Most of what paranormal investigating does includes trying to bury those old stories and bring the most probable ones to the surface. Gathering and presenting evidence is the rule of thumb, and urban mythology gets in the way of that. That might be the very reason a good investigator needs to know about what is out there. A good story can get our blood going, but if we are too eager to accept it, or consider ourselves so professional we ignore it, a vital piece of the puzzle might be left out.

These stories resonate because they are manipulations of a truth, but they also resonate a fragment of something based in a possible reality. In other words, it's an eventual lie that might have been true at one time. Dr. Michael Bell, author of *Food for the Dead: On the Trail of New England's Vampires*, talks of one form of folklore being the oral tradition of a society passed on. In many ways it's as crucial to a society as media contact or written history, but because of folklore's nature, it can change as it gets passed. When that twist happens it becomes something different, and with many changes it becomes harder to see the truth that remains. This is essential to investigating ghost stories you hear. Even if they fall into any of the categories we'll talk about here, there might still be an element of truth in it.

Investigators have to be ready to take the grain from the shaft.

The Wild Goose Chase

IF A STORY IS TOO GOOD to be true, someone has been falling for it for years. There are stories in the paranormal that make the rounds and send investigators out searching in vain for a ghost of a ghost. Even the most experienced investigator can be fooled, and even the most cynical researcher can sometimes be heard uttering a story whose words have been repeated over and over for decades. It is not their fault entirely. The tale is too neat and makes too much sense.

Just the Facts

When you get an e-mail or hear a story that makes the hair on the back of your neck stand up, how do you react? If you are like most people, you probably retell it. Usually, there are some parts that do not make sense, but you add reasons for those. You probably just forgot what the person had told you. To make it more interesting, you say it happened to a friend of a friend of yours, even though the friend is far removed. This makes you part of the story and really doesn't hurt anyone. After all, the story is true and you only changed it so someone else could feel it as intensely as you did when you were told. An urban legend is born. More precisely, an urban legend is allowed to live another day.

Figure 12.1
A haunted hotel turned dormitory. It is the subject of ghost stories and urban legends.

When I hear the same story, I do one thing. I ask for more details, which I usually can't get from the teller. Most times, I see the story for what it is, but either way the researcher in me kicks in. I then go to one or two of my favorite websites that focus on urban mythology and run a few keywords of the story through their search engine, and I usually end up on snopes.com. If I get it in an e-mail or as part of a blog, I cut and paste a sentence, unedited, and get the same result. In less than five minutes, I have proven the evidence was nothing more than a campfire story. I debate whether to send it back and tell them, usually deciding it is not worth the argument. Most tell me they know it is a legend in some places, but their story really happened. There's no winning.

But the story is so good. We are drawn in by the romantic notion of the truth of it, and that is what makes it so dangerous. As investigators, we hold ourselves up to be the protectors of truth, but too often a respected colleague sends me a forwarded e-mail telling me a serial killer is loose or a missing child was taken from the mall. Serial killers are active and children turn up missing every day, so the specific cases we hear about and pass on make sense to us as something that could be true. We're not trying to lie.

We'll look a bit later at the influence of the Internet on paranormal investigators, but for now we can at least bring it up. Most websites cut and paste information from one source, usually adding a bit of commentary or some element they might have heard in addition to that. This method invites urban legends to make it around the world and back, like the old game "Telephone," and the origin of the story is too far removed to be of any use. Be careful when beginning an investigation because you read about it online. It probably won't be a ghost your hunting.

But It Was a Great Story

Many of these stories have been around for years, even decades, and knowing truth from fiction may help keep a ghost hunter from wasting time on a case he will never solve. The goose chase is not worth it. Knowing these stories helps investigators in other ways. Witnesses or people passing on information may be tainted by these tales, so it is important for us to know what is what for ourselves. You might become smarter and not let your surroundings mold how you think, but a non-ghost hunter who hears a story while in the cemetery is going to just know it's haunted when they talk to you. It also helps us understand some basic human needs, and while looking for spirits may seem to have everything to do with the world of the dead, it also has much to do with the world of the living.

Folklore Motifs

EVERYBODY LOVES A GOOD campfire story, and when we hear about the man with the hook we jump and understand there probably was never an escaped mental patient who went to Lover's Lane and tried to attack some experimenting teens. The story is so well known it dies there, and when we retell it, our audience understands the same thing. This all changes when ghosts slip into the narrative. There is something about the mythological phantom that hit us in the stomach instead. Truth or tale, there is always something truthful about it.

Figure 12.2
This asylum is notorious in its community.
Picture courtesy of Brian Paulson, EPRA.

Why They Work

Urban legends persist because they do fool us. They speak to us and touch some of our most primal and base instincts. They make the unexplained known and offer some insight into a world we don't understand. They talk about our fears and what scares us in the dark. The interesting thing about urban legends is that most of them have been around for decades. They do not point at what we are scared of today but rather what we as people fear. That universal lump in our throat makes them persist.

Think of a haunting surrounding that old abandoned mental asylum down the street. We are scared of what we might have done to those people there, and frightened we might one day be them. Then there are the scary darkened corners and sweating walls. These are all the elements we have been told to avoid since we were kids.

Other kinds of stories draw us in. It makes perfect sense that we would be scared or touched most by the child ghosts who often inhabit ghost stories. An older man who died after a long sickness is heartbreaking, but a child never dies of natural causes. It makes us think of the immense sorrow for his parents and forces us to confront the mortality of our own offspring.

One of the most obvious draws of the urban legend is the same thing that draws an investigator to a real haunting. It says something about our soul and what happens to us after we die. It touches upon religion and explains very passionate situations in easy to understand words and scenarios. The ghost is an archetype.

Urban legends allow us to see the wrongful death, one of the great fears we all share, but there are other common themes just as powerful. Many have to do with unfinished business and needing to find peace with this life before we can move on. They talk about love, especially unrequited love. More importantly, many allow the dead to find redemption somehow. Especially in a Christian society, even when the individual might not consider themselves Christian, redemption is an important part of the death process. Whether it be through righting a wrong or getting revenge, the soul may have the chance to get it right.

Sift through the stories you are told for some common hauntings. The fact of the matter is that most hauntings have a tragedy involved with them, but almost as many have a mundane, unconfirmed tale that led to the surviving spirit. Especially if you can't get a source for the story and you have not investigated it yourself, be careful of stories you hear about these subjects:

- **Hitchhikers**
- **Women in white or green or gray or brown or...**
- **Nuns who have affairs or start cults**
- **The Underground Railroad**
- **Attacked babysitters**
- **Any and all college hauntings**
- **Unrequited love or star-crossed lovers**
- **Card games gone wrong**
- **Falling mine shafts**

Figure 12.3
Haunted Stonehill College in Massachusetts. Most of the activity there is nothing more than legend.

Location, Location, Location

Be prepared to raise an eyebrow when you hear a story, especially when it comes second or third hand. Raise both of them if the story takes place in one of these locations. While there are many reasons these places may be haunted, there are too many stories that allow the place to make the haunting. The best way to tell whether any of these famous locations might be the site of an urban legend is to notice if one familiar tale gets stacked upon another.

For example, the bridge is haunted by a suicide victim who jumps because his lover never showed up to meet him there one night, or if you are on the bridge and honk three times, he will appear in your headlights.

- **Bridges**
- **The woods**
- **Places of death/sickness**
- **The water**
- **Railroad tracks**
- **Bars and restaurants**

Figure 12.4
Haunted woods.

Folklore as the Haunting

IT IS A CLASSIC TALE OF HORROR touching upon all of the sentimental hot buttons. A busload of young schoolchildren is getting its daily lift to school when their bus passes over a set of well traveled railroad tracks. For some reason, the bus stalls as the train approaches. The driver tries furiously to get the vehicle moving as the train bears down on it. It is too late. He tries to evacuate the children through the front, but the collision is too quick and too violent. All those inside perish.

Figure 12.5
A cemetery where ghostly legends abound.
Picture courtesy of Luanne Joly, Whaling City Ghosts

The thing is this. The little souls survive after death to help those in the same situation. When a car stalls out on those same railroad tracks, it is mysteriously pushed to safety. People sometimes see little children behind them or hear giggling when it happens. You can go down to the tracks and recreate it yourself. Just put your car in neutral and watch your car move safely to the other side, uphill even, and if you sprinkle talcum powder on your bumper, you will be amazed at the little handprints that appear on it.

I Know That Story

Don't get too excited. You've heard the story before, and if it didn't take place in your town, you're sure you've heard it from the one next to you. Sorry. It never happened. There has been only one accident in this country where a school bus was hit by a train, and all the tiny Texas schoolchildren got out before anyone got seriously hurt. Locations all across the country have these mystery areas where a car in neutral appears to go uphill, but the experience is an optical illusion and the vehicles are actually moving downhill. The powder on the bumper can also be explained by dirt and fingerprints already on it that are only lifted when the talcum is added.

The story remains a constant on message boards and e-mail chains, and I get requests to investigate the scene from peers eager to record the laughter of small kids. I have to tell them it isn't true and usually they tell me they know it is a tale told in some states, but the one they heard of locally is indeed true. I tell them I am busy that weekend, but ask them to please share the evidence when they get back. I usually don't hear back from them about it, and I let it drop.

This is the first type of relationship between hauntings and legends. The legend is the haunting. In this case, the ghost is the subject of local folklore, unproven but engaging, and people believe it because it is rooted in enough truth, and spotted with enough detail, to make it feel true. There have been fatal accidents involving school buses where trains weren't involved, and we all feel anxious once in a while when we send our children off to school. Besides, don't we want to think if innocent souls die they will somehow become angels in death?

Riding the Legend

Another good example is the onslaught of hitchhiker and roadside ghosts seen all across the country. People are seeing ghosts on the side of the road looking to hitch a ride to somewhere. The drivers ultimately find their passenger is a ghost when they disappear somewhere during the ride. There are dozens of variants of the story, from driving through a person in the middle of the road to bringing the ghost to a dance and then having her disappear after she asks to go home. Some even claim the hitchhiker to be Jesus who predicts when the world is going to end. It is one of the most popular and widely circulated urban legends, and often is passed as a true story. You can trace the story from community to community much like hitching a ride across the country.

These myths have had a collective effect on our culture. The story becomes a haunting in and of itself. There are often no firsthand witnesses to the haunting but rather a character, such as Resurrection Mary in Chicago, is just well known or a stretch of road becomes synonymous with a ghost. People retell the stories to be part of the bigger picture. They become part of the lore and their section of the story travels on.

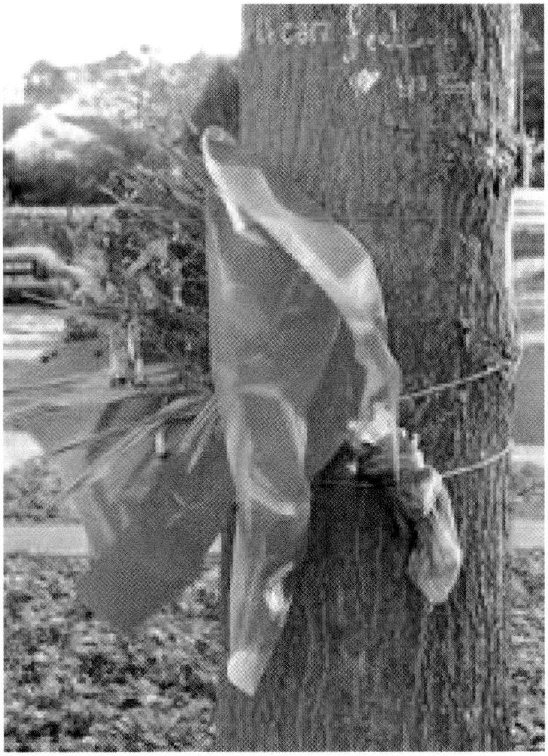

Figure 12.6
A roadside memorial thought to be haunted by a teenage girl.

Over time, the ghost becomes unquestioned in the community. This does not mean some of these reports are not true; rather, many times a classic myth becomes so well known people think they see it. Something that might be explained away becomes the ghost because the area is known for it. A sketchy person walking into the woods becomes otherworldly.

Ain't It Supposta Be?

WHY DON'T THEY JUST TEAR down that house? It's falling apart, with broken stairs held together by jutting, rusted nails and shattered windows. On the right night, you can look inside and see figures moving where it is just dark enough so that they appear as shadows. I heard a person was killed there once, a whole family, in fact, and they never found the man that did it. The family was never able to sell the house, especially after the sister who survived went crazy. John was there last Halloween because we challenged him to spend the night. He lasted longer than the radio show that was set up in the basement as a promotion for their station. My sister says she has heard the crying when she walked up there once, and Lisa's best friend's brother has heard the screaming and the gunshot. They should just tear that place down.

That creepy old house down the street. It is a fixture in most towns, and although there is a way to go down to the town records and find who owns it, no one actually ever does. Instead, the community is content to have it be abandoned, owned in many ways by the town itself, and have the stories told about the house be its history. No one ever remembers the name of the murdered family, and it happened long enough ago that people in the town remember something about it, maybe from when they were kids. The whole town knows it just has to be haunted. Ain't it supposta be?

Looking the Part

The house becomes the main character in the ghost story because it looks the part, like it put on a Halloween costume a decade ago and has never taken it off. It has to be haunted because the media has set hauntings in houses that look like it for years. The rotting floor boards, the ripped curtains blowing in the breeze, set the mood because of our expectations. Some places are thought to be haunted because they look like they should be. It touches something that has been made part of our paranormal personality from the earliest horror stories we have heard. So much of haunted folklore depends on mood, and these types of houses transport you deep into your own fear about the haunted house. The backstory might be much more mundane than the community wants it to be, but there is a need to have the house, and the town never really wants to know differently anyway. What would they talk about during Halloween?

Figure 12.7
This building in Boston just has to be haunted.
Picture courtesy of John M. Nevulis.

Well, That's Where I'd Be

Ghost hunters make their bones on those haunted sites in the community they hear about from other people. Rather than a family experiencing a ghost and calling them in, they find a supposed haunted location, gear up, and go out to see what they can find. Too many investigators run headlong into an investigation based on the reputation of a place. The building has been rumored to be haunted for years, so they know they'll get something if they go. These types of places are the same in every community. Go from town to town and ask if there are any ghosts, and people will list them with bullet points. They are the locations that are haunted because it makes sense they would be. The catch is, so many of them are ideal places to get false evidence because of the environment they are in. Old buildings have a lot of dust, and that dust becomes orbs or spirits and streaks of souls.

Burial grounds are a good example. Cemeteries are ground zero for ghost hunters. When they have nothing to do, they travel to the most popular one in the area and gather evidence. The dead are there. The reason it should be haunted is the same reason the rumors surrounding them should be ignored. Of all the variables that make a cemetery a bad place to investigate, the most compelling might be the uneasy investigator with his feet planted firmly in the one place ghosts just have to be. There are too many things late at night to be scared of in graveyards, and most have nothing to do with the supernatural. You scare yourself because something should jump out at you. That adrenaline is enough to amp up your senses, making phantoms out of noises you would ignore or be able to explain during the day.

Aside from the haunted house, the abandoned hospital or jail is perfect for a story. If they were going to make a movie about demons trying to take over the world, they would set it in one of these buildings. New England is great for old hospitals that are more moss than stone now, and investigators pass stories among themselves about the ones they have been to. All of them sound the same after a while, and when they are told second and third hand from another group, I know it is more legend than legitimate. The same is true for abandoned mines and old railway stations.

Figure 12.8
This door opens and closes by itself and leads to an attic with a questioned past.

Figure 12.9
Another attic haunted by footsteps and voices.

Things can hit closer to home though. People have a fear of what is close to them. Your basement and attic are the unfamiliar places in your house and some of the scariest places known to man. Even if they were empty when people moved in, they still feel there is something left from a previous owner there, and the fact that we don't spend much time there makes them off limits somehow. The cobwebs and new shadows tell us it is the perfect soil for a good ghost story, and that becomes the breeding ground for an urban legend to imprint itself.

Figure 12.10
The haunted basement to a restaurant where there has been activity.

I Heard It Somewhere: Folklore as the Root

AN OLD MAN BECOMES SOUR to the world as his body slips away from him. His son has moved in to help him and when he needs something, he bangs an old rusty can against the wall and screams his name out. The man dies and the son moves on. The new family moves in and hears the sound of metal banging against the wall and a name being called out. Once the pipes are checked, we can start to look at other reasons for the noises. If the old family can be contacted and we discover the story of the old man, we can connect the dots and all is well.

Most hauntings are not wrapped up like this. Most happen in a vacuum and give no indication of the why. We are left with the what and the when, and in our need to explain everything away, we fall into a classic bear trap. We pull an explanation out of what we have heard somewhere else, and the story makes perfect sense to us.

Folklore as the root of a haunting is probably the most common connection between myth and the reality of a ghost. There is evidence gathered and people have had experiences, but there is no backstory. Long ago, societies blamed bad things on seen and unseen creatures, like fairies or leprechauns. Airplanes crashed or disappeared because of gremlins in World War II. As people advanced, they replaced these monsters with gods or demons, and now they filled in the blanks. Today, stories help us find the blame, and haunted places take the lead in finding scapegoats.

A Real Ghost, but the Names Are Changed

I was investigating a very haunted location when I came across a trusted peer who had witnessed something there. It was a common party area in a forest, and this particular part was an old quarry with a high ledge and a bottomless pond. He had gone there to down a few and meet with people, and as he arrived, he noticed the silhouette of a woman off to his left near the edge of the rock. He looked to his friend to ask her name and when he turned back she was gone. Dumbfounded, he asked if anyone else had seen her, and his friends laughed. They told him that he had just seen the Lady of the Ledge.

Figure 12.11
The Lady of the Ledge's view for eternity.
Picture courtesy of Jeff Belanger, Ghostvillage.com.

Years ago, she had been waiting for her lover to show up, but he was delayed because his parents didn't approve of her. Thinking she had been rejected, she jumped to her death rather than live without him. It is a familiar story and most likely never happened on that particular spot, but in place of knowing her background, people found it easy to fall on a story that has been told for centuries. The man did see something unexplained there, and there had been more than a dozen suicides at the location, so the story has an, "it could be true," element to it. A lonely ghost becomes the Lady of the Ledge, and her story is romantic enough to last for generations.

In place of a true history, we are comfortable with making one up. Many ghost hunters look to one day prove the existence of ghosts, which really means proving to the nonbeliever the potential for the supernatural. Often, the spark to begin investigating is a personal experience, but many times, the true push happens when the person reads a well crafted book about true hauntings. The best part of these stories is when the ghost is later revealed to be old Uncle Caleb who lost his life when the horse threw him off. That is why a strange spirit is seen in the trees and no grass will grow in that part of the field.

Being able to come up with that ending when everything makes sense is almost a way to prove the ghost exists. How else could the backstory and the modern haunting have so much related? Unfortunately, in the rush to have that ending, and to have it make sense and prove the haunting, an urban legend is allowed to suffice for the story.

Urban Legends: Ghost Hunter's Rumors

In many cases, urban legend is a euphemism for rumor. Unsubstantiated stories become history when they can be told enough, and no one does this better than investigators. We don't mean to; we just like the puzzle solved. When there is no reason for a place to have a spirit and there is an old hospital in the town (and there is always an old hospital in the town), an escaped mental patient did it. There are so few of these cases that are real, but we put everything on the emotionally challenged.

In a real baffling location urban legends can live on top of each other. It would seem like this confuses things, but in reality it makes it easier. When so many stories exist together, you just know they can't all be true, especially if the stories change from person to person. The nun was practicing witchcraft or got into an accident or was having an affair with the priest. There is such a mess, but it is presented with such a neat package. The only trouble is separating fact from fiction, which is part of the fun of a researcher's job.

Some Classic Roots

When in doubt, point the finger at a minority, and point it twice if the culture is weird or unusual to you. There are too many hauntings in the North that get their origins from death, for some reason by fires, along the Underground Railroad. That time in history mystifies us, and there is probably something to be said for the guilt of slavery, and any hidden room or secret passage outside was once a stop for escaped slaves. Better yet, they're all haunted.

Figure 12.12
A haunted Native American reservation.

Let's not forget the ancient Indian burial ground. If you don't know why your house is haunted, say it is built on sleeping Native Americans and even the most hardened cynic will nod his head at you. The excuse is a quick fix and convenient, so most stop their digging there. We are at least the second people on this land, and we displaced so much of the Native American culture, that it is plausible our house is planted on an area that once had sacred value to another culture.

In fact, there have been very few hauntings traced back to Native Americans and the way they buried their dead. The excuse tells us more about ourselves and our ideas about Native Americans.

A great giveaway when trying to separate true hauntings from their folklore counterparts is to look at the phrasing of the story. How many times have you heard them called "ancient Indian burial grounds," those four words together in that order. If it sounds like a cliché and walks like a cliché, it might be an urban legend.

Religion is not safe either. Witchcraft has been made to take the stand for hauntings throughout the country, and demons are the source of much of the ghostly activity in the southern part of the United States. The real bad guys are the cults, although usually what kind of cult is left out of the story and the listener doesn't ask.

It is assumed the cult is a pack of Satanists, and who likes them anyway. They are one of those groups most people are unified against. Paranormal activity, especially in wooded areas, often comes back to a cult in the forest. It is hard to tell if they bring the ghosts or if they are drawn in by them, but they are mentioned side by side with the unexplained.

More on the Word Game

Much like the witness motif, there are certain words that should make the alarms go off in your head. As mentioned before, these are not keys that a lie is about to happen, but they are signs that a classic myth is about to be passed off as true. Beware when you hear:

- **The college tried to cover it up to keep the enrollment up.**
- **It happened about 20 years ago.**
- **I heard this from a guy in town.**
- **Some nights, when the moon is full...**
- **There is this hitchhiker...**
- **It was an escaped mental patient.**
- **But the family was rich and real important in the town...**
- **In my dorm...**
- **There were these children...**

Figure 12.13
A haunted pond on a college campus.

When you point out how often these phrases have been heard before, you'll get a dirty look, but you might be a bit closer to peeling away that layer of untruth that clouds investigators getting closer to the real deal.

Reevaluating the Old Stories

WE HAVE BECOME so sophisticated we can look down at years of stories and chuckle at how silly they were back in the day. We have come a long way. The fact that we still believe these stories and fall for the urban legends we are told tells us we are not as wise as we thought. There is a comfort to them that forces us to be ignorant.

It works the other way too. Many of the stories we pass off as folklore might, in fact, be true hauntings passed off as we made that great leap from rural superstition to modern cynic. If only we had the technology and the open mind at the same time, some of those old stories might offer us a better insight in the supernatural world.

What to Do with All This

It's a lot to swallow, and some of it might contradict itself. There is an inherent link between urban legends and true hauntings. Our ideas are molded by those old tales, and witnesses have heard them over and over again when they experience something. They might find their way into your investigation, and it is part of your job to weed them out, to take the time to rethink and examine what someone has said or the reputation of a haunted place.

There is another connection though, and this link is one of the reasons the paranormal field goes through cycles of popularity and why so much of the mainstream world will always believe there is such a thing as ghosts but never really believe in them. Local folklore and a good ghost story satisfy the same need to have that single emotional response, to see the world turned on its ear and have a clear narrative that calls our very soul into question.

Now that is all very poetic, but as you continue to keep a diary of your investigations it should become a necessity to come up with some visual way to represent the urban legends you are told as if they were facts. I suggest highlighter or some kind of word processing distinction. The more you hear from people, the more you will be able to see trends in certain areas and their connections to other stories.

But Keep Pressing On

The fact is clichés exist because there is an ease to them. Urban legends seep into our haunted lives, but that might not take away from the cream of the crop. Characterize something that seems too familiar, but don't dismiss it. Enjoy the urban legend when you hear it, as long as you understand it as a story. Stories are the reason most of us got into this originally.

The urban legend might have more truth than you think. It might only be a legend giving backstory or a person trying to communicate the unknown to you through filters the world has created for them. Ghosts have a strange way of finding the living, and maybe a scary looking place is where they know you'll be waiting for them. Maybe an old hospital has enough energy to draw other spirits in. Maybe a school, with energetic youth whose minds are more open to things, allows a ghost wandering in the dark to find light. After all, I still can't explain how I got an EVP of a young girl saying, "Help me," in Spanish while looking for Maria.

Figure 12.14
A rock dungeon rumored to be haunted.

Resources

A

Online Resources

Adventures Beyond	www.adventuresbeyond.com
Alchemy Lab Web Ring	www.alchemylab.com/webring.htm
Alien/UFO/Ghost Research Society	www.AlienUFOart.com
Alphaland	www.alphaland.com
American Ghost Society	www.prairieghosts.com
The American Society for Psychical Research	www.aspr.com
An Unknown Encounter	www.barcon.com
Archive X Stories	www.wirenot.net/X
Center for the Study of EVP	www.ghostshop.com
Chat Ghosts	http://www.psychics.co.uk/ghostchat.html
The Committee for Skeptical Inquiry	www.csicop.org
Deadframe Spirit Photography	www.deadframe.com
Earthbound Ghosts	www.erols.com/rcod
Ghost Hunters, Inc.	www.angelfire.com/tx3/ghosthtml
Ghost Hunters Society	http://members.tripod.com/GhostHuntersSociety/Home.htm
Ghost Research Society	www.ghostresearch.org
Ghosts and Other Haunts	www.go.to/nzghosts
Ghostvillage	www.ghostvillage.com
Haunted American Tours	www.hauntedamericatours.com
Haunted Places	www.haunted-places.com
International Ghost Hunters Society	www.ghostweb.com
The L.I.F.E. Foundation	www.paranormalhelp.com
Obiwan's Paranormal Page	www.ghosts.org
The Paranormal Network	www.mindreader.com
The Shadowlands	www.shadowlands.net
Sight Seekers	www.sightingseekers.com
True Ghosts	www.trueghost.com
Universal Ghost Guide	http://universalguide.com/myth/myth-ghosts-4.htm
New England Society for Psychic Research	www.warrens.net

Paranormal Groups and Sites by State

Alabama

Northern Alabama Paranormal Research Society
www.naprs.us/index.htm

Alabama Ghost Hunting Society
http://ghostinvestigator.tripod.com/ghostinvestigators

Alaska

Investigation of Paranormal in Alaska
http://hometown.aol.com/articphox/myhomepage/profile.html

Arizona

Phoenix Paranormal Investigations
http://ppi.org.uk

Ghosts to Ghost Arizona
www.arizona.ghost2ghosts.co.uk

Arkansas

Arkansas Paranormal Investigations
http://hometown.aol.com/articphox/myhomepage/profile.html

Central Arkansas Society for Paranormal Research http://hometown.aol.com/articphox/myhomepage/profile.html

California

Bay Area Paranormal Research Society
www.bayareaparanormal.com

American Paranormal Investigations
www.ap-investigations.com

Southern California Paranormal Detectives
http://www.paranormaldetectives.org

Colorado

CCPI www.candcparanormal.com

Rocky Mountain Paranormal Research Society
www.rockymountainparanormal.com

Connecticut

Connecticut Paranormal Research Society
www.cprs.info

Northwest Connecticut Paranormal Society
http://northwestconnecticutparanormal.com

Cemetery-Graveyard Investigators
http://www.myspace.com/c_gi

Delaware

Delaware Ghost Hunters
www.delawareghosthunters.com

M and M Investigators
www.m-and-m-investigators.com

Georgia

Georgia Paranormal Society
www.GeorgiaParanormalSociety.com

Georgia Haunt Hunters
www.geocities.com/gahaunt

Florida

Infinity Paranormal Investigations Network
www.infinityparanormal.com

Daytona Beach Paranormal Research Group, Inc.
www.dbprginc.org

Hawaii

Kwaidan
www.geocities.com/Area51/Hollow/6166/

Idaho

Idaho Spirit Seekers
www.idahospiritseekers.com

Illinois

Haunted Chicago
www.hauntedchicago.com

TRIPAR Research Organization
www.triparinvestigations.org

Ghost Research Society
www.ghostresearch.org

The Mesa Project
www.mesaproject.com

Indiana

Crossroads Paranormal
www.crossroadsparanormal.com

Proof Paranormal
http://proofparanormal.com/index2.html

Circle City Paranormal Exploration
www.c-c-p-e.com

Iowa

Iowa Center for Paranormal Research
www.iowacenterforparanormalresearch.com

Kansas

Miller's Paranormal Research
www.millersparanormalresearch.com

Kentucky

Kentucky Paranormal Research
www.kyghosts.com

TM Ghost Hunters
http://tmghosthunters.com

Louisiana

South Louisiana Ghost Hunters
www.southlouisianaghosthunters.com

Maine

Maine Supernatural
http://mysite.verizon.net/vzeqnk8x/

Northeast Paranormal Society
http://spiritsofmaine.tripod.com/index.htm

Central Maine Researchers and Investigators of the Paranormal
www.centralmaineparanormal.com

Maryland

Maryland Paranormal Investigators
www.angelfire.com/md/MPInvestigators/index.html

Massachusetts

Massachusetts Paranormal Crossroads
www.masscrossroads.com

New England Ghost Project
www.neghostproject.com

The Berkshire Paranormal Group
www.berkshireparanormal.com

South Coast Paranormal Investigators
www.myspace.com/southcoastparanormal

Michigan

Faces from the Grave
www.facesfromthegrave.mirrorz.com

West Michigan Ghost Hunters Society
www.wmghs.com

Minnesota
Minnesota Paranormal Investigators
minnesotaparanormalinvestigators.com

Minnesota Ghosts
www.minnesotaghosts.com

Mississippi
Observations
www.orbservations.com

Missouri
Missouri Ghost Hunting Society
http://ghosthaunting.com

Montana
Montana Paranormal Research Society
www.mtprs.org

Nebraska
Great Plains Paranormal Research Society
www.gpprs.org

Nevada
Nevada Spooks
www.nvspooks.com

Las Vegas Society of Supernatural Investigation
www.lvssi.org

New Hampshire
East Coast Transcommunication Organization
www.ectoweb.com

Northeastern Paranormal Investigations
www.northeasternparanormal.com

New Jersey
New Jersey Ghost Hunters Society
www.njghs.net

New Journey Ghost Research
www.njgr.org

New Mexico
New Mexico Paranormal
www.newmexicoparanormal.com

New York
Long Island Paranormal Group
www.liparanormalinvestigators.com/2

Western New York Paranormal
www.wnyparanormal.org/e107/news.php

New York Paranormal
www.newyorkparanormal.i8.com

NYPAPS
(New York, Pennsylvania Paranormal Society)
www.freewebs.com/xxghostsandspiritsxx/

North Carolina
Coalition of Autonomous Scientific Paranormal Entity Researchers
www.geocities.com/casper_research/Main_page

Eastern Paranormal
www.easternparanormal.com

North Carolina Paranormal Research Society
www.ncprs.net

North Dakota
North Dakota Ghosthunters and Paranormal Investigators
www.ghostinvestigator.tripod.com/ndgis

Ohio
Ghosts of Ohio
www.ghostsofohio.org

G.H.O.S.T. (Ghost Hunters Ohio Search Team)
www.ohioghosthunter.com

Oklahoma
Ghost Haunts of Oklahoma and Urban Legend Investigations
www.ghouli.com

Native American Ghost Society
www.myspace.com/Prettysaro99

Oregon
Salem Spirit Trackers
http://home.comcast.net/~noticky/wsb/html/view.cgi-home.html-.html

Pennsylvania
Ghosts of Gettysburg
www.ghostsofgettysburg.com

Blue Moon Paranormal Investigations
www.bluemoonghosthunters.com

Rhode Island
Haunted Paranormal Research Society
www.hauntedprs.org

NEAR (New England Anomalies Research) Paranormal
http://nearparanormal.com

Greenville Paranormal Research
http://www.greenvillepr.tk

South Carolina
Carolina Paranormal Research
http://carolinaparanormal.net

Tennessee
Bell Witch
www.bellwitch.org

Tennessee Ghost Hunters
www.tnghosthunters.com/

Texas
The Society for Psychical Research
www.spr.ac.uk/expcms/index.php?section=1

Lone Star Spirits
www.lonestarspirits.org

Texas Paranormal Society
www.txparanormalsociety.com

Utah
Paranormal Investigations Team of Utah
www.piteamofutah.com

Vermont
Vermont Agency of Paranormal Organized Research
www.teamvapor.org

Paranormal Investigators of New England
http://pinewengland.blogspot.com

Virginia
Hampton Roads Paranormal Research Group
www.geocities.com/Area51/8497

Washington DC Metro Area Ghost Watchers
www.dchauntings.com

Washington
Amateur Ghost Hunters of Seattle-Tacoma
www.aghost.us

Washington State Paranormal Investigations and Research
www.wspir.com

West Virginia
West Virginia Ghost Hunters
http://ghosthunterwv.tripod.com/westvirginiaghosthunters

West Virginia Paranormal Researching and Investigation
www.wvpri.com/page2.htm

Wisconsin
Wausau Paranormal Research Society
www.pat-wausau.org

Jason Jrakeman
www.jaesonjrakman.com

Paranormal Media: Magazines, Television, and Radio Shows

Alabama ParaSpiritual Research Radio www.apsrradio.com This is one of the true gems of the paranormal radio community. They also offer a network of shows from other hosts, including Shadow Talk.

Beyond Reality Radio http://beyondrealityradio.com Think of this as TAPS radio, although they cover much more than ghosts. The show can be heard on the air in Rhode Island but online as well.

Blog Talk Radio www.blogtalkradio.com This is the main page for Blog Talk Radio. Once on the site you can search for paranormal radio shows by topic.

Coast to Coast AM/Somewhere in Time www.coasttocoastam.com This is the main site for the Coast to Coast and Somewhere in Time radio shows, the most successful of their kind. The show can be heard in most areas in syndication, but for a fee you can subscribe to hear it live and gain access to the archives.

Darkness on the Edge of Town Radio Show www.darknessradio.com The home of Darkness Dave, one of the most respected and knowledgeable people working today. He has his own style, which people either love or hate.

FATE Magazine www.fatemag.com *FATE* (Fantastic Adventures and True Experiences) is probably the most respected paranormal magazine covering all topics weird and unexplained. It also offers some radio shows hosted by icon Hilly Rose.

The Ghost Chronicles and Ghost Chronicles International www.toginet.com The Ghost Chronicles is a live show twice a week and with archived episodes. The same crew features more in-depth shows, usually on location, at www.ghostvillage.com.

Ghost Magazine http://ghostmag.com This is one of the most respected of the new paranormal magazines and offers a scientific approach to the topic. The site has information on the publication, but not much more in the way of content.

Ghostly Talk www.ghostlytalk.com Doug and Scott take listeners on a journey into the paranormal. They feature top guests and have a well maintained archive.

Haunted Times www.hauntedtimes.com This is the main site for *Haunted Times Magazine* and offers a message board and information on the publication. The site also has online content and articles.

The Lou Gentile Show www.lougentile.com This show has been around, it seems, since the beginning.

Mysteries Magazine http://mysteriesmagazine.com This publication is one of the better of the new magazines out there and has monthly articles on new ideas, famous cases, and newer supernatural ideas.

Parahub Radio www.parahub.org Listed as one of the best paranormal radio shows on the web today, the show is strong and the site offers a new perspective on the paranormal.

Psi Talk Radio Webcast www.psitalk.com This site is a way station for some of the most popular paranormal radio shows, including Dark Matters Radio, The Lou Gentile Show, and News for the Soul. Think of it as a great first stop.

Spooky Southcoast www.spookysouthcoast.com Located in Southeastern Massachusetts, this radio show has gained a national following. It features shows on such varying topics as ghosts, UFOs, and odd technology.

Shadow Talk Paranormal Radio www.shadowtalkparanormalradio.com They have been in the business a while and their show and guest list are a tribute to that.

Unsolved Mysteries www.unsolvedmysteries.com This website is a meeting place for those into the unknown. Mainly a message board type format, it allows posts on all aspects of the unexplained.

The Paranormal Glossary

B

Amorphous: Without definite form or shape.

Angel: A nonhuman entity who's believed to be aligned with God.

Anomaly: An experience, occurrence, or object outside of the normal.

Apparition: A spirit that a witness can see.

Apport: The appearance or disappearance of an object during a ghostly experience.

Astral projection: Voluntarily or involuntarily leaving ones body and traveling somewhere else.

Automatic writing: A method of spirit communication where a spirit uses the hand of the living to write words or draw pictures.

Bilocation: The presence of a person or object in two places at once.

Channeling: Communication by a spirit through a human being where the spirit comes through the channeler.

Channeler: Someone who allows a spirit to temporarily possess his body to allow for communication with the living.

Clairvoyance: The ability to communicate with the other side, see the future, or be given other information using only the mind.

Collective apparition: A ghost that is seen by several witnesses at the same time.

Cleansing: Using occult or nontraditional means to remove something supernatural from a place.

Corpse light: The glow sometimes seen around the spirit of the departed.

Crisis apparition: A one-time paranormal experience where the spirit is seen at the time of its death by a loved one as a way of saying goodbye or communicating information.

Demon: One of many nonhuman spirits. Although the term is commonly used in the Judeo-Christian tradition, the term applies to many different spirits and traditions.

Demonologist: Someone who is an expert on demons and nonhuman entities and who is called upon to perform exorcisms.

Discarnate: Another name for a ghost.

Doppelganger: The spirit of a living person viewed by that person. Doppelgangers are seen as a bad omen, usually as a sign of impeding death.

Dowsing: Locating objects by the use of a divining or dowsing rod.

Ectoplasm: Anything physical left behind by a ghost or other entity. Many believe spirits use it to actually make themselves take some kind of physical form.

Electromagnetic field (EMF): Natural and unnatural fluctuations in the magnetic fields in an area. This field can be measured, and high readings often indicate the presence of a ghost.

Electromagnetic field meter: One of several devices used to measure EMF and detect a ghost.

Electronic voice phenomena (EVP): A term used to describe the noises and voices that are recorded on traditional audio or videotape, but that aren't audible to the human ear—often believed to be voices from the other side.

Elemental: An inhuman spirit who is closely tied to the elements.

Extrasensory perception (ESP): An awareness of outside happenings or information not attained through the normal human senses.

Familiar: Any animal who is used by a witch for surveillance or for casting spells. A familiar can also be the witch in animal form.

Full-bodied apparition: A ghostly encounter where the complete human ghost is seen.

Ghost: The disembodied essence of someone.

Ghost light: Unexplained lights often associated with paranormal activity.

Haunting: The interaction between the paranormal and the normal.

Infestation: A haunting that implies multiple spirits or something demonic. The word is also associated with a rise in the intensity of a haunting.

Inhuman spirit: A spirit that was never a human. The two most common forms of inhuman spirits are elementals and demons.

Medium: A person who has a special gift and believes he or she can act as a bridge between the world of the living and the other side.

Metaphysics: A field of study dedicated to the nature of reality and an individual's distance from it.

Near death experience (NDE): The experiencing of temporary death or loss of biological life where the subject goes through an archetypal event.

Necromancy: Speaking to the dead, most frequently used to determine the future.

Night terror: The sudden overwhelming of a person during a nightmare or unexplained nocturnal occurrence.

Obsession: The process by which a demon gains its initial access to a targeted human. The subject literally becomes obsessed with the demon.

Old Hag Syndrome: A nighttime experience where one wakes to a heavy force on the chest and is unable to move. Folklore tells of an old woman who sits on you and steals your breath while you sleep.

Orbs: A phenomenon in the shape of a floating ball of light; often thought to be trapped souls.

Out-of-body-experience: Leaving one's body during an unexplained event, most times during a near death experience.

Paranormal: A term used to describe unusual activity that involves ghosts, apparitions, spirits, hauntings, poltergeists, etc. This term defines anything for which there is no scientific explanation.

Parapsychology: The study of phenomena, real or supposed, that appear to be inexplicable to presently accepted scientific theories.

Pendulum: A crystal or rock suspended from a chain; used for divination or spirit communication.

Phenomenon: A term used to collectively categorize an event or occurrence that cannot be explained by science or the natural world.

Physical mediumship: A form of mediumship in which the spirit communicates using both the physical energies and consciousness of the medium.

Planchette: A pointing device used in conjunction with a channeling board.

Poltergeist: A phenomenon that is more often experienced than seen. A poltergeist will often interact with its environment by moving objects, making noises, or making itself known in a variety of other ways.

Possession: The result of a demonic attack where a demon may take complete control of its victim for an unknown purpose.

Precursor noise: Any noise or signal recorded during an EVP signaling the beginning of a communication.

Progression hypnotherapy: The act of visiting past lives through the use of hypnosis.

Psi: A term used to describe psychic ability or power.

Psychic: A person who uses feelings or abilities to engage nonphysical forces.

Psychokinesis: The ability to move objects using only one's mind.

Residual haunting: A term used to describe a spirit that is trapped in a continuous emotional loop in a specific location.

Sixth sense: A term used to describe psychic ability or psi.

Spirit: Any entity who is not part of the known natural world.

Spirit world: The ambiguous place spirits go after death. This term does not imply any religious idea but rather a general dimension or place.

Spiritual guide: A spirit that watches over a living person and offers wisdom or guidance. Some may refer to one as a guardian angel.

Supernatural: Anything beyond the accepted definitions of the natural world. There is a difference between paranormal and supernatural.

Table tipping: One of the original forms of Spiritualist ghost communication where the responses of the spirit are related through the movements of a table or similar device.

Telepathy: Communication using the mind as opposed to other senses.

Time slip: A displacement where the witness experiences a different time, usually while in the same place.

Trance mediumship: A form of mediumship in which the medium shares his or her energy with a spirit through the use of trance.

Urban legend: Any story told as having happened to a friend of a friend. Many reported hauntings are recycled urban legends.

Vortex: Any type of rip or natural energy hole where energy from one place is pulled into or drawn to another place.

White noise: The clatter produced by traditional media forms behind the intended sound.

Xenoglossy: The ability to write or speak in a language not known.

Sample Forms C

South Jersey Ghost Research

A division of G.H.O.S.T.

Ghost Hunters Organization of Study and Training

Investigators Log

Date: ________________ Time: ________________

Investigator: ______________________________

Location: ____

Weather:____

Other Investigators Present____

____

Equipment: Camera Video Camera Tape Recorder Digital Camera

EMF Thermometer Night Vision

Film Speed_________ Brand____________ Exposures___________

B&W Color Infrared APS

Audio Tape: Micro Cassette Standard Cassette

length 60min 90min 120min

Video Tape: VHS VHS-C 8mm Digital 30min

Length 60min 90min 120min

Thermometer: Standard Electronic Infrared

Phenomena witnessed by investigator

Time:	Phenomena:
________	____
________	____
________	____
________	____
________	____
________	____
________	____
________	____
________	____

Investigators initials_______________

South Jersey Ghost Research

A division of G.H.O.S.T.

Ghost Hunters Organization of Study and Training

Phenomena witnessed by investigator

Time: _______ Phenomena: _______________________

Other Comments: _______________________

Investigators initials: _______________

South Jersey Ghost Research

A division of G.H.O.S.T.

Ghost Hunters Organization of Study and Training

Final Record

Roles of film used: ________________

Audio tapes used: ________________

Video tapes used: ________________

Number of Psychic Photos: ________________

Number of EVP recorded: ________________

Phenomena captured on film: ________________

Summation:

____
____
____
____
____
____
____
____
____
____
____
____
____
____
____
____
____
____
____
____
____

Investigators initials____________

INTERVIEW QUESTIONS

1. ADDRESS OF SITE: ______________________________

2. HOW MANY OCCUPANTS AT LOCATION: ______________________________

3. OCCUPANTS NAMES AND AGES: ______________________________

4. OCCUPANTS OCCUPATIONS: ______________________________

5. OCCUPANTS RELIGIOUS BELIEFS: ______________________________

6. TIME OF OCCUPANCY AT THE LOCATION: ______________________________

7. AGE OF THE SITE: ______________________________

8. HOW MANY PREVIOUS OWNERS: ______________________________

9. HISTORY OF SITE: (TRAGEDIES, DEATHS, PREVIOUS COMPLAINTS) ______________________________

10. HOW MANY ROOMS IN THE SITE: ______________________________

11. HAS THE LOCATION BEEN BLESSED: ______________________________

12. HAS THERE BEEN ANY RECENT REMODELING: ______________________________

13. ANY OCCUPANTS ON MEDICATION: ______________________________

14. ANY OCCUPANTS USING ILLEGAL DRUGS: ______________________________

15. ANY OCCUPANTS DRINK ALCOHOL HEAVILY: ______________________

16. ANY OCCUPANTS INTERESTED IN THE OCCULT: (OUIJA, SEANCES, PSYCHICS, SPELLS) ______________________

17. ANY OCCUPANTS CURRENTLY SEEING A PSYCHIATRIST: ______________________

18. HAVE ANY RELIGIOUS CLERGY BEEN CONSULTED: ______________________

19. HAS THERE BEEN ANY MEDIA INVOLVEMENT: ______________________

20. HAVE THERE BEEN ANY OTHER WITNESSES BESIDES THE OCCUPANTS: ______________________

21. HAVE THERE BEEN ANY ODORS: (PERFUMES, FLOWERS, SULFUR, EXCRETMENT) ______________________

22. HAVE THERE BEEN ANY SOUNDS: (FOOTSTEPS, KNOCKS, BANGING) ______________________

23. HAVE THERE BEEN ANY VOICES: (WHISPERING, YELLING, CRYING, SPEAKING) ______________________

24. HAS THERE BEEN ANY MOVEMENT OF OBJECTS: ______________________

25. HAVE THERE BEEN ANY LEVITATIONS: ______________________

26. HAVE THERE BEEN ANY UNCOMMON COLD OR HOT SPOTS: ______________________

27. HAVE THERE BEEN ANY PROBLEMS WITH ELECTRICAL APPLIANCES: (TV, LIGHTS, KITCHEN APPLIANCES, DOORBELLS) ______________________

28. HAVE THERE BEEN ANY PROBLEMS WITH PLUMBING: (LEAKS, FLOODING, SINKS, TOILET BOWLS)

____

29. ANY OCCUPANTS HAVING NIGHTMARES OR TROUBLE SLEEPING:____________________

30. HAVE THERE BEEN ANY PHYSICAL ATTACKS: ____________________

31. ARE PETS AFFECTED: ____________________

32. WHEN WAS THE FIRST OCCURRENCE OF THE PHENOMENA: ____________________

33. WHAT WERE THE WITNESSES' REACTION DURING THE PHENOMENA: ____________________

34. WHAT WAS THE DURATION OF THE PHENOMENA: ____________________

35. WHO FIRST WITNESSED THE PHENOMENA: ____________________

36. WERE THERE ANY OTHER WITNESSES: ____________________

37. WHAT TIME WAS THE FIRST OCCURRENCE OF THE PHENOMENA: ____________________

38. HOW OFTEN DOES THE PHENOMENA OCCUR: ____________________

39. DO THE OCCUPANTS FEEL THE PHENOMENA IS THREATENING: ____________________

40. WHAT DO THE OCCUPANTS BELIEVE IS HAPPENING: (IS IT SUPERNATURAL) ____________________

41. DO ALL OF THE OCCUPANTS AGREE ON WHAT IS HAPPENING OR DO THEY THINK IT'S NONSENSE:

____

South Jersey Ghost Research Release Form

Research, Assistance and Understanding
Phone: 609-218-7447 **Email:** sjgr@theshadowlands.net
Website: http://theshadowlands.net/southjersey/

I, ____________________________ , have the authority to allow access to S.J.G.R. members and affiliated persons to ____________________________ located in _________________ for the purpose of conducting an investigation into possible paranormal occurrences or conducting field research at this location. The investigation process has been explained to me and I give S.J.G.R. permission to conduct one at this location. S.J.G.R. releases the owner of the location from any liability for injuries and/or damages incurred during the investigation. S.J.G.R. assumes responsibility for any damages to the property during the investigation.

Signed_____________________________ Date___________
Witness_____________________________ Date___________

South Jersey Ghost Research
Release of Information and Evidence

Research, Assistance and Understanding
Phone: 609-218-7447 **Email:** sjgr@theshadowlands.net
Website: http://theshadowlands.net/southjersey/

S.J.G.R. respects your right to privacy. All of your personal information will be kept confidential. S.J.G.R. would like to use some or all of the information and evidence collected during the investigation for possible inclusion in our website, newsletter and other future media considerations. Please check the level of confidentiality you would like to request:

___ S.J.G.R. may not release any part of the investigation to the public.

___ S.J.G.R. may release the information providing that the identity of witnesses and clients is changed and the exact address of the location is excluded.

___ S.J.G.R. may release any/all of the information and evidence collected during the investigation.

___ Other
comments/requests____
____
_

Signed____________________________ Date___________
Witness____________________________ Date___________

South Jersey Ghost Research

Phone: 609-218-7447 **Email:** sjgr@theshadowlands.net
Website: http://theshadowlands.net/southjersey/

Proposal for Permission to Conduct a Field Investigation for ANY Cemetery & Crematorium or place

To Whom It May Concern:

I represent a small group of student researchers, in the field of paranormal studies.

As part of our ongoing education, we must coordinate our research efforts on historical sites, including cemeteries, churches, parklands, etc.

We seek permission for the three of us to have access for 1 (ONE) evening, preferably this week sometime, it would be after regular gate hours, for a duration of 3 hours, from 8pm until 11pm, in order to conduct the following field investigation:

1. Photography, standard and infrared, 3 rolls (24 exposures per roll), for location verification
2. A small tape recording unit, for documentation of our efforts
3. A few other tools, such as flashlights (for obvious reasons), compass, candles for emerg. light source, and spare film, batteries and tapes, as backup, and a small hand-held electric field sensing device, as well as a notebook to record the steps as we go through them.

We expect this to be a dry run for future coordination of professional research, upon earning our certification. It will also establish base readings so that we may more ably gauge when future readings are anomalous.

Our research is dependent on clear weather, and will have to be postponed if fog, rain, high winds, snow or other inclement weather occurs on the set date and time. We will notify you of any cancellation, and if there is a need to reschedule, your permission will again be sought.

We understand, and fully respect that we will be on private property at all times, and all due consideration will be given, so that no damage come to any burial sites, mementos, or any part of your property. If through accident, or neglect on our part we do cause damage, we will repay your organization in full for the cost of repairing it.

We each have the utmost respect for all those who have a loved one buried here, and solemnly promise there will be no intoxicant consumption, horseplay, or any other disagreeable conduct, just the research as mentioned above will be done, for the duration permitted, and on the agreed site(s).

We will also notify the appropriate division of Metro Police of the date and time of our study, so that there won't be a false alarm.

We agree that we undertake this research at our own risk, and understand that your organization is not responsible for any injury or damage to the students or their instruments, while on your property.

We agree to conduct the entire study out of view of passerby, and the general public, so as not to arouse their interest.

We ask that if you give your permission, please leave a current copy of your property's map with the caretaker, so that we can accurately make our way to our location, with no needless walking around.

Please give us your consideration, in this matter, if you require any other conditions to be met, we will accommodate them into our proposal, and sign to it. The other two students will disclose their names and contact information, and sign to your terms as well, on the date of the study. We will also provide ID, if requested.

Yours truly,

____

your name
96 Main Street, City, State
Home: (555) 555-8772   Work: (216) 555-1224

Index

H

I

J

K

L

M

Q

R

License Agreement/Notice of Limited Warranty

By opening the sealed disc container in this book, you agree to the following terms and conditions. If, upon reading the following license agreement and notice of limited warranty, you cannot agree to the terms and conditions set forth, return the unused book with unopened disc to the place where you purchased it for a refund.

License:

The enclosed software is copyrighted by the copyright holder(s) indicated on the software disc. You are licensed to copy the software onto a single computer for use by a single user and to a backup disc. You may not reproduce, make copies, or distribute copies or rent or lease the software in whole or in part, except with written permission of the copyright holder(s). You may transfer the enclosed disc only together with this license, and only if you destroy all other copies of the software and the transferee agrees to the terms of the license. You may not decompile, reverse assemble, or reverse engineer the software.

Notice of Limited Warranty:

The enclosed disc is warranted by Course Technology to be free of physical defects in materials and workmanship for a period of sixty (60) days from end user's purchase of the book/disc combination. During the sixty-day term of the limited warranty, Course Technology will provide a replacement disc upon the return of a defective disc.

Limited Liability:

THE SOLE REMEDY FOR BREACH OF THIS LIMITED WARRANTY SHALL CONSIST ENTIRELY OF REPLACEMENT OF THE DEFECTIVE DISC. IN NO EVENT SHALL COURSE TECHNOLOGY OR THE AUTHOR BE LIABLE FOR ANY OTHER DAMAGES, INCLUDING LOSS OR CORRUPTION OF DATA, CHANGES IN THE FUNCTIONAL CHARACTERISTICS OF THE HARDWARE OR OPERATING SYSTEM, DELETERIOUS INTERACTION WITH OTHER SOFTWARE, OR ANY OTHER SPECIAL, INCIDENTAL, OR CONSEQUENTIAL DAMAGES THAT MAY ARISE, EVEN IF COURSE TECHNOLOGY AND/OR THE AUTHOR HAS PREVIOUSLY BEEN NOTIFIED THAT THE POSSIBILITY OF SUCH DAMAGES EXISTS.

Disclaimer of Warranties:

COURSE TECHNOLOGY AND THE AUTHOR SPECIFICALLY DISCLAIM ANY AND ALL OTHER WARRANTIES, EITHER EXPRESS OR IMPLIED, INCLUDING WARRANTIES OF MERCHANTABILITY, SUITABILITY TO A PARTICULAR TASK OR PURPOSE, OR FREEDOM FROM ERRORS. SOME STATES DO NOT ALLOW FOR EXCLUSION OF IMPLIED WARRANTIES OR LIMITATION OF INCIDENTAL OR CONSEQUENTIAL DAMAGES, SO THESE LIMITATIONS MIGHT NOT APPLY TO YOU.

Other:

This Agreement is governed by the laws of the State of Massachusetts without regard to choice of law principles. The United Convention of Contracts for the International Sale of Goods is specifically disclaimed. This Agreement constitutes the entire agreement between you and Course Technology regarding use of the software.

THE BOBBY GOLD STORIES

BY THE SAME AUTHOR

Nonfiction

Kitchen Confidential
A Cook's Tour
Typhoid Mary

Fiction

Bone in the Throat
Gone Bamboo

THE BOBBY GOLD STORIES

ANTHONY BOURDAIN

BLOOMSBURY

First published in Great Britain in 2002 by Canongate Crime, an imprint of Canongate Books Ltd.

Published by Bloomsbury, New York and London
Distributed to the trade by Holtzbrinck Publishers

Library of Congress Cataloging-in-Publication Data
has been applied for.

ISBN 1–58234–233–4

First U.S. edition 2003

1 3 5 7 9 10 8 6 4 2

Typeset by Palimpsest Book Production Limited,
Polmont, Stirlingshire, Scotland
Printed in the United States of America by
R.R. Donnelley & Sons, Crawfordsville

CONTENTS

BOBBY IN COLOR

Bobby Gold at twenty-one, in a red-and-white Dead Boys T-shirt, blue jeans, high-top Nikes and handcuffs, bent over the hood of the State Police cruiser, arms behind his back, wished he was anywhere but here. The beach would be nice, he thought, as the trooper to his right read him his rights. The beach would be great. Cheek pressed hard against the hot metal of the car's hood, Bobby wondered: if he held his head just right – so that his ear cupped against the blue-and-white car – would he be able to hear the ocean?

The rented Chevrolet Caprice sat on the shoulder, between two cruisers, bathed in flashing red and blue lights. Styx had come on the radio just as they'd pulled him over. He had been happily listening to "Monkey Man" by the Stones, singing along, in fact, volume all the way up when he'd seen the lights in his rear-view mirror, and in the excitement and confusion of the moment, had neglected to turn the radio off. Now Styx was playing on the radio, always and forever the soundtrack to any future memories of this ugly event. Damn, thought Bobby.

Bobby wondered how the rental company dealt with a situation like this. Would he be charged for the extra days that the car was held for evidence? Who would come and pick it up?

What if the cops tore the car apart? This was a worst-case scenario as there were three kilos of cocaine hidden inside the spare tire – and another two kilos behind the seats. Would the guy from Avis take a taxi to the police impound lot, and then drive the car away – or would another employee drive him over, then follow in convoy? As the cops pulled him upright by his hair and walked him over to the rear of one of the cruisers, held his head as they pushed him into the back seat, Bobby found himself curiously detached from events around him.

He would not be sleeping with Lisa tonight – that was for sure. He wouldn't be lying in the bed they shared in the Stimson Dormitory, listening to Brian Eno and sniffing Merck cocaine and smoking hydro. Lisa would not, later, when the quaaludes kicked in, look him in the eyes and turn up the corner of her mouth in a dreamy smile while she sucked his cock. Not tonight. Tonight he was going to jail.

His parents, the already disappointed-in-their-son Dr. and Mrs. Sherman Goldstein, were not going to be happy about this. The words "This is the last time –" echoed in Bobby's head as he vaguely remembered some previous outrages he'd committed: the time he'd passed out in his parents' bed with a checkout clerk from the Pathmark, a fully packed bong still in one hand. The time he'd wrecked their car – sinking it into a water hazard on the green of the local country club. The time he'd been expelled from Horace Mann. The time he'd been expelled from the Englewood School for Boys. The shoplifting misunderstanding . . . He hoped that if his parents – after wailing and bemoaning the miserable fate that brought such a disgrace of a son into the world – couldn't do anything to help him, maybe Eddie could. Eddie could fix anything. He'd been in trouble his whole life – and yet he'd never spent a night in jail. Eddie, Bobby hoped, would know what to do.

Bobby Gold in an orange jumpsuit, handcuffs and leg irons shuffled into the courthouse and sat down next to his parents' attorney. Things did not look good. Eddie had not been any help. He wasn't even in court today. Bobby examined the jurors' faces, not liking what he saw.

The old bat at the end, juror number twelve, was shaking her head disapprovingly. She had a daughter in college, Bobby recalled from voir dire. She was thinking about all that coke – all that pharmaceutical-grade cocaine, headed in Bobby's car to supply college kids. Might as well have been her daughter's college – to get her daughter hooked, turn her daughter into a coke-sniffing, dangerously underweight coke-whore, tossing off scabby drunks at some imagined truck stop for her fix. Juror number four didn't look too friendly to Bobby's cause either – a retired jarhead with two sons in the service. With that haircut, he was a definite guilty vote. Things did not look good.

When they gave him ten years, Bobby was not surprised.

Bobby Gold in an orange jumpsuit stood quietly in line for tuna noodle casserole, coleslaw and lime jello. The other convicts on line in front of him and behind were thick-necked, over-muscled gladiators compared to the scrawny, pencil-necked Bobby. He'd have to exercise – and fast. He'd have to get big, bulk up, get tough. Tomorrow he'd get a tattoo.

That would be a start. Something badass. He had to get big. It was going to take a lot of lime Jell-O.

He was adding muscle. He read the muscle magazines after his cell-mate was done with them. He went to the prison library and read up on anatomy, nerve clusters, bones, pressure points, martial arts. He'd been – supposedly – pre-med in school, so he could order books from outside. He knew what to look for.

Bobby Gold in a towel in the communal shower asked his buddy LT how to get the other convicts off his back. Two *cholos* from the Mexican gang had tried to jump him earlier in the week, and yesterday, one of the Muslims, a whippet-thin ex-junkie who called himself Andre, had taken a parker roll right off of Bobby's tray. What to do?

"You'll have to kill somebody, little brother," said LT, rinsing the shampoo from his eyes.

"Who?" asked Bobby. "Who should I kill?"

"Anybody'll do," said LT.

Bobby Gold on a gurney with squeaky wheels, two knuckles pushed all the way back to his wrist, was hurried to the prison infirmary in restraints.

His nose was broken, ribs cracked, spleen ruptured. There was a three-inch puncture wound below his right shoulder where air whistled from a lung. A chunk of Andre's flesh was still stuck between his molars from when Bobby took a bite out of his cheek. Bobby felt a little bad picking Andre, but he hadn't been big enough yet to tussle with the other convicts. And Andre had asked for it. Bobby was watching *One Life to Live* in the dayroom – and fucking Andre had changed the channel to the fucking *Jeffersons*. Hadn't even asked if anyone minded. Bobby had looked over at LT and LT had smiled and shrugged.

He didn't think he'd killed the smaller man, though he'd certainly tried everything he could. After Bobby had kicked him in the balls from behind, he'd kneed him in the head, stepped on his neck and then broken both his own hands whaling on Andre's face. When Andre's buddy shanked him from behind with a sharpened toothbrush, he ignored it . . . When Andre grabbed him, clarity bit him hard until he let go. He kept hitting him until Andre's eye went sideways in its socket and stayed that way. Bobby kept hitting him until the guards came and pulled him off. Just like LT had said he should do.

From now on, thought Bobby, he'd have as many fucking parker rolls as he wanted.

Then he passed out.

Bobby Gold, in a red-and-white Dead Boys T-shirt, blue jeans, and high-top Nikes, stepped through the high electrified fence at the perimeter of the prison. It was February, and he was freezing. He looked around to see if anyone had come to meet him, but there was no one. Lisa hadn't written him, so she sure as hell wasn't coming. His parents had turned their backs on him forever.

Where was Eddie?

BOBBY AT WORK

Bobby Gold, six foot four and dripping wet, squeezed past an outgoing delivery of Norwegian salmon and stood motionless, smelling of soggy leather, in the cramped front room of JayBee Seafood Company, taking up space. Men in galoshes, leather weight-belts and insulated vests jockeyed heavily loaded hand-trucks around him. No one asked him to move.

Everybody smoked – their wet cigarettes held in gloved hands with the tips cut down. Men ticked off items on crumpled invoices with pencil stubs, stacked leaking crates of flounder, mussels, cod, squid, and lobster, swept crushed ice into melting piles on the waterlogged wooden floor. At an ancient desk by the front window, a fat man with a pen behind his ear was making conciliatory noises into the phone, blowing smoke.

"Yeah . . . yeah . . . we'll take it back. Yeah . . . I

know . . . the dispatcher missed it. Whaddya want me to do? What can I say? I'll send you another piece – no problem. Yeah . . . right away . . . center-cut. I got it. Right . . . right. It's leaving right now."

When he hung up, the fat man called back to somebody in the rear. "Send twenny pounds of c.c. sword up to Sullivan's! And bring back what he's got!" Then he looked up, noticed the large figure in the fingertip-length black leather jacket, black pullover, black denim pants and black cowboy boots, obstructing commerce in his loading area.

"Yo! . . . Johnny Cash! Can I help you with something?"

"I come from Eddie," said Bobby Gold, his voice flat, no expression on his face.

The fat man at the desk rolled his eyes, took a deep hit on a bent Pall Mall and jerked a thumb towards the rear. "He's in the back office."

Bobby pushed aside long plastic curtains that kept the cold from escaping a cavernous, refrigerated work area. Salsa music was blaring from a portable radio at one of six long worktables where more men in long white coats smeared with fish blood packed seafood into crates and covered it with ice. But the dominant sound here was a relentless droning from the giant compressors that kept the room chilled down to a frosty thirty-eight degrees. They were gutting red snappers around a central floor drain, and there were fish scales everywhere – like snowflakes in the workers' hair, clinging to their knives, on their clothing. Black and purple entrails were being pulled from the fishes' underbellies, then tossed carelessly into fifty-five-gallon slop buckets. Against one wall, a triple stacked row of grouper seemed to follow Bobby's progress across the room with clear, shiny eyes, their bodies still twisted with rigor.

Another room: white tile, with a bored-looking old man working a hose while another picked over littleneck clams and packed them into burlap. Bobby's boot crushed a clam shell as he swept through a second set of plastic curtains and into the rear offices. Two bull-necked women with door-knocker-sized earrings and bad hair sat talking on phones by a prehistoric safe, a sleeping Rottweiler between them. Bobby opened Jerry Moss's door without knocking and went inside.

"Oh, shit," said Jerry, a sun-freckled old man, hunched over a pile of price quotes and bills of lading.

"Hi, Jer'," said Bobby, sad already. The old man

looked particularly tired and weak today – as if a good wind could blow him over. Bobby noticed with unhappiness the bottle of Maalox on Jerry's crowded desk, the dusty picture frame with Jerry's immediate family clustered around a fireplace, the half-eaten brisket sandwich peeking out from its wax paper wrapping.

"Is it that time again?" said Jerry, feigning surprise.

"I'm afraid so," said Bobby.

Jerry sat back in his cracked leather swivel chair and sighed. "So I guess this means I gotta take a beating ... Is that right, Bobby? I gotta take a beating?"

Bobby just nodded, regretting everything that got him here and everything that was going to happen. He felt as trapped as the old man. It had been like that lately – the feeling bad part. Even with the tough guys, the mouthy, think-they're-smart assholes who he'd straightened up in recent weeks – the big-shouldered power-lifters who'd thought they didn't have to pay because of their hulk-sized chests and their bad attitudes – Bobby no longer took pleasure in proving otherwise. The technical satisfactions of a job well and precisely done just didn't cut it anymore – replaced by a growing sense of . . . shame – a tightening in the stomach.

Jerry Moss was sixty-two years old. He'd had, as Bobby well knew, two heart attacks in the past year, and a recent bypass operation. His last trip to Florida, the old man had come back with a small melanoma on the left cheek which had had to be surgically excised. And he was suffering as well from conjunctivitis, shingles and a spastic colon. He was falling apart by himself.

"How bad does it have to be?" asked Jerry, shifting uncomfortably in his chair.

"It's got to be an arm – at least," said Bobby, controlling his voice. Any hint of reluctance now would give the old man hope – and there wasn't any. "That's what he said. An arm. And, of course, the face. You know how that is . . . There's gotta be something for show."

The old man winced and shook his head, studying his desk top. "That's just fucking great . . . I guess it don't matter I got the money now, does it? I mean . . . shit, Bobby – he knows I'm gonna pay . . ."

"He knows that, Jerry."

"I mean . . . Bobby . . . Boobie . . . I got the money right here. I can pay now, for fuck's sake. This second. It's right there in the safe."

"Jerry . . . he doesn't care," said Bobby, sleepwalking through this part, trying to think about a faraway beach, running an advertising jingle through his head, wanting to get it over with. "It's not about that and you know it. I'm not here to collect. You're late. That's the point. That he had to ask."

"An arm . . ." mulled Jerry. "Shit!" He looked pensively down at his body, as if taking inventory. "That's just great . . . That's just . . ." He struggled for a word . . . came up with ". . . boffo."

"What can I say?" said Bobby, shrugging.

"You could say, 'Forget it,'" said Jerry, more exasperated than frightened. "You could say, 'What the fuck' and walk away from it . . . That would be a nice fucking thing to say . . ."

"Never happen," said Bobby. "Not today." He lit a cigarette and sat down across from Jerry. He could see the fear starting to come on, welling up visibly now behind the old man's glasses, sweat forming on Jerry's upper lip as the memory of the last time Eddie had had to send him a message began to come back.

That time had been awful, Bobby knew. He'd been on vacation and Eddie had sent two oversized kids from Arthur Avenue to do the job, and predictably, things had gotten out of hand. They'd whaled the shit out of Jerry for fifteen minutes – beaten him within an inch of his life. If memory served, they'd broken both of the old man's legs, his collar-bone, forearm, nose and instep – then smashed his teeth so badly he'd had to have them all replaced. He now wore complete upper and lower plates – they made him whistle slightly when he spoke.

"How many times has it been now, Jerry?" asked Bobby – though he knew the answer. "I mean … Jesus …"

"This'll make four," replied Jerry, almost defiantly, poking his chin out slightly – a bit of business that didn't quite make it as bravado.

"It's pathetic … Really. You're not a young man … Why the fuck you gotta be such a fucking donkey?"

Jerry just smiled weakly and shrugged his shoulders – looked out the dirt-streaked window at the rain coming down.

"Nobody likes this, Jerry," said Bobby. "I certainly don't like it. You think I like this shit? Coming here?"

"Oh yeah?" barked the old man, raising his voice so it cracked slightly. "Those two retards he sent over the last time? They liked it, Bobby … they liked it fine! Those two behemoths? They had a great fucking time, those two . . . I swear to God . . . the one kid? He's dancing on my fucking stomach? Guy's getting a fucking boner!! Oh yeah . . . Those two . . . they was all over me like a bunch a drunken Cossacks. They fucked me up good those two. Real good . . . They were having themselves a real good fucking time busting me up like a day-old fucking biscuit."

Jerry had gone pale recalling the incident. He tried quickly to buck himself up. "Hey . . . I should look at the bright side, right? At least he sent you this time. I should be grateful. I should be relieved. Am I right or what?"

"I brought some pills," said Bobby, reaching into his wet leather jacket, coming out with a bottle of Demerol. "Take three now. I'll wait . . . I'll wait around for them to kick in, okay? Then it won't hurt so bad . . . That's the best I can do for you, Jerry. The pills . . . they help a lot." He passed the bottle over to Jerry, watched as the old man tilted his head back and dry-swallowed three. He was used to taking medication.

"Drink?" offered Jerry, motioning to a fifth of Dewar's on the dirt-encrusted windowsill. "Since we're gonna be here a while . . ."

"Yeah . . . sure, thanks," said Bobby. He fetched

the bottle, poured two drinks after blowing the dust out of two promotional coffee mugs on Jerry's desk. Bobby's mug read "JayBee Seafood" with a cartoon drawing of a leaping salmon on the side. Jerry's mug had a picture of a smiling Fred Flintstone on it, and the words "Yabadaba-Doo!" in bright red block letters.

"Cheers," said Jerry. He poured his drink down in one gulp, coughed, then asked for another. Bobby poured.

"Why don't you just pay the man on time," said Bobby. "Like you said . . . you got the money. Why piss him off like this – for nothing?"

"Liquidity problems," explained Jerry, looking at the younger man like he was explaining the bond market to a pool boy or a gardener. He swept his arm through the air. "Cash flow . . . You know . . . It's ponies and pussy, pussy and ponies," he said. "And the dogs. I went the dog track down there at Hialeah? I don't have to tell you what happened," Jerry smiled weakly. "That ain't ever gonna change, Bobby . . . so why shit anybody? What? Am I gonna tell you it ain't never gonna happen again? C'mon!"

"If you say so . . ."

"I get to pick the arm?"

"Sure," said Bobby. "Your choice. You pick it."

"I hope I pick better than I pick winners."

"Yeah . . . no shit."

"The left. I think. Yeah – the left," said Jerry. "I'm a lefty, but" – he lowered his voice – "I jerk off with my right."

"Too much information, Jerry. I didn't need to know that."

"What – I'm too old to jerk off? I need that arm! First things fucking first!"

"Whatever you say."

"How long . . . how long you think before I can use it again?"

"Three weeks in a cast," said Bobby, talking about something he knew for sure. "Four weeks tops. And the new casts they're making these days – they're much more lightweight. You'll be able to get around with it sooner."

"Fabulous," said Jerry.

They were both quiet for a while, Bobby sipping his Scotch, gazing idly out the window into JayBee's rear alleyway, listening to the rain pelt the thick panes of alarmed glass and the distant whine from the compressors. The Rottweiler, awake now, poked his head into the room, a filthy squeaky toy between his massive jaws. Seeing no one interested in playing with him, the big dog turned and left, the toy making hiccuping sounds.

"What's the dog's name?" asked Bobby.

"Schtarker," said Jerry, uninterested. "That's Yiddish, if you didn't know. People used to say that about you."

Bobby let that go – consulted his watch.

"Few more minutes and I'll be ready, okay?" said Jerry. "I'm startin' to feel them pills."

"No problem," said Bobby. "I don't have to be at the club for a while. I've got time."

"How's that working out for you?"

"Good," said Bobby. "It's going good . . . I'm head of security now."

"Nice for you."

"Yeah . . . It's okay."

"You ever get anybody there I'd like? You know . . . somebody . . . somebody I could take Rose to see? She loves Neil Diamond. You ever get Neil Diamond there?"

"No . . ." said Bobby. "We had . . . let's see . . . we had . . . Lena Horne once . . . we had Vic Damone and Jerry Vale. We had him."

"Yeah? . . . Good?"

"Yeah . . . they were good. You know . . . Not my kind of music, but good."

"Bobby . . . If you ever get anybody there . . . you know . . . that Rose would like . . . I'd appreciate it. If you could get us in. She'd love that. If I actually took her out sometime. They got the dinner and the dancing and everything over there, right?"

"Yeah . . . the whole deal. And the food's not bad."

"Lamb chops? I like a good lamb chop."

"Yeah . . . we got that."

"Beautiful!"

"I'll put you on the list anytime you want to bring her," said Bobby.

"Eddie . . . He ain't gonna mind?"

"As long as you fucking pay on time, Jerry, he won't give a shit. You can do the fucking hokey-pokey on the table – he won't care – he's never there anyway. Just call me when you want to come."

"Thanks . . . I appreciate that."

"So," said Bobby. "You ready?"

"Shit," said Jerry, exhaling loudly.

"Take off your glasses, Jer' . . ."

"You gotta do that?"

"Do what?"

"The face . . . You gotta do the face?"

"Jerry . . ."

"I dunno . . . I thought . . . maybe just the arm would be enough . . ."

"Jerry . . ." repeated Bobby, standing up.

"Awright . . . awright . . . Jesus Fuck . . . Lemme get a tissue at least."

"I brought a handkerchief," said Bobby, reaching again into his jacket, this time for a neatly folded cotton square. "Here. Keep it."

"Always prepared," muttered Jerry, sourly. He removed his glasses and put them carefully on the desk. "They teach you that in the Boy Scouts? What did you used to have to say? 'A Boy Scout is . . . trustworthy, loyal, helpful, friendly, obedient, cheerful, thrifty, brave, courteous, kind, clean and –'"

Bobby hit him across the nose with the back of his hand. Quickly. It was a sharp, precise blow that knocked Jerry into his chair-back.

"Shit!" said Jerry, honking a red streak onto his shirt front, then covering his face with the handkerchief. He rocked silently in his chair for a moment while Bobby looked around the room for a fat enough book to finish with.

"Get it over with!" hissed Jerry. "Do it now . . . while I'm distracted!" He rolled up his shirt sleeve.

Bobby found what he was looking for – a thick, hardback copy of *Mollusks and Bivalves of the North Atlantic*, and quickly placed the book in front of Jerry on the desk. Jerry knew the drill. He compliantly laid his thin, blue-veined arm against the spine so that the hand was raised, then closed his eyes. "Do it!" he said.

When Bobby brought his fist down on Jerry's radial ulna – the thinner of the two bones between wrist and elbow – there was a muffled snap, like a bottle breaking beneath a pillow.

"Ohhh . . ." moaned Jerry, tears squeezing from the corners of his eyes.

"Oh . . . Bobby . . . that hurt. Fuck me. . . it hurts . . ."

"It's over now, Jerry," said Bobby. He wanted to comfort the old man now – wished he could put his arms around his shoulders – even kiss him on the cheek like he'd had to as a child.

"It hurts," said Jerry. "It hurts worse than I remembered." Bobby went out and found a clean apron on top of a locker. When he got back, Jerry was still rocking back and forth, the injured limb held close to his body, his eyes still closed.

"C'mon, Jerry. Here we go," said Bobby. He fashioned a serviceable sling out of the apron, helped the old man's arm into it, then primly adjusted it around his neck.

"Motherfuck!!" said Jerry, through clenched teeth. "It's hot. It feels hot . . . and it hurts . . ."

"Hey . . . It's over," was all Bobby could think of to say.

"Yeah . . . thanks," said Jerry. "Thanks for breaking my arm." A thin dribble of blood ran from one nostril, collecting on his lip. The whites of his eyes were turning red – as intended. Bobby felt the urge to lean over and blot the nose with a tissue, but resisted.

"It could have been those kids from Arthur Avenue, Jerry," said Bobby, lamely.

"Yeah . . . you're right. He coulda sent the kids," said Jerry, bitterly. "I love this! Like I'm supposed to be grateful? You broke my fucking arm!!"

"What hospital you want to go to? I can drop you at St. Vincent's, you want."

"Fuck you, Bobby. I'll walk over to Roosevelt."

"St. Vincent's is better . . . You won't have so much of a wait, Jerry. It's cleaner. C'mon . . . I'll take you in a cab . . ."

"Get the fuck outta here Bobby, okay?"

"It's raining, Jerry . . ."

"I know it's fucking raining, Bobby Gold . . . Stop it, already . . . You did what you hadda do. Now get the fuck outta here and leave me alone."

"I'm sorry, Jerry. It's my job. This is what I do . . ."

Jerry looked up at him with sudden and unexpected clarity. "I know . . ." he said. "That's what's fucked up about you, Bobby. You are sorry. You got no fucking heart for this shit – but you do it anyway, don't you?" He turned his face away, as if looking at Bobby disgusted him. "What the fuck happened to you, for fuck's sake? Nice Jewish boy . . . educated . . . and you're beatin' on old men – your uncle . . . your own mother's brother, for a fuckin' living. Some fuckin' life you got, Bobby . . ." His voice cracked, barely audible. "Little Bobby Goldstein, all grown up. Your father – he must be very proud . . ."

Bobby flinched. "Fuck you, Jerry . . . I wouldn't have to do this shit – you paid your debts on time. Don't start talking about family – the way you live – all right?"

"Awright . . . I'm sorry," said Jerry. "I'm sorry . . . I shouldn't have said that . . ." He looked out the window, voice steadier now, and sadder. "Who am I to judge a person?"

It was coming down hard on 9th Avenue when Bobby and Jerry emerged from JayBee Seafood. The old man was looking drugged and dreamy now, his eyes pinned from the Demerol, mouth slack at the corners.

"Let me get you a cab," offered Bobby for the last time, signaling with his hand.

Jerry waved him away. "You take it. I'm not fucking helpless here, Bobby. I can take care of myself. I was having guys busted up worse than this when I was half your age – those two guinea cocksuckers he sent the last time? Next week, the very next week – from my hospital bed – I call Eddie and have him send those two down to see some other schmuck owes *me* money – so I ain't gonna curl up and die cause I gotta stand up for another ass-kicking, all right? Now get lost, you little pisher . . . tell that midget gonniff cocksucker you work for he can send somebody over tomorrow to pick up the money. Now leave me alone . . ."

When Bobby left him, standing hatless and coatless in the rain, looking up 9th Avenue toward Roosevelt Hospital, the old man was weeping. Bobby saw him holding the handkerchief to his nose as his cab pulled away from the curb. He watched him through the raindrop patterns of the cab window as Jerry slowly started to walk, one foot in front of the other, shoulders hunched protectively over the broken arm, growing smaller in the distance.

BOBBY THE DIPLOMAT

Bobby Gold in work clothes – black sport jacket, black button-down dress shirt, skinny black tie, black chinos and comfortable black shoes – pushed open the double doors onto the mezzanine level of NiteKlub. Below, on the dance floor, heads were bobbing in the smoke and the strobes, the heavy bass tones from the half-million-dollar sound system vibrating through the concrete. Fifty feet away, on his left, the mezzanine bar was doing big business, stacked three-deep with customers. He saw Del, the mezz security man, hurrying toward him.

"Bobby! This is outta control! Have you seen this?"

Bobby looked around, saw, as his eyes adjusted to the light, what was happening.

They were kids. The whole fucking crowd. Not one of the customers clamoring for drinks over the upstairs bar looked to be over seventeen. They were everywhere: chunky girls with teased hair wearing camisoles, skinny boys with baggy jeans and sneakers that glowed in the dark – teenagers, shirtless, dressed up, dressed down, in makeup, wearing wigs, sunglasses, drag, full nightclub battle-dress – and they were running wild. In pairs, in packs, eyes lit with X, with booze, with animal tranquilizers, ketamine, Mom's pilfered Valiums, ephedrine, mushrooms and God knows what else. Every one of these little bastards was a potentially ticking time bomb. At the small bar, they signaled noisily for Long Island Iced Teas, Kamikazes, tequila shooters, Lite beers and rum and cokes. Bobby could scarcely believe it.

"You gotta do something about this," said Del, in despair. "And look . . ." he added, "check this out." He drew Bobby over to the booths running along the mezzanine wall and yanked back a curtain to reveal a short blond girl, legs in the air on the middle of a dinner table, her drunken boyfriend in a warm-up jacket grunting over her, his pants down around his ankles. Another boy sat slumped in a chair by her head, unconscious, his mouth open, snoring. The girl looked right up at Bobby with uninflected, porcine little eyes. She was chewing gum.

"They're going at it everywhere," said Del, disgustedly. "I found two in the air-conditioning room before. More in the dry goods area. They're fucking all over the place like little bunnies. Can you believe this shit?"

A young girl in a brassiere and blue jeans hurried past them, fell to her knees and vomited into the base of a potted palm. "Remind me to never have kids," said Del.

"You have kids, don't you?" said Bobby, reaching for his radio.

"Yeah . . . well, remind me to not let them grow any more."

Bobby trotted to the lobby, calling into his radio for Tiny Lopez on the street security detail.

"Tiny! . . . What's your twenty?"

"I ousside, man. Whassup?" said Tiny, a three-hundred-eighty-pounder whom Bobby had placed out front for crowd control.

"We're shutting it down. Tell the friskers. I'll let them know at the desk," said Bobby. He squeezed past a long line of kids who were ascending the main staircase, signaled the downstairs bartenders that something was up, drawing a finger across his throat to give them the sign to stop serving. The lobby was packed. It took him two solid minutes to make it the last few yards to the front desk, where Frank, a silver-haired charity-case pal of Eddie's, was stamping hands, standing next to two young promoters in shiny sharkskin suits. Bobby shouted to the security men at the door to close it down, alerted Tiny to what was going on over the radio, and had the two friskers move together to block off access at the choke point.

"Shut the doors," he said, "Nobody gets in."

One of the promoters was in green sharkskin, the other, orange. Green sharkskin looked up. "What the fuck, man?" he said. "What are you doing?"

Bobby pushed through the crowd of bodies until he towered over him.

"That's it. Show's over," he said. "I'm shutting it down."

"What?" exclaimed orange suit.

"You heard me," said Bobby, struggling to keep his voice under control. "Frankie," he said, "who's been carding these people?"

Frank nodded at the two promoters, neither of whom looked to be of age themselves. "Eddie said they was in charge of the door. They . . . they said that Eddie said it was okay."

"What the fuck you think you're doing here?" Bobby demanded of green suit – clearly the alpha male of the two. He saw right away that the kid was going to get up in his face. Orange suit moved closer, shoulders back, trying to look bigger than he was. Bobby outweighed both of them together.

"Whass goin' on?" said orange suit in a whiny voice. "Why we stopping?"

"You costin' us money, bro'," protested green suit.

Bobby slapped him across the face and he fell against the wall like a stunned trout. He grabbed a fistful of sharkskin with his right hand and a fistful of sharkskin with his left and dragged the two promoters into the cloakroom where it was a little quieter, pushed them both up against the coat racks.

"What kind of fuckin' jerks am I talkin' to here?" he demanded.

"What the fuck you talkin' about?" said green suit. Orange suit was too shaken to talk.

"Eddie said – "

Bobby slapped him again.

"Let me explain something to you, asshole," said Bobby, speaking softly.

"This is a business. What do you think's gonna happen – one a these girls you letting in here goes home late, drunk outta her mind, her parents find her puking all over the doorstep with jiz all over her dress?"

"We're straight with Eddie, man. This is our event!" ventured orange suit, finding a little courage.

"Yeah? You know what I think Eddie said?" said Bobby. "I think he said that you two morons promote the event. That's what I think he said. I think he said that you two do the advertising. That you get the door and we get the bar. That's what I think he said. I don't think he told you two shit stains to let every fifteen-year-old in the five boroughs in the door without carding them. I don't think he asked you twerps to get his liquor license pulled for him!"

"He's gettin' fifteen percent a the door!" howled green suit. "This is costing us money, bro'!"

"Listen carefully," said Bobby. "And watch my hands. Because if I want any more shit outta you, I'm gonna squeeze your fucking head . . . Nobody else is getting in this place until everybody in the club has been carded and checked and all the minors are out of here. You two are half smart? You'll step outside yourselves and make the announcement that everyone is expected to produce valid ID. Not those knock-offs you can buy a few blocks over. We're talking driver's license, passport, photo fucking ID, got it? I'm having my people go through this club to check everyone who's already here. Anyone under twenty-one is out. The sooner we get that done, the sooner we can all go back to making money. Is that understood?"

The two promoters looked at their shoes, humiliated.

"I want to talk to Eddie," said green suit.

"You want to talk to Eddie?" said Bobby, incredulous. "Here," he said, offering green suit his cell phone. "I'll give you the number. You can call him right now. Interrupt the man's business and explain to him why he's gonna get sued when one of these underage teeny-boppers plows Daddy's Lexus into a bus load a fucking nuns. You want to explain that? Tell him not to worry? That you got it under control? That you definitely ain't gonna put his business in jeopardy, get his license yanked? That he can count on you two to make sure he doesn't wake up tomorrow and see his fucking picture on the cover of the *Post*? . . . Here!" Bobby said, shoving the cell phone under green suit's nose. "C'mon, tough guy. Call him."

"Fuck it, man," said orange suit.

Green suit just glared at him while Bobby continued holding the phone under his nose. When he finally averted his gaze, Bobby turned his back and walked away, giving instructions into the radio.

After calling in additional security from the exits, Bobby put together a flying squad to move about the club, checking ID and escorting those without to the doors. He moved about the club, overseeing the operation – and everywhere he went there was trouble. Outside the Blue Room, he saw his man Rick holding a struggling youth in a full nelson. Rick had a red welt over his right eye, and was having a hard time controlling the kid without hitting him. A teenage girl was crying on a banquette while her boyfriend was being subdued. A bottle was thrown, and another security man rushed towards the source.

"Little bastard cold-cocked me," said Rick, through bloody teeth, as he frog-walked the kid down the stairs. "He must weigh eighty pounds!"

"Get him out," sighed Bobby. "And try not to humiliate him in front of his girlfriend. He might come back with a slingshot."

Another security man, Melvin, with a bad gash over his nose, carried a young man in overalls down the stairs, yelling, "Coming through!" Furniture was kicked over. More bottles were thrown. Bobby radioed the sound booth and told the head of tech to shut off the music and turn up the house lights.

It took nearly an hour to clear the club. When it was over, only a small group, those who'd actually been twenty-one, huddled by the bar, waiting for it to reopen. Half of Bobby's security team of thirteen able-bodied men and one woman had been scratched, punched, hit with flying objects or in some way injured. Before reopening the bars, Bobby positioned two extra people in the street and doubled the force at the door – in case some of the ejected kids came back with retribution in mind.

When things were finally under control, an older-looking crowd filing into the entrance in orderly fashion – first frisked, then escorted through the metal detectors, then carded, money taken and hands stamped, Bobby looked up to see Frank gesturing worriedly at the door with his chin, pointing out two men who were standing patiently at the head of the VIP line.

One of them was a crew-cut hard case in a turtleneck and trench coat. The other was a fiftyish gent with snow-white hair, thin lips and flashing brown eyes in a dark suit and camel-hair overcoat. Tommy Victory. Bobby could see the kid in the green suit smirking at him from nearby. Bobby went right over to Tommy, knowing this was trouble, and respectfully offered a hand.

"Tommy. How are you?" he said.

"Bobby," said Tommy, looking irritated. "I understand there was a problem here." He looked around for a second, said, "Is there someplace we can talk?"

"Yeah, sure," said Bobby.

He took the two men upstairs and through the Blue Room into the tiny office the banquet department used during the day – and closed the door behind them. Tommy plunked himself down behind the banquet manager's desk without bothering to take off his coat and gestured for Bobby to sit across from him. The big man with the crew cut stayed on his feet, remaining behind and slightly to the right of Bobby, his hand resting ominously on his shoulder.

"My nephew called me a while ago," said Tommy. "I'm in the middle of a late supper with some friends . . . and the kid calls me. He says you hit him. Is that true, Bobby?"

Bobby could feel crew cut's hand tighten on his shoulder.

"Which one's your nephew, Tommy?" Bobby asked.

"Kid inna green suit. He says you smacked him around."

"If I'd known he was your nephew, Tommy, I would have been a little more diplomatic," said Bobby. "I would have called you directly."

"So what's the problem here, Bobby?" asked Tommy. "Why you go and have to put a hand on my nephew? What he do? He's a good kid!"

"Tommy . . . They were letting in children. Fourteen, fifteen years old. They coulda got our license yanked. There were teenage girls upstairs getting fucking gangbanged on the dinner tables. It was outta control."

"So? So you hadda hit the kid?"

The crew-cut bodyguard's hand started to move around. Bobby could smell his aftershave.

"Tommy," said Bobby. "I'd like very much for us to talk about this like men. Straighten out any misunderstandings. Make amends. Whatever. But, with all due respect to you? If this cocksucker behind me doesn't take his hand offa my shoulder like right now, I'm gonna snap it off at the wrist and shove it up his ass."

Bobby could feel anger and alarm running like a current through crew cut's hand. He was getting ready to turn around, when Tommy smiled and put up a hand.

"Richie," he said. "Give the man some room."

Then he laughed, a long wheezy laugh. "He'd do it, you know. Bobby here? He's one crazy, bad-ass motherfucker. Am I right, Bobby?"

Richie didn't seem so sure. Though he'd released his grip on Bobby's shoulder, he still loomed close.

"More room," said Tommy. "Give him some space to fucking breathe. Believe me. You don't want to fuck with this guy. Friends a mine was upstate with this testadura. He's got some sorta kung-fu shit or something. Studied fucking medicine whiles he was up there – like . . . where the bones are and shit. So he knows how to fuck a guy up. He's like a ox, this guy."

"He don't look like much to me," said Richie. The first words out of his mouth.

Bobby said nothing, his eyes on Tommy.

"Think?" said Tommy, smiling. "Tell that to Terry Doyle. You remember Terry? The middle-weight champeen? He was up on a rape charge when Bad Bobby was there. Terry liked dark, young, good-looking fellas like Bobby here – and this was before Bobby was big like he is now. Ol' Ter' tried to help Bobby wash his back in the shower one day – him and a bunch a his pals. They say he felt like a fuckin' dishrag when they came for him. Sounded like a bag fulla chicken bones when they loaded what was lefta

Terry onto the fuckin' gurney – wasn't no bone over a foot long that wasn't busted. His head looked like a beach ball you let the air outta. You don't want to tangle with this guy, Richie. Just leave it at that. I got confidence we can straighten this out."

"Thanks, Tommy," said Bobby.

"I still say you didn't have to smack the kid," said Tommy. "That just isn't right. It's disrespectful. A few kids drinkin' . . . gettin' rowdy . . . That's still no reason."

"One of the kids upstairs," began Bobby, "getting poked on the table? I recognized her. It was Christine Failla. She can't be more than fifteen."

Bobby watched the color drain out of Tommy's face.

"Paulie's kid?"

"The same," said Bobby.

"Minchia!!" hissed Tommy, screwing up his face in an expression of distate – and worry. "Jesus Cheerist!! . . . I was at her first communion for fuck's sake!"

Bobby shrugged and said nothing, content to let Tommy think things through now.

"You sure it was her?"

"Me and Eddie were at her confirmation. Out on the Island."

"I missed that," said Tommy. "I was in AC that week. Jesus . . . Paulie's little girl. You're sure?"

Bobby nodded gravely. "I saw that, I figured I hadda move fast. What am I gonna do? I can't tell anybody. Your nephew? I don't know who the fuck he is. Even if I did – mean, Tommy . . . What's Big Paul gonna say? He finds out his baby girl is gettin' porked onna dinner table in Eddie's club? A buncha drunken frat boys watchin' the whole thing? I don't think he'd be too happy."

Tommy exhaled loudly and actually shuddered visibly. "You did the right thing, Bobby. You did what you hadda do. Where is that fucking nephew a mine – I'll give him a fuckin' beatin' myself . . ."

Bobby smiled reassuringly. "Forget it. I cleared the club. Everything's cool."

"Jesuss . . ." said Tommy. "Fifteen . . . Listen . . . This goes no further than this room. Nobody . . . and I mean nobody finds out. Paulie hears about this . . . even a hint . . . and I don't even want to think about it.

"My nephew doesn't know, right?" said Tommy, standing up.

"He doesn't know."

"Good. He's a sweet kid – but he's got a mouth

on him. His mother didn't hit him enough. That's the problem."

"Kids today," said Bobby.

"No shit."

"So we're straight on this?"

"Sure," said Tommy, making for the door. He stopped and shook Bobby's hand, warmly.

"I'm in your debt."

Later, Bobby stood in nearly ankle-deep litter on the empty dance floor, watching the bartenders break down and count out. He felt badly about besmirching the reputation of a fifteen-year-old girl who – as far as he knew, was safely tucked into bed with her stuffed toys somewhere out on Long Island – and could well have been all night. In truth, he hadn't seen Chrissie Failla since Eddie had pointed her out, years earlier, waiting for the pony ride at Eddie's kid's birthday party in Westchester. But it had been a necessary lie. Tommy V had put him, and Eddie, in a tough spot. Smack a made guy's nephew and people have to make hard decisions. Appearances have to be kept up. Allegiances affirmed and reaffirmed. Somebody somewhere sits down with a bunch of old men who aren't even close to the situation and then somebody has to get hurt.

Bobby knew how that worked.

And it wasn't going to happen here.

Not this time anyway.

BOBBY EATS OUT

Bobby Gold in black Armani suit (from a load hijacked out of Kennedy), skinny black tie, black silk shirt and black Oxfords sat on the banquette of 210 Park Grill and looked uncomfortably at Eddie Fish's sourdough dinner roll. Eddie had torn the thing apart but hadn't eaten any; the bits of bread and crust lay scattered on his plate like an autopsied crime victim. When the drinks came, vodka rocks for Bobby, Patron straight up with a side of fresh lime juice for Eddie, Bobby drained his in two gulps, exhausted already.

At thirty-eight years old, Eddie Fish had not once in his life had to wash his own shirt, clean an ashtray, pick up after himself or take public transportation. He was a little man; five-foot-four in heels, and impeccably dressed today: a charcoal gray pinstriped suit from an English tailor, ultra-thin Swiss timepiece, hand-painted silk tie, shirt from

Turnbull and Asser, and Italian shoes made from unborn calfskin. His nails were buffed and polished, and his hair, trimmed twice a week by the same man who'd cut his father's, was neat and curiously untouched by gray. Eddie Fish's skin was golden brown, burnished by strong Caribbean sun, and his pores were clean and tight after a morning visit to his dermatologist. He looked pretty much like the man he imagined himself to be: a successful businessman, a nice guy, a democrat and a citizen of the world.

"They love me here," said Eddie Fish, one arm over his chair back, motioning for a waiter.

"Can't you just pick something and order?" pleaded Bobby, knowing it was hopeless.

"I need a minute," said Eddie, his eyes darting around inside his head like trapped hamsters.

The waiter arrived and asked if they were ready to order.

"Would you like a few moments to decide?" inquired the waiter politely after Eddie ignored him, his nose buried in the menu.

"No . . . no. Stay," commanded Eddie.

For Eddie Fish, menus were like the Dead Sea Scrolls, the Rosetta Stone, the Kabbalah and *Finnegan's Wake* all rolled into one impenetrable document. There were hidden messages, secrets that had to be rooted out before it was safe to order. There was, there had to be, Eddie was convinced, some way of getting something better, something extra – the good stuff they weren't telling everybody about. Somebody somewhere was getting something better than what appeared here. Someone richer, taller, with better connections was getting a little extra and Eddie was not going to be denied.

Brow furrowed, the muscles in his jaws working furiously, he scrutinized each item on the menu, each listed ingredient, his eyes moving up and down the columns, then back again.

Bobby had decided on onglet medium-rare thirty seconds after picking up the menu and he looked around the room, killing time, waiting for Eddie. It was mostly women here; long-legged ones with foreign accents and faces pulled tight, a few weedy-looking men who looked like their moms had dressed them. They were packed in three-deep at the bar, a host hurrying to air-kiss new arrivals. Their waiter, still waiting on Eddie, looked nervously at the rest of his rapidly overflowing station.

"The oysters . . ." began Eddie. "Where are they from?"

"Prince Edward Island, sir," replied the waiter. "Nova Scotia. They're excellent."

"You have any Wellfleet oysters?" inquired Eddie, looking grave. Bobby nearly groaned out loud. Eddie wouldn't have known a Wellfleet oyster if one had climbed up his leg, fastened itself on his dick and announced itself in fluent English. He must have seen them on another menu.

"I'm sorry, sir. No. We don't have them," said the waiter. "We only have the Prince Edward Island's."

"And . . . what kind of sauce do they come with?" asked Eddie. "I don't want any cocktail sauce . . . that red stuff. I don't want that."

"They're served with a rice-wine wasabi vinaigrette," said the waiter.

"Like it says on the fucking menu . . ." he could have added.

"Uh huh . . ." said Eddie, processing this last bit of information, wondering no doubt if the waiter was trying to trick him somehow. Wasabi . . . Wasabi . . . Was that a good thing or a bad thing?

Bobby saw something being resolved. A decision had been made on the oyster question. "Can you ask the chef to make me some of that sauce with the shallots in it? What do you call that? Mignonette! I want mignonette sauce. It's like . . . red . . . red wine vinegar and shallots . . . and some black pepper. The shallots – you gotta chop 'em up real small. Can you do that?"

"Mignonette," repeated the waiter, thinking visibly. Which would be worse, thought Bobby: telling Eddie fucking Fish, known gangster associate, that he couldn't have the fucking mignonette with his oysters – or approaching a rampaging prick of a three-star chef in the middle of the lunch rush and telling him to start hunting up some shallots and red wine vinegar?

"I'll have to ask the chef, sir," said the waiter. "But I'm pretty sure we can do that for you."

By the time he started in ordering his entree, Eddie had kept the waiter at his elbow for five full minutes, the rest of the poor man's station shooting daggers at him from their tables. Eddie, oblivious to Bobby's discomfort, began the tortuous process of grafting together elements from different menu items, designing an entree for himself, figuring out the way it should be served, instead of the way everyone else was getting it. Only fools, as Eddie liked to say, settled for less.

"The hanger steak. How is that prepared?"

"With saffron cous-cous, sir," said the waiter. "It's pan-seared, then roasted to order and served with a reduction of Côte de Rhone, demi-glace and caramelized whole shallots. It's very good." The waiter's offer of an opinion doomed that selection. Eddie wasn't having any.

"And the tuna?"

"That's grilled rare ... served with roasted fingerling potatoes, braised fennel ... and a citrus herb reduction," said the waiter, the first hint of frustration creeping into his voice. It made no impression on Eddie. The poor bastard could hop up and down holding his crotch, get down on one knee and bark like a dog – it wouldn't make any difference to Eddie, who seemed to slip into some kind of a fugue-state when ordering from a menu.

"Okay ... Okay ..." pondered Eddie. "How about ... let me ... get ... the ... the monkfish. The saddle of monkfish."

"One monkfish," repeated the waiter, gratefully, the clouds beginning to part, one foot already pointed towards the kitchen.

"But ... let me have that with ... with the sauce from the hanger steak," said Eddie. "And like ... the roasted finger potatoes. That sounds good ... And what came with the tuna? What was the vegetable with that?"

"Uh ... braised fennel," stammered the waiter.

Bobby saw the light go out in his eyes. He got it now. He understood, finally, what was happening. Eddie was never letting him go. All hope was gone. This vicious, malevolent little creep wasn't going to be happy until his whole station was up in arms, until his other customers were so pissed off they tipped ten percent, until the chef was pushed to the point of murder. Chefs blame waiters for the sins of their customers, the waiter was probably thinking – and this chef, when he saw Eddie Fish's order, was going to unscrew his head and relieve himself down his neck.

"Forget the monkfish," said Eddie, changing tack, "Let me have the turbot instead. Yeah. I'll have the turbot. It's fresh?"

"Yes, sir," said the waiter. "It came in this morning."

"Then I'll have the turbot. Grilled . . . with the balsamic reduction and baby bok choy from this pork dish here . . ."

"Yes, sir," said the waiter, picturing his imminent dismemberment in the kitchen.

"Wait!" commanded Eddie, as the waiter began to turn away. "Before you bring the fish . . . could you lemme have a Caesar salad?"

"I'm sorry sir," said the waiter. "We don't have – "

Eddie was not deterred. He'd expected this. "It's

simple. You tell the chef, take some egg yolks . . . and some garlic. Fresh garlic . . . and some anchovies . . ."

It went on like this . . . and on. It always did. Bobby had known Eddie since college. Nearly twenty years – and every meal was like this. When the order was, at long last, finally taken, the waiter dispatched to the kitchen to meet his fate, Eddie was still looking at the menu, unsatisfied. He'd study it for a few more minutes, to see, Bobby thought, where he might have gone wrong, doing an after-action report in his head, analyzing where he might have missed something. By now, Bobby had completely lost his appetite. The customers at the tables around them glared, murmuring in French. Bobby, easily the largest man in the room, felt like a circus bear, staked in place, trapped and uncomfortable.

Eddie straightened his tie and put down his menu.

"Isn't this place great? You can't get reservations here. Six month wait."

"You murder these waiters," said Bobby.

"Are you kidding me? They love me here!" said Eddie, shooting his cuffs, then rubbing his hands together in anticipation of his oysters and his Caesar. "You know how much I tip when I come here?"

Yeah, thought Bobby. Twelve percent.

* * *

Knowing the back-of-the-house of the restaurant business as he did, Bobby could well imagine how much they loved Eddie Fish here. They probably had a nickname for him. Catching sight of Eddie, moving brusquely across the dining room to his favorite table (without waiting to be seated), they probably said, "Oh, shit! Here comes that malignant little shit! Please, God . . . Not my station! Not my station . . ." Or, "Here comes the Pomeranian. Look out! That cocksucker can keep his twelve percent. You take that table. I'm NOT waiting on that fuck."

What the chef thought of the troublesome Mr. Fish, Bobby could only imagine. Considering what havoc he played with the man's scrupulously thought out menu, Bobby would be surprised if there wasn't some small way in which the chef revenged himself. If he hadn't already hocked a big, fat phlegm-ball into one of Eddie's from-scratch Caesars, he was clearly a man of Herculean endurance.

Bobby recalled overhearing one of the NiteKlub cooks, talking about what one could do to a particularly hated customer's food.

"Copper oxide, dude," the cook had said. "You can get it in, like, hobby shops, for chemistry sets. You sprinkle that shit in somebody's food, bro'? They gonna slam shut like a book – then it's lift-off time!

We're talking projectile vomiting! We're talking explosive diarrhea – that motherfucker's going off like a fucking bottle rocket!"

"What's so funny?" said Eddie, noticing Bobby smiling serenely. His oysters had arrived, and he speared one with a fork, ran it around in his mignonette.

"Nothing," said Bobby, startled out of his reverie. "I was just thinking."

"Oh yeah? . . . Well, think about this: I got something for you to do tonight."

"What?"

"A tune-up. You gotta go out to Queens and see a guy."

"I work at the club tonight."

"Yeah? Well, get somebody to cover for you. This guy needs a talking-to right away."

"Shit, Eddie . . . You don't have anybody else? I'm over this shit. I don't want to do it anymore."

"I don't have anybody big enough. This guy is a fucking gorilla. You should see him. He looks like a fucking building with feet. And tattoos. You never seen so many. I think this goof's been in jail."

"What he do, Eddie? He doesn't sound like a customer."

"He's not. I brought the Jag in to be fixed – this guy," said Eddie, pushing away his plate of oysters, only half of them eaten. "He was supposed to put in a new carburetor. New, Bobbie. New. My regular guy comes back from vacation, takes a look under there, says it's a reconditioned piece a equipment. Fucking guy ripped me off."

"So? Call him up. Tell him what a dangerous man you are. Tell him to put a new fucking carburetor in for Chrissakes ... What's the problem?"

"This guy doesn't listen to reason. We had a few words on the phone. I make a few suggestions. He tells me to go get fucked. He's a real hard-on this guy. A tough guy. A Nazi. No shit!"

"A Nazi?"

"He has, like, swastikas all over his neck – on his arms. I saw this character when I brought the car in, I couldn't believe it."

"Why you going to Nazi fucking mechanics, Eddie?"

"He came recommended. What? I don't care for the guy's politics. I don't give a fuck he's got Yasser Arafat, John Tesh, Willie Nelson tattooed on his fucking face – he was cheap. And this other guy said he was good. It's a fuckin' chop shop he runs out there. Tommy V's crew brings him some cars now and again. You know . . ."

"Great. I gotta go all the way out to Queens. Get into it with some fucking hero from AB – "

"AB?"

"Aryan Brotherhood, Eddie. It's a jail thing. Guy's flashing swastikas all over his body, he's probably AB."

"Oh . . . Then you probably know the fucking guy. It'll be like old home week. Go break his kneecaps and reminisce about the good old days. I can't have this asshole getting over on me, Bobby. It's bad for business. People talk, you know? Tommy's people hear this fucking animal talking about how he pulled one over on me – where does it end? Next thing you know, I'm taking it up the ass from every deadbeat fuck in town."

"Peachy. And it's gotta be tonight?"

"Tonight, Bobby. It's gotta be tonight."

Their entrées arrived, but Bobby's appetite was long gone. He picked at his hanger steak, transfixed by the way Eddie chewed with his mouth open.

"Remember in school?" said Eddie, apropos of nothing, spraying food as he talked. "You weighed, what? One-fifty? One-sixty? I could have taken you! . . . Remember we were going to take off Kenny – the guy with the Merck coke? You wouldn't do it. You said he was too big. Remember?"

"Yeah," said Bobby. "I remember."

"That worked out. Jesus, we make money on that or what? I musta put like a six-to-one cut on that shit . . . That worked out okay."

"Okay?" said Bobby, snarling. "Okay? I got pinched with that shit! I did eight fucking years for that shit! I did your fucking time! Maybe you remember that part?"

"Oh, yeah," said Eddie, wiping his mouth with the end of a napkin. "I forgot."

Lenny's Auto Parts was located in Long Island City, on a deserted street lined with warehouses and fish wholesalers. Lenny's was at the very end, by the Long Island rail tracks; a big, unruly yard heaped with compacted and uncompacted cars, mountains of rusting fenders, windshields, chassis and tire rims, just barely contained by a corrugated steel fence. Next to the house, a garage with graffit-covered steel shutters. A dog barked somewhere when Bobby got out of his taxi. The light on the second floor was the only sign of life on the block, a single window situated over a dark office space, approached by a rickety outside staircase which wound around what looked like it was once a two-family house.

A Harley was parked out front, on a small square of untended lawn, the grass littered with candy wrappers and beer bottles. Bobby clumped up the stairs, not bothering to be quiet, and banged twice on the door.

The man who answered was enormous, a scowling, fat bastard with redwood-sized arms, a tangled beard with what looked like bits of potato chips caught in it, and a dense mural of tattoos, both professionally and self-applied, which said, "prison prison and more prison."

The knocking had clearly awakened the big man. As soon as he opened the inner screen door, his eyes still focusing, the words, "What is it?" coming out of his mouth, Bobby hit him with a short, chopping right straight into his windpipe. As he staggered back, Bobby crouched down, feet planted, and as the big, hairy beast struggled for his first gasp of air, gave him a roundhouse wallop to the temple. He fell flat on his back with a tremendous crash and didn't move.

"Whatchoo do to my brother?" came a voice from the back of the room. Bobby looked to his right, across a shabby, communal living space littered with beer cans and take-out containers. Sitting in a clapped-out reclining chair, sipping beer from a tall-boy, was an even larger man – also bearded, also heavily tattooed. Worse, Bobby recognized him.

"Bad Bobby!" said the man. "Dude! You really fucked my little brother up. What brings you to mi casa, bro'?"

"Lenny?" said Bobby, flustered.

"Yeah," said the man in the chair, scratching an iron cross over his thorax. "When you knew me I didn't go by that name. That's Frank there on the floor. He's gonna be pissed when he wakes up. Got a temper, that boy."

Bobby noticed with dismay the twelve-guage Ithica shotgun leaning against the side of the chair. Fortunately, Lenny seemed to be making no attempt to reach for it.

"LT . . . LT, can't believe it," said Bobby.

"Right."

"I'll be dipped in shit!"

"Come on in. Siddown, have a beer."

Bobby crossed the room, stepping over the crushed cans, the Styrofoam containers. A TV flickered silently in the corner, two chubby lesbians going at it with a bright orange dildo on a shag rug on the screen.

"So," said Lenny, when Bobby was sitting down

on a rickety lawn chair by a beer-can-covered card table. "You got business with little brother? Or you got business with me?"

Bobby thought he heard snoring, looked over against the right wall and saw a black woman sleeping on a bare mattress. She looked pregnant.

"My old lady," said Lenny. "I got a kid too. In the next room. He's got the asthma. Got him hooked up to one a those machines. Try not to wake him."

"I guess I got business with you," said Bobby, grabbing a warm beer from a half-emptied six-pack on the card table. "LT. I can't believe it . . ."

"Bad Bobby comes calling. After all this time . . . Who woulda thought. Made nice work of little brother too. You look good. You keeping in shape."

Bobby just shrugged. He was uncomfortable with the situation. LT had been the head of AB at Greenhaven when Bobby had been up there. He'd taken the then gangly and dangerously unprotected young Bobby under his wing, assigning other gang members to look after him. They'd become buddies, playing chess in the day room, exercising together in the yard, talking about history – particularly military history – the fact that LT was essentially a Nazi, and Bobby a Jew, adding a certain playful nature to their relationship.

"So, what's the problem? And who do I got a problem with?" said Lenny.

"Eddie Fish has a problem," said Bobby. "Something about a carburetor you sold him."

Lenny threw his head back and started to wheeze with laughter, his whole body shaking.

"THAT asshole? You comin' all the way out here – the middle of the fuckin' night – chop down my bro' like a freakin' tree – over a fuckin' carburetor? Oh, Bobby. I thought things was gonna be different for you when you got out. We all thought you was gonna go back to school. End up a lawyer or somethin'. Aww, Jesuss. I'm sorry to hear this."

"I'm not too thrilled with how things worked out either," said Bobby, his ears burning. Pity from a 350-pound white supremacist car thief not going down well.

"Let me clue you in, here, Bobby. That little shit comes out here with that fuckin' Jag a his. Says he wants a deal on a new carb. I says I got a new carb right in the back. Cocksucker doesn't want to pay for it. You know who I am? He says. You know who I'm with? Now lissen, Bobby, you know me. I don't give a fuck who he's with . . . I'm with some people too – and when they come by my shop? They talk nice to me. I ain't nobody's nigger, right, Bobby? So shithead tells me how much he wants to pay – which is not much. I couldn't get a used carb out of a fuckin' Ford for what he's offerin'. So I tell the kid I got to clout me one out of this nice XJ I happen to know about. Thing's a year old. Practically new. I give it to this Fish asshole at fuckin' cost. This kid I got working for me? He's used to taking cars, Bobby. To order. The whole fuckin' car. Not rootin' around under the fuckin' hood like some kid who's just beggin' to get grabbed. I made a couple a calls to some people and asked about this Eddie fuckin' Fish that's supposed to be such a big shot? And you know what they told me? 'Fuck him.' Do what you can. But don't bend over backwards, you know what I mean? I did the right thing." Lenny took a long draught of beer and shook his head. "What are you doing hanging around with that fuck, Bobby? From what I hear? He's gonna get fuckin' clipped any day now. The people he thinks he's such friends with? They ain't such good friends." He took another long slug from the can and stared at Bobby while he finished his thought, eyes getting hard. "Not like us."

On the floor, Lenny's little brother stirred. Holding his throat, he raised up on one elbow and stared at Lenny and Bobby sitting amiably together. "What the fuck?" he rasped.

"Be cool, bro'," said Lenny, his voice betraying no concern. "You just stay where you is – right there."

"Fuck that!" said not-so-little brother, managing to clamber onto all fours. "I'm gonna –"

"You ain't gonna do nothin', Frankie," said Lenny. "Unless you want me to get outta this chair and give you the biggest asswhuppin' a your life. You wake the kid and I'm gonna be real mad at you, little bro' . . . Real mad."

"Listen, Bobby," said Lenny. "As you can see, things are gettin' a little tense and all around here. Tell you what. Tomorrow? You tell that little Christ-killer you work for to come round with his fuckin' Jag. Me and little brother put a nice shiny new one in for him, no charge. Cause it's you? I'm happy to do it. But after that, I don't want to see him no more. Next time he comes around here? There might be some folks waitin' for him. Guy's a fuckin' insect. I don't care what he tells you. The people who count? He's nothin' with them. Only reason he's still alive is some folks figure he ain't worth killin'. Whether you want to tell him that is up to you, bro'. But you know me. I tell it straight."

"Thanks, LT," said Bobby. "I really appreciate it. You were always good to me. Never understood why . . . But you were always good to me."

Lenny smiled and leaned back in his chair, his eyes narrowing to slits. "You ain't a white man, Bobby Gold. That's for sure. But you almost white. And we white men gotta stick together."

"What about her?" said Bobby, indicating the sleeping black woman on the mattress.

"Oh, that?" said Lenny. "That's love, Bobby. That's a whole different thing."

Bobby nodded as he stood up to go.

"Listen," said Lenny, helpfully. "You better put Frankie over there to sleep for a while on your way out. He's gonna be all hot and bothered and I don't want him waking the kid or causing a ruckus, he goes followin' you out to the street. Better he sleeps for a while."

"What?" said Frank, trying to scramble to his feet as Bobby approached him on the way to the door.

"Sorry, Frank," said Bobby. He side-kicked him behind the ear as he passed by, doing it with his toe rather than the heel. The impact pushed him onto his face. He stayed down.

"Thanks, LT," said Bobby.

"Be good, Bad Bobby . . ."

"I'm tryin'," said Bobby.

BOBBY IN LOVE

Someone was snoring. Nikki opened her eyes, instantly aware of a jumbo-sized, king-hell hangover, her mouth tasting of tequila – afraid to look.

There was a used condom in the ashtray on her nightstand. Nice touch, she thought, pain boring into her skull like a dull drill-bit. Just perfect. She raised herself onto one elbow, feeling nauseated, pushed some long, brown hair out of her face, and examined the hand that was resting limply on her bare hip. Seeing the thick, diagonal callus at the base of the man's index finger, her heart sank. Whoever he was, he was in the business. This was bad. Everybody would know. All the other NiteKlub cooks; the chef, the sous-chef, even the floor staff – they'd all know about it by tonight.

Nikki knew how these things went in the small, incestuous subculture of cooks and kitchens: first, the initial report, then the reviews, then additional commentary. Word would spread. Kitchen phones would be ringing all across town. "Did you hear who the sauté bitch went home with last night?"

Who had she taken home anyway?

Nikki turned over, carefully, so as not to wake the sleeping man. She held her breath, then pulled down the covers to take a look. It was Jimmy Sears.

"Oh, NO!" she yelped, sitting bolt upright now. She delivered a sharp blow to Jimmy's well-muscled shoulder.

"Get up!! ... Wake up you asshole!! ... Oh, shit ... oh, FUCK!!"

"Morning," said Jimmy, sleepily, already looking much too pleased with himself. He rolled over onto his back, a morning hard-on poking out from under the sheets, rubbed his eyes and stretched. She considered braining him with the lamp. That would keep his mouth shut. Maybe she could even dispose of the body – bit by bit – if she had her knife kit. She could break him down like a side of veal. How hard could that be? She knew veal, beef, lamb, venison, chicken, rabbit, pork ... how different could human anatomy be? But her knives were at the club, rolled up in their leather case and safely stashed in her locker – and who was she kidding anyway? This was awful. Of all the rotten people in the world to get drunk with, take home, let between her legs – this had to be the worst-case scenario.

Jimmy, while cute – and hung like a donkey – was the sleaziest, most loud-mouthed Lothario in the restaurant universe: a braggart, misogynist, prevaricator and all-around bullshit artist. To make matters worse, he was the NiteKlub chef's arch rival. This wasn't just an embarrassment. This was treason.

Nikki flashed back to when she'd worked for Jimmy – how she'd heard him, on countless occasions, bragging to his entire crew how he'd bagged some round-heeled hostess or rebounding bar customer – the excruciatingly clinical details: the way Jimmy would imitate the noises a girl had made when he'd "walked her around the room like a wheelbarrow," how she'd "looked like a glazed donut" when he'd blown his load all over her face. The room seemed to tip sideways for a second, and Nikki ran for the bathroom.

She made it to the bowl with no time to spare, hurled yellowish bile into the porcelain, seeing stars. She was in there a long time, intermittently lying naked on the cold tile floor, and crawling back to the toilet, her stomach muscles convulsing with the effort of trying to squeeze out what was no longer there.

After ten minutes or so, staring up at the ceiling, the sink making drip drip sounds, she tried listening for Jimmy in the bedroom, hoping he was gone. She thought she heard the refrigerator door closing.

Memory was returning. She recalled Siberia, last night ... the crowd at the bar, people jammed around the jukebox, Tracy, the owner, dancing with a pastry chick from the Hilton, remembered herself on the couch in the back room, drunk on tequila shots, Jimmy's tongue down her throat – and her with her fingers down the front of his pants, teasing the head of his oversized dong.

"Please kill me now," she said to the bathroom ceiling, "I'm ready ... I deserve to die. Please ... just get it over with ..."

When she finally stood up, her vagina hurt. She was horrified by what she saw in the mirror: eyes, mascara-smudged sinkholes, the skin around them puffy and bruised-looking from throwing up. Her hair was a rat's nest, sticking out at all angles like it had been teased with a weed-whacker. There were purple marks on her outer thighs where Jimmy, no doubt, had held her while he'd drilled away with his legendary wonder-penis. She couldn't really remember the sex yet – but then Jimmy would be happy to remind her.

She swallowed three aspirin, fighting to keep them down while she ran the water, waiting for the room to fill with steam before she stepped into the shower. She was in there a long time, trying to boil Jimmy Sears out of her pores. When she was done, she brushed her teeth twice, combed out her hair, wrapped herself chin-to-ankles in a long, terrycloth robe and, finally, stepped warily back into the bedroom.

Jimmy, still naked, had made breakfast: two perfectly fluffy yellow omelettes sat plated on the kitchenette counter – a spoonful of pilfered beluga on each one. Jimmy's signature garnish: two antennae-like chive sticks projected up from each mound of pearly gray fish eggs.

"I was saving that caviar," said Nikki.

"I didn't use it all," said Jimmy, pouring champagne.

"Where'd you get the champagne?"

"I ran out to the corner."

"You got dressed . . . ran to the corner . . . bought champagne, came back . . . and took your clothes off again?" said Nikki, horrified.

"Hey . . . It's a special occasion."

This was enough for Nikki. "You're not staying. And I'm not eating."

She avoided looking straight at Jimmy. For all his faults, he had a good body. All the surfing, skiing, in-line skating, handball, golf and tennis (when he should have been in his fucking kitchen) had made Jimmy tan and cut, his stomach ribbed with muscle. Even at thirty-nine, he had a boyish, almost irresistably ingratiating smile that seemed to invite conspiracy and bad behavior . . . He was, thought Nikki, watching him reposition an omelette so that the knife and fork faced her, sort of charming.

He had to go. Now.

"Get dressed and get out, Jimmy," she said. "You can take breakfast to go. Take it home to your wife, or your girlfriend or whoever it is these days you're lying to. Just leave." She sat down on the bed, dizzy again, a sudden stabbing pain in her groin. "Jesus . . . what did you fuck me with? A pineapple?"

Jimmy shook his head, smiling like a little boy who'd just successfully lifted a comic book, and sat down next to her. He brushed his lips against her shoulders. She shook him off.

"Just leave, please."

He began to dress. J. Crew polo shirt, khaki pants, Gap blazer, Cole Haan loafers (no socks of course), a baseball cap with the name of a band on it. God, thought Nikki – how could I have fucked this asshole?

"Whatever you say," said Jimmy, fully expecting, it appeared, that she would change her mind.

"I say," said Nikki. Dressed, at least, Jimmy was easier to despise. She looked at the floor, noted with displeasure the trail of clothes she'd worn last night – evidence of her stupidity – a reconstruction of events possible from the shoes kicked into opposite corners, the underwear hanging over the rocking chair. The brassiere must have come off last – it peeked out from under a pillow.

"You're losing your hair," she said.

"I am not!" protested Jimmy. "Bullshit!"

"In the back. You're losing your hair. You're going bald."

"I am not going bald!" insisted Jimmy, zipping up his pants but not going anywhere until this issue was resolved. "I use stuff . . . and it's working!"

"It's not working," said Nikki, tossing him a loafer. "Maybe you should get that spray. The skull-paint? Maybe that'll work . . . But the Rogaine? The minoxadyl or whatever it is? It's not taking. Believe me."

"You can be a mean bitch, Nikki."

"Yeah?" said Nikki, lip curling as she moved in close. She was taller than Jimmy by three or four inches – and face to face she looked down into his eyes. "You think you seen mean? Lemme tell you this then, chef . . . I hear one word about this from anybody . . . ever . . . One fucking word about last night – and I'm gonna tell every cook, every waitress, every chef, dishwasher, bartender and busboy in town that yes – I did take you home and fuck you – that I got you drunk, took you home and fucked you. And I'm gonna say that you cry 'Mommy' when you come. I'm gonna say that you came in about two seconds, cried for your mommy, wet the bed in your sleep . . . and left a big tuft of hair on my pillow when you got up in the morning. Now get the fuck out of my apartment, you bald fuck. I gotta go throw up again."

"Are you saying you didn't have a good time?"

"Truth be told, Jimmy? I can't remember one way or the other . . . But I'm sure you were spectacular. Feel better? Now get out."

Jimmy walked to the door and stepped out into the hallway, shaking his head. Nikki slammed the door after him. She heard him on the other side, saying under his breath, "Cunt!"

"Got that right, asshole," said Nikki. She began dressing for work.

Bobby Gold, in black jeans, black, short-sleeved T-shirt and black trainers, walked up the steps of the empty club. On the second floor mezzanine, he heard a toilet flush, waited for whoever it was to emerge. The mezzanine was still a mess from the night before – the maintenance crew still busy waxing the dance floor. The door opened and a girl came out, dressed in chef's whites. Bobby had seen her before in the kitchen – they called her the "sauté bitch" in there, he seemed to recall.

"Hi," she said.

"Hi," said Bobby, a little flustered. He didn't spend much time with women – and he was thrown by how good she looked in the sexless, double-breasted uniform and checked polyester pants. "You're in early aren't you?"

"Yeah," she said. "Prep for the party tonight. I gotta get the stocks going."

"Oh," said Bobby. She was tall – maybe five-ten, with long, dark hair that smelled like it had just been washed and her eyes – dark, almost Asian-looking – flashed with intelligence. There was the hint of a smile – the slightly sour, self-deprecating smirk of someone who's had their ass kicked and survived the experience.

"You a fan of classic comedy?" she asked, seemingly apropos of nothing.

"What do you mean?" Bobby asked, "Like what? The Marx Brothers? Fields? Chaplin?"

"I meant more like Lenny Bruce," said the girl. "Remember him?"

"I saw the movie – if that's what you mean. Dustin Hoffman played him, right?"

"Yep," said the girl.

"Good movie."

"Yeah . . . well . . . I don't know how to tell you this – but there's a guy doing a really good Lenny Bruce imitation in one of the stalls in there," she said, jerking her head in the direction of the bathroom.

Bobby thought no way she meant what he thought she meant. He hurried into the bathroom, walked quickly down to the last stall – the only one still closed – and leaned against the door. It wouldn't open. When he pushed, it felt as if someone had piled a stack of flour sacks against the other side.

He entered the next stall, stood on top of the toilet and peeked down over the divider.

She was right about the Lenny Bruce thing. There was a man in there – pants down around his ankles, one sleeve rolled up, a syringe hanging out of his arm, just below a tightened belt. He was dead, and he was blue, slumped over to one side with his legs jammed against the stall door, eyes staring straight up at Bobby like a lifeless flounder's.

Bobby got back down from the toilet and went back outside. The girl was smoking, sitting on a banquette, watching for his reaction. She'd gone in there, he realized, found the body and calmly sat down for a piss, before exiting.

"See what I mean?" she said, smiling.

"It's Lenny all over," said Bobby, unable to take his eyes off of her.

He was in love.

BOBBY GETS JILTED

Bobby Gold in black Levis, black trainers and black T-shirt, the word SECURITY printed in white letters across the chest, pushed open the swinging kitchen doors and stepped into the noise and heat. He hesitated momentarily by the door, fully aware that this place – of all the various rooms, areas, offices and fiefdoms in NiteKlub – was not his territory. Here he was an outsider, an interloper, completely unaware of the local language and customs. Dinner was winding down – all the entrees were out, only the *garde manger* chef still plating a few forlorn desserts – and the cooks were breaking down their stations, wrapping up *mise-en-place* in clean metal bains and crocks and wiping down their areas. Out in the main dining room, the waiters were beginning to strip the tables, hauling and rolling them off the dance floor. When the last few dinner customers put down their dessert forks and called for their checks, the THUMP, THUMP, THUMP of bass tones would come rumbling through the kitchen walls, then the smell of chocolate from the smoke machine – sucked in by the powerful range hoods. The Intellabeam system would wink on, bouncing filament-thin rays of colored laser beams off tiny dancing mirrors controlled by computer and joystick in the sound and tech booth. There was maybe a half-hour before the front doors were opened and the lines of people, already two deep and wrapping around the corner onto 8th Avenue, were let in. Two hours from now, every foot of floor space in the main room, mezzanine, Blue Room – even the entranceways, stairs and bathrooms – would be jammed with people.

Bobby stood near the door, unsure why he was even here. He'd told himself, climbing the back service stairs, that he was hungry, that he'd stop by the kitchen to see if there was any staff gruel leftover. But that was something he'd never done before. The truth was, he'd come to see the girl. The cook, the one they called Nikki – to look at her if possible, to get close enough, maybe, to smell her hair – just for a second, to look in those eyes, the ones that hurt when they looked at you. He had no plan – unusual for Bobby, who planned just about everything these days

– and that made him nervous and uncomfortable. He certainly wasn't going to ask her out, as he'd long ago forgotten how to do such things, and the whole thought was ridiculous anyway.

He hadn't had a woman for years.

From where he stood, awkwardly trying to figure out what to do, he could see Eric, the sous-chef, counting out dinner dupes by the printer, spiking the little slips of paper onto a spindle, his hair plastered to his skull with sweat. A shorter cook (he thought they called him Lenny) was scraping down the grill with a wire brush, bobbing his head along with the speed metal on the radio, bitching in kitchen patois about some violation of protocol that Bobby didn't understand.

"You want truffle jiz? Get your own truffle jiz, cabron. I tired a you raiding my motherfuckin' meez everytime I turn around, *pinchay culero*. Every time you go in the shit, you sticking your hands in my fucking bains."

Next to him, an Ecuadorian pasta cook named Manuel smiled serenly, shook his head and apologized. Insincerely.

"I sorry my friend," he giggled, turning toward Eric, who had clearly heard all this before. "Chuletita no like I touch the station. He like I touch the pinga. *Si! Verdad!* Touch his pinga is okay. Culo, no problem. He like that. But no touch the station." He reached over and swatted a dirty side-towel at the back of Lenny's head, before dropping down to his knees to mop out his low-boy refrigerators. Two cooks, Segundo and Eduardo, were dumping a tray of indifferently roasted chicken legs into a hotel pan on the pass. Billy, the skinny white boy with the pierced tongue on the *garde manger* station, listlessly tossed salad in a large stainless-steel bowl with his hands.

In the corner behind the line, Nikki was heaving a stack of dirty saucepots and sauté pans into a cardboard-lined milk crate, a cigarette hanging from the corner of her mouth, her chef coat unbuttoned. Bobby saw the pink and red bum marks – like tribal markings – on her forearms, and thought they were the sexiest thing he'd ever seen. Her hair was popping out of its ponytail, long strands falling over her face, and Bobby could not help but be fascinated by how the muscles on her arms swelled and jumped as she slung, one-armed, one heavy load of pans after another loudly into the crate. She hadn't seen Bobby yet. As she leaned over the stove, to remove the burner covers, he stared at the way the boxy, checked poly pants stretched over her ass.

"I'm hungry!" complained Joe, the head tech,

with a hoarse, froggy voice. Billy, who relied on Joe for cocaine now and again when the busboys and bar-backs didn't come through (Bobby knew this from observing Joe's mid-shift runs around the corner to the Full Moon Saloon – and the ensuing not-very-discreet sequence of hand-offs and bathroom visits which inevitably followed) was all too willing to make something special for his patron. No chicken leg and wilted salad for Joe.

In the noise and clatter of the kitchen, Nikki still hadn't seen Bobby, who continued to stand there as if invisible, ignored by the cooks and their protégés from the floor. Unlike Frank, now tucking into a porterhouse steak on a broken chair in the corner, Bobby did not share the impounded guns and drugs from the door with the kitchen crew. He didn't let the cook's friends in for free – or give them drink tickets. No one had dared ask him. Everyone eating something other than the staff gruel in the kitchen at this moment had some kind of special arrangement with one cook or another. The waitress, Tina, was a vegetarian. The usually surly cooks had fixed her up with some grilled vegetables and cous-cous. Because she was cute. Because she flirted with the cooks. Because once or twice a year, after a few drinks, she took Eric, the sous-chef, into the liquor cage and sucked his dick. She sat on the ice cream freezer while she ate; a few powerless busboys and newbies poking unenthusiastically at their chicken legs nearby as they slunk off to eat in locker rooms, stairwells and hallways. Even Hector, the night porter, was being taken care of. He was eating a thick slice of pork loin with sauce and mashed potatoes, probably a payback for giving the kitchen a regular cut of all the pilfered goodie bags from NiteKlub industry parties and fashion shows. He also, apparently, threw them the occasional oddity or archeological find he'd come across when clearing out banquettes, or exploring the sub-cellars the club shared with the hotel next door. There was a covert cooks' lounge, Bobby knew, located in a disused storage closet on the fourth floor, which Hector had furnished nearly single-handedly with stolen hotel furniture, pilfered carpet remnants, even a jury-rigged phone line, so the cooks could call their dealers.

A runner arrived with a tray of cocktails for the kitchen: a large pitcher of Long Island Iced Tea, a pitcher of beer, a few Stoli grapefruits for the Chef – who was now hidden away back in his office, no doubt packing his nose with the new hostess. As soon as he'd dispensed drinks and returned from the Chef's office, two steak frites appeared (one for the runner and one for the cooperating bartender) as if by magic on the slide, and the runner wordlessly scooped them up and headed for the door.

Bobby, who'd forgotten to eat since yesterday's breakfast, approached the tray of chicken legs.

"Don't eat that shit," said Nikki, who'd apparently been aware of him for some time. "I'll make you something."

Bobby, surprised, stood upright, stammered, as suddenly all the cooks were staring at him.

"Uh . . . sure. Thanks . . . Th-that'd be nice."

"What?" said Eric, glaring at Nikki through the pass. "Did I hear right?"

"I said I'd make him something," said Nikki. "You got a problem with that? Or does he have to suck you off first?"

Tina, on the ice cream freezer, blushed slightly and the other cooks laughed.

"Whatever," said Eric, backing down. He looked at Bobby, a sustained stare for a few seconds, then went back to counting his dupes. Lenny, the grill cook, however, kept staring, a look of unrestrained hostility fixed on the new intruder.

"It's not necessary, anything special . . ." said Bobby, not wanting to get in the middle of some arcane tribal political situation. "I can have this. I can have the chicken."

"No way," said Nikki, pushing wet hair out of her face. "No way you eat that mung. I make you something nice . . . Fish okay?"

"Yeah. Great," said Bobby, no longer thinking about food at all, really. Trying not to look at the pale expanse of bare flesh between Nikki's sports bra and check pants underneath the open jacket. It looked smooth and hard.

"Ricky!" Nikki barked, calling over a runner. "Get him a chair and a setup!"

The runner dragged over a chair from the nearby wall phone, disappeared for a minute and came rushing back with a rolled up napkin and silver. Bobby sat down at the end of a long steel worktable in the center of the kitchen, feeling all the cooks' eyes on him.

"You want something to drink? We got beer, Iced Teas – anything else you want. Just ask Ricky," said Nikki from behind the line.

"Water. Water is good," said Bobby, uncomfortable with all the furtive looks and barely concealed scrutiny.

"Ricky!" she yelled, again. "Bring him una boteilla de Pellegrino! Rapidemente!"

Richard, the Chef, poked his head in the kitchen, a clot of white powder hanging from one nostril, a snap undone on his check pants. "Eric! How many?"

"About three hundred," said Eric, not looking up, the last dupe just hitting the spike.

"Smooth?"

"Like Lenny's ass. Like a well-greased machine. No bumps. We didn't get weeded at all."

"Returns?"

"Just the one. A refire steak."

The Chef grunted and went back to his office and whatever he had been doing.

Though there were at least twelve felonies, or violations of club policy, in evidence at this precise moment, Bobby didn't care. He watched Nikki prepare his dinner, absolutely transfixed by her smooth, economical movements behind the line. She seasoned a thick slab of monkfish, grinding black pepper from a mill, then rubbed it with sea salt. She fired up the stove and noisily slapped a pan on it, waiting for it to get hot. Without looking, one hand darted out, grabbed a wine bottle with a speed pourer, and drizzled a little olive oil into the pan, stood back a few seconds, waiting for it to get hot, then laid the fish in the pan with a sizzle and gave it a shake.

Twirling, she fired up another burner, reached for

a small saucepot and positioned it over low flame. Bobby saw butter go, a little oil, some shallots. He was amazed how quickly her hands moved, how effortlessly she seemed to handle her knife, chopping the shallots into uniform small dice before scooping them into the saucepot. When Lenny saw her pouring hard pellets of arborio rice into the pan, stirring it with a wooden spoon, he looked shocked. She nudged him out of the way and reached into his lowboy.

"Hey, bitch," he protested, "don't fuck with my meez!!"

"Shut the fuck up, bitch," said Nikki. "I need stock. Gimme some . . . And some porcinis. Some porcinis would be nice."

"Fuck, man . . . they all the way in the back," complained Lenny.

"Suck my dick," said Nikki, ignoring him. "I need stock. I need porcinis. And haul me out some truffles while you're in there, cupcakes." She gave Lenny's fat ass a gentle pat as he ducked into the low reach-in refrigerator to get her what she wanted.

She laid out a few crayfish tails from her own stores, a bottle of white truffle oil, turned to stir the rice, poured in a little stock when Lenny finally managed to extract some from his crowded refrigerator, stirred the risotto with the wooden spoon. Judging the fish ready to turn, she flipped it with a pair of tongs, put the whole pan in the oven and casually kicked the oven door closed with the side of a food-encrusted clog.

"Damn!" said Lenny, seemingly appalled. "You making the man truffle risotto?"

Nikki just turned wordlessly back to her cutting board, reached down once again into Lenny's box to retrieve some arugula, turned, stirred the risotto again, added a little more stock and stirred again – then lowered the heat, looking satisfied, lost, seemingly in thought. Bobby saw she was chewing her lower lip.

"How do you like your fish?" she asked Bobby.

"Uh . . . I don't know . . . Whatever . . .' said Bobby. Noticing that she seemed to shake her head slightly at this, he corrected himself. "Okay . . . uh . . . medium rare." This seemed to please her.

"Good. You didn't look like a well-done." As she turned back to the stove to once again give the risotto a stir, she said "Good" again, softly this time.

In went the crayfish tails, the mushrooms and the truffle peelings. She reached down into the oven, a side towel protecting her hand, and removed the fish.

Bobby watched as in a small saucepan she heated a little sauce from a cooling crock a few stations down, whisked in a little knob of whole butter, lowered the flame. Pulling the risotto off the stove, she folded in some arugula, then carefully piled a neat mound in the center of a plate, spun back to the stove and gingerly transferred the fish from pan to plate, resting it at an angle atop the risotto. When the sauce seemed reduced to her liking, she drizzled some around the plate with a large spoon, then stepped back to examine her work, head tilted, seemingly unsatisfied with something. She reached for a bottle of truffle oil over Lenny's station, reconsidered, and then, looking both ways, quickly dodged back into Lenny's lowboy and removed a single, fresh white truffle from inside a moist towel. She was shaving a few paper thin slices over the plate with a small grater when Eric looked up from his cocktail and his stack of dinner dupes.

"White truffle!? White fucking truffles you're giving the guy?" he spluttered, speaking as if Bobby weren't sitting right there. "Fresh fucking white fucking truffles? Why don't you just yank down his fucking pants? Give him a nice sloppy fucking blow job?"

"I'm thinking about it," said Nikki, squaring off, giving him a hard, confrontational look.

Bobby turned crimson. Ordinarily, in such circumstances – not that there had been any circumstances like this in recent memory – his first instinct would have been to stand up, walk over to this Eric guy and squeeze his carotid for him, maybe lift him up off the ground by his throat, give him a few smacks, a few pointed words. But this wasn't about him at all. Nobody was watching him. All the cooks were paying attention to a contest of wills between Nikki and the sous-chef, anxious to see how things were going to turn out. There was something else going on here, too, Bobby saw. All kinds of history – beyond a simple struggle for control. The other cooks looked worried, protective, defensive; Lenny and Billy actually moved closer to the lone woman behind the line, defending her – lonely, but also, somehow . . . hurt.

Eric threw down the stack of dupes with a look of disgust and a "Fuck it," and stalked back to the locker area.

"This okay?" said Nikki, bringing Bobby his meal.

"It looks . . . wonderful," said Bobby. "I hope I didn't get you in trouble." He was trying to get the blow job comment, and Nikki's response, out of his mind.

"Fuck him."

Bobby took a bite of fish with his fork. "It's amazing," he said.

Nikki hopped up onto the stainless-steel work-table and watched him as he chewed, a look of almost clinical detachment on her face. After he took another bite, she leaned forward, reached over and tore off a little piece with her fingers, popped it in her mouth and tasted, pleased with herself. Leaning forward the way she was, Bobby got a good look straight down the valley between her breasts, every tiny bead of sweat coming suddenly, vividly, into focus, Bobby wanting suddenly, and in the most terrible way, to lick them off. Instead, he took a bite of fish, a little risotto. It truly was amazing.

"Really, really good. Thanks. So much," he said, trying desperately not to stare at her tits anymore, focussing intently on her eyes.

"Bon apetit," she said, hopping down off the table and removing her apron. She crumpled the food-smeared cotton/poly object into a tight ball and hurled it casually across the kitchen, where it dropped neatly – all air – into a laundry bin. "Three points," she muttered.

The other cooks were melting away one by one. Bobby and Nikki were almost alone in the large kitchen, when, looking like she was getting ready to leave, she turned back to him and asked, "What are you doing later?"

Flustered, Bobby found himself saying that he was working – which was patently obvious.

"Until three," he finally managed to say.

"You got a girlfriend or something?"

"Uh. No," said Bobby, no phrase book available for this conversation. Totally at sea.

"So. You want to meet me later for a drink?" she asked. Just like that.

Bobby hadn't had a "date" since before prison. "After work?" he asked, feeling terribly tongue-tied. "I uh . . . okay. Sure. That would be nice."

There. He'd said it.

"Sooo . . . I'll go home. Shower all this fish jiz off, change – and I'll see you back here at three . . . Meet you out front." With that she turned her back and was gone.

She had a drink at the mezz bar on the way out. The bartender there never denied her anything. She'd fucked him in the dry goods area at the last Christmas party – an experience she was unlikely to repeat. His cock, she remembered dimly, leaned noticeably to the left. And he'd smelled of patchouli.

The glass in her hand suddenly empty, she had another one, as she felt, strangely enough, nervous about her imminent meeting with the mostly silent and (they said in the kitchen) dangerous Bobby Gold.

"You know what that guy does?" Lenny had said in the locker room, his voice lowered to an insistent whisper. "He's like a bone man! He busts people up for Eddie Fish! He's a fucking gangster, Nick! I heard that he maybe even kills people!" Lenny had been waiting for her in there when she arrived to peel off her soggy, reeking whites.

"Bullshit," said Eric, unseen on the other side of a row of graffiti-covered lockers.

"He's a fucking faggot. What's with the all-black clothes? Who does he think he is? He's all talk. Another punchy-ass doorman been sprinkling steroids on his fucking Froot Loops. Probably got balls the size a cashews."

Nikki, in her underwear, peeked around the corner. Eric was cutting a few lines of coke on the lid of a plastic fish tub, a shaker glass of Long Island Iced Tea sitting on the floor next to him.

"Think so?" she said. "I'll let you know."

"I'm tellin' you, man. He's into some serious shit," said Lenny. "I know . . . I heard from reliable sources.

He's been to prison – for like a long time. For murder or some shit."

"Bullshit," said Eric, unwilling to believe anything so interesting about the quiet security man who his number-one line cook was clearly planning on fucking. "All those muscle guys are faggots," he sneered. "They all take it in the twins."

Seeing that Eric was too high and drunk to talk to – and not caring what he said anyway – Nikki struggled into her jeans, pullover and leather jacket, slung her knife roll over her shoulder and prepared to leave. Lenny looked stricken.

"It'll be fine," she told the chubby little line cook, pinching his cheek. "I'm just having a drink with him."

She left him in the locker room looking dejected, shaking his head.

They all wanted to get in her pants. That was the problem.

Back at the mezz bar – another drink. This one the last. She was worried. All the tall, thin women around her, with their carefully applied makeup, their club clothes. Nikki caught sight of herself in the mirror above the bar and didn't like what she saw, an outcast, a line cook, a guy with a cunt. She watched herself drain yet another drink, looking like nothing more than the kitchen slut – stringy brown hair, a pullover shirt from the fish company, baggy jeans and sneakers. The scent of smoked salmon still lingered on her fingers.

"What the fuck am I doing?" she asked herself, more than once, as she walked somewhat unsteadily over to her 11th Avenue apartment. She hauled herself up four flights of narrow stairs, the hallway smelling of cabbage and boiled corned beef, unlocked her door and, after peeling off her clothes, poured herself another drink and headed for the shower.

Bobby Gold at three-thirty in the morning. Standing outside NiteKlub. Feeling bad.

Nikki woke up fully dressed, sunlight blinding her.

"I can't believe it!!" she wailed, her eyes filling.

Her shoes were still on. A black Danskin top, tiny black leather skirt. "I can't believe it! I can't fucking believe it!! I am such an . . . asshole!"

The bed was barely disturbed. She'd come home last night, best as she could reconstruct it, showered, washed her hair, done her fucking nails (toenails too, she noticed). She'd brushed. She'd combed. She'd dressed. Jesus fucking Christ – she'd even waxed!

Eau de toilette . . . lipstick . . . mascara – even rolled a joint for her three o'clock meeting with the moody security chief. Then she'd rested her head on her pillow for, what? . . . One fucking second? And promptly fallen asleep.

She'd jilted him. The tall, morose Bobby Gold would have been disappointed. She knew that. She could tell he could be hurt. Something about the way he wore his hair long, the way his long forelocks hung down over his face, concealing his feelings.

"Shit!!" she rasped, kicking her best knock-me-down-and-fuck-me shoes onto the floor petulantly, wondering how long he'd waited. Standing there in the dark and the cold outside NiteKlub.

Story of my life, she thought. More questions to which she'd never know the answer. Another road not traveled. Another missed chance. Now she'd never look inside, past those dead shark eyes, past that look – of resignation, acceptance – she'd never know what the other thing was in there, that thing she'd seen for a second or two outside the bathroom that day, the whatever it was that she'd glimpsed somewhere at the sea bottom.

If she'd gotten him in the sack, she'd have known. Another vain, body-worshiping jerk, in love with his own reflection? She didn't think so. He wasn't a cook. There wouldn't have been the bluster, the cynicism. The false bravado, the endless talk about dick dick dick. No smell of garlic and seafood, no corn starch caked under his balls – none of that towel-snapping, jock-like, locker room mindset that Nikki now lived and breathed, it felt sometimes, with every pore and atom.

For the first time in six months, she thought, I put on a skirt. Do my nails. Wax my fucking pussy – and then I pass out.

She wriggled out of her clothes and lay face down on the bed for a while. She had to be at work in three hours. In three hours, she'd have to put on those scratchy poly-blend kitchen whites again, the damp, food-spattered clogs, she'd pick up her knife roll and walk down the long flight of steps to the kitchen and the noise and the boys who loved her but would never understand her . . . the endless, relentless flow of incoming orders, the soul destroying . . . stupidity of it all.

What would Bobby say when he saw her again? What would she say?

She had to get out of this someday. She needed a plan. She thought, for the first time, about what Lenny had been talking about a few days ago in the walk-in. His latest, knuckleheaded get-rich-quick scheme. For a few seconds, Nikki pictured herself on a Caribbean beach, in a bathing suit. A tall umbrella drink in her hand. No burn marks on her wrists. Where would she live in such a place? And with whom? She couldn't picture a house. Or a person.

When she found she was wearing earrings, she hurled them against the wall and started crying again.

Then she did something she'd never done even once in her entire career.

She picked up the phone and called in sick.

BOBBY GETS BLUE

Bobby Gold, in a blue funk, sat slouched back deep in the stained couch, one leg slung over a torn armrest, drinking vodka. Timmy Moon, behind the stick, washed glasses and hummed along to Junior Walker on the jukebox, ignoring the sole customer at the bar – a fastidiously dressed old man in an ancient suit, currently snoring into a puddle of beer. There were two gum-ball machines in the corner, leased, Bobby knew, from Metro Vending – Eddie's company. A joker-poker machine blipped and clicked and beeped against the far wall under the chain-link-fenced piece of glass that had once been a picture window. No one had been able to see through the grime-encrusted square for decades. The poker machine, occupied at this moment by a pencil-necked building super named George, was also Eddie's (Magic Carpet Entertainment Inc.) as was the cigarette machine near Bobby, and the condom machine in the bathroom. Bobby had once joked with Eddie about the condom machine, pointing out that "no one at Timmy's has had an erection for years." The beer in the taps was from a distrubutor associated with Tommy Victory (dba Zenith Distributors), and the vodka Bobby was drinking – what was it – his sixth, seventh? – was from Xanadu Beverage Inc. – also Eddie's – in partnership with Tommy, of course.

Timmy, now lighting another Parliament from the end of its predecessor, did the occasional work for Tommy V – as he had for Tommy's father before him. Part of a long and glorious tradition of murder-for-hire going back three generations of Moons. Timmy's son, James, Bobby had recently heard, had been arrested for menacing and possession of a handgun. Bobby remembered seeing James, only a few years earlier, hanging out with his friends on the corner, skateboards and baggy pants and new, white sneakers, wool caps pulled down low over their eyes, in conscious emulation of Latino prison gangs Bobby knew only too well.

The music changed to U2, a development as predictable as the over-aerated Guinness in Timmy's taps, or the wet mass of toilet paper clogging Timmy's toilets, or the inescapable outcome of an evening spent drinking at Timmy's: a hangover, a nose clogged with undissolved mannitol and unexplained cuts and bruises. The place smelled of vomit and Lysol, something one got used to after a while, and the sweat of the old men who drank up their social security checks there in the afternoons. It was nighttime now, late night, the high-end crowd. Soon, the place would be crowded with bartenders and waiters and cooks, come over after last-call had been announced at more legitimate establishments.

Bobby was punishing himself. He was feeling bad – angry that he'd allowed his hopes to rise, something he'd been very careful not to do since being upstate. This was the price, he thought glumly, of allowing yourself to believe in other people. This is what happens.

All day and into the evening, he'd tried, really tried, not to look in the kitchen – or anywhere in the direction of the kitchen. He'd convinced himself he wasn't hovering by the door at four o'clock when Nikki was scheduled to come in – and he'd pretended to himself that he neither cared nor wondered when she hadn't shown up for her shift. There'd been a short stab of pain every time the door opened and it wasn't her. And when it was clear that she wasn't coming it only made things worse, because now, not only was he wondering why she'd led him on and then not shown up as promised, but where she could be right now – and what she might be doing.

He felt sick. And the vodka wasn't making things better. Bobby lay his head back on the couch and stared up at the painted-over tin ceiling, Sam Cooke on the box now, angry, angry about how all this had snuck up on him unasked for.

Two hairy bastards in leather jackets and work boots came into the bar holding a car radio, slapped it on the bar in front of Timmy and demanded to know how much he'd pay for it.

"Not interested, gentlemen," said Timmy, not inquiring if the two would care for a drink.

"How 'bout you, buddy? You want a radio? It's a Blaupunkt. Get fifty bucks for it. Sell it to you for twenny, my man."

"Fuck off," said Bobby, not bothering to even look.

"What you say to me?" said the larger of the two – a bearded asshole with a much broken nose and dried blood caked under one eye.

"He tole you to fuck off," said the other one.

"Get the fuck outta my bar," said Timmy, holding a cut-down 10-gauge now, what was left of the barrel resting on the bar. A few inches away the sleeping man continued to snore, undisturbed, such was the relaxed, even mellifluous tone of Timmy's request.

"What's the matter with you?" said Timmy after the two had left. "Why are you provokin' a pair a cunts like that?"

Bobby held up his glass, motioning for more vodka, but Timmy shook his head and came around the bar. "You ain't drinkin' here tonight, Bobby Gold," he said. "You're stinkin' . . . and you're lookin' to get yourself jammed up for no good reason that I can see. So be a good guy and fuck off home. Don't you got a cat or somethin' to look after? You ain't doin' nobody any good being here tonight."

He began wiping down the cable-spool table in front of Bobby with a wet bar rag. It was the nicest Bobby had ever seen him. Even drunk, he could see that.

See? He did have friends, he thought to himself, as he picked his way to the door. Timmy Moon. Greatest guy on earth. A man who cared. Looking after him like that, making sure no harm came to him. Concerned. Fuck everybody else.

Bobby careened out the door and walked right into Nikki.

"Whoa there, cowboy," she said. "I've been looking for you."

The Apex Coffee Shop was off the lobby of a run-down tourist hotel on 48th Street. Bobby drank burnt coffee and tried to focus on the plate of eggs in front of him.

"Eat it," said Nikki, across from him. "You'll feel better. Jesus, you were drunk. I've never seen you that way."

Bobby said nothing, just poked at his eggs with his fork. He hadn't said anything at all since she'd found him, just let her lead him like a trained camel a few blocks away to the overlit coffee shop, watched as she'd ordered for him, sat there until the food arrived, looking at her.

She was in a black leather motorcycle jacket, jeans and a T-shirt, but something was different about her. She was wearing makeup – a little around the eyes, he thought – and was that lipstick? He thought it was.

"I'll wait till you sober up a little before I apologize," she said, tearing off a piece of toast with short but polished fingernails, the nails cut or chewed in parts, her hands pocked with pink welts.

"I'm okay now," said Bobby. "You don't have to apologize. For what?"

"For not making it last night. I'm not like that," she said, looking away and fumbling for a cigarette.

"I got loaded," she said. "Pissed fucking drunk . . . and I fell asleep."

"It happens," said Bobby, trying to be noncommittal. "No big thing."

"Irregardless . . . It happened to me," said Nikki, reaching across the table and taking his hand. "And I'm sorry." She squeezed his fingers and withdrew her hand awkwardly. "You know, not for nothin' – but I got all dressed up and everything. I put on a fuckin' dress."

She laughed suddenly, Bobby smelling vodka on her for the first time, realizing that she too was drunk. "I even waxed my cat," she said, an unbecoming half laugh, half derisive snort escaping from her mouth.

"Your what?" said Bobby – picturing his own cat, shorn of hair, trying to imagine her putting up with such a thing.

"My pussy, jerk," said Nikki, lowering her voice. "First date and all. I wanted to make a good impression."

Bobby didn't know what to say. He stared into his coffee, feeling dizzy, imagining the cleft between her legs devoid of hair, partially groomed, au naturel . . . When she pretended to pick a piece of lint off the sleeve of her jacket, betraying a welcome nervousness, he said, "Fully waxed? Or like . . . only some?" astonished that the question had escaped his lips.

"I left a little bit over the top," said Nikki, standing up and calling for the check.

"C'mon. I'll show you."

"Where we going?" he asked, seeing things more clearly, yet somehow even more out of control. "Where you live?"

"Let's go to your place," she said, tugging him west. "You live near here right? The door guy – the big one – said so."

Making a mental note to fire the loose-lipped doorman, Bobby stopped in his tracks and considered things. No one had ever been inside his apartment. He tried to picture it, as if for the first time, trying to imagine what it would look like to an outsider.

"I need to look at your record collection," she said, taking his arm in hers and leaning against him. "I see any Billy fuckin' Joel in there and this ain't gonna happen."

"Jesus? What you got in here? Fort Knox?" complained Nikki, her hands inside Bobby's jacket as he fumbled with the last lock – a custom-made deadbolt put together for him by an Albanian thief when he'd moved in. The place was clean, he knew.

Any guns or cash or "evidence of wrongdoing," as he'd once heard such things referred to, were – as always – securely put away in the concealed floor safe. But Bobby was embarrassed when he flicked on the light. There was something too severe, almost fanatical, about his apartment, he knew. The too-clean, too-polished hardwood floors, the raw brick walls, the always-dusted sound system, the set of free weights neatly arranged in the corner and the heavy bag hanging from the ceiling. His mattress, squared away as usual and tight as a snare drum, rested on a low unfinished wood platform, a copy of *Grey's Anatomy* on the simple, mail-order nightstand. The refrigerator, he knew, was empty save for a V-8 and a few wedges of leftover pizza in the freezer.

But there was no Billy Joel to be found, he comforted himself. Returning from a long piss in the too-clean bathroom, he found Nikki smiling by his collection of old vinyl, a copy of the first Modern Lovers album in her hand.

"You're an interesting man," she said, putting the record back in its place, alphabetically between Harold Melvin and Ennio Morricone. She got up, sat down on the bed and began peeling off her clothes, Bobby instinctively looking away for a second before returning his gaze to her sleek, well-muscled back as she bent over to remove her shoes, the crack of her ass, the way her dark hair moved around on her naked shoulders.

"Can you, like, get the light?" she asked, sliding under the covers. "If you're too drunk to fuck, we can do that tomorrow. Right now, I just want to sleep with you." She sat upright for a second, an innocuously worried look crossing her face. "If that's okay?"

Bobby undressed in the bathroom. Took a long shower, washing the stink of Timmy's couch off himself; stood there in the bathroom, forlornly looking at himself in the mirror. He hadn't looked at himself like this in a long time.

When he emerged from the bathroom, in robe and boxer shorts, she was asleep. The cat, who had materialized after no doubt hiding (she'd never seen anyone other than Bobby since he'd taken her in), snoozing by her head. Bobby folded the robe carefully over the single chair, sat for a long time on the edge of the bed, wondering whether to remove the boxer shorts or not, feeling both silly to have put them back on and uncomfortable about taking them off. Finally he whipped them down, pulled up the sheet and got into bed. Nikki didn't move.

In the middle of sleep, he felt fingers on his chest,

Nikki's leg working itself between his, her head moving to rest against his shoulder, the absolutely amazing sensation of her breasts brushing against his stomach. His penis immediately stiffened, raising the sheets. He lay there, motionless and afraid, not sure what to do next. A contented noise – it could have been "Mmmnnn" – came from Nikki's mouth, but that was it. She snuggled a bit closer, then her breathing became more even and she stopped moving entirely. Bobby stared up at complete blackness, tiny flares of color exploding in his head.

"Now that's a penis!" someone was saying. Bobby woke – the room flooded with light from the streakless windows – to see Nikki, resting on one arm next to him, covers pulled down, looking at his cock. He still had a hard-on, a painful one, and he reached instinctively for the covers but she swatted his hand away. She straddled him quickly, leaned forward and kissed him lightly on the lips, then whispered in his ear. "You're a nice guy, Bobby Gold. Aren't you? That's the big secret, isn't it?"

She reached down to grab hold of him, raised herself up for a second, then impaled herself on his erection. The cat woke up, looking alarmed, and fled.

BOBBY AT THE BEACH

Bobby Gold in a black Speedo, his hair still wet from the surf, took a long sip of beer and looked at the pigeons.

"Rats with wings," he said. "Beach should be for seagulls. Not pigeons."

"Lighten up, grouchy," said Nikki. "It's a city beach. City beach? City birds."

"I just don't get why people feed them," said Bobby, watching an old man in a walker sprinkle breadcrumbs on the boardwalk. "I mean – it's not like they don't get any food. You ever see a starving pigeon?"

"Cooked a few pigeons in my time," said Nikki, wiping sweat from between her breasts. She was wearing a tiny little bikini. Color: black – in deference to Bobby, the two of them pale in their dark suits, dark sunglasses and dark hair.

"Yeah? How do they taste?"

"Like chicken."

The beach was crowded. It was Sunday and barely a foot of sand wasn't occupied with beach chairs, umbrellas, brightly colored blankets, volleyball players, inflatable rafts, body boards and sunbathers. Bobby and Nikki sat on the edge of the boardwalk, drinking beer from plastic cups and staring out to sea.

"I could live at the beach," said Nikki. "If I had enough money? I could definitely live at the beach. Not this beach . . . More like Cape Cod, maybe the Jersey Shore."

"Maybe. I could see that. Not Florida."

"No. Definitely not Florida." Nikki drained the last of her beer, crumpled her cup and hurled it into a trash can a few feet away.

"Nice shot," said Bobby.

"Three points."

"Two," said Bobby.

"I'm thinking of doing something illegal," said Nikki, apropos of nothing.

"Yeah? Like what?"

"I need money. I want money. I'm thinking about a career change."

"From saucier to what? Arsonist? Home invader? Bank robber?"

"No . . . I don't know yet. I'm looking for an opportunity. To you know – steal or something. I want to steal a lot of money and then retire to the beach."

"You don't expect me to –"

"No way! Please . . . I was just sayin'."

"And I ain't setting you up with anybody either. What are you fucking thinking? Who put this shit in your head? You been talking to somebody at the Club?"

"No. I just saw a movie on TV last night. *Bonnie and Clyde*? It looked like fun."

"You watch the end? They get killed at the end."

"Not that part. The taking the money part. The driving around real fast in cars part."

"You'll get grabbed. Believe me. Some genius, some fellow criminal mastermind'll snitch and you'll go to prison. You don't want to go to prison. I'm telling you. You may get plenty of sex there – but the food blows."

"I know, I know. Don't worry . . . I don't know . . . I just want to do something illegal."

"You want to do something illegal?" said Bobby, standing up and taking her hand. "Come with me . . ."

He led her down the wooden ramp to the beach, walking quickly to the right, Nikki hurrying to keep up. It was slightly less crowded at the rear, mostly volleyball players waiting their turn.

"Where we going?" said Nikki.

"Just come on. We're going to do something that's

illegal in all fifty states. We're gonna break the law, break the law."

"Yeah?" said Nikki, interested.

After about four hundred yards, Bobby stopped, looked around, and ducked under the boardwalk, yanking Nikki after him.

"Oh," she said. "I think I get it."

He stuck out a finger and pushed her back onto the cool sand, got down on all fours and pulled off her top.

"People can see us," she giggled.

"Public lewdness. Indecent exposure," said Bobby. He peeled down her bikini bottom, flipped her over and put his tongue up her ass. "Sodomy," he added. She jerked like she'd been hooked up to a car battery, moaned and rolled over again, grabbing Bobby's hair to pull his face into her crotch. Bobby's cock protruded almost entirely out of his Speedo. He peeled the Speedo off and lay down next to her.

"I'm gonna get sand in my cunt," she said, throwing a leg over him and working him inside. "Go away, kid!"

A teenager with a volleyball was standing transfixed, a few yards from the edge of the overhanging boardwalk. He blushed and scampered away.

"Corrupting the morals of a minor," muttered Bobby, pushing into her as far as he could go.

BOBBY GETS SQUEEZED

Bobby Gold, in black Ramones T-shirt, black denims and black Nikes, smeared bone marrow on toast and sprinkled sea salt on it before taking a large bite. His mouth was still full when the man came over and stood by his table, looking at him.

"What the fuck are you eating?"

Bobby raised an eyebrow and finished chewing. The man was tall, about forty-five, with the tired, mean face of an old cop. He wore blue slacks with knife creases, new, white running shoes, and a V-neck T-shirt with a windbreaker over it. His Glock, Bobby guessed, under his left kidney, beneath the T-shirt. There was another gun, something smaller, in an ankle holster on the right. From the man's expression, he did not look like he was going to shoot Bobby – or arrest him. At least not today.

"Bone marrow," said Bobby, swallowing. "It's wonderful."

"Yuck!" said the cop. "I can't believe you eat that shit."

Blue Ribbon Bakery on Bedford Street in the Village was not a place Bobby expected to see cops. Cops ate out in packs, usually at cop-friendly places where raised voices, heavy drinking and the occasional freebie were not unheard of. Blue Ribbon was not like that. This cop had either recognized him from his sheet – or, more likely, come looking for him. Bone marrow was a secret pleasure – something Bobby usually indulged in alone. He'd never told Eddie about the place, afraid of being embarrassed, and Nikki couldn't get through a meal without smoking, so he always came here alone. It pissed him off that the cop had clearly decided to brace him here.

"Do I know you?" said Bobby.

"No. I don't think so," said the man, taking a seat at the corner two-top.

"Have a seat," said Bobby. "I guess."

"Do I look like a cop?"

"Yes. You do," said Bobby. "It shows all over."

"Yeah," said the cop. "That's what my wife says."

"Is there a problem?" asked Bobby. "I done something wrong?"

"This is a social visit," said the cop. "For now,

anyway." He snapped his fingers for a waiter – who was visibly displeased at being summoned in such a fashion – and ordered a coffee.

"Bad Bobby Gold," said the cop. "I'm Lieutenant James Connely of the Organized Crime Strike Force. Your name keeps popping up in an investigation we're taking part in and I thought we'd have a chat."

"Investigating what? I'm a doorman. I work security at NiteKlub. Anything we have to report we report to Midtown South."

The cop waved away what Bobby was saying, ignored it completely. "Please? Okay? We both know the drill, okay? You're nice and polite. You make it look like you're honestly attempting to answer my questions – but you're confused by them because of your immaculate state of innocence. I make some suggestive remarks. Then you simply tell me to fuck off – talk to your lawyer – and how dare you interrupt my bone marrow. Either way you tell me shit and play Dumbo. Okay? Either way you listen. 'Cause you're curious."

"I'm curious?"

"You should be. Things are happening. Things that are gonna be affecting you and that nice job you have. Or should I say jobs?"

"You gonna tell me what you're talking about? Or we just gonna play I Know More Than I'm Tellin'? You win, by the way."

"I'm gonna tell you. I'm gonna tell you right now," said the cop, not acknowledging the arrival of his coffee. He didn't even look at it. "That little freak you work for? Mr. 'Eddie Fish'? We're picking up that this goof is gonna get himself greased any minute now. Did you know that? I hear you're close. Like brothers, you're so close. Did you know how bad things were?" Bobby just shook his head slowly and kept his mouth shut.

"Eddie is no longer in such good odor with his former associates. People are talking. They're saying Eddie has been unreliable lately. Making a pest of himself. They say that he's popping pills which make him stupid – or should I say more stupid – and some people, apparently have had quite enough. He hasn't been showing up at sit-downs. You know that? They don't like that out there, you know. They really take that the wrong way. They ask a person to come in for a nice talk and he doesn't, they start getting all sorts of ideas. Eddie hasn't been keeping his appointments."

"Maybe he's been sick. I don't know."

"He's not sick. Eddie's suckin' that glass dick. He's

poppin' a fuckin' drugstore full a goofballs – he's sitting around his fuck-pad on Sutton Place in his undies and ordering take-out. You know that. The man is toast. Tommy V is running the show for him at the club. Did you know that? Of course not. You wouldn't notice something like a new boss, would you Bobby?"

Bobby just shrugged.

"Shrug all you like. Don't mean shit to me. Alls I'm tellin' you is that your old pal is finished. As soon as he steps out for a sandwich or a blow job, somebody's gonna do him. They got a patch a land-fill all picked out for him. And my question to you is: what do you, Bobby 'Gold,' né Goldstein, gonna do then? You gonna work for Tommy? You think they gonna let you live?

"You, they're actually scared of. Eddie's just annoying. What do you think is gonna happen, they drive out Eddie to his final resting place? They gonna let his bestest friend, Big Bad Bobby, live on? Bad Bobby who, they say, did two big bastards up in prison there? The guy they call when somebody needs his bones busted? Eddie Fish's oldest and closest friend and fellow tribe member? You don't think they're worried you might want to do something stupid like take revenge when Eddie goes? You got no job security in what you been doing, Bobby. I can tell you that for free."

"I can't say I know what you're talking about," said Bobby.

"I know you can't say," said the cop, smiling. "But you know. You know exactly what the fuck I'm talking about."

The cop took a long sip of his coffee and let out a grateful sigh. "That's good," he said. "That's good coffee."

"What do you want?"

"Gee. What do you think I want?"

"You want me to snitch. You want me to wear a wire. You want to be my new best pal so you can keep me out of jail, keep me from going to prison. You want to provide me with a new secret identity, large-breasted women, a house in Arizona next to Sammy Bull's. You want me to call you late at night and breathe heavily into the phone so you can go round up miscreants, arrest people I know. You want me to start giving Tommy V long lingering looks so I can get close to him and then tell you what he dreams about. Forget it. Nobody tells me shit. I don't give a shit about Eddie. And I'm retiring . . ."

"Retiring?" laughed the cop. "Retiring? What are

you gonna do? What can you do – other than bust people up into nice little pieces?"

"I'll find something. I can always work security."

"What security? Who's gonna hire you? You're an ex-con! You can't get bonded. Nobody who's not mobbed-up is gonna give you a fuckin' job. What are you gonna do? Stand next to an ATM machine the middle of the night? What are you gonna put on the application where it says last place worked? NiteKlub? People gonna say, 'Oh, that's the place where that Eddie Fish got killed!' Your boss. Not too good at your job, they might think. Forget it. You'll be screwed. You'll be dunking fucking fries at Chirpin' Chicken."

"I was thinking of going back to school," said Bobby, telling the truth for the first time.

"Now that's nice. That might work," said the cop. "I saw your old transcript, you know. You weren't stupid once . . . Had a nice future up there until you got grabbed driving for Eddie. Eddie skated on that scot-free didn't he? And what does he do when his old pal, the guy who went to prison for him, gets out? He hires him as a fucking bouncer. He makes his old buddy into a trained ape. You could have been, what? A doctor? You were pre-med, right? Things coulda turned out real different for you, you hadn't started listening to Eddie."

"Eddie had nothing to do with it," said Bobby, irritated. That episode of his life was a sore point, as Connely clearly was aware.

"Yeah, yeah, yeah, Einstein," said the cop. "That's what you said then. It got you five years. You think your friend Eddie could have done eight to ten? I don't care how early you got out. He woulda snitched off everybody he ever knew. He snitched you off, didn't he?"

"Bullshit!"

"Oh yeah? Think? Listen up, moron. Wake up and smell the coffee. How do you think they picked you up with that carload a dope, genius? You think they're that smart up there? You just looked suspicious – so they pulled you over, happened to have a warrant? Eddie got grabbed two days earlier. He traded the load – and your ass – for a nice cushy community service, licking envelopes at some friend of his daddy's office. His father put it together for him. You didn't know that?"

"He had nothing to do with it."

"I got the fucking arrest record. Eddie Fish, detained while enjoying the services of a prostitute and found to be in possession of a controlled substance. You want to see the CI report? The one where he put it all on you? Told the nice troopers what kind of car you'd be driving and where and when? You surround yourself with bad people, Bobby. You're not a good judge of character."

"Fuck off. This conversation is over," said Bobby. "You want to talk more, call my lawyer."

"Awww . . . Is that any way to be? With an uncertain future in front of you – and a new girlfriend – I thought at least you'd want to listen."

At the mention of Nikki, Bobby slowly moved his hand across the table and pushed the cup of coffee onto the cop's lap.

"Ooops. Terribly sorry," said Bobby, without any attempt at conviction in his voice.

Connely stood up and separated the wet fabric of his pants from his crotch, shaking his head.

"That wasn't nice," he said. "These are Haggar slacks. Not polyester. All cotton. I'll never get that stain out."

"I know the feeling," said Bobby.

It was the people doing the little things around Eddie who saw him at his worst: the drivers, the waiters, bartenders, the doormen who saw him stumble home late, the deli owner at the corner who sold him ice cream when he was too high to talk, the clerk at the video store who rented him pornos. Eddie didn't notice them – so he figured they didn't notice him. They did. The elevator man had seen plenty. Bobby saw that as soon as he stepped inside the gold-and-mirror-paneled chamber and told him what floor he wanted. The man rolled his eyes, repeated the floor and pressed the button. Bobby took the ride in silence, still not sure what he was going to do.

The cop had been telling the truth, of course. Bobby could see that now. It's no accident that the rich seemed untouchable. They never hesitate to sacrifice their friends.

The thing to do was to kill him. That's what Eddie would have done, same situation. It's what Tommy V would do – probably what he's going to do, thought Bobby. Right upstairs, charge inside the apartment, pick that treacherous little fuck up by the armpits and throw him off the balcony – thirty-four floors down. Emotionally, it was the right thing, in that it was the traditional thing to do when betrayed. And intellectually . . . it might be the right thing too. Eddie was a terrible liability right now. Had been for a while. There were plenty of people who would be happy – even grateful – to see him go. The fat men out in Brooklyn would not be unhappy – that's for sure. As a career move it was almost a necessity, the way things were going. Still want that nice job at the club? Want those fat stacks of unaccounted-for bills to keep coming? No problems with the Italian contingent? A life free – or at least freer – of aggravation? Kill the midget. Hit him once, right on the Adam's apple, pick him up and throw him out the fucking window. Say something Arnold or Clint as he goes down, something like, "Have a nice flight," or, "See you on the street."

The bell tone rang once when the elevator arrived at Eddie's floor. Bobby looked at the elevator man and mused on whether he would choose to remember him. He glanced at the corner of the ceiling where he knew the camera would be. The window wouldn't do. He heard music from inside the apartment, Curtis Mayfield, "Little Child Running Wild" . . . knew that Eddie was in a sentimental mood, playing records from the good old/bad old days. Bobby leaned on the bell, heard the music turn off and the shuffle of feet.

Eddie was dressed in a silk bathrobe, no shirt, dress pants – the bottom half of a charcoal-gray pinstriped suit. He wore no shoes or socks and he hadn't shaved or bathed in days. Bobby was shocked at how bad he looked – usually, no matter what he was doing, Eddie remembered to get a haircut, have himself shaved if his hands shook. This was not like him. There was a white crust at the corners of his mouth, and the eyes were wild, jangly little pin-pricks surrounded by dark, raccoon-like circles.

"It'sh you," he said, opening the door and then tottering back to a leather couch. "Just thinking about you . . . about school." Bobby looked around the apartment. There were half-empty take-out cartons everywhere: an uneaten turkey sandwich from a deli on top of the wide-screen TV, a half-order of Pad Thai on the cocktail table, bags of Cheetos and chips which had been torn open at the sides, Chinese spread across the floor, a completely melted box of Eskimo Pies forgotten in the sink at the bar. Eddie was drinking single-malt Scotch and washing it down with Coronas. He must have – at one point – thought about limes. There were two of them on the cocktail table next to the remote control. *The Wizard of Oz* was on the tube, volume down. Eddie turned up the music again: "Freddie's Dead" this time.

"I hate the flying monkeys," said Eddie, swatting at something that wasn't there on his face. "Always hated those fucking monkeys. Remember that time we dropped acid and went to see this?" Bobby remembered. Eddie and he and two girlfriends had gone to see it at the college auditorium, tripping their tits off. One of the girls, Eddie's he thought, had never seen it before. The acid was really starting to kick in when the flying monkeys started getting busy, tearing up the scarecrow and tossing his limbs about, grabbing Dorothy and the dog. The girl couldn't handle it. Started bugging right there. They'd had to leave. Fortunately Eddie had had some thorazines. They'd cooled her right out. Yes, it was Eddie's date, Bobby remembered. He'd gone back to his dorm with the other girl. They'd listened to Roxy Music and John Cale and then she'd given him a memorably dry-mouthed blow job in his small, overheated room. She'd smelled of sweat and patchouli, he recalled. He hadn't been able to come. Hadn't been able to sleep. Just laid there in the dark, the girl's arm across his chest, watching the explosions of color behind his eyes, heart racing.

"What the hell's the matter with you, Eddie?" he said, sitting down across from his old friend. "Your life looks like it's turning to shit."

"It is shit," said Eddie. "Fuckin' guineas ruinin' my fuckin' life. Got the IRS crawlin' up my ass, got Tommy's people tryin' to put me outta business, the cops with their noses up my ass, and my wife . . . my wife's takin' the kids and the house."

"Maybe you're taking a few too many pills, Eddie? You thought of that?"

"I know. I know. I need them. I got a preshription. The doctor says I gotta take them."

"Which doctor?" Eddie always had five or six writing scripts for him at any given moment. His fucking dermatologist wrote him Demerol and Dilaudid and Ritalin and Tranxene. Bobby looked at his friend and boss, sagging into the couch in his bare feet and stained dress pants, and knew he was looking at a dead man. What could Eddie say now that would make him feel any better? "I'm sorry"? Seeing Eddie dead would give Bobby no pleasure at all. He could easily just reach over – the state he was now – pinch off his nose with one hand, clamp the other hand on his mouth and watch him go. Eddie was too fucked up, too out of shape to put up much of a struggle.

"This place smells like a Chinese whorehouse," said Bobby, getting up and sliding open the glass doors to the balcony. "Jesus! Get some fucking air in here." He stepped out onto the balcony, looked out across the East River and the Coca-Cola sign and Yankee Stadium. It was freezing cold, a few snowflakes floated down and then up again with the updraft from the street. Eddie joined him after a few seconds, his robe wrapped tightly around him, his hand gripping fabric under his chin. Eddie collapsed into a chaise lounge, spilling his drink.

"I'm fucked," said Eddie. "Unless something happens to Tommy, I got no future. You gotta make him go away, Bobby. You gotta do him."

"I gotta do Tommy Victory, Eddie?" spluttered Bobby. "You want me to do Tommy? A made fucking guy? What good is that gonna do, Eddie? What the fuck good is that gonna do for anybody?"

"Show them who to respec'," said Eddie, eyes nearly closed. "Show them who they're fuckin' with . . ."

"That'll work. That'll work great. How long you think they gonna let you live after that? Are you outta your fuckin' mind? You gotta get permission do something like that – and you ain't ever getting permission, Eddie. You even ask, they'll kill you right there. When's the last time those guys ever sided with a Jew over a guinea?"

"Bugsy Seigel," shouted Eddie. "Meyer Lansky!"

"Two Jews."

"Uh . . . give me a minute . . ." mumbled Eddie. "I'll think of one."

"It never happened, Eddie. Never. And you ain't no Meyer Lansky. You're a fuckin' stumblebum.

You're an unreliable, stuttering, drooling, out-of-control fuck-up with his hand in the fucking cookie jar – and you ain't earning enough – you haven't been earning enough for a while – to make them overlook it any more."

"Fuck you! What do you know? You don't know me, man . . ."

"I know you, Eddie. I know you in my fucking bones. I known you since I was a skinny kid. I know you for eight fucking years in the jug, smellin' dirty socks and dried jiz and loose farts, you asshole. You sold me out. You fucking dropped a dime on me. And I ain't killing nobody for you no more and I ain't hurtin' nobody no more for you. You can pop your fuckin' pills and drink your fuckin' Coronas and fuck your he-shes and do whatever you want to do 'cause you're not even worth me killing anymore. You're dead already. Worse than dead. Look at yourself!"

Eddie just lay there, staring out into space from under heavy lids. Bobby could hear him breathe, a thick, rasping sound. A few seconds later, he was asleep.

Bobby took a yellow cab over to 9th Avenue, the Bellevue Bar at 39th, and found a seat at the end.

He should probably call Tommy, arrange a sit-down, work out an arrangement in keeping with the new, inevitable restructuring. He should have killed Eddie. Rented a car, taken him out for a drive. Problem over. Anybody still loyal would understand. And Eddie's enemies would appreciate the gesture. But he just didn't have it in him.

There'd be people trying to kill him soon, Bobby understood. If he said nothing. Met with no one. Did nothing. If he just sat here every day, drank himself into insensibility day after day, let them do what they had to do – let the gears turn, the world outside go on without him – sooner or later, someone would come through that door and kill him too.

Nobody at the bar talked to him. When Bobby nodded, the bartender came over and gave him another drink. Soon he was drunk, tapping his fingers to the jukebox. "Love Comes in Spurts," Richard Hell and the Voidoids. He was deciding whether he wanted to try and live, about what would have to be involved. He'd need a gun. And a car. And money. He had the airweight and the H&K in the floor safe of his apartment, with a stack of emergency money totalling about 50K. He could get a car no problem. Just a phone call and a taxi to Queens. His Aryan "brothers" would help – for a while – where the Italians would be unsympathetic. He wouldn't kill Eddie. He wouldn't set him up. But he'd leave him to the wolves this time.

His cell phone rang and he heard objects noisily knocking together on the other end. A second later, "Pusherman" off the Curtis Mayfield album was playing over the receiver. Eddie, in a sentimental mood, playing him tunes over the phone. The soundtrack to better times.

BOBBY'S NOT HERE

Bobby Gold nowhere in sight; 5:30 A.M. in the NiteKlub office with Lenny, in ludicrous-looking ski goggles, working the power saw, Nikki wetting the blade down with water from a kitchen squeeze bottle. Halfway through the second metal pin on the revolving money drop in the safe and Lenny is bathed in sweat, his goggles beginning to steam up.

"Jesus! This thing is taking forever!" says Lenny, turning off the drill for a second and listening for the sound of the floor waxer. "You sure that guy's still got his Walkman on?"

"He's always got his Walkman on," says Nikki, wiping Lenny's brow with a paper towel, hands – like Lenny's – in surgical gloves from the kitchen. "C'mon. You're almost through there. Keep at it."

Lenny turns on the drill and proceeds, bits of metal bouncing off his goggles, stinging his face, lodging in his teeth.

"Ouch!" he complains. "That hurt!"

"Pussy," says Nikki.

Finally the sound of the saw changes pitch, the shelf falls free of the last pin. Lenny yanks it out and hurls it into a corner. "I've gotta piss like a racehorse."

"Use the trash," suggests Nikki, pointing at a plastic wastebasket.

While Lenny empties his bladder, Nikki reaches her arm (longer than his) down into the safe and starts pulling out banded stacks of cash. There are a lot more of them than they'd expected.

"Uh . . . Lenny," she says. "You see this?"

Lenny, zipping up his fly, turns and looks. The pile of cash on the floor is large – and getting larger. "Holy . . . shit!"

"No kidding! . . . Holy . . . shit is right!" says Nikki, suddenly damp, a few strands of hair glued to her forehead. "There wasn't supposed to be that much – was there?"

"Let's get the fuck out of here," says Lenny.

Lenny leaves first: down the back kitchen stairs, through the service entrance to the hotel. Nikki drops the duffel full of cash out the window and into his arms before following a few moments later. Two hours later, the money divided up and hidden

– for the moment under a pile of sweaters in Nikki's closet – the two are sitting in the cellar of Siberia Bar, leaning forward, heads close, talking.

"What's the matter?" asks Lenny, bothered by Nikki's stunned expression, the way she keeps shaking her head.

"I'm alright."

"No. Really. What's the matter?" he repeats.

Nikki slams back her third vodka shot, her eyes beginning to fill up. "Everything is different now, isn't it?"

"What do you mean?" says Lenny, playing the tough guy.

"I mean . . . How do we go to work tomorrow? It's gonna be a shit-storm in there. How do I look anybody in the eyes? They'll fucking know."

"Who are you worried about? The Chef? Ricky? What? Nobody's gonna think it was us! Who would think it was us?"

"There was so much. There wasn't supposed to be that much. I'm worried. I admit it. I'm worried."

"Fuck them. They're idiots. They'll never find out as long as we don't tell them."

"I'm worried about Bobby. I don't want him to lose his job."

"Bobby!? Bobby!! That security goon? Fuck him!

He's not a cook! He's not one of us! What do you care about that asshole? Are you fucking that guy?"

"Yes," says Nikki. "Yes. I'm fucking that guy. I've been fucking that guy for months!"

"I can't believe this!" shrieks Lenny. "You're doing the head of fucking security?!" His hands trembling, Lenny takes a pull on a beer, missing his mouth and slobbering on his chin. "You're not going to tell him anything? You're not that stupid."

"I won't say anything," says Nikki.

"You better not!" Lenny thinks about this for a while. "In fact . . . In fact . . . if it looks like he's getting close to figuring anything out – you better tell me. You will tell me, right?"

Nikki waves him away, dismissing the prospect. "I think you should bug out tonight, Lenny. You can have the money. Okay . . . maybe I'll keep some . . . but you can have most of it. Go to fucking Florida or something. But you should go. That's a lot of money there. You should be fine."

"What are people gonna say, I disappear the day they find somebody cracked the fucking safe? They'll know!"

"We didn't think this out too good, did we?"

"What do you mean? Stick with the plan. We stick with the plan. That's what we should do!"

"The plan? There was no plan, Lenny. You know what my fucking plan was? You know how stupid I am? My plan was to take the money and get out of the fucking business for a while and maybe rent a nice place somewhere where there's water and maybe a beach and buy some clothes and a TV and like . . . live like a normal person for a while. That was what my plan was, Lenny. You know . . . a nice boyfriend . . . hole up behind some white picket fucking fence with a garden and like, live like a regular person. You know . . . he goes to like . . . work . . . wherever that is . . . and I putter around the house. I order shit outta catalogs . . . make myself a midday martini . . . watch soap operas . . . cook, like, tuna noodle casserole. Friday nights he comes home, we get dressed up, go out to dinner and maybe a movie – after which we go home and he throws me on a big four-poster bed and fucks me till my nose bleeds."

"Are you fucking kidding me? Are you nuts? I feel like . . . it's like *Invasion of the Body Snatchers*!! What is with you? My fucking partner is going Suzy Homemaker on me? What the fuck!?"

"I always wanted to putter," says Nikki, glumly, not looking at Lenny when she says it.

"Putter? You want to putter?"

"You know. Do normal shit. Whatever it is people do. You know. When they're not like us."

"This is great," says Lenny, returning from the bar with a Jäger shot and two beers. "This is great. I don't even know you anymore. You couldn't a said this before? You're going out with the head a fuckin' security . . . you got some weird-ass idea you're gonna turn into some kinda suburban housewife or some shit. We put down the biggest score of our fucking lives – I'm thinking, buy a couple a kilos a coke and turn that over and, like, open our own place or something – "

"I'm not opening a restaurant with you, Lenny, I said that. I always said that."

"I thought you were kidding. I thought . . . Jesus, Nikki," says Lenny. "I thought you liked me. I thought. You know . . ."

Nikki just shakes her head and then leans forward and gives Lenny a sisterly hug. He tries clumsily to kiss her but she turns her head away, avoiding his mouth.

"I see. I see what it is now," says Lenny. "I'm outta here tonight. I'm outta here tonight before you fucking tell the fucking ape-man and blow everything. You . . . you . . . fucking whore!"

Nikki is up in a flash. She reaches back and pops

Lenny a good one in the right eye that knocks him back into his seat. Two customers look up quizzically but immediately look away as Nikki glares right back at them and Lenny bursts into tears.

Nikki cradles Lenny in her arms on the hardwood floor of her tiny apartment. They're both still in their coats. Lenny is still crying, his nose running profusely, chest heaving with suppressed sobs. Nikki is petting the back of his head like he's a child, saying, "That's okay . . . that's okay." Though, of course, nothing is okay now.

The money has been divided, Nikki keeping only a relatively small share – getaway money should things really turn sour. It's morning already – and Nikki can't remember a time the cheeping birds and early morning garbage trucks have sounded so sinister. Lenny's money is in an airline bag, ready to go.

"You should get out of here," says Nikki. "Take your money, get on a train. Go someplace nice and live a little. Get yourself a fucking girlfriend. You're a rich guy, now, Lenny. You'll have to beat them off with a stick."

"I want you to be my girlfriend," snivels Lenny, his face collapsing all over again.

"That ain't gonna happen, Lenny," says Nikki, wiping tears off his receding chin with her sleeve.

Lenny gone, morning commuter traffic in full swing outside her window, Nikki lays on her bed, staring at the ceiling. This was something she never should have become involved in. "Story of my life, right?" she says out loud.

Her cut, still in the nearly empty duffel bag, sits on the floor – more an affront than a windfall. It isn't the prospect of cops she is worried about. Or the chaos and paranoia and whatever else awaits her when she goes in for work today – if she goes in for work today. It wasn't Eddie Fish – who always struck her as a pathetic little shrimp anyway – or what he might do. She could stand up to an interrogation. She'd hide the money somewhere and she'd ride it out. She doesn't feel guilty about taking money from a dishonest shithole like NiteKlub – probably go out of business in a few months anyway (à la carte dinners were getting slower and slower and the party business was drying up for the season). The owners had already skimmed their money out, that was for sure. Only a matter of time till they were all out of work. They deserved it. They'd probably barely notice the money had gone missing. One night's fucking receipts – okay, there had been a disconcertingly large amount in there this time – but what would really happen now? It isn't getting caught that bothers her. She wasn't going to get caught. It isn't guilt. Or fear – not much anyway. Who'd suspect a chick? Especially now, with Lenny gone? She closes her eyes and tries to forget about the whole thing – pushing the office, the safe, the bag of money on her floor out of her mind. But something keeps intruding. Keeps waking her up, eyes wide open, her breathing getting faster, a painful, swelling ache in her chest.

It's Bobby.

That bothers her. It really does.

BOBBY TAKES IT ON THE LAM

Bobby Gold, in a hastily thrown on black leather jacket, white T-shirt, black denims and sandals, a Heckler and Koch pistol between his legs, stomped on the gas and blew right by a tractor-trailer. "Roadrunner," the old Modern Lovers tune about cruising Route 128, was on the radio, volume cranked up – appropriate to the circumstances as Bobby and Nikki were on exactly that road, middle of the night, Massachusetts highway, headed for the Cape.

"I forgot to pack a bathing suit," said Nikki, from the passenger seat. "Does the music have to be up so loud?"

"Just this song," shouted Bobby. "Greatest album ever made. What do you need a bathing suit for? It's winter."

"The hotel. Maybe the hotel will have a pool."

"We ain't stayin' in no hotel, baby. Not this trip. People are angry with me. They want to kill me. We stay in a hotel we gotta use a credit card. We use a credit card and it shows up on my statement. Wrong person sees my statement? Bang Bang Dig Dig time."

"Shit! I thought at least there'd be a pool."

"You're the one wanted to break the law. You're the one wanted to be an outlaw. Welcome to the wild world of interstate flight."

Bobby's cell phone rang from inside his jacket. He slowed down slightly, reached, flipped it open and listened. It was Eddie.

"You've killed me," said Eddie, his voice thick with pills.

"How did I kill you?" said Bobby, annoyed.

"Threw me to the wolves. You left me out on a limb. I've got nobody. I've got nobody anybody's scared of."

"Buy yourself a pit bull. Hire a security guard. Do the Witness Protection thing. I don't give a fuck. I'm gone."

"You're with that bitch?"

Bobby flushed with anger, surprised at the question. "What the fuck you talking about?"

"That rotten bitch from the kitchen. She busted into the safe last night and took the fucking receipts, Bobby. That's the bitch I'm talking about. She with you?"

"I got to get back to you, Eddie," said Bobby. "Call you right back."

"Uh . . . sweetheart?"

"Yes," said Nikki.

"Have you been a bad girl? Is there something you're not telling me?"

"Well . . . depends by what you mean by 'something' . . ."

"How about this. Did you by any chance break into the club's safe last night?"

Nikki said nothing for a while as she considered her answer. A 16-wheeler blew by them on the highway followed by silence.

"I might have done something like that. I'm very mechanically inclined. My brother works in a machine shop."

"That's nice. That's very nice. And last night, when you and whoever helped you in this bone-headed fucking venture were taking stacks of money out of the safe. Did it occur to you, perhaps, whose money exactly it was you were absconding with?"

"Well . . . I guess we figured it was Eddie's."

"And who does Eddie owe money to do you think? Who do you think Eddie's partners are?"

"Some German asshole. I've seen him. He's always trying to fuck the waitresses."

"That's what we call in the business the 'straw owner,' cupcakes . . . That's what they call on television cop shows 'the front man.'"

"Uh-oh," said Nikki. "You're about to tell me whose money it really was, aren't you?"

"Yes. Yes I am," said Bobby.

A little while later they were crossing the Buzzard's Bay Bridge onto the Cape and Route 6. Bobby's phone went off again and he rolled down the window on the driver's side, hurled it out over the rail into blackness.

"Your phone's ringing," said Nikki.

"I know," said Bobby.

"This guy you mentioned is not a very nice man, I take it?" said Nikki.

"You could say that," said Bobby.

"I got nineteen thousand dollars," said Nikki. "Would he like, hunt us down and kill me for that?"

Bobby did a little quick math in his head, abandoning his equations after a few seconds.

"Well . . . let's just say he's not exactly going to be looking for his money back. It'll cost him half the nineteen by the time he finds us. Thing is, with Tommy, guys like Tommy? It's the principle of the thing, you see. That's the problem."

thought he could hear an occasional sniffle between cigarettes. He kept his eyes on the road, speed just under the limit, thinking about what to do next. A place in town was now out of the question. He knew somebody who could hook them up with a dune shack which would have to do until they figured out what to do next. Terrible things were going to happen in New York. People were going to die. Eddie being "boy most likely to." He figured he'd wait. See who fell and who survived before he made any rash moves. With luck, something bad could happen to Tommy in the shake-out to come. Letting some girl sauté cook take his crew off for a night's receipts didn't look good. Such things were bad for you, the business Tommy was in. With any luck, a few whispers, some young Turk would maybe make the problem go away. Maybe Eddie would turn state's evidence, go off to Arizona and rehab, keep Tommy and his people hunkered down filing motions and answering summonses. On the other hand, maybe Tommy would come after them with everything. Maybe Tommy would go have a nice talk with Paul and tell him what a terrible thing that Eddie's man Bobby did – how he cast aspersions on Paulie's sainted, no-doubt-virginal daughter to get out of a previous jam, how he was a thieving, cowardly, and potentially dangerous problem who had to be taken care of immediately – along with his puttana. This, of course, was the more likely scenario.

"Pull over," said Nikki.

"What? Why? You sick?"

"No. I'm horny. I get horny when I get scared."

She was already unsnapping Bobby's blue jeans when he pulled over to the side of the road.

"Slide over," she said, her feet over the dashboard as she yanked off her pants.

"This is not smart," said Bobby. "This is not smart at all."

She straddled him on the front seat and pushed down.

"Oh."

"Yep."

"You're a dangerous woman. You're going to get us both killed," said Bobby, already way way way beyond caring.

"I know," said Nikki. "Feels good though, doesn't it?"

After a month, when nobody came, when no strangers had been noticed in off-season Provincetown, where people tended to notice such things, they began to visit town more often, usually for breakfast at the Tip for Tops'n on Bradford Street, or for dinner at a Portuguese fisherman's joint where Nikki liked the squid stew. Nikki took a job part-time at a pizzeria, spinning pies, and Bobby did a little roofing and carpentry, a little day labor at the boatyard. It was cold and crisp during the day, but with brilliant, sharp-focused light, the sunsets spectacular, and the sound of foghorns and boat whistles, the smells of fish and salt spray, the slowed down, more relaxed life of an off-season resort town making Cape Cod seem much farther away from whatever was happening in New York.

Bobby read the *Times*, religiously, looking for news of dead organized crime associates, and Nikki read *Vogue* and *Marie Claire* and *Bazaar* and planned her wardrobe for the spending spree they were going to have whenever they made their next move. Whatever that was. At night it was freezing cold in their beach shack – and on really cold nights, they'd leave the oven on with the door open and huddle naked under four or five blankets, noses cold, giggling, and curiously without care. Bobby kept the H&K under the pillow for the first few weeks then moved it to the night table. They fucked almost every day and spent hours just staring wordlessly down at the sea. They shot pool at the Governor Bradford, bought a cheap TV set from a Portuguese fisherman and watched snowy, blurry reruns of old sitcoms under the covers, Bobby getting out in the cold to move a clothes hanger/antennae around the room from time to time – for better reception. Nikki cooked now and again – usually something simple, but occasionally a classic French feast, serving *paté de canard* and salmon with sorrel sauce on paper plates, washed down with fine wine in plastic cups. Bobby never asked her about the stolen money or why she should have done something so stupid and suicidal. It was assumed that at some point they'd really run away. Bobby favored the Far East. Nikki was partial to the Caribbean or Mexico.

Nineteen grand, Bobby might have pointed out, was not going to be enough for both of them.

In April, Eddie Fish made the papers. A full-cover shot in the *New York Post*, Eddie interrupted at dinner, a mouthful of veal chop with the sauce from the chicken, laid out on the cold tile floor, shirt pulled up, head leaking black onto white, dead as dead could be. His eyes were half open and there was food on the shirt.

"I think I need more guns," thought Bobby, heading back to the dune shack. "I really do."

But when he got back Nikki was asleep, dozing really, midafternoon, one arm thrown over her eyes, mouth slightly open, blankets just below her breasts. Bobby quietly got undressed and slipped under the covers with her. She curled into a ball and worked her way dreamily under his arms, seeking warmth. He felt her slowly unravel, throwing a leg over his, then a hand around his back, the other one seeking something, finding it. Her head disappearing completely under the covers.

When he woke up it was dark and he couldn't hear the generator. The window by the bed flew off its hinges, blew apart, glass suddenly in his hair. It took a second to realize that people were shooting at them; window, door, through the walls, the reports of three, maybe four weapons muffled by the sand, whipped away in the wind.

It's always the little things you remember when terrible things happen.

Bobby would remember the splinter he got when he jumped out of bed, his bare feet scrambling for purchase on the floor. He remembered the way his fingers felt useless and rubbery as he tore open the drawer and grabbed for the H&K. He would always remember the sound Nikki made when he shoved her out of bed onto the floor – and that his cock stuck to his leg for a second as he ran for the door firing.

He'd remember that the first man he saw was wearing a shooter's vest and earmuffs and that when Nikki was hit she made an "Ouch!" noise like she'd just cut herself on a grapefruit knife.

He was free all right. Cut loose from everything. Eddie gone. NiteKlub gone. Family ... long long gone. And Nikki? Not here. That was for sure. He missed everything about her. Her hair. Her sardonic smile. The not knowing what was going to come out of her mouth next. Her scent. Recalling it made his chest hurt.

He was the driver now. No longer a passenger in a tightly circling cab. And he had seen the world – the eastern part of it anyway: Bora Bora, Singapore, Japan, China, Vietnam, Laos, Thailand, Cambodia, a blurry film strip of temples, *wats* and mini-bars, transit lounges, buffet breakfasts, noodle shops, maimed beggars, stone-faced soldiers, brown-skinned children in mud and rags calling "hello!" "bye-bye!" from riverbanks and stilt-supported houses. He'd seen moon-faced whores and eager cyclo-drivers, smoked opium in a tin-roofed shack under a driving rain, stayed in cheap neon-lit hotel rooms: bed, fan, TV set showing only Thai kick-boxing and MTV Asia, "karaoke-massage" in the lobby and someone else's hair on the complimentary plastic comb and everywhere the smell of wood smoke, the overripe camembert odor of durian fruit, fish sauce, chicken shit and fear. The soundtrack to the new not-so-improved Bobby Gold Story was the sound of a million throbbing generators, the endless droning of yet another pressurized cabin, the whoosh of turbines, the low-throated gurgle of turbo-props, the admonitions in pidgin English, Thai, Khmer, Vietnamese and Chinese that one's seat cushion could be used "as a flotation device" and to refrain from using cell phones or electronic devices.

He'd bought a gun in Battambang – an old Makarov pistol with extra shells. Partly for self-protection, as what constituted a crime in these parts depended largely on how much money one had in one's wallet and who one's cousins were. But also with the half-formed idea that one of these days he might want to put the gun in his mouth and pull the trigger. It seemed a romantic place to die, Siem Reap, in the shadows of Angkor Wat and Angkor Thom – to be found dead under the big stone heads at Bayon; the reports, if any, of his demise to read something like, "found dead of a gunshot wound in Siem Reap." It just as well might read Battambang, or Pailin, or Vung Tau or Can Tho or Bangkok. It made little difference, as there was, really, no one left back home to read or care or be impressed by such a romantic demise.

"Oh yeah, the dude with the ponytail? The guy

who used to work security? He was fucking the sauté bitch, right?" was what they'd say in the kitchen

"He was doing Nikki, right? Whatever happened to her, man? She was good on the line," was what they'd say. Then someone would notice a song they didn't like on the radio and go to change the station and then they'd talk about something else.

It was a very nice hotel – though an empty one. Black-and-white tiled floors, ochre colored walls with mahogony and teak moldings. The ceiling of the bar was decorated with finely drawn murals of elephants and Khmer kings and the agreeable waiters wore green and white sarongs and knew to a man how to make a proper Singapore Sling or a dry martini or vermouth cassis.

Bobby was well liked at the hotel as he was neither Russian nor German and didn't insist on bringing whores to his room like the other guests. He spent his days at the temples or at the riverbank and his evenings at the bar slogging through Malraux and Greene and Maugham and Tim Page, trying to absorb their enthusiasms. Their lives so different than his own. "I love you," she'd said and squeezed him tightly, her fingers sinking into his back. He'd kissed her and tasted blood and then she'd slipped – as Jim Morrison once put it – into unconsciousness.

He'd been drinking too much . . . and smoking bad weed – the rough-tasting Khmer smoke that cost only a stack of worthless riels per kilo and the anti-malarial pills he'd been taking once a week were putting the screws to his head, giving him nightmares. He'd wake up, middle of the night with his chest pounding after a particularly violent dream, smelling blood, his arms actually aching from fighting off full-color phantasms.

Here's one dream Bobby had:

Bobby Gold at eight years old, in blue jeans, high-top sneakers and pale blue T-shirt, standing in the schoolyard, a ring of faceless children around him in a tightening circle. It was dodge ball they were playing – and Bobby was it – the bigger kids, pale and dead-eyed, aiming the big rubber ball at his face. Suddenly the action switched and it was Eddie Fish standing in the perfectly round gauntlet, Bobby holding back the ball, taking aim, throwing it. Eddie cowering, the ball (Bobby could smell the rubber, read the manufacturer's name: "VOIT") striking Eddie flush on the nose, smashing it flat, the blood coming, coming, not stopping, as Eddie, in shorts, screaming silently and Bobby's head filling with the smell of rust, of school erasers, Juicyfruit, disinfectant, latex paint, the taste of chewed pencils. The others come at Eddie with garden hoes now, striking first the hard schoolyard asphalt, then flesh, Bobby hearing the sound as metal buried itself in bone, felt the vibrations in his spine with each solid whack.

He woke up in cold, wet sheets, gasping, then smoked a half a pack of 555s, afraid to go back to sleep.

An ancient Antonov to Phnom Penh, seats broken, seat belt useless at his side, the cabin filled with steam a few minutes after take-off – the other passengers actually laughing when the stewardesses handed out the in-flight meal, a plastic-wrapped sandwich and a roll in a cardboard box – wings yawing dangerously as the plane touched down. Overnight in Bangkok in a gigantic airport hotel, a twenty-minute walk to his room from the lobby, a Filipino trio singing "Rock the Boat" in the lounge, Tiger beer in the mini bar. Transfer at Narita. A packed flight – tourist class – to LAX, taxi to a Japanese-owned hotel in West Hollywood.

* * *

The cocktail lounge was filled with well-dressed people talking on cell phones in amber-colored light. The women were well made-up, hair done, heels, the men in jackets with recently polished shoes. They sat in plush, upholstered chairs and overstuffed couches, drinking novelty drinks off tiny little tables. British techno-soundtrack music issued from hidden speakers. A waiter offered Bobby a complimentary spring roll from a tray. He'd never felt so detached from his own country. It smelled of nothing here, only air-conditioning, the figures around him in the lounge moving dreamlike through space like characters in a film. A woman at the next grouping of chairs looked at Bobby then whispered something to her date – he turned around for a second, glanced at Bobby, then snapped his head away as if frightened. Bobby sat there like a stone obelisk, his ice melting in his drink, horrified. There was something indecent in all this affluence. He'd just come from a place where everything smelled, where children tugged your sleeve and begged for your leftovers, where amputees slithered legless across the street and the police felt free to open fire at any time. He felt like he was on another planet, the languid movements of the young, graceful crowd somehow a cruel and terrible affront to the way he knew the world to with little signs announcing family names over identical mailboxes, driveways filled with SUVs, muscle cars, children's toys. Just outside of town was a mega-mall with food court, deca-plex cinema, a chain hotel with heated pool and "convention facilities." The "old" part of town dated back only to the forties; similarly identical homes – built like the newer ones all at once – these to accommodate the wartime aviation and munitions industry who'd once had factories in the nearby desert. And a single strip of shabby businesses: superette, hardware store, a movie theater turned furniture outlet, city hall, police department, bowling alley, a few shops selling nostrums and notions.

She worked at Duke's Pizza, spinning pies in the front window. She had her hair tied back with a red kerchief – to keep it from burning in the oven, and she wore a tight white T-shirt that revealed a slight impression of nipple, a long, sauce-stained apron. From across the street, he couldn't see where the bullet had entered. She was spinning pie now, two fists working the dough ever larger, a twirl with the fingertips of the right hand, and then the pie disappeared up and out of frame, reappearing a second later. Nikki looked grimly satisfied as she slung the floppy, white object back and forth between her wrists. A single strand of hair worked loose from the headband hung over her face, giving her an appearance of heartbreaking earnestness. Below the window frame, she ladled sauce, sprinkled cheese, then moved the finished pizza on a long wooden paddle into the back of a deck oven, yanked it free with a hard, unhesitating jerk of the arm, muscles flexing.

He rolled up his window, ducking back as she pushed away the strand of hair from her face, blew out, stared out the window at the empty street, squinting in the midafternoon glare.

Nikki in hiding. New name. New address. She'd snitched him off – as arranged bedside at the hospital – in return for protection. He looked up and down the street and saw no one who looked like a cop or a fed or a U.S. marshal. As arranged, she'd sent him a single postcard, care of a rooming house in Goa, telling him where she was and that she was okay.

She'd had nothing to say – no "direct knowledge" as lawyers like to phrase it – about Tommy Victory. Bobby had been all she'd had to offer and he'd insisted. She'd needed something to pay the toll – and an organized crime "associate" with multiple bodies on his résumé had seemed like an easy out. She'd been in the hospital for three months – and physical therapy for a year after that. He'd had to do something.

"Why?" she'd asked him. "Why does it have to be you?"

"Because it's all we've got," he'd said. "Because they might come back. Because what Tommy's people want from you is too high a price for anyone to pay." The person they'd send, if they could find her, would have been someone just like he had once been. A professional. Someone who knew how to hurt people, how to ask hard questions. Someone who didn't flinch when people screamed. Someone for whom another life extinguished was just another day at work.

Because Tommy knew that Bobby was out there somewhere. Because he knew what he was likely to do.

Bobby left town quietly, saying nothing. He didn't call her at the shop. He didn't even wave.

He dropped the car in Tucson, rented another – under yet another name – and made the long, long drive cross-country, New York finally appearing beyond the George Washington Bridge. He bought a banged up .38 Airweight from a Serbian safecracker he'd known upstate and checked into a no-tell motel just across the river in Fort Lee.

* * *

Tommy Victory, in a smart tweed jacket, brown turtleneck and pleated slacks, approached his Lincoln town car in the cool autumn Connecticut dusk. A dead leaf stuck to his loafter, and he stopped to peel it off distastefully with a fingertip before standing by the rear passenger door of the idling car. He knocked on the smoked glass window for his chauffeur/bodyguard, and when no response came, opened the door, irritated, and heaved himself inside, mouth already open to chew out his sleeping driver.

He wasn't sleeping. Tommy could see that right away. His head lay on the seat back at an unnatural angle, the neck broken. The door on the far side suddenly opened and Bobby Gold, looking thinner and tanner than he'd remembered him, was sitting next to him, grabbing him by the hair and pulling his head back. The .38 broke a tooth as it went in Tommy's mouth. Tommy's last thought was of bridgework as he heard the words, "Hello, Tommy," matter-offactly spoken as Bobby pulled the trigger, pushed the barrel ever deeper down Tommy's throat.

Bobby emptied the gun, the car filling with cordite smell, the report deafening in the enclosed space. When Tommy sagged back onto new leather, a single perfect smoke ring issued from his open mouth.

* * *

Bobby Gold, in a purple-and-blue sarong, feet bare, drank Tiger beer and watched children washing their hair in dark, brown, muddy water at the riverbank. A water buffalo strained to pull a cart with a missing wheel in a rice paddy in the distance. A Khmer in a khaki shirt and shorts, a red krama covering his head from the sun, collected sticks from the roadside. Bobby brushed a persistent fly away from the corner of his mouth and lit another 555, sat there smoking, yearning for pizza.

A NOTE ON THE AUTHOR

Anthony Bourdain is the author of *Kitchen Confidential: Adventures in the Culinary Underbelly*, which spent fourteen weeks on the *New York Times* bestseller list, and the Urban Historical *Typhoid Mary*, as well as *A Cook's Tour*, which was turned into a successful series by the same name for the Food Network. His mystery novels include *Bone in the Throat* and *Gone Bamboo*. He is the executive chef at Brasserie Les Halles in New York City.

A NOTE ON THE TYPE

This old-style face is named after the Frenchman Robert Granjon, a sixteenth-century letter cutter whose italic types have often been used with the romans of Claude Garamond. The origins of this face, like those of Garamond, lie in the late-fifteenth-century types used by Aldus Manutius in Italy.